THE PRICE

THE PRICE

WHAT IT TAKES TO WIN
IN COLLEGE FOOTBALL'S
ERA OF CHAOS

Armen Keteyian
and John Talty

HARPER

An Imprint of HarperCollins*Publishers*

THE PRICE. Copyright © 2024 by John Talty and Lights Out Productions, LLC. All rights reserved. Printed in the United States of America. No part of this book may be used or reproduced in any manner whatsoever without written permission except in the case of brief quotations embodied in critical articles and reviews. For information, address HarperCollins Publishers, 195 Broadway, New York, NY 10007.

HarperCollins books may be purchased for educational, business, or sales promotional use. For information, please email the Special Markets Department at SPsales@harpercollins.com.

FIRST EDITION

Designed by Kyle O'Brien

Library of Congress Cataloging-in-Publication Data has been applied for.

ISBN 978-0-06-334525-6

24 25 26 27 28 LBC 5 4 3 2 1

From Armen to Dede, the love of my life for going on forty-five years, and to our grandson Brooks and granddaughter Kaia, our two new bundles of joy

From John to my son, Jack, my reason for everything I do, and my mom, Kathie, who has encouraged my writing career every step of the way

Contents

Prologue

JIM HARBAUGH LOOKED OVER AT Nick Saban, seemingly incredulous that he had gone *there*.

The press conference the day before a playoff game was typically awkward, with most of the game's storylines long played out and everyone just ready to get on with it, but this one especially so. The Michigan sign-stealing scandal loomed over the Rose Bowl, inflamed by Alabama players saying earlier that week they had changed their pregame preparation out of fear their iPads could be hacked. It was yet another impugnation of Harbaugh and his Michigan Wolverines, who had become college football's biggest villains that 2023–24 season.

Saban and Harbaugh had a complicated history. There was mutual respect for what the other had accomplished, but not much warmth between them. Harbaugh's 2015 barnstorming camp tour of SEC country irked Saban, who said it was "bad for college football." Harbaugh returned fire, posting, "Alabama broke NCAA rules & now their HC is lecturing us on the possibility of rules being broken at camps. Truly 'amazing.'" When they later met in the 2020 Citrus Bowl, some believed Saban was trying to send a message when he let running back Najee Harris score a touchdown with twenty-six seconds left in a game that had already been decided in the Crimson Tide's favor.

Against that background, Saban and Harbaugh mostly played nice, sitting a few feet apart from each other as journalists lobbed general game questions at them. Then, with the last question of the press conference, a reporter asked Saban if he was concerned about Michigan's sign-stealing scandal. After initially saying that he wasn't particularly concerned, Saban started off on the "integrity of the game," as Harbaugh fidgeted listening to the Alabama head coach talk about his program. Saban wrapped up his answer this way: "We just have to adapt to how we communicate with the quarterback, and we'll change it up and try to not put our players at a disadvantage in any way." At those words, Harbaugh turned to his right, looked at Saban, and smirked over the Alabama head coach even dignifying the question. Saban had a chance to shut down the sign-stealing talk and instead said Alabama was adapting to it so it wasn't at a disadvantage. It was one more arrow, one more indignity, for the black hat of college football.

The next day, the sun-dappled San Gabriel Mountains proved the perfect Southern California backdrop for a battle between a feared dynasty led by an aging king and an iconic Midwest program boasting the most wins in college football history—undefeated No. 1 Michigan versus No. 4 and once-beaten Alabama playing for a shot at a national championship in the sport's most iconic venue.

It had been a harrowing journey to Pasadena for both head coaches and their teams. Saban's Crimson Tide had been left for dead after an early season home loss to Texas and a slipshod win over South Florida, only to recover and reel off ten straight wins to sneak into the College Football Playoff over Florida State for the final spot. Many believed it was Saban's finest coaching job in seventeen seasons in Tuscaloosa.

On the other side stood a head coach who found himself in the middle of one controversy after another. Forced to serve two separate three-game suspensions, the face of the notorious sign-stealing scandal was adamant he had done nothing wrong. Harbaugh claimed he was guiding "America's Team," yet it seemed like everyone, from the NCAA to the Big Ten to an administration losing its patience with his irregular ways, was lining up against him.

As the teams readied for kickoff, Saban and Harbaugh skipped the usual pregame pleasantries. Saban seemed to truly enjoy the pregame handshake, the one moment inside a football stadium you could reliably find him smiling and looking like a normal human being. But on this day, there would be none of that. It was time for battle. By the end, one was headed to the national championship and the other to an uncertain future.

The Rose Bowl offered a perfect snapshot of what college football had become. On the surface, it was as strong as ever, with the marquee Alabama-Michigan matchup delivering ESPN a monster 27.2 million viewers, the most for a college football game in a decade and the highest-rated non-NFL sporting event since 2018. Dig a little deeper, though, and even the sport's most successful coaches, like Saban and Harbaugh, were questioning their place in it. The last four years had taken a serious toll on coaches who insisted on control and hated change that disrupted their organizations. From the COVID-19 pandemic, which eliminated all semblance of normalcy, to the transfer portal and name, image, and likeness combo that hit college football like a nuclear bomb, coaches had been on their heels and couldn't keep up.

"There's no rules, no guidance, no nothing," said Clemson head coach Dabo Swinney, who has won two national championships. "It's out of control. It's not sustainable. It's an absolute mess and a train wreck, and the kids are going to be the ones who suffer in the end."

It wasn't just the coaches either. The disruptive change the sport faced impacted athletic directors, compliance staffers, athletic trainers, and on and on. To many inside the system, it felt like college football was coming apart at the seams.

"The unhappiness and dissatisfaction level are off the charts," said one high-level crisis management consultant with a broad base of college clients. "I'm going to project eighty percent of my presidential clients, commissioner clients, AD clients, and my coaches are miserable."

The misery of the adults was a financial boon for the college students. Never had players more power or freedom or more ability to capitalize financially on their skills and transfer without consequence time and time again in what had quickly turned into free agency, with the NCAA increasingly unable to stem the tide. It was about time, after the damning decades-long refusal of NCAA leadership to share an abundance of commercial riches with the very body largely responsible for that wealth, the athletes themselves.

It was against this backdrop that the authors of this book spent more than a year reporting deep inside college football—from the Nick, Kirby,

Jimbo, and Lane show in the SEC, to Harbaugh's way and the sign-stealing scandal (and much more) in Ann Arbor, to a bustling beach town outside San Diego and rare access to the recruiting of one of the top high school quarterbacks in the Class of 2024. We traveled from one coast to the next, one corner of the sport to the next, from inside the collectives taking advantage of a brave new world to an embattled enforcement staff trying to stop them, conducting more than two hundred interviews to understand how one of America's most popular sports got to this moment and what its fragile future might hold. It tells the story of the toll being paid—financially, physically, emotionally, and psychologically—by every single soul who cared about the game.

Welcome to *The Price* and what it takes to win in an era of chaos in big-time college football.

CHAPTER 1

The Old King I

ON THE OTHERWISE QUIET NIGHT of May 18, 2022, all it took was seven words out of Nick Saban's mouth to set the college football world on fire.

"A&M bought every player on their team," the Alabama head football coach said almost nonchalantly. He was speaking to a group of wealthy supporters at a downtown Birmingham, Alabama, restaurant. The evening, featuring Saban, Alabama basketball head coach Nate Oats, and NFL Hall of Fame quarterback Joe Namath, who failed to show, was meant to raise awareness for the World Games, a second-rate Olympics that would later turn into a financial boondoggle for the city of Birmingham.

Few were at the restaurant for the World Games. Instead, this was an opportunity for Alabama fat cats to sidle close to the Crimson Tide's resident football genius and hear how good his upcoming team would be. No one in the room, including the University of Alabama system chancellor Finis St. John IV, expected Saban to go nuclear on Texas A&M, an SEC rival.

There were some nervous chuckles and acknowledgments as Saban's comments hung in the air. Then he kept on rolling, pondering aloud about the ramifications of Texas A&M "buying" every player in a recruiting class ranked as the nation's best.

"We didn't buy one player," Saban continued. "I don't know if we're going to be able to sustain that in the future, because more and more people are doing it."

The comments, initially disseminated by AL.com reporter Mike Rodak, spread like wildfire. At first, there was disbelief that the words were real until the accompanying video showed that, yes, Saban really did go there. For Saban to publicly accuse not only a fellow SEC school, but a member of his coaching tree, felt like a Mafia boss breaking omertà, an unspoken vow of silence to never rat out a fellow member of the family. Said a senior NCAA investigator: "The SEC has a code and the code is that we do not turn each other in."

Saban's blowing off steam that night resulted from a long buildup, including months of private complaining over what he believed to be blatant disregard for the sanctity of the sport. He even privately lobbied ESPN commentators Stephen A. Smith and Paul Finebaum to call out what A&M and other programs were doing behind the scenes.

Those efforts hadn't materially impacted anything the night he walked into the Fennec for the World Games fireside chat. Jim Dunaway, a local radio host leading the Q&A portion of the night, went over every question ahead of time with Saban. The Alabama head coach knew the Name, Image, and Likeness—NIL—question was coming at the end and was ready to unload on the issue. Local media was supposed to stop filming after the first fifteen minutes of the event, but they kept the cameras going when no one asked them to leave. What they saw was the king of college football noticing a rising threat just beyond the palace wall. He was already dealing with his former protégé Kirby Smart of Georgia riding high off defeating him in the national championship game four months earlier, challenging him for college football's throne. Now he had to deal with Jimbo Fisher of A&M securing the top recruiting class ever . . . and off an 8-4 season. Saban couldn't accept that. Not the Saban who once told his Alabama boss he was "a horseshit football coach, but nobody will out-recruit me." Now he was losing the recruits he wanted—the lifeblood of his program—to what he saw as an inferior program and inferior coach because he refused to match what in his mind he believed to be illegal offers. He didn't face any internal punishment because his bosses knew what he was up against and supported his efforts to raise awareness.

"Using NIL as a recruiting inducement is a clear violation of NCAA rules on NIL, and we know it's happening because we are being asked to match A&M," said a high-ranking Alabama source.

Saban didn't expect his comments to go as wide as they did, but those familiar with his thinking believe he had two goals in purposefully sharing the unvarnished truth that night. First, he was trying to rally the troops, to remind the wealthy benefactors in attendance that all the good times and championships they'd enjoyed over the years wouldn't continue if they didn't start contributing more money. Saban saw the writing on the wall and knew if he couldn't fire up his base to give, shake off the complacency, and realize that success is always ephemeral, his program would start to slip.

In Nick Saban's kingdom, everything always came back to recruiting. He knew better than anyone that the best-laid plans could only be achieved with the right players to execute them. He traversed the country, putting in thousands of hours each year to find the best players who best fit his system. He knew that as good a coach as he was, if the supply of top high school players around the country to Tuscaloosa every year was disrupted, everything he built could be dismantled. At seventy years old, he was in legacy mode, even if he'd never admit it publicly, and he knew the end was far closer than the beginning.

The second thing he hoped to do that night was send a message to Southeastern Conference commissioner Greg Sankey that the conference—and the sport's leaders at large—needed to step in and do something. Mike Slive, Sankey's predecessor, had stopped all the conference infighting and established a spirit of "We keep things in-house," but Saban's private complaints within the conference had gotten him nowhere. According to those familiar with his thinking, he thought that if he started getting louder and louder about it on this night, only a mile and a half away from SEC headquarters, Sankey would have to do something.

And Sankey did step in, though not in the way Saban wanted.

IN COLLEGE STATION, TEXAS, JIMBO Fisher, the man accused of buying his incoming class, exploded in outrage. Fisher and Saban, who had worked together at LSU in the early 2000s, were always deferential to each other publicly, but they had a strained relationship. Each was a hard-charging alpha personality with doctorate-level mastery of obscenities and putting up with zero bullshit. The two were a powder keg ready to blow by the end of their four years together in Baton Rouge. On that May night, Fisher seethed that a man he knew had never done anything to stop wealthy LSU boosters from paying players back in their days together was now calling him out as a cheater in front of the whole world. Former players, those who received money while playing for Saban and Fisher at LSU, couldn't believe Saban went there either.

"As soon as I heard Coach Saban say that I was like 'What is he doing?'" said former Tiger Elice Parker. "Does he really think the same thing isn't happening at Alabama? Shit, it happened at LSU."

Parker, a Zachary, Louisiana, native, was the old man of Saban's early LSU teams. He spent four years with the Marine Corps after high school before coming to play football for LSU in his early twenties. He was never a star at LSU—he excelled on special teams but was a backup on offense—but still benefited financially from the tremendous local interest in the Tigers. It was common practice, he said, for players to get taken care of, and everyone knew the deal when one of the stars started driving a new SUV. After LSU games, boosters would come into the locker room and reward players who performed well.

"I had multiple times where I got the nice game handshake," Parker said. "The bigger-named athletes just got a healthier handshake than what I did. It wasn't a million dollars, but it was a whole lot of money to us as college kids."

Saban understood the dynamics around big-time college football. In one of his first staff meetings at LSU, he had laid out his expectations with his staff.

"If any of you are ever caught cheating, you're immediately fired," Saban told them. He waited for a beat and said, "But, of course, we can't control what the boosters do."

Fisher was there for that meeting and, more than twenty years later, was ready to bare it all, to let everyone know the Saban he knew, the truth about a man who had won seven national championships. He vowed to his deputies he wouldn't back down from a fight with the big bully over at Bama and demanded a next-day press conference to set the story straight. Texas A&M athletic director Ross Bjork and Creative Artists Agency (CAA) superagent Jimmy Sexton, Fisher's agent, pleaded with him to stand down, to take the higher road, but he couldn't hear it. Fisher believed it was a vicious personal attack, and the only way he could respond would be to go scorched earth.

At the press conference, an incensed Fisher unloaded on his former boss. He went completely off script from the talking points his A&M colleagues had prepared for him. "It's despicable that a reputable head coach can come out and say this when he doesn't get his way or things don't go his way," Fisher said. "The narcissist in him doesn't allow those things to happen. It's ridiculous when he's not on top. The parity in college football he's been talking about? Go talk to coaches who've coached for him. You'll find out all about the parity. Go dig into wherever he's been. You can find out anything."

Citing their shared West Virginia roots, Fisher suggested Saban should have been slapped more as a child. Fisher said people like Saban "think they're God," but that he knew how the man they worship in Tuscaloosa conducts business. He practically begged the reporters assembled in the room to pack up their bags and investigate Saban's behavior that very minute.

"We build him up to be the czar of football," Fisher said. "Go dig into his past or anybody who's ever coached for him. You can find out anything you want to find out. What he does and how he does it. It's despicable. It really is."

Fisher's fiery comments came despite Commissioner Sankey explicitly warning Fisher not to cross the line in retaliating against Saban. This wasn't the first warning the SEC commissioner had given Fisher about going after one of his SEC coaching peers.

Now Sankey, traveling back from an event in New York City, was nonplussed, to put it mildly, that Fisher directly disobeyed his request and turned his conference into a media circus. Texas A&M wanted Sankey to suspend Saban for his comments, but after Fisher returned fire, he was forced to reprimand both. He couldn't believe Texas A&M came complaining, only to let Fisher do *that*.

"He came off like a buffoon," said a high-ranking SEC official. "No one can control him at Texas A&M."

As for Saban, he tried to call Fisher to apologize, but Fisher refused to answer and reiterated multiple times that he and his former LSU boss were done. Deep down, Jimbo was in pain. He couldn't understand why a man he had given four of his prime coaching years to would take such an unnecessary public swing at his character. But Jimbo (like his former mentor) never backed down from a fight. Other members of that LSU staff were disappointed, albeit not surprised, that the two would let the intense desire to sign the top players torpedo their relationship.

"Just two fucking testosterone-ridden babies," said one LSU assistant coach on the staff with Saban and Fisher. "If you got something you don't like about the other guy, say it to the other guy. But they're competitive as shit and emotions burn white hot with high-testosterone guys."

Mark Emmert wasn't surprised either. The NCAA president had hired Saban while serving as LSU's chancellor and knew both men well. How each reacted played true to what he saw in Baton Rouge. "Nick doesn't just launch things out into the world by accident. He's very disciplined for the most part," Emmert said. "Jimbo a little less so. Jimbo is a little more like the rest of us, I suppose; when he says things, he says things." That Saban, Fisher, and the SEC became the focal point of the NIL discussion did amuse him though. The SEC, specifically Sankey, was the most difficult party to deal with, he said, when the NCAA futilely tried to create NIL rules. Now the problem had come home to roost in Birmingham. "To have two SEC coaches throwing rocks at each other was fun," Emmert said.

Fisher had his share of supporters, but the coaching industry generally favored Saban in the hostilities. They thought the Alabama head coach was out of line calling Texas A&M out by name—he later publicly apologized for it—but Fisher's vitriolic attacks on Saban's character didn't land much support.

"He fucked up when he attacked Nick personally," said one SEC coach. "If they did like him, they wouldn't admit it, because he went against the Godfather of college football."

• • •

DESPITE GROWING UP ONLY ABOUT fifteen miles away from each other in West Virginia, Saban and Fisher were fourteen years apart in age and had never crossed paths before working together at LSU.

While working as Michigan State's head coach in 1999, Saban watched film of a Cincinnati–Ohio State game while preparing his team for its game against the Buckeyes. Ohio State won, but Saban was impressed with how well Cincinnati played on offense, totaling 525 yards and 26 first downs. Knowing Cincinnati's head coach, Rick Minter, had a defensive background, he became intrigued about the man behind the prolific offense and put Jimbo's name on a list in case he ever needed an offensive coach.

That came in handy a few weeks later when Saban got the LSU job. He called Minter personally for permission to interview the Cincinnati offensive coordinator. Fisher not only had a burgeoning reputation as an offensive whiz, but he had experience recruiting the South as an assistant at Auburn. In thirty-four-year-old Jimbo Fisher, Saban saw a younger man who grew up like he had, including the accompanying hard edge. There was soon an Odd Couple feel, however, between the meticulous Saban and the easily distracted Fisher.

"Jimbo is like a mad scientist," Minter said. "He's chaotic *and* organized. He's like an accountant . . . [whose] desk looks like crap but he knows where every folder is. He's a brilliant mind, but he comes off as scattered."

In addition to Fisher, Saban's staff included two future NFL head coaches (Freddie Kitchens and Adam Gase), two future Power 5 head coaches (Derek Dooley and Mel Tucker), and well-known career assistants like Pete Jenkins, Rick Trickett, and Sal Sunseri. Saban himself was far from football royalty when he arrived in Baton Rouge. He was well respected within the coaching community but had never even won a bowl game as a head coach. He wasn't a particularly popular hire at LSU despite coming off a 10-2 season in his final year at MSU, something he was well aware of. They'd even say it straight to his face that first year in Louisiana, according to members of his staff.

After he was officially introduced as LSU's new head coach, someone came up to then chancellor Mark Emmert and informed him he had just hired an asshole. Emmert knew Saban's reputation, saying he was "pretty gruff especially at that time," but told the man he wasn't concerned about it. "I've got people to go to dinner with," Emmert told him. "What I really needed was a football coach."

Saban became obsessed with outworking, outrecruiting, and outscheming every opponent. The pace was severe for everyone involved, especially those who had never worked with Saban before.

"He wasn't much fun in 2000," his defensive line coach Pete Jenkins said. "Mel Tucker and I got him the worst year of his damn career."

Trickett, who had worked with Saban at West Virginia in the late 1970s, had a sense of what he was getting into. Saban, Fisher, and Trickett had all grown up in coal country with demanding fathers who had healthy appetites for work. "Big Nick" Saban, who owned a gas station in Monongah, was never one to offer his son many attaboys or pats on the back; instead, he always zeroed in on his mistakes. It shaped Nick's worldview and set him on a never-ending pursuit of perfection. "Fear of failure, fear of having nothing, fear of your family not being able to provide," Trickett said, explaining what powered all three of them. "Seeing how hard your dads worked and not having much."

The stories of Saban's time in Baton Rouge are part legend and part horror story. He was laser-focused on being the best and would keep pushing and pushing until he got there. The long hours didn't matter. The punishing tempo at practices didn't matter. Players throwing up in the 100-degree Louisiana heat? Get the next guy in there. It wasn't malicious or vengeful; it was a man who thought he had the map to the palace and wouldn't let anything slow or distract him from that journey. He had a burning desire to be great and put every ounce of himself into trying to elevate the people around him to accomplish that. You either got on board with the mission or you sought life elsewhere. Coaches and players from that era described him as a thoroughbred horse with blinkers on—it was all about what was ahead and not about anything else happening around him.

A famous example of Saban's one-track mind, passed down from assistant to assistant over the years but never previously reported, occurred early at LSU. On a Tuesday morning in September, Saban and his defensive staff were game-planning for a Saturday home game against Auburn when he was interrupted. A secretary ran into the room and informed Saban that a plane had just hit the World Trade Center in New York City. Confusion started building in the room, but the work continued. Later, she ran back into the room and told Saban a second plane had now hit the second World Trade Center building. To many Americans, that moment on September 11, 2001, signaled that the country was under attack. In that LSU staff meeting, panic unfolded as the coaches tried to understand what was happening and what it might all mean.

Seeing the reaction of his staff, Saban said, "Boys, there are some screwed-up people in the world," he said. "Now, what are we going to do when we're in Cover Two against these routes?"

Saban continued with the regularly scheduled practice later that day, with some players on the team having no idea what was happening across the country because their head coach never addressed it. (Saban would later apologize to a newspaper for having his "head in the sand" in not addressing 9/11 with his team that day. He'd have to apologize again in 2007, when he clumsily compared an Alabama loss to 9/11 and Pearl Harbor.)

Years later, as Saban assembled his first Alabama staff in Tuscaloosa, his assistant coach Kirby Smart used the story to explain to the new coaches what they had just signed up for. "This guy is all football all the time," Smart told them. "When he's in the office, he's not thinking about anything else."

Saban never wanted to waste a second and fastidiously followed his schedule. "He's very decisive and he doesn't have any time for bullshit," said one longtime staffer. "If he thinks something is a waste of his time, he's going to treat you like it and walk out of the room." In 2004, Saban's final season at LSU, Louisiana governor Kathleen Blanco, the first female governor in the state's history, came to talk to the team. Saban allotted ten minutes for Blanco's talk. As a few seconds trickled past the ten-minute mark, Saban got up, stepped in front of the governor, and said it was time to practice.

"He cuts it off in the middle of the speech," offensive lineman Steve Arflin said. "I'll never forget that. Cut off the governor of Louisiana so we could get started because it was seventeen seconds into his schedule."

The results were undeniable, but the pace was unrelenting. By 2002, Saban was on his third defensive coordinator in as many seasons. To survive the LSU era under Saban, you had to have thick skin, near superhuman stamina to keep up with the hours, and the ability to perform under pressure. "He was hard as hell to work for, but he outworked everybody on the staff," Jenkins said. "His expectation level for his assistants is way the hell up there." He was constantly cranking up the heat on his coaches, whether on the practice field or in the meeting rooms, but if you went in the tank when he got after you, then he lost all confidence in you. Fisher and a young Will Muschamp had the disposition to handle Saban's antics and give it back to him, creating spirited practices and staff meetings.

Saban and Fisher were fiercely competitive, which often spilled onto the practice field. It was an elaborate chess match with the players as pawns, albeit with much more profanity than anything between Kasparov and Karpov. Saban, a defensive mastermind, and Fisher, the offensive mad scientist intent on showing off his brilliance, clashed often in those practices. Fisher actually liked to try to get under Saban's skin.

"Jimbo was funny," Arflin said. "He was a nice yin to Saban's yang. Saban was always serious and rarely let loose at all. Fisher would do that a little bit."

Saban and Fisher both had talent in another department. Saban "is one of the greatest cusser-outers of all-time," said LSU offensive lineman Peter Dyakowski. "if not the greatest of all-time." Only Fisher, who said "goddamn more than anybody I've ever met in my life," according to Arflin, could vie with him.

There was a "real rivalry" between the two, according to Dyakowski, but the players believed it was mostly two highly competitive guys going at each other. Saban built a culture where every practice repetition was treated as if it were the most important thing, and everyone from the coaches down to the players had to buy into that philosophy. Early on, there was resistance. "We didn't like him because practice was so hard," said offensive guard Brandon Hurley. "Senior guys [would] have a countdown in their locker with how many more practices they had left." Later, the team bought into the system when the results showed there was a method behind the labor demands.

"He had this talent for fostering incredibly well-conditioned angry men by the time it came to Saturday," Arflin said. "You're just pissed and you want to take it out on someone."

Twenty years later, Jimbo Fisher showed some of those pissed-off feelings didn't always go away.

TWO WEEKS AFTER THE SHOTS heard 'round the college football world, all eyes were on Saban and Fisher as they arrived in Florida for the SEC's annual spring meetings. Everyone involved, from the SEC to the pair's shared agent, Sexton, worked to tamp down the situation and ensure there were no fireworks on the beach. Still, it would be the first time Saban and Fisher had seen each other in person since the drama, and they had to share a meeting room with twelve other SEC coaches for the next day and a half.

Saban struck a contrite tone, according to those in attendance, realizing he created unnecessary headlines that overshadowed the real issues. Fisher, meanwhile, came in swaggering and unrepentant about his vicious words against the Alabama head coach. Saban seemed thrown by Fisher's attitude. He said publicly that he had no problem with his former assistant but didn't back down from the context of his comments. Fisher wouldn't acknowledge the situation at all, taking a page out of Bill Belichick's playbook, and repeatedly said "We're moving on" when asked by reporters about his relationship with Saban. He did nothing to shut down speculation that the relationship between the two was irrevocably damaged.

How each handled the situation further illustrated the Godfather-like roles they played within the SEC. While the ages didn't quite match, Saban was Michael Corleone and Jimbo was Sonny. Saban, who rarely held grudges, believed it was all business, not personal, when he called out schools using NIL as pay for play. For Jimbo, of course, everything was all personal, and he couldn't help but react emotionally.

That night, in a swanky beach restaurant near the SEC's meetings, the Saban-Fisher brouhaha dominated a dinner conversation. Behind the personality showdown were more complicated matters. A source intimately familiar with Alabama's NIL situation explained the existential crisis that the Crimson Tide was facing.

"If Nick Saban retired tomorrow, we're fucked," the source said.

This person described Alabama's NIL operation as trying to plug the leak on the *Titanic*. Alabama purposefully took a cautious approach to NIL in its first year of existence, but the program had quickly fallen dangerously far behind its SEC peers. Alabama was still recruiting at a high level because of the magnetic pull of Saban, who sold his track record of developing NFL player after NFL player, but it had nothing to sustain the program should he ever retire.

"As soon as Saban leaves, this thing is a house of cards," the source said. "It's all going to fall apart."

And even the long-term benefits of playing for Saban didn't always win against cold, hard cash. Alabama's languishing NIL operation cost it top recruits, which is what had led Saban to air his grievances publicly in the first place. The top-end number Alabama could hit at that time, in the low six figures, paled in comparison to the seven-figure numbers thrown around by other schools for elite players. Things might have been different if Alabama was even in the NIL ballpark. Fisher's all-star recruiting class was a clear shot across the bow about what Alabama was up against.

"I think Bama would probably have three or four more five-stars last year if NIL wasn't a thing, which is pretty crazy to think about," said Jackson Zager, an NIL agent who represented top recruits. "I know there were a few that would have gone to Bama."

And if the NIL agents like Zager knew it, Saban did too.

The Alabama head coach was conflicted though. He desperately wanted to win but worried about NIL's corrosive effect on his meticulously cultivated culture. As another top NIL lawyer said at the time, "They are really weird. They don't really pay traditionally. They don't do that." The world had been turned upside down so much that not violating NCAA rules to pay players was now considered nontraditional.

In fact, Alabama had a chance to add a high-profile transfer, the kind of difference maker that the 2022 team needed, but Saban declined because of the asking price. "I'm not going to let some kid own my ass for a million dollars," Saban told a confidant. He'd rather have a level playing field where every player on the team got the same base amount, and then the true star players could earn more based on the national platform playing at Alabama provided. It frustrated him that recruiting was devolving into just how much money was offered up front rather than the bigger, long-term goals he always successfully sold to top recruits.

It wore on Saban, who prioritized recruiting above all else. Consider that on his very first day as Alabama's head coach, he called for a staff meeting to explain his vision of Crimson Tide football. He wanted everyone who worked in the building in any capacity to be there.

When the entire staff arrived, from coaches to janitors, Saban delivered the core mission to his new employees. "Everything we do," Saban said, "is about recruiting. Everything we do."

He advised that if a recruit—or a recruit's parent—walked into the building and the bathrooms were dirty, it would reflect poorly on the entire program. It was the same if a secretary, who he explained was the first link to the football program, didn't answer the phone a certain way. Every piece mattered, and it all impacted his recruiting efforts.

In his first year as Alabama's head coach, Saban was so relentless on the recruiting trail that the NCAA changed the rules because of him. At the time, head coaches could go on the road in the spring to visit prospects. But after working constantly from the season to recruiting to spring practice, come May, head coaches weren't exactly eager to hit the road. But Saban, knowing how badly he needed the right players to fulfill his vision of Alabama football, was everywhere that spring. Wherever he went, he might start with a recruit's morning workout at 6:00 a.m. and then traverse the state, hitting as many as eight or ten schools that day. "No other coach in college football was doing that or wanting to do that," said Geoff Collins, his first director of player personnel at Alabama. "He was a machine. He set the tone for everyone in the organization, because if he's out there grinding like this, we need to be doing this or even more so." After enough coaches complained about it, the NCAA banned head coaches from in-person spring evaluation in a rule change known as the "Saban rule."

No one spent more time with Saban than Collins that first year. Before becoming a head coach at Temple and Georgia Tech, Collins was in charge of Saban's recruiting department, a highly valued but rather stressful position. He'd start the day sitting in on defensive staff meetings with Saban, join him for the full staff meeting later that morning, then spend two hours going over recruiting tape together before practice. "It was relentless attention to detail, maniacal obsession with getting everything fixed and getting the process in place," Collins said. "I'd have two hours, just he and I, every day, and you'd think after spending that much time, there'd be some levity and some light moments. I can't say that there were. It was here's how we are going to maximize every second of every day."

After a nonstop sprint from Saban's arrival in January, an exhausted staff was finally readying to go on its first vacation in July. NCAA rules prohibited coaches from calling or hosting recruits during that time, giving everyone a chance to get a brief break in before fall camp started in August. Saban, seemingly aware of the torture he just put his new staff through, made a big deal about wanting everyone to enjoy their time off, spend time with their families, and recharge, because when they returned to the building, it was on. He gave the same speech multiple times as vacation neared, promising not to call any of them during the break.

Finally, the first day of vacation was upon them.

Collins heard his phone go off and looked at the time. It was 6:45 a.m. The call, coming from a blocked private number, meant only one thing: Saban was on the other line. "I was like, 'Dog, I thought you weren't calling us during this break?'" Collins said. "I didn't realize that conversation was not applying to me and my role. I talked to him like four or five times a day every single day during that vacation."

This is who Nick Saban was. A man who willingly eschewed enjoying vacations—during which he watched recruit films—and always had football on his mind. It was rarely fun—the winning was the fun part he'd tell players after yet another grueling practice—but this is what he recognized was necessary to be the best. The results only emboldened him. After calling Collins every day during vacation, Saban and the rest of his staff signed a Julio Jones–headlined recruiting class that at the time was one of the best ever. From 2011 to 2021, Saban signed the nation's top recruiting class nine times, including an unprecedented seven-year streak atop the 247Sports rankings. Saban annually signing the best players became the surest bet in sports. The one blip came in 2018, the first year of the early signing period, which allowed players to sign letters of intent starting in December instead of in February. Saban underestimated the impact that would have on the recruiting calendar and didn't push to have recruits get on campus earlier, and it led to only the fifth-best recruiting class that year. The following year, Alabama adjusted its approach and again had the top group of prospects. Saban was inevitable.

This man had a tried-and-true methodology, from the types of players he targeted to how he recruited them, and believed he could control his destiny through recruiting.

But by 2022, he wasn't sure he could anymore.

"If there's one thing Nick likes, it's control," said Charlie Weems, the former chairman of the LSU Board of Regents.

Weems had helped hire Saban at LSU and became a close confidant during his time in Baton Rouge. After Saban left LSU for his brief tenure with the Miami Dolphins in 2004, it didn't take long for Weems to hear from his friend about how different things were in the NFL. Saban told him that in college, if he needed a good quarterback or cornerback, he'd just go out and recruit the best one. And he loved how he could mold a player with his famous process. In Saban's college kingdom, it was a true meritocracy. It didn't matter where you came from or who you knew, the best-prepared player always won.

In the NFL, he had to deal with the draft, salary caps, and other complications that limited his success. It had been his dream to be an NFL head coach, but it didn't take him long to realize where he could truly excel was back in college football. The NFL robbed him of his greatest gift: control.

"I can't do everything that I can do," Saban told Weems. "I've got guys you can't motivate and have the same control over."

The fear now keeping him up at night was that college football had become the same.

CHAPTER 2

Michigan Man

IT WAS A LITTLE PAST nine in the morning the Thursday before Memorial Day weekend. One hundred days before the 2023 season kicked off, and Jim Harbaugh was sitting in his office overlooking a pristine indoor practice field on the back side of Schembechler Hall, wearing a gray sweater and—you guessed it—khaki pants. He fidgeted a bit, the culprits, one suspected, the two soda cans taking up residence on a desk cluttered with paperwork and the smokeless tobacco he occasionally spit into a nearby trash can in defiance of a surgical procedure back in 2012 to correct an irregular heartbeat.

For most any coach the subject at hand was a heart attack in waiting: the chaotic state of the game. It was a subject in which this head football coach had long since decided, for better or worse, to take a stand. Fundamental to this stand was the belief that old school values of player development, 143 years of football tradition, 44 Big Ten titles, an iconic stadium, eleven national championships, backed by a prestigious U of M degree, and—how should we put this—an *invested* alumni base would win out over the short-term promises of the portal and NIL collectives.

"You're telling me people are being distracted by it, people are losing their shit," he said. "This game, football, has been the foundation of my life, done so much, taught me so much, and I've seen it be good for so many.

"Football is ninety-eight percent of what I have. Who I am as a person came from the game of football, a kid who made a sport of everything from five years old to fifteen or sixteen. A real nobody. To have a seat at the table now, all that came from football. The work ethic. The discipline."

On this day, seven months shy of his sixtieth year of life, Harbaugh was nothing less than a Michigan Man on a mission, preaching principles destined to carry enormous weight against the headwinds to come in the months ahead.

"I don't treat my kids at home any different than players on the team or the players on the team any different than my kids at home," Harbaugh said. "I got one goal for them: get to the point where they can take care of themselves, and aren't afraid of any challenges, aren't afraid to take on any new challenges. Once you get them there, then your mission is to make them the best version of themselves on and off the field, in their lives. That's the way I was taught as a lad by my dad. That's the way I was coached here at Michigan. Regardless of any adversity, distractions, you're teaching young kids, college kids, to be steadfast. No matter what the changing winds, changing currents. Stay on your mission. Stay steadfast in your goals, your values, and your faith. The most important thing."

Faith, Family, and Football. In many ways the preordained Holy Trinity for the youngest son of Jack and Jackie Harbaugh. His mother was a spitfire, the rock on which a family rested. His father, a football lifer who spent more than fifty years coaching under the bright lights of high school and college football—with pit stops at places like Perrysburg and Xenia, Ohio; Morehead State and Bowling Green, Iowa; Michigan (under Bo Schembechler); and Stanford, before accepting head coaching jobs at Western Michigan then Western Kentucky, where Jack won a Division I-AA national championship in 2002, in his fourteenth and final season at the school.

Oldest son, John, then in his seventeenth year as head coach of the Baltimore Ravens, and Jim (younger by fifteen months) shared the same bedroom growing up, a line of white athletic tape, quite naturally, dividing it in half.

In grade school John and Jim played sports year-round: basketball, hockey, football, wrestling, and baseball. Young Jim up and out by 6:00 a.m. on Saturday for wrestling, changing his clothes in the family car in time for a basketball game at 10:00. By the time he was eight, he kept statistics on his batting average in baseball, scoring average in basketball, and touchdowns in football.

Given their ages and combative DNA, John and Jim grew to be best friends and relentless competitors, never giving an inch in anything—basketball, baseball . . . or chess. As the story goes, Jack once woke up in the hospital, recovering from surgery, only to find his two boys arguing over a board at 2:00 a.m. During more restrictive winter months, they devised a test of wills using only a deck of cards. The rules were simple. If you turned up, say, a seven, it meant seven push-ups. A face card was ten, aces fifteen, and the Joker twenty. Depending on the draw, you could pull as many as four hundred push-ups in an hour.

AS PART OF A FEATURE on the Harbaugh family by ESPN's Marty Smith prior to the playoffs, the origin story of "Who's got it better . . ." was brought to life. It all stemmed from the day seven-year-old Jim and nine-year-old John stepped out of the house ready for a ride to school.

"Where's the car?" asked Jim.

"No car today, boys," his father replied. "We're walking."

So they walked. Basketball in hand, one hundred dribbles with the right hand, a hundred more with the left, back and forth, back and forth, traveling, so to speak, on their way to school.

At one point their father shouted:

"Who's got it better than us?"

"Nobody, Dad! Nobody!"

AFTER A STELLAR CAREER AT Palo Alto High in 1982, the prodigal son returned to his Midwest roots. By the time his college career was over, Jim Harbaugh was an all–Big Ten quarterback, had set a school record in career passing yards (5,449), and finished third in Heisman Trophy balloting.

Drafted in the first round by the Chicago Bears in 1987, he would go on to play 177 games for four different teams over fourteen seasons in the NFL. In 1995 he earned Pro Bowl and AFC Player of the Year honors after leading the Indianapolis Colts to the AFC Championship Game.

Harbaugh once recalled his icy Windy City welcome. One fine spring day he walked into head coach Mike Ditka's office in Halas Hall shortly after being drafted, only to have "Iron Mike" give him a team sweater and the cold shoulder.

"You know," Ditka said, "we've got four other quarterbacks here already."

"I really didn't get the feeling he wanted me," Harbaugh said. "From everything I heard, it seemed he wanted a different player."

Three years later Ditka named him the team's starting quarterback.

ENTERING HIS NINTH SEASON AS the Man at Michigan, Harbaugh had lost none of his famous fire. He loved his 2023 team—junior quarterback J.J. McCarthy, senior running back Blake Corum, starting guard Zak Zinter, defensive tackle Kris Jenkins, defensive back Mike Sainristil, leaders of a band of brothers that remained at Michigan when they could have gone pro or into the portal to try to capture an elusive national championship.

This devotion was underscored by the fact that just a few months earlier, Harbaugh himself had turned down the head coaching job and life-altering Walmart money from the owners of the Denver Broncos to remain in Ann Arbor—despite a perilous NCAA investigation hanging over his head, one centered around impermissible contacts with recruits and other sundry minor violations during a COVID-19 "dead" period, and the serious charge that Harbaugh had lied to investigators about two chance meetings with recruits and their families during that same dead period.

"I swear the only reason he turned down the Broncos was loyalty," said a source with direct knowledge of the negotiations. "He had these guys coming back. He explained it to me. He was apologetic about it. 'I owe it to these guys. These guys have every reason to expect me to be there when they come back, and I have to be there for them.'

"He wasn't disregarding the [NCAA investigation] facts. 'These are all possible outcomes, and none of them are good for me. One or two could be really bad for me. This opportunity at this stage in life is a once-in-a-lifetime opportunity.' Nonetheless, he stayed. Only because of his loyalty to J.J., Blake, those other guys coming back."

With the Broncos offer in mind, Harbaugh was asked how hard it would have been to leave Ann Arbor, better known to locals as A2. "Seems to be a pretty damn big magnetic pull here. Is that a fair assessment?" he was asked.

"Yeah. That is fair. That is more than fair," he replied before offering a chuckle. "Who's got it better than us? Nobody."

THAT "BETTER THAN US" BOAST carried more than a touch of irony. In many precincts Harbaugh had long since been voted the runaway winner in any Most Polarizing Coach in America poll, alternately described as controversial, complicated, unique, unorthodox, idiosyncratic, and, more often than not, quirky. A highly intelligent road-less-traveled guy who delighted in pushing boundaries, exploiting gray areas, in zigging where others zag, in what Harbaugh himself once called "outsmarting the system."

To wit: early on at Michigan, Harbaugh discovered there was no national rule on how many offseason summer camps a head coach could conduct. So in 2015 he set up the satellite tour—in reality, planting U of M recruiting flags deep in the SEC's backyard, leaving the likes of Saban and other coaches fit to be tied; offered educational "team bonding" trips in early May to countries like Italy and South Africa at a cost of some $6,000 per man; and made the controversial hire of a high school football coach from New Jersey as the team's director of player personnel and recruiting (Chris Partridge—remember that name), who just happened to influence the commitment of one of his star high school players and future pros to Michigan (safety Jabrill Peppers), before bringing another future NFL star (Green Bay outside linebacker Rashan Gary) along for the ride.

ATTORNEY TOM MARS GOT HIS first taste of this Harbaughian stew in the spring of 2018. At the time Mars was representing former Ole Miss quarterback Shea Patterson in his attempt to receive a waiver from the NCAA to transfer to Michigan and become immediately eligible to play. In the ensuing years, Mars would spend countless hours engaged with Harbaugh on an array of topics—eligibility, Netflix movies, abortion, politics, and, oh yes, his trials and tribulations with the NCAA.

"I think Jim is a complex person. In some ways they broke the mold when they made Jim Harbaugh," Mars said. "I mean that in a good way. Some people have described him as quirky. I find personality traits that are unusual, endearing. I'd give him the highest rating in leadership, motivation, integrity. Definitely a principled guy. And loyal to a fault."

That's not to say, as Todd Anson, a Michigan law school grad and long-time friend and adviser, put it, Harbaugh wasn't capable of taking his laser focus on football to comic extremes. Case in point: The time Anson was invited to stay at the Harbaugh's new home in Ann Arbor shortly after Jim was hired, while Sarah and the kids were still back in California finishing out the school year. Arriving at the house, Anson said he discovered nothing but a blow-up mattress in a spare bedroom, not a bath towel or roll of toilet paper in sight, and a fridge full of nothing but cold air. A trip to Costco soon followed.

"At times," said Anson, "Jim can be a very narrow human being."

JAMES JOSEPH HARBAUGH OFFICIALLY ARRIVED on Michigan's bucolic campus from San Francisco on December 30, 2014. By then he was in the twentieth year of a coaching life that began as an unpaid assistant under his father at Western Kentucky, scouting and recruiting high school athletes while still playing in the NFL. Upon retirement, a two-year stop as quarterback coach in Oakland (2002–2003), highlighted by a trip to Super Bowl XXXVII before taking the head job at the University of San Diego in the Pioneer League, where he won twenty-nine games in three years. Next stop: Stanford. Over four seasons Harbaugh firmly established himself as a turnaround artist, breathing new life into a struggling Cardinal program. From 4-8 his first season to 12-1 his last, with some very public clashes with his peers—like USC coach Pete Carroll—along the way.

Then the 49ers came calling. Over four seasons Harbaugh performed a bit of Bay Area magic, advancing to three NFC Championship games and Super Bowl XLVII against his brother and the Baltimore Ravens, before an ongoing battle with general manager Trent Baalke greased his exit.

Harbaugh's return to Ann Arbor was hailed as nothing less than the revival of Michigan football. Two months earlier, Jim Hackett had been named interim athletic director, replacing a beleaguered Dave Brandon, who had resigned under pressure.

Hackett was not any interim AD. He had just retired after thirty years with the Grand Rapids–based office furniture giant Steelcase, becoming the youngest CEO in company history at the age of thirty-nine. After an eighteen-month stint in Ann Arbor, Hackett would later become CEO of the Ford Motor Company. His thinking about complex business problems and solutions was deeply influenced by the theoretical research coming out of the Santa Fe Institute, an independent nonprofit founded by several scientists who had previously worked at the Los Alamos National Laboratory helping develop the atomic bomb. The institute's research was dedicated to the "multidisciplinary study of . . . complex adaptive systems," not unlike an athletic department the size of Michigan's.

Hackett's first day on the job was October 31, 2014, a not-so-happy Halloween. Brady Hoke was in his fourth season as head coach of a generally underwhelming run—at least by Michigan standards—at the tail end of a dismal 5-7 campaign, including another blowout loss to Ohio State.

"I only see a few games, including the Ohio State game, and Brady's contract is up," Hackett said. "No one told me that."

So, much like a Los Alamos scientist, Hackett did some deep thinking and decided he needed to make not a one-year but a five-year decision on his next head coach.

"That's what led me to say I have to end the relationship [with Hoke] now," said Hackett, "because I can't give you a new contract. I'll let the world know what kind of wonderful man you are, because he is, and I did that in a press conference, and then I started to work."

As it so happened Hackett had been a reserve center on one of Bo's teams when Jack Harbaugh was the defensive backs coach. Before practice when the centers and quarterbacks were working on exchanges and Harbaugh senior was working with the punt returners, they started to talk. A long-lasting friendship was formed.

"I hadn't let Brady go, but I knew I was going to," said Hackett, "so I called Jack and said, 'I can't tell you what's going on, it wouldn't be right, but let's just say I found myself in a situation where I've got to deal with Brady's contract and I don't continue it,' and he knew where I was going."

Hackett told the senior Harbaugh he would like to speak with his son but only if there was hope. He didn't need or want a media circus.

"Jim," replied Jack Harbaugh, "I think if you're interested in recruiting him, I think he would love that."

That's all Hackett needed to hear. He said his first call with Jim Harbaugh came right before the Ohio State game. Hackett's telling, nine years later, is something out of a *Saturday Night Live* skit.

"He answered the phone. I said, 'This is Jim Hackett.'"

Harbaugh: "Is this the guy who taped me in the locker?"

Seems young Jim had tagged along with his dad to quite a few Michigan football practices and—stop us if you've heard this before—was a complete pain in the ass. Running around, throwing the ball everywhere, creating the kind of havoc only a hyperactive four-year-old can create.

So one day some pissed-off offensive linemen picked him up and taped him inside a locker.

Hackett: "So I said to him, 'No, man, I'm the one *who cut you out.*'"

After the laughter died, the two men started talking—and kept talking, every weekend for six or seven weeks. All the while Hackett was trying to figure out the "idiosyncratic" behavior people were talking about, trying, in his words, "to get to the bottom of the moral compass."

"You've met some competitive people, they are so competitive, that's why they're dominant," said Hackett. "I grew up with three older brothers. I have a brother like that. Here's what you get in the package, they can't lose, so what happens next? Do they cheat? How far are they willing to go?

"My book on Jim is he'll go right to the line to see if you'll catch him. He's trying to be really clever . . . like the summer camp thing. Jim's cleverness is not cheating. He just knows the rules better than you. [Former Cleveland Browns coach] Paul Brown was like that. Bo. Woody. Belichick. All those guys are like that. Jim fit a niche for me."

Now all Hackett had to do was pry him away from the 49ers. Fortunately, Harbaugh's battles with GM Baalke had reached a breaking point.

So Hackett got on the phone with Jed York, the 49ers' young owner, told him he wanted Harbaugh, and worked out an exit strategy.

A month after the Ohio State game Michigan had their man signing Harbaugh to a seven-year contract.

• • •

SIX YEARS LATER, ONLY DEAR friends and the faithful believed Hackett, now running Ford Motor, had made the right choice.

In Harbaugh's first five years his Wolverines lost between three and five games every year—including five straight to Ohio State—never ranking higher than 10th in the final polls. The sixth year, the COVID-19 pandemic shortened 2020 season, the maize and blue bottomed out, winning just two of six games.

"If you did a poll of Michigan fans, I'm not sure Harbaugh comes back," said John U. Bacon, chronicler of all things Michigan athletics and author of *Endzone: The Rise, Fall, and Return of Michigan Football*. "People forget that pretty quickly."

Certainly not Harbaugh. One cold December night he walked down a hill to his parents' house and poured his heart out.

"I remember, it was about seven o'clock," his father Jack told *Sports Illustrated*'s Michael Rosenberg. "He sat down on the couch with us. And he said, 'I just want you to be ready. Tomorrow I could be fired. . . . I'm not going to be the coach at the University of Michigan. The reason I tell you is because when you see it, I want you to be prepared.' And then he got up and went home. Walked up the hill."

Faced with a problem of his own making, Harbaugh pivoted. He took stock and revamped his coaching staff—letting six older assistants go. In their place he hired younger coaches full of innovative ideas and recruiting zeal, landing the likes of five-star quarterback McCarthy.

A control freak by nature, Harbaugh ceded more power to key players and coaches, particularly Biff Poggi, who took on the role of consigliere and conduit to the locker room. Perhaps most importantly, he doubled down on the man since hailed as the team's X-factor: director of strength and conditioning Ben Herbert, a certified perfectionist with an inspiring spirit.

"In the weight room it's like Nirvana," said Harbaugh during our interview. "That's the center of our player development, with Ben Herbert and his staff. I spend as much time as I can down there."

Finally, seven years into his time in Ann Arbor, a revamped form of Michigan football emerged—bigger, stronger, mentally tougher, defensive minded, and far more versatile. At the same time that the team's DNA was changing, Harbaugh retained his unique ability to own a room—whether in the locker room or when speaking to a recruit and his family in his office for two and a half hours about everything under the sun, be it his new lawn mower or leaf blower. To turn things up a notch, he added a "Beat Ohio" drill, an intense team workout that weeded out guys who, in Harbaugh's words, didn't want to "push the train." The results became clear in 2021, when the Wolverines went 12-2 and recorded their first win over Ohio State in a decade, earning a spot in four-team postseason playoff.

Of course, that season also marked the beginning of the Name, Image, and Likeness era. Based on pure numbers alone Michigan should have dominated right from the start. It boasted not only one of the largest living alumni bases—an estimated 670,000 people—but more than 25,000 annual donors, and raised between $500 million and $700 million a year, among the top ten universities overall, including between $15 million and $25 million for athletics.

Despite those numbers, Michigan found itself stumbling out of the starting blocks, trailing Miami, USC, Ohio State, and a smattering of SEC schools—Texas A&M, Tennessee, Georgia—that shot out like cannons. Unlike other blue-blood programs housed under a single collective roof, Michigan had decided to take a shotgun approach: as many as a half dozen collectives or marketing groups eventually vying for donor money and influence, bearing names like Valiant, Champions Circle, Stadium & Main, and Hail! Impact.

Compounding the problem, according to multiple sources, athletic department staffers were reluctant to embrace the new normal, taking their cues from the athletic director Warde Manuel.

"For a good year we didn't hear a thing out of athletics [about NIL]," said one senior university official. "It came from Warde. He stayed quiet on what we should do. You cannot steer a donor to a student-athlete. You cannot make those deals happen. We had no guidance really up until December 2022. Otherwise, it was I don't know what to tell you. We're neither for or against it. Warde's silence made me think we were pretty much against it."

Others in the know about Manuel, who played defensive tackle under Bo on the same 1986 team as Harbaugh, were less charitable, describing him as an obstructionist.

"There was an uprising by coaches against Warde," said one university official. "Telling him 'We can't compete anymore, you're killing me, I'm going to get fired, you won't allow us to compete.' NIL was number one in terms of tension."

In our interview, Manuel pushed back hard on the notion he was reluctant to embrace NIL, saying he had been an outspoken proponent for student-athletes publicly and privately.

"In terms of collectives, I wanted to make sure whoever we developed the collective around, we did it the right way in terms of inducements for our student-athletes," he said. "Some may say I was slow. But I've always worked and always had open communication with our collectives. I wanted to make sure our student-athletes were not taken advantage of. If I'm going to be blamed for that, then blame me."

"Warde is very measured, methodical, and it hurts sometimes," said one high-ranking athletic department official, "especially in today's environment, where things happen with the snap of your fingers. It slowed us down."

It wasn't until the summer of 2023, nearly two full years after NIL became the law of the land, that Harbaugh got involved, crisscrossing the country in support of Champions Circle, by now the official NIL partner of U of M athletics.

"There are other people who are not sitting idle," he told a group of donors at an event in Chicago in June. "We can sit here and go, 'Hey, we're Michigan. Let's just be idle. We are in a great spot!' Other people are not idling right now."

Asked directly a month earlier about Manuel's role and whether Michigan's NIL structure had kept pace with other elite programs, Harbaugh dodged the question.

"I don't know what you're referring to," he said. "It's well documented. I have put something out there [support for Champions Circle]. I'm coaching the team. I have a little sign over there—just coach the team. Making sure they are getting an education, which I still think is the most powerful thing I can do for them."

• • •

TENSION BETWEEN THE TWO MOST powerful people in most athletic departments—the AD and his head football coach—is nothing new. One side is keenly focused on keeping the entire ship afloat, the other, on the bright shiny object right in front of their face. Winning. Costs be damned.

Follow the U of M timeline back far enough and longtime staffers are among the first to point out Schembechler and nationally renowned AD Don Canham didn't always see eye to eye during their twenty-year marriage. But Hall of Fame head coaches no longer command $150,000 a year in salary and bonuses as Schembechler did; instead they're closing in on *one hundred times* that amount.

In addition, in 2023 alone Michigan's football revenue topped $140 million. In short, the stakes had skyrocketed, and along with it the tension between two singular forces, particularly when one of those forces has, in Harbaugh's case, a dance card marked with the Minnesota Vikings, Denver Broncos, Los Angeles Chargers, and Atlanta Falcons.

"We called it Harbuary," said one former U of M administrator. "Every January we'd all watch Harbaugh to see what pro team he was talking to."

For departmental detectives, the Harbaugh-Manuel relationship had long since devolved into something of a parlor game on social media and fan blogs featuring a rotating cast of characters. For example, when Manuel was hired in January 2016 from the University of Connecticut, Harbaugh's choice was said to have been well-respected West Virginia AD Oliver Luck, the father of Andrew Luck, who had starred at quarterback for Harbaugh at Stanford. Manuel's subsequent top-down reporting hierarchy discouraged drop-in visits. In addition, after the post-COVID season and ensuing lower football revenues dropped precipitously, Manuel cut Harbaugh's guaranteed $8 million salary (plus incentives) in half. And even though he signed a five-year extension in 2022, it's never really been about the money for Harbaugh, so much as the feeling of being *wanted*, having an outspoken advocate he could count on, that had his back with the Board of Regents.

Manuel called speculation he had anything less than an honest relationship with a head coach he called "smart, passionate, a great colleague" flat-out ridiculous.

"Jim and I, from my perspective, had a very open, great relationship in that there was communication," Manuel said. "When I called, he picked up the phone. When he called, I picked up the phone. There was never the stuff that was out in social media that we don't talk; all of that was ridiculous. Our relationship was very open, direct. There was never a time there was a break."

Manuel was the first to admit he had little or no interest in taking to social media to calm the critics or rally support for his coaches.

U of M president Santa Ono turned out to be that vocal advocate. Just three months into his new post, following another stellar 13-1 season in 2022 and a second consecutive trip to the CFP, Ono, a man who enjoys the spotlight, took it upon himself to break yet another logjam of contract talks between Harbaugh and Manuel.

Among Harbaugh's reported demands at the time: the desire to be the highest paid coach in the Big Ten—around $9 million per year plus up to another $3 million in incentives—and a large assistant salary pool of $8 million. Meanwhile, the dalliance with the Broncos continued.

Having successfully stepped into that breach, on January 16, 2023, Ono posted this tweet, perceived by some as a not-so-subtle dig at his athletic director.

I just got off the phone with Coach Harbaugh and Jim shared with me the great news that he is going to remain as the Head Coach of the Wolverines. That is fantastic news that I have communicated to our Athletic Director Warde Manuel. #GoBlue!

That same day Harbaugh released a statement of his own, expressing "love" for his relationships at Michigan, mentioning Ono by name but no one else.

"My heart is at the University of Michigan," he said. "I once heard a wise man say, Don't try to out-happy happy."

HARBAUGH'S DEATH MATCH WITH THE NCAA began that very month, when the university received a draft Notice of Allegations (NOA). Four of the alleged infractions were Level II and viewed as relatively minor: recruiting and coaching during the COVID-19 dead period. Specifically, texting recruits, having off-field analysts involved in on-field coaching activities, and coaches evaluating summer workouts via Zoom during the shutdown.

The fifth and final violation was by far the most egregious: a Level I charge that Harbaugh misled or lied to investigators.

By now Tom Mars was Harbaugh's attorney. As the NCAA had long since discovered, he was not just another advocate. Mars had finished first in his law school class and made the top score on the bar exam, quickly establishing himself as one of Arkansas's most respected trial lawyers and representing defendants in a variety of complex cases ranging from contract disputes to class action, RICO, and defamation suits. In 1998 he had left a booming private practice to become the director of the Arkansas State Police and later served as senior vice president and general counsel for Walmart for five years.

By his own admission, prior to 2017 Mars had no interest and knew next to nothing about college football. Then, one day, a close friend told him former Ole Miss head football coach Houston Nutt was ensnared in a NCAA investigation alleging he had allowed ineligible students to play in 2011 and 2012. At one time Mars and Nutt had lived right next door to each other when Nutt was the head coach at Arkansas.

Mars was intrigued. In a subsequent drive from Atlanta to Starkville to meet a Mississippi-based reporter, he listened to the audio version of *The System*, a 2013 bestseller on the state of big-time college football coauthored by one of the authors of this book.

"I was pretty much addicted to the book," Mars remembered. "Ended up finishing it. One hundred percent of what I knew about college football."

To better understand the sport, Mars said he spoke with some of its most respected voices—Dennis Dodd at CBS Sports, Dan Wolken at *USA Today*, and Pat Forde, then at Yahoo Sports now at *Sports Illustrated*. Armed with more insight and information, Mars reached out to the general counsel at Ole Miss with an offer on behalf of Nutt.

"I said, 'Look, Houston would probably just accept a private letter of apology (from the university) that he can stick in a desk drawer in case he needs it,'" he remembered. "He said that was out of the question."

So Mars did some more digging. Eventually, he filed a lawsuit against the school. By the time he was done digging, Bible-thumping Ole Miss coach Hugh Freeze was out of a job when a university-funded independent investigation discovered a number of cell phone calls to an escort service and Nutt had a financial settlement. The requested private apology was now quite public.

"Certain statements made by University employees in January 2016 appear to have contributed to misleading reports about Coach Nutt," the statement began. "To the extent any such statements harmed Coach Nutt's reputation the University apologizes, as this was not the intent . . ."

A few months later the father of quarterback Shea Patterson called seeking a waiver so his son could transfer out of the Ole Miss mess and become immediately eligible to play. Mars knew nothing about eligibility or waivers but quickly realized NCAA rules were open to interpretation. And, if carefully applied, to public pressure.

"In this NCAA transfer space at least, that's like a country club," he said. "People like to do what they do, but don't throw rocks."

Much to the NCAA's dismay, Mars decided to fire a few in the form of a fourteen-page statement he wrote on Patterson's behalf, chock-full, he said, "of the worst stuff at Ole Miss."

By now the association was well aware Mars had the likes of Dodd, Wolken, and Forde on speed dial.

A deal was proposed, Mars said, NCAA style: Make a waiver request but please remove all the egregious Ole Miss recruiting misconduct previously outlined in excruciating detail in a state court complaint.

"If you will withdraw all that nasty stuff you put in the Michigan waiver request file, and replace with bullet points, one sentence each, do that to-morrow, then the next day the NCAA will announce a new exemption to the year residency required based on mitigating circumstances affecting the student-athlete's welfare and safety beyond their control. They will make it effective immediately," Mars said. "They don't want the world to know they made this up today and instead present it like they've been studying this for months."

From that point on Mars said his phone started ringing off the hook, emails pouring in. Within a year his commercial and corporate law practice had morphed into 75 to 80 percent college waiver and eligibility cases—football, tennis, volleyball, basketball, baseball players—then head coach contract disputes. The loudest and most successful: quarterback Justin Fields's racially charged transfer from Georgia to Ohio State.

That's when, out of the blue, Mars said, Jon Duncan, the NCAA's vice president of enforcement and the association's general counsel, called offering him a five-year contract as an independent advocate on the newly formed Complex Case Unit (CCU).

"I had just had a conversation and several texts with Jon, who I think is one of the most high-integrity, classy, solid lawyers I've ever dealt with," said Mars. "They intended to appoint three lawyers and asked me if I would be interested in one of those positions. My immediate knee-jerk reaction was why me? Is this because you want me out of your hair? And Jon immediately said no. Not at all."

Whatever the intentions, after a year or so both sides conceded the complex marriage was not working out. The first eleven months Mars said he had sat on the sidelines wondering why he wasn't assigned any CCU cases. Finally handed a few, he passed on them all, still ticked off. That's when, Mars said, he received a letter from Enforcement saying the Committee on Infractions had concerns about possible conflicts of interest because of his past representation of players and his current work with coaches. The committee wanted supplemental information—information, Mars said, he had already supplied.

"I sent them the info, and I just decided I'm probably not a good fit for this organization," Mars said. "So I invoked a phone agreement with Jon Duncan, and I bailed."

Instead, Mars became the perfect fit for a Michigan Man investigators had come to view as a liar and a cheat.

CHAPTER 3

Oppenheimer

STRANGELY ENOUGH, THE MOMENT THAT changed college football forever came during a college basketball game.

Lord knows John Paul Vincent "Sonny" Vaccaro had seen enough of those, tens of thousands over the years.

The year was 1997 when Vaccaro's epiphany appeared in the form of Dwayne "Pearl" Washington, a New York City playground wizard performing his eighties magic at point guard for Syracuse University. Vaccaro was no stranger to sitting courtside. That night, however, he was at home on the West Coast watching a rerun of an old college hoops game from the mid-eighties on ESPN Classic. Seeing Pearl, he began to think for the first of countless times that a legend was lighting up the screen, entertaining him long after his college playing days were over, and was not getting a plug nickel for it.

It would take ten more years before Vaccaro finally said enough is enough and walked away from the game he had changed to undertake a knight-errant quest against what he would call "the most fraudulent organization that ever lived," and in doing so, lighting the fuse for the atom bomb to come.

"I say this to you, you'll think I'm crazy," Vaccaro said in the summer of 2023. "I was Oppenheimer. There's no question. I was Oppenheimer."

THE NATIONAL COLLEGIATE ATHLETIC ASSOCIATION was officially formed in 1906. But it really arrived on October 1, 1951, with the hiring of

Walter Byers, a college dropout and former sportswriter, as its first executive director. Just twenty-nine years old when he got the job he'd keep for the next thirty-six years, Byers ran the NCAA like a third-world despot—obsessive, intimidating, ruthless—lifting the association to new heights in exposure, influence, and prestige. The unforgiving fiat of his dictatorial rule: college athletes were strictly amateurs. Playing college sports was not a job but an "avocation" that should be "protected" from exploitation by "professional and commercial interests."

This commandment was sorely tested four years into Byers's reign when twenty-six-year-old Ray Dennison, an Army veteran and a right guard for Fort Lewis A&M junior college in Durango, Colorado, died thirty hours after his head collided with an opponent's knee during a kickoff return. Dennison's widow and the mother of his three children later filed a claim with the state for workmen's compensation death benefits. The Colorado Supreme Court ultimately ruled in favor of a school that, it decided, was "not in the football business." The family didn't see a dime, but the football field at Fort Lewis would later be named in Dennison's honor.

After Dennison's death, Byers and the NCAA came up with the deliberately ambiguous term "student-athlete," which provided leadership the leeway to decree there was no need to compensate the athlete in question with anything more than books, tuition, and housing.

In his 1995 memoir *Unsportsmanlike Conduct: Exploiting College Athletes*, Byers explained how he purposefully had the term embedded in all NCAA rules and regulations as a way to evade efforts by several states to classify college athletes as employees, and thus allow them to collect workers' compensation in the event they were injured or, like Dennison and dozens of others before and after, died on the football field.

Byers, long since retired to his ranch in Kansas, unloaded some cold-blooded truths, a sinner suddenly seeking salvation. He wrote, "Collegiate amateurism is not a moral issue; it is an economic camouflage for monopoly practice." Here it was from the horse's mouth. According to the man who had shouted "amateurism" from rooftops for decades, it wasn't about the sanctity of amateur sport. No, it was about protecting a monopoly and its eye-catching commercial appeal.

"That's where we start with the original lie of amateur sports that athletes are amateurs who play for the love of the game; they're students, not employees," said Marc Isenberg, an NIL expert and adjunct professor at the University of Southern California. "That was the most effective business model that they could ever create for the last seventy, eighty years because they used it every single time—it was almost like *Rain Man*, five minutes to Wapner, over and over again, and the people who mattered started to believe it, college presidents, state legislatures, judges."

As time marched on, Byers and those who later sat in his seat either supercharged that appeal or stood by as membership or conference commissioners seized control. In the process, big-time college sports, in the searing words of civil rights historian Taylor Branch, grew into a form of modern-day slavery. In his groundbreaking 2011 *Atlantic* article, "The Shame of College Sports," Branch wrote "amateurism and the student-athlete" are "cynical hoaxes" and the NCAA let off "an unmistakable whiff of the plantation."

Branch opened his piece with Vaccaro, by this time a true power broker, addressing the esteemed reform-minded Knight Commission on Intercollegiate Athletics in a closed hearing in 2001 at the Willard Hotel in Washington, D.C. Asked by Bryce Jordan, president emeritus of Penn State, why a university should be an advertising medium for the shoe and sports apparel industry, Branch reprised Vaccaro's unblinking response.

"They shouldn't, sir," he replied. "You sold your souls, and you're going to continue selling them. You can be very moral and righteous in asking me that question, sir," Vaccaro added with good irrepressible cheer, "but there's not one of you in this room that's going to turn down any of our money. You're going to take it. I can only offer it."

DESPITE THE ANTITRUST RULING IN *NCAA v. Board of Regents of the University of Oklahoma* in 1984, what a lower court had deemed a "classic cartel" continued to operate with impunity. By then, Byers's attention had turned to the corporate appeal of the Division I Men's Basketball Tournament. In 1982, CBS Sports announcer Brent Musberger first shouted the phrase "March Madness" after hearing it used to describe the Illinois High School Association Boys State Basketball Tournament. The NCAA quickly adopted March Madness as did corporate America—unleashing a tidal wave of advertising, forerunners of the NCAA's nineteen official Corporate Champions and Partners of today.

As millions and then billions of dollars poured in and tournament and playoff payouts skyrocketed, demands on those generating the revenue turned the sacred "student-athlete" term upside down. In revenue-generating televised sports *athlete-students* were spending as many as forty-seven weeks a year working out, practicing, and playing.

In one of the more powerful passages from his memoir, Byers mocked the NCAA's exalted mission of protecting athletes from commercial exploitation. "This is not about amateurism," he wrote. "This has to do with who controls the negotiations and gets the money."

GROWING UP IN TRAFFORD, A single-stoplight town in steel-country western Pennsylvania, Sonny Vaccaro hawked daily papers by the factory steps and sold fruit off the back of a pickup truck. A superb high school athlete (baseball and football) whose college career as a running back was derailed by injury, he bounced between part-time jobs for decades—grinding out a living as a schoolteacher, coach, gambler, and concert promoter.

In 1965, at the age of twenty-five, Vaccaro cofounded the Dapper Dan Roundball Classic, the first national high school all-star game. Over the next twelve years he spent countless hours in stifling gymnasiums coaching grassroots basketball teams and evaluating players. A long and winding road that in 1977 led to Beaverton, Oregon, and the office of Phil Knight, the chairman and CEO of Nike, at the time a fledgling running shoe company. By the time Vaccaro walked out of Knight's office he was on the Nike payroll—five hundred dollars a month as a "consultant"—with the putative title Head of College Basketball.

Vaccaro had pitched the Nike cofounder and company executives a deceptively simple way to supplant Converse at the top of the college basketball food chain. In the late 1970s, he said, most coaches were making $25,000 to $30,000 a year, plus a few extra dollars coaching at summer camps.

"We pay the coaches," he said.

"Is that legal?" someone asked. "The NCAA allows that?"

"There's no NCAA rule against it," Vaccaro said.

Forty-eight hours later Vaccaro was in Las Vegas, where he signed up his first coach and a big one—longtime friend Jerry Tarkanian, hot off UNLV's first trip to the Final Four—for $5,000 up front with the promise of another five grand along with a stack of Nike shoes, T-shirts, sweatsuits, and bags. Over the next two years Vaccaro would sign seventy more coaches to sneaker deals.

SEVEN YEARS INTO THIS WHIRLWIND Nike existence Vaccaro gained a new level of fame when he signed twenty-one-year-old Michael Jordan out from under Adidas. It was nothing less than the richest endorsement deal in NBA history: $300,000 a year plus a $250,000 signing bonus and a cut of his signature shoe revenue. Seven years and a world of influence later, Knight fired Vaccaro in a ten-minute meeting, with Vaccaro believing it was the result of Knight's resentment over his growing celebrity.

Vaccaro later worked for Nike rivals Adidas and Reebok, memorably signing high schooler Kobe Bryant to an unprecedented five-year, $5 million Adidas deal.

But the constant battle for generational talent and market share wore thin on Vaccaro, adding to his deepening despair as college sports rose, one level after another, into a multibillion-dollar business, and rules and schools took increasing advantage of a labor force ill-suited to challenge the artificial suppression of wages.

By 2007 Vaccaro had reached what he called an "inflection point" over the financial abuse of student-athletes, particularly Black basketball players, and shifted sides. Having created an infamous "cesspool" around the influence of shoe money on recruiting, he now wanted, if not to drain the swamp, at least to try to balance the commercial scales. He quit Reebok with two years remaining on a $500,000 a year contract and put an end to his prestigious ABCD summer camp featuring future NBA lottery picks, his high school all-star game, and the Big Time Tournament in Vegas.

He had found a new calling: challenging a cartel.

Vaccaro's crusade began in earnest in the spring of 2007 when he accepted an invitation to speak at Duke's law school. In that speech he raged against what he dubbed "the Machine," leading to countless other offers to speak—at Harvard, Yale, Indiana University, MIT, Howard University. The idea of taking the NCAA to court was never far from his thoughts, an idea that suddenly felt real after an old friend, labor lawyer Rob Ades, came to hear Vaccaro speak at Howard.

Ades agreed the association had likely engaged in discriminatory civil rights and antitrust behavior but cautioned over lunch with Vaccaro that class action cases can take five years or more to reach a conclusion, especially against an organization with millions of dollars at its disposal.

Vaccaro would not be deterred. He told Ades he would just keep speaking out until some senator took notice. Ades had a better idea. He suggested Vaccaro speak with Kenneth Feinberg, the New York lawyer chosen to handle the September 11th Victim Compensation Fund.

Two days later, as Vaccaro was getting ready to deliver a talk at the University of North Carolina, his cell phone rang. Ken Feinberg was on the line.

Vaccaro detailed how for fifty years the NCAA had routinely wrested away the rights to name, image, and likenesses from current and former players with their signing of the seemingly benign Student-Athlete Statement without legal representation. Twenty minutes into Vaccaro's soliloquy, Feinberg broke in.

"I'm going to have someone call you," he said. "He's a lawyer who specializes in these types of issues."

Two months later Vaccaro entered the D.C. law office of Michael Hausfeld to find an impeccably tailored man with an equally impeccable reputation. Hausfeld didn't know much about sports, but like Vaccaro, he was a crusader. In the 1990s Hausfeld won his first big case—against Texaco, for discriminating against minority employees, resulting in a monetary settlement of $176 million. He later sued Exxon on behalf of Native Alaskans after the *Valdez* oil spill, and a bank in Switzerland on behalf of Holocaust survivors. For a man in search of a cause, the NCAA was an inviting target: imposing, imperial, without peer. Hausfeld ended his meeting with Vaccaro with a promise and a pledge. He was in. All in.

Vaccaro later said he could have cried when he heard those words. Then Hausfeld told him he needed to find a lead plaintiff. No problem, thought Vaccaro, his Rolodex was full of Hall of Famers and former All-Stars. But when he started calling, he hit one dead end after another, the voices on the other end sympathetic but intimidated at the prospect of a long legal fight against an organization known for playing rough. He kept making calls.

IN 1995, ED O'BANNON LED the UCLA Bruins to a national basketball championship and was named the tournament's Most Outstanding Player. Fourteen years later he happened to be at a friend's house watching his son playing the EA Sports NCAA *March Madness 09* video game when he noticed a left-handed Bruin player matching his exact height, weight, bald head, skin tone, and his number 31 on the screen. Funny, he thought, nobody had asked his permission to use what certainly looked like his image and likeness, much less pay for it.

That moment was fresh in O'Bannon's mind when Vaccaro, a longtime friend of the family, called asking if Ed would consider becoming the lead plaintiff in an antitrust suit against the NCAA. O'Bannon's short-lived NBA career had long since ended; he was married and working as a marketing executive for a prominent Las Vegas car dealership. In short, he was doing fine, had a lot on his plate, and maybe more to lose than to win by getting involved in an epic lawsuit.

He told Vaccaro he needed some time to think.

Ten days later O'Bannon called back. He had done a lot of thinking.

"I'll do it," he said. "I'll be your lead plaintiff. I'm with you 'til the end."

EDWARD C. O'BANNON, JR., ON Behalf of Himself and All Others Similarly Situated, v. National Collegiate Athletic Association, aka, The NCAA, and Electronic Arts, Inc.; Collegiate Licensing Company, aka, CLC, an antitrust class action lawsuit, was filed in the United States District Court Northern District of California on July 21, 2009. O'Bannon and several others sued the NCAA claiming the organization violated U.S. antitrust laws by not allowing athletes to get a share of the revenues generated from the use of their images in broadcasts and video games.

Two months earlier former Arizona State and Nebraska quarterback Sam Keller had fired the first shot. In federal court in San Francisco he sued EA and the NCAA, citing the same *O'Bannon* argument. In response,

NCAA spokesman Bob Williams had said in a statement the association was confident the case would be dismissed.

"Our agreement with EA Sports clearly prohibits the use of names and pictures of current student-athletes in their electronic games," Williams said. "We are confident no such use occurred."

In the lawsuit Keller charged the NCAA and Collegiate Licensing had allowed the video game maker to replicate team logos, uniforms, mascots, and stadiums with "almost photographic realism." Keller's attorney Rob Carey told the Associated Press his client wasn't interested "in getting compensation for himself."

The same month the Keller lawsuit was filed, NCAA president Myles Brand passed away from pancreatic cancer. A philosophy professor who rose through academia, Brand was the first college president to lead the organization, a former Indiana University president who had summoned the courage to fire legendary IU basketball coach Bobby Knight after a confrontation with a student. In January 2003, Brand took over the NCAA, attempting to be a reformist—vowing to put academics first and improve the overall experience for "student-athletes" while at the same time warning against what he viewed as an escalating "arms race" among big-time revenue-generating programs.

In an early speech before the National Press Club in Washington, D.C., Brand said he wanted to "turn down the volume on commercialization."

"This escalation—this spiraling—of success demanding even more success has good people of noble intentions chasing both the carrot and their tails," he said.

Escalation was hardly unique to major football and basketball programs. As Brand would discover, a love of money had filtered through the halls of the national headquarters as well: the NCAA was on the verge of signing a fourteen-year $10.8 billion deal with CBS Sports and Turner Broadcasting, essentially just for the right to televise three weeks of March Madness every year.

GREG SHAHEEN FIRST CROSSED PATHS with Myles Brand as an undergraduate at IU. Shaheen was an Indiana boy through and through, born in

Kokomo, a basketball junkie who had volunteered to direct traffic around the hometown RCA Dome during the Final Fours in 1997 and 2000. In the spring of 2000, Tom Jernstedt, an assistant executive director of the NCAA who oversaw the Final Four, asked Shaheen to join his basketball staff. After Knight was fired in the fall of that year, a young Shaheen moderated a series of luncheons with Brand to help heal the lingering wounds of the Knight dismissal.

"Myles was humorous, far more disarming than he was made out to be," Shaheen said. "At the luncheons it was interesting to watch the faces around the room as they changed. He was very human. 'I'm doing the right thing. Here's how you can be a part of it.'"

In 2005 Shaheen was working the Final Four in St. Louis when he was given a briefing on the NCAA's basketball licensing operation as it related to EA Sports and something called "likeness." As part of the presentation, Shaheen watched a video game between Big Ten rivals Indiana and Purdue, thinking the look and feel of the game did not appear generic. He asked the licensing staff a simple question: How is this not likeness?

"The answer was we don't define likeness that way," Shaheen recalled. "My mom, who still at that point had no idea what I was doing for a job, for the life of her wouldn't understand video games, but I was sure would look at that and go, yeah, that's likeness."

Shaheen needed to know more. He started with the programmers at Electronic Arts looking to bring as much reality as legally possible into the game. Then, at the NCAA's annual convention in 2006—after being unequivocally told to stay away—he crashed the national meeting of the Division I Student-Athlete Advisory Committee (SAAC), the leadership and liaison group between nearly one hundred sixty thousand student-athletes and athletic administrators and the NCAA. The group hadn't been looped into the conversation, but over the next several months and years, Shaheen kept showing up to let them know the latest. He believed the NCAA and SAAC needed to work together to produce a fair and equitable NIL solution.

EA Sports and its corporate partners were on board, Shaheen said. EA's primary interest was replacing a game that wasn't selling with a far more compelling version, complete with random injuries, pop quizzes, and player suspensions for taking shady third-party money.

In August 2007, Shaheen wrote an email informing senior staff of his SAAC efforts and EA's interest in improving the game. He estimated the NCAA was leaving upwards of $8 million a year on the table by not allowing EA to license the name, image, and likenesses of actual college basketball players. That email, Shaheen later conceded, was typically the first exhibit presented in every subsequent NIL litigation the association found itself involved in.

"The names and likeness are rigged into the games now by illegal means," Shaheen had written. "Meaning that many of the video game players have the features, it's just that our membership doesn't benefit from it."

In 2008, Brand appointed an NIL task force to study the matter. It ultimately produced a watered-down proposal, but an encouraging sign for anyone who believed *O'Bannon v. NCAA* loomed as a watershed moment in college sports.

"We're going to have to deal with this," Shaheen said. "You can't say you're all about student-athletes, and bring in billions of dollars in various rights fees and so forth showing their performance and have a blind eye toward the commercial reality that it's their performance, and their remarkable stories that attract people, that have value."

In August 2009 Brand asked Shaheen, now six years into a well-respected job of running the Men's Basketball Tournament, for an update on the NIL task force. Four weeks later, Brand was dead.

"Basically, upon Myles's death, anybody who had not gotten their way immediately moved in and started," said Shaheen before pausing. "It's scary. You don't know who to trust. It exposed the fact that the board of directors and executive committee of presidents really counted on the president for leadership. Who's going to succeed Myles and what does that mean?"

ARRIVING FROM THE UNIVERSITY OF Washington in November 2010 to succeed Brand, Mark Emmert oversaw the NCAA for twelve years in a tenure marked by inaction, ineffectiveness, and complaints, from both inside and outside the organization. He was a well-paid ($2.7 million annually) punching bag by the end, with conference commissioners and prominent athletic directors becoming increasingly bold in their public complaints about a man they deemed a feckless leader.

Acknowledging the "incredibly trying times," Emmert used his final moments in the spotlight during the NCAA's "State of College Sports" presentation in 2023 to champion a track record that included health and wellness improvements, major strides in graduation rates, and the work done in the "human development business." As he wrapped up, he told the assembled university presidents and college sports stakeholders, "I've loved working with the organization and I'm really excited to see what's next."

They gave their embattled leader a standing ovation.

The next day, in a nondescript conference room hidden away from the hustle and bustle of the convention, Emmert was asked about that moment. "Here's how I interpret it: They appreciate and understand my focus, despite what others have thought, of how do you make this better and better for students?" Emmert said. "How do you keep them focused on things that are changing their lives? We've done that well, and I'm really proud of that."

Emmert's critics would push back on that perceived success. A year earlier, he came under fire for obvious inequities between the men's and women's NCAA tournaments, disparities so striking the organization had to hire an outside law firm to investigate how it got that bad. There was a laundry list of mishaps that occurred under Emmert's watch, from an ill-advised attempt to punish Penn State in the Sandusky child sex scandal, that went beyond the NCAA's purview, to undervaluing the NCAA Men's Basketball Tournament TV rights in a deal that aged poorly, to a flawed legal strategy that resulted in loss after loss and allowed chaos to overtake major college athletics. "Lost the locker room," is how Mountain West commissioner Gloria Nevarez described the end of Emmert's tenure.

Asked about his biggest regret, Emmert instead landed on the NCAA's losing public relations battle. Emmert had largely remained in the shadows during much of his NCAA tenure, absent a press conference or national interview here and there. If he could do it all over, he said, he would have spent more time vocalizing the truth about the byzantine nature of the organization, which was blamed for everything but had less power to make material change than the average person realized. As Emmert reiterated, the NCAA president didn't have unilateral power to do whatever he wanted. His critics painted him as aloof and disinterested, but he had the ability to be charming and warm, working hard to stay in the good graces of his bosses (the NCAA Board of Governors) even as the industry wanted little to do with him by the end.

"I had one of our commissioners yell at me for not doing something the way [NBA commissioner] David Stern would have done it," Emmert said. "What the hell does that have to do with me? *In my dreams* I had David's authority."

One high-ranking Power 5 conference official admitted there was truth in Emmert's defense. This person placed far more blame on university presidents and chancellors, who frequently didn't have a good grasp of the issues and were rarely capable of coalescing around a topic. They were prone to hyperbole, as issues that now look quaint, like cost of attendance and feeding the players, were hyped as existential crises. "Imagine if you were the president of a totally insane population," the high-ranking official said.

Harvey Perlman, who served as the University of Nebraska's chancellor for fifteen years, used to be part of that population. Perlman, now a law professor, was a sports fan, but even if he wasn't, he understood the importance of big-time athletics at a place like Nebraska. "There's only two things that will get you fired as a president," Perlman said. "One is athletics, the other is medical schools. Fortunately, I didn't have to deal with a medical school." In his time as chancellor, Perlman got an up-close look at the inner workings of the college athletics system. He was on the powerful NCAA Board of Governors. He served first on the Bowl Championship Series Presidential Oversight Committee, which evaluated the idea of a College Football Playoff, and then served as chair of the board of managers for the College Football Playoff Association. He chaired the Big 12's board of directors. After countless hours spent interacting with fellow university presidents, Perlman came away with a pessimistic view of the operation.

"There are too many constituencies that have to play a role in any kind of decision-making, which means that hard decisions cannot be made," Perlman said. "Any decisions that are made are generally delayed beyond the point where they're not particularly effective.

"To think that kind of organization can govern this mammoth industry with all of the money associated with it is foolhardy."

Taking over from Brand, Emmert thought he knew what he was in for, but he soon learned what Perlman already knew. After his first meeting with all thirty-two Division 1 basketball conference commissioners, Emmert realized he was in over his head and didn't comprehend what they were even fighting about. He arrived wanting to be a change agent, seemingly taking pleasure at picking apart the NCAA's "picayune" rules during an early barnstorming tour meant to sell the NCAA's new leader's reform plan. He quickly focused on allowing athletes to receive full cost of attendance with an additional $2,000 stipend—money that went toward expenses beyond tuition and room and board—and thought he could push it through the system. The membership revolted, successfully pulling off an override vote, and delayed it going into effect for three years. "It's been a knife fight every time you want to give them something more, but we got it done," Emmert said. It took him about two years just to understand the lay of the land and how much fell under his purview, things that went far beyond just big tentpole events like the NCAA Tournament. It was a position that came with rarefied stature within the sport, but more headaches than Emmert expected when he took the job.

"Did I ever feel frustrated?" Emmert asked rhetorically. "You mean except from the day I started 'til the day I quit? Except for that time?

"The solutions to a lot of these problems are not rocket science. Some of the solutions are pretty self-evident and some of the frustrations that get tossed at the NCAA, including me as the president, I completely agree with. I want to shout at them, 'You're right.'"

When given a chance to embrace others looking for major reforms, though, Emmert's NCAA had repeatedly fought to maintain the status quo. An Upton Sinclair quote, detractors said, best explained the mentality: "It is difficult to get a man to understand something when his salary depends on his not understanding it."

THE DAY AFTER MICHAEL HAUSFELD filed the O'Bannon lawsuit in July 2009, Andy Schwarz and his business partner Dan Rascher sent a memo detailing why they should be added to the team.

An excitable and chatty antitrust economist, Schwarz held degrees from Stanford, UCLA, and Johns Hopkins, and had been waging war against the NCAA since 1999. It started innocently enough, with an academic research paper titled "Neither Reasonable nor Necessary: 'Amateurism' in Big-Time College Sports," which set him on the path to destroying what he believed to be a cartel. As he learned more and more about the NCAA's sham of an amateurism defense, he concluded that it wasn't just an antitrust issue, but a civil rights one.

He and Rascher had spent years trying to entice a law firm to take on the NCAA in an antitrust lawsuit before finally landing a pair of well-known firms to sue to allow schools to pay the full cost of attendance, with former Stanford defensive back Jason White as the lead plaintiff. The 2006 lawsuit, the first by college athletes to achieve class action status, could have been a game changer, but the lawyers sold their clients down the river for $8.5 million in fees as part of a settlement that left Schwarz demoralized. He wondered if maybe it was time to just sit on the sidelines after investing so much energy only to get burned at the end.

The potential of an O'Bannon lawsuit reinvigorated him. Hausfeld didn't immediately hire Schwarz, despite his aggressive pitch, but after seeing him speak at a conference in Santa Clara in 2011, eventually added him to the team.

For everyone involved, from Schwarz to Vaccaro on down, the fight was personal. And nobody felt it more personally than Ed O'Bannon.

"He was mocked," recalled Vaccaro. "He was mocked. He was mocked. Nobody wanted to be around him. Nobody wanted to touch him."

To no one's surprise, the NCAA's massive legal team went to work on federal judge Claudia Wilken. They buried her in a blizzard of briefs and motions—motions to dismiss, against class certification, bending and molding the sacred word "amateurism" any way they wanted. It was a tried-and-true method for the NCAA as it attempted to bleed out an opponent, but its stall tactics backfired. As the case dragged out through four years of delays, the media coverage of O'Bannon's plight shifted public perception increasingly in the plaintiff's favor. "Every time a Boomer dies, the NCAA loses one of its wings," Schwarz quipped.

Finally, Judge Wilken issued her initial ruling, giving the O'Bannon side a qualified win, certifying the *O'Bannon* plaintiffs as a class, while limiting the class by removing potentially tens of thousands of former players.

The case finally went to trial in the Ninth U.S. Circuit on June 9, 2014, 1,784 days, nearly five years, after it was first filed. In an omen of things to come, that very same morning the NCAA announced it had settled the Sam Keller lawsuit—awarding $20 million to "certain Division I men's basketball and Division I bowl subdivision football student-athletes who attended certain institutions during the years the [EA] games were sold."

Once again, in the O'Bannon case, NCAA attorneys sold the status quo: the value of access to higher education, the dark days associated with "professional" sport. In her ninety-nine-page ruling issued on August 8, Judge Wilken handed the association yet another loss in what had become a string of them, ruling that the NCAA could not prevent athletes from selling the rights to their names, images, and likenesses, and that such restraint violated antitrust laws.

Predictably, the NCAA appealed. When the Ninth U.S. Circuit Court of Appeals upheld the vast majority of Wilken's ruling, the long-standing legal dam broke. Electronic Arts had already agreed to pay $40 million to tens of thousands of current and former players and shut down its college basketball division. As part of Wilken's decision, schools were allowed to offer not just full scholarships but "full cost of attendance," adding an additional $3,000 to $6,000 to an athlete's bank account every year.

Judge Wilken's decision left Schwarz with mixed feelings. It was a historic win, one that would prove to be the spark for the legal battles to come, but in the moment, after working nearly three thousand billable hours in one year on the O'Bannon case, it felt like a measured victory rather than cause for all-out celebration. "She opened up the door, but she didn't open up the door all the way," Schwarz said.

The fight wasn't over.

Schwarz tried to find a law firm to take another run at the heart of the White lawsuit, succeeding in what eventually became known as the *Alston* case. Schwarz also tried to build a college basketball competitor to the NCAA, called the Historical Basketball League, that would pay basketball players to attend historically black colleges. If the NCAA wouldn't let its athletes make money, he thought, there was a market opportunity to create a better product by paying athletes. The idea never quite came to fruition the way he envisioned, with private equity and venture capital funds perhaps skittish about investing in an NCAA competitor with the slogan "Amateurism is a con."

And then Schwarz met a Bay Area woman named Nancy Skinner, who told him at a fall 2015 Oakland Rotary Club luncheon that she was running for state senate and looking for ideas. He pitched her on creating a bill that would allow California college athletes the unfettered right to commercialize their name, image, and likeness rights. Schwarz, not knowing if Skinner even had a real shot of winning her election, didn't give it much thought until she did. "I blunder into things," Schwarz said.

As Skinner started working on California Senate Bill 206 in what would eventually become known as the "Fair Pay to Play Act," Schwarz worked on the landmark *Shawne Alston v. NCAA* case that again came under Judge Wilken's purview on the Ninth Circuit. The natural successor to the O'Bannon case, Alston zeroed in on the NCAA restricting "non-cash education-related benefits," which violated antitrust law.

On June 21, 2021, the U.S. Supreme Court, in a rare 9–0 decision, eviscerated the association's antitrust arguments. In a concurring opinion, Judge Brett Kavanaugh ripped the NCAA's decades-long denial of a basic human right under the guise of amateurism:

> The NCAA couches its arguments for not paying student athletes in innocuous labels. But the labels cannot disguise the reality: The NCAA's business model would be flatly illegal in almost any other industry in America. . . . Price-fixing labor is price-fixing labor. And price-fixing labor is ordinarily a textbook antitrust problem because it extinguishes the free market in which individuals can otherwise obtain fair compensation for their work. . . . Nowhere else in America can businesses get away with agreeing not to pay their workers a fair market rate on the theory that their product is defined by not paying their workers a fair market rate. And under ordinary principles of antitrust law, it is not evident why college sports should be any different. The NCAA is not above the law.

Emmert did not regret taking the case all the way to the Supreme Court, saying it was the well-accepted strategy at the time and anyone who said otherwise was relying on revisionist history. Kavanaugh's opinion stung, but he couldn't muster much of a defense. "Who am I to disagree with a Supreme Court judge?" Emmert said. "I believe that if you get a decision where this particular court, which is divided, it's pretty polarizing between the right and the left, and they agree on something, you better pay bloody attention to it."

Ten days after the *Alston* ruling, the NCAA's problems amplified with the start of the new NIL world.

CALIFORNIA GOVERNOR GAVIN NEWSOM HAD signed Schwarz and Skinner's "Fair Pay to Play Act" into law on LeBron James's *The Shop* show on HBO on September 30, 2019. The bill had been somewhat watered down from Schwarz's original idea, and the compromise was that it wouldn't go into effect until January 2023, but it was still a massive grenade aimed at the NCAA's headquarters.

"I don't want to say this is checkmate," Newsom said, "but this is a major problem for the NCAA."

In response, the NCAA threatened to ban every single California university from competing in NCAA-sanctioned events and called the NIL bill "unconstitutional" and an "existential threat."

A month later, the NCAA did what it does best: it created a working group to study the issue. But unlike many of its other groups, which were dead on arrival, this one had some heavy hitters among its roster: Big 12 commissioner Bob Bowlsby, Ohio State athletic director Gene Smith, Big East commissioner Val Ackerman, and University of Georgia president Jere Morehead, among others. The NCAA Board of Governors put a January 2021 deadline to establish a new set of rules "in a manner consistent with the collegiate model," a phrase Myles Brand had popularized.

The group featured some true believers, hardliners against athletes being paid, but during the year-plus it worked on the topic, the inevitability of the outcome prompted evolution. The group came up with some "guardrails"—a favorite word of college administrators—that would prevent universities from using NIL as recruiting inducements but that would allow athletes to hire agents, financially capitalize on their likeness, and create a third-party entity to oversee the situation.

"We wanted to put things in that would create transparency, create structure, and create things that weren't an ordeal for young people to put in place," Bowlsby said.

As the working group debated a solution, other states started following California's lead. Florida, through the work of attorney Darren Heitner and Representative Chip LaMarca, became the second state to pass an NIL-related bill on June 20, 2020. It was very similar to the California bill, but most importantly it pushed up the timeline: Florida's law would go into effect on July 1, 2021. With Florida leapfrogging California on the timeline, it ratcheted up the pressure on the NCAA to come up with a solution and fast. Instead, the NCAA seemed to focus its energy more on begging Congress for a federal solution, with Emmert making frequent trips to Washington, D.C., to ask for help.

Ahead of the January 2021 NCAA convention, held virtually because of the COVID-19 pandemic, the Division I Council was expected to finally vote on the NIL working group's proposal. And then, on the eve of the vote, the proposal was pulled from the docket. Emmert blamed it on a prominent conference opposing it—"The SEC was very unhappy with it," he said—and an inquiry letter from the Department of Justice's antitrust division that indicated the organization was entering murky waters moving forward. There was a strategy behind the SEC's opposition to the proposal. A high-ranking official at one SEC school said that the SEC had purposefully lobbied NIL "like shit" to set up a possible NCAA breakaway. "With a Democratic Congress ready to load an NIL bill up with unionization, collective bargaining, lifetime health care all under guise of granting antitrust? Kill that bill and breakaway is the only answer," the source said.

Bowlsby, who admitted not every conference was singing off the same sheet music, said the SEC "wanted several of their states to have rules that weren't all the same so that was the chaos." And he acknowledged that the Justice Department's inquiry warning of antitrust issues was legitimate. But in his mind, the NCAA was going to get sued either way, and the least it could do was clearly state what its rules were so there was no ambiguity, and it could adjust them down the line if needed. He begged Emmert up until the last days before NIL went into effect on July 1 to do something, anything, to prevent a chaotic world of no rules. Instead, the day before the laws went into effect, the NCAA retreated into its shell and essentially said there would be no universal rules, and schools should just follow whatever its state laws allowed. That mentality set off a new arms race for state legislators to create the most permissive NIL state laws—twenty-seven different states had NIL laws as of July 1—creating a world in which schools in the same conference and in neighboring states could operate under completely different rules.

"To leave the membership with no guidance is just irresponsible, and that's what they ended up doing," Bowlsby said. "Leaving the membership with no guidance, leaving states to make their own rules, and now we deserve what we got."

AS NIL UPENDED COLLEGE SPORTS, the lawsuits didn't stop. The one that had a chance to break the NCAA once and for all, filed by former Arizona State swimmer Grant House and two other athletes, argued that some fifteen thousand current and former players had been denied NIL money and a slice of broadcast revenue prior to 2021. In November 2023, in the same U.S. District Court in Northern California, the same Judge Claudia Wilken certified *House* as class action, meaning, short of a massive settlement, the NCAA could be forced to pay treble damages dating back to 2016, to the tune of more than *$4 billion.*

In her ruling, Judge Wilken wrote that she found "ample support for [the] plaintiffs' assumption that student-athletes NIL in broadcasts have value, and their value is at least ten percent of the revenues of Defendants broadcast contracts."

The case was scheduled to go to trial in January 2025, but the specter of another thunderous defeat spurred a chorus of critics, coaches, and conference commissioners to charge that it was past time to share with the Division I athletes largely responsible for nearly $20 billion a year in media rights, bowl, tickets, royalties, licensing, and other revenue.

Looking back on a two-decade fight with the NCAA, from the White lawsuit to O'Bannon to Alston to now House, Schwarz saw an NCAA organization that made the wrong turn at every step. It was too aggressive in settling the White lawsuit, he believed, which paved the way for O'Bannon. The NCAA's lawyers had numerous opportunities to settle the O'Bannon case but preferred to rack up billable hours on useless motions. An O'Bannon settlement would have lessened the need for Alston. At every opportunity, the NCAA took a hard line rather than acknowledging the changing landscape and coming to a reasonable resolution.

"They kept doing things that put blood in the water instead of getting out of the water and getting some gauze," Schwarz said. "At core, they're not a business, they're a cult."

CHAPTER 4

The Prince

LIKE A PROUD SON JUST wanting his surrogate father's approval, Kirby Smart was hurt.

In the immediate aftermath of his greatest professional accomplishment, winning his first national championship, his former boss, the man he had just defeated for football glory, was gracious. There looked like real joy in Nick Saban's eyes that the disciple who followed his "Process," the closest version of himself, had achieved college football immortality.

Immediately after Georgia defeated Alabama 33–18 in the Lucas Oil Stadium on January 10, 2022, Saban told Smart he was proud of him and said later that night, "I love Kirby."

"He did a great job for us for a long time," Saban said. "If we had to lose a national championship, I'd rather lose one to one of the former assistants who did a great job for us and has done a great job for his program and his team. If any team deserves [it], they deserve it."

Saban was very generous in that moment, Smart would later write in his book *How 'Bout Them Dawgs!*, complimenting the Bulldogs on their toughness and how they outplayed his program in the fourth quarter. "I know Coach Saban was disappointed, but I felt that in some strange way he was happy for me," Smart wrote. "We have competed hard against each other, but we are friends—not bitter enemies."

But just like Saban could instantly turn the page on a win, he did the same with any appreciation for his protégé turned rival who had denied him an eighth national championship. Any love and affection for Kirby's big moment was gone the next day. He was ready to kick his ass again.

And with that feeling came what Smart thought were excuses. Saban brought up his younger receivers' inability to step up in place of star Jameson Williams, who got hurt in the third quarter of the title game. The more Saban talked about it, the more it became about what Alabama hadn't done right compared to what Smart and Georgia had accomplished. At the Alabama Football Coaches Association convention two weeks after the game, Saban told the assembled coaches, "We lost the national championship game basically because we had three corners out, both starters and the best backup. We're playing with some guys that didn't have a lot of experience. It eventually got us in the fourth quarter."

There was an internal reason for Saban doing that, to set his team up for another run the following season, but Smart couldn't help but be hurt.

"Why can't he just be happy for me?" Smart asked one friend.

KIRBY PAUL SMART IS A Georgia man through and through, but his origin story starts in Alabama. The second of Sonny and Sharon Smart's three children, Kirby was born two days before Christmas, December 23, 1975, in Montgomery, Alabama.

He spent the first seven years of his life in a town known as Slapout—now officially Holtville—living in a double-wide mobile home that the Smarts lived in for free on school grounds. In 1982, the Smart family moved to Bainbridge, Georgia, where Sonny became the high school's defensive coordinator before later becoming its successful head coach. At the peak of the Vince Dooley era, Kirby fell in love with Herschel Walker and the Bulldogs.

Even as a kid, Smart was intensely competitive—his family had to stop playing board games because of how seriously he took them—a trait he maintained as he aged and became one of college football's most successful coaches. Like Saban, Smart's father coached him, but there was more outward affection shown, which would serve as a core tenet of Kirby's coaching style. His father taught him that you could—and should—steadfastly hold your players accountable, but you had to show you loved them too. It could be tough love, but there had to be love in there somewhere if it would work long term.

Smart was self-aware as a teenager about what set him apart. He knew he didn't handle losing well but believed it only made him compete harder rather than go in the tank. At Bainbridge, he was a successful football player, class president, math league most valuable player, and ultimately class salutatorian. Kirby set the stage for what was to come in his address at his high school graduation.

"I don't know what will carry you to the next level. . . . I do know what got me here and what I believe will carry me to the many challenges that wait in my future," he told his classmates. "For me, it has everything to do with winning and losing, because competition is why I'm here."

Like his future mentor, Smart was an undersized defensive back—he stood at about five foot ten—but had a tireless work ethic, high football IQ, and a desire to be great. He was one of the last players Georgia head coach Ray Goff offered a scholarship, a butterfly effect moment that could have dramatically changed college football history had Smart gone to Valdosta State or Georgia Southern, as it once looked like he might.

Rocking what one teammate called his "Charlie Brown haircut," Smart played with Will Muschamp, Hines Ward, Richard Seymour, Champ Bailey, and other legendary Bulldogs in Athens. He set a Georgia record (since broken) with thirteen career interceptions, a fun fact he'd frequently remind his defensive backs at Georgia twenty years later. Even as a college player, he spent hours breaking down film and had the memory and recognition skills to deploy it on the field successfully. It's a cliché to say he was like another coach on the field. More accurately, he was *better* than some of the coaches. He tried out for the Indianapolis Colts, but after he got cut in the preseason, he wanted to get into coaching, just like his father.

His first job was as an administrative assistant at his alma mater, but his first real coaching job was as Chris Hatcher's defensive backs coach on a Valdosta State staff that included a young Muschamp. After two years at Valdosta, twenty-six-year-old Smart jumped to Tallahassee to spend two seasons as a graduate assistant on Bobby Bowden's Florida State staff. And then it was time to work for the man who, in many ways, defined the rest of his career.

Muschamp didn't do his old teammate any favors when he recommended Smart for the most challenging job on Saban's staff: defensive backs coach. As a former defensive back at Kent State, Saban loved coaching the defensive backs and was never capable of being hands off with that position. Saban was remarkable at delegating responsibilities and trusting his staff to execute them how he wanted, embracing a version of Bill Belichick's "Do Your Job" mantra. The one exception was the defensive backs. "The highlight of his day is going into those defensive backs meetings and being around those players," said George Helow, who twice worked for Saban at Alabama. "He loves it, and it's like a joyful moment for him to get to coach and teach those guys." If you were Saban's DBs coach, it meant you spent all day with him, from the whole-staff meeting to the defensive meeting to the position meeting. It might be no surprise then that Saban went through three defensive backs coaches in his first four years at LSU before he landed on Smart as number four. "If you're his DBs coach, you're not really the DBs coach," said Harlon Barnett, who played safety under Saban at Michigan State and joined his LSU staff in 2003.

In their first year together, Saban was on Smart constantly. Yelling at him, cursing at him, pushing and prodding him to do more. Smart told friends that while his title said he was a position coach, he was actually a glorified graduate assistant for Saban. Coming off his first national championship, Smart was on the receiving end of Saban's complete and total aversion to complacency without enjoying the spoils, as brief as they were, of the previous season's title. Saban delivered his unrealistic expectations in his typical trenchant manner.

But Smart had the thick skin and disposition to handle Saban. The ubercompetitive Saban recognized himself in Smart. Smart, now twenty-eight, went full speed in everything he did, from recruiting to coaching to playing in Saban's noon pickup basketball game. "You don't want him guarding you," said Leroy Ryals, LSU's tight ends coach. "This is like YMCA basketball, it's half-court, but, buddy, he's playing to win." Stacy Searels, LSU's six-foot-four offensive line coach, had the unfortunate experience of facing Smart on the court. "He fouled more than anybody I've ever seen," Searels said. "He would guard me, and I have a height advantage, but he could bruise a thigh worse than anybody just to block you out."

After the season when Saban left to coach the Miami Dolphins in the NFL, Smart returned to Georgia and switched to running backs coach on Mark Richt's staff. It was the only year of his career that Smart coached on offense, but it proved worthwhile. It gave him a different perspective, one that helped him later when he became a head coach and oversaw the entire operation.

He returned to Saban's side in 2006 as defensive backs coach before following his mentor to Tuscaloosa. He spent that first season as the secondary coach before transitioning to defensive coordinator as Saban's right-hand man. Smart already knew how to work hard, but Saban's demands amplified those efforts. He had a front-row seat to the construction of college football's greatest dynasty as he, Saban, and the rest of an all-star staff recruited the country's best players, demanded the best out of them, and won at a clip rarely seen in the sport. Saban taught Smart that teams won championships through the line of scrimmage and they needed the accompanying elite talent there to win big. He showed him how to manage a big organization to hold everyone accountable regardless of their job title or perceived power. Saban would yell at a walk-on player just as hard as a star player and be as forceful in his expectations of the student equipment manager as a top assistant like Smart. It served a useful purpose: it showed everyone in the organization that Saban cared about what they did and that they played a role in the organization's success.

Saban and Smart saw the world similarly and had the requisite work appetite to take the college football world by storm. One year, Saban called Smart from a blocked number on Christmas and told him to call back later that morning. When Smart did, Saban, already getting antsy being around his in-laws and not working all day, pretended Smart had a pressing situation that required him to go to the office. Saban being Saban, as he started working from the office that Christmas, got pissed that he was the only one there and started calling people into the office.

Smart worked for *that* guy for eleven seasons. While other coaches came and went, either sick of Saban's unrelenting approach or seduced away to become a head coach, Smart was remarkably patient. He had multiple job opportunities, which he'd discuss with his boss, but Saban, knowing the seemingly limitless potential of his top pupil, advised him to wait for a job he could win big at, helpful advice Saban would no doubt one day rue.

One SEC school interviewed Smart for its head coaching opening and was blown away by his intelligence and plan to succeed. The school ultimately didn't hire him, though, because in a rare bit of self-awareness, it knew it didn't have the necessary resources for him to flourish. They believed Smart needed a similar infrastructure to Alabama's to win big, and only a few schools fit that mold.

Helow, who worked as a defensive intern at Alabama with Smart—before a fast rise up the coaching ranks that took him to Florida State, Maryland, and Michigan—believes Smart's patience is his strongest attribute, which no one discusses. Smart lived out the philosophy that, at times, the best decision you can make is to say no.

"When I was there, he had a lot of opportunities to take jobs at really good schools," Helow said. "It's hard to do that when people are throwing millions of dollars at you and you're sitting here working for Nick Saban, who is the most demanding coach in college football and tends to micromanage a lot of stuff in a positive way."

By 2015, Smart was ready to be a head coach. South Carolina was in hot pursuit of the SEC's top assistant coach. For a moment, it looked like he'd depart for Columbia.

And then Mama called.

GEORGIA COULDN'T GET OVER THE hump under Mark Richt. He was a good man, beloved by fans and players, but he couldn't win the big one. Some thought he was too nice and didn't have the killer instinct to do what was necessary to win it all. He had come awfully close multiple times, including the excruciating last-second loss to Saban's Crimson Tide in the 2012 SEC Championship Game. Had Chris Conley not slipped and instead gotten into the end zone, Georgia would have gone on to play a Notre Dame team it likely would have crushed in the national championship game. But that was college football, and coming close wasn't enough.

Greg McGarity, the school's athletic director, knew the stakes. Like most Power 5 schools, football drove the bus at Georgia. When the football team prospered, so did the rest of the athletic department. There wasn't anything going horribly wrong under Richt, but McGarity had a gnawing feeling that Georgia could be more than it was. He was Florida athletic director Jeremy Foley's deputy during the Urban Meyer years and knew what it looked like when a program was legitimately competing for national championships. Georgia no longer looked like that under Richt. With South Carolina circling Smart, McGarity knew that now was the time if he wanted to make a significant change.

Georgia fired Richt on November 29, 2015, and Smart's name quickly emerged as the obvious replacement. Media reports leaked out on December 1, four days before the SEC Championship, that Smart was expected to be the next Georgia head coach. Still, he wouldn't officially finalize the deal until after the game in Atlanta.

The two sides knew each other well—Georgia president Jere Morehead had even taught Smart when he attended the school as a finance major—and when they met that Sunday in Atlanta it was just making sure everyone was on the same page about what needed to be done to excel at the highest levels. For a long time, Georgia had tried to be above the college football arms race. It seemed never to want to fully commit to spending major money on facility upgrades and huge staff. That had to change.

"Our whole mantra was we want to go big, and Kirby, you have to guide us on what that means," McGarity said. "We didn't want to leave anything on the table. Our commitment to Kirby that night was, 'Tell us what you need, and we'll get it done.'"

Saban raved to McGarity about Smart's impact on his Alabama program and his bright future, but he had one request: Could Kirby stay on through Alabama's playoff run? It was an easy yes for McGarity as long as Smart was good with it, believing his future coach being part of one last national championship in Tuscaloosa could only help his recruiting sales pitches moving forward.

Smart did double duty, trying to assemble a last-minute recruiting class at Georgia while building a defensive game plan, first against Michigan State in the Cotton Bowl and then Clemson in the national championship game. Smart helped Saban win his fifth national championship in Glendale on January 11, 2016, and then quickly turned the page.

Anyone who thought Smart would remain a subservient courtier to Saban after leaving the kingdom didn't truly know him. He deeply respected and appreciated everything Saban had done for him, but he was too competitive to ease off the gas and defer to his former boss. He had already seen too many Saban assistants come and go to head coaching opportunities and not fully commit to the lifestyle. Derek Dooley, the tight ends coach on Saban's LSU staff, flamed out in three seasons at Tennessee. Will Muschamp, at one point the head-coach-in-waiting at Texas, had initial success replacing Meyer at Florida but was fired after four seasons. (Coincidentally, Muschamp landed the South Carolina job after Smart took the Georgia one instead.) There was a ruthlessness to Kirby that previous Saban acolytes didn't share. They either didn't have the stomach for it or couldn't withstand the withering pace.

If Smart won, he couldn't be afraid to ruffle feathers back in Tuscaloosa.

It started with swiping Mel Tucker (defensive coordinator) and Glenn Schumann (linebackers coach) away from Saban. The Alabama head coach knew rival schools would try to raid his staff annually, but it especially irked him when former assistants he helped get head coaching opportunities took key staff members with them. Schumann was Alabama's defensive game-planning secret sauce, playing an important behind-the-scenes role in putting together the strategy alongside Saban and Smart. Smart tried to hire Scott Cochran, the program's strength and conditioning coach and the glue to the program, but Saban successfully fought to keep him.

The move that had Alabama ready to declare war was when the program believed Smart took the Crimson Tide's recruiting evaluations on his way out the door and used them against his former employer. The belief within the Alabama program was that Smart told mutual recruits where they stood on Alabama's recruiting board, particularly if it could be construed as negative, and parsed negatives out of the program's evaluations to hurt Alabama's standing with recruits. It was a brilliantly cutthroat move that enraged Saban and damaged their relationship.

It was a clear shot across the bow at Alabama, and it wouldn't be the last. Months later, Smart heavily pursued Alabama graduate transfer Maurice Smith despite Saban stating he wouldn't release the defensive back to another SEC school. Smith was slated to be a starter for Saban, and not only did he have zero interest in letting him walk to Athens, but he had the SEC bylaws on his side. The fight over Smith went public with the Smith family criticizing Alabama's handling of the situation, which it claimed included throwing out Maurice's personal property and banning him from working out with the team. SEC commissioner Sankey eventually relented on Smith's behalf, granting him two waivers to play at Georgia, giving Smart another win over his former boss and leaving Saban fuming.

Smart would always go above and beyond to land players he believed could help his program, regardless of whether it upset any feelings. He even made his assistants take video cameras out on the road to film recruits at their high school practices—a rarity at that level, according to multiple coaches—so that he could watch it all back in his Athens office and not have to rely solely on game film. Mary Beth Smart, his wife, summed up Kirby's philosophy well in his book: "He is passionate about recruiting as he is about anything. He knows recruiting is where success begins."

THE INFLUENCE OF ALABAMA IN Athens was everywhere, and Smart didn't shy away from it. When he first arrived at Georgia, he told Claude Felton, the school's Hall of Fame sports information director, to call Alabama and ask for its media policies, because that's how Georgia football would do things moving forward. Smart wanted to roughly double the size of his recruiting staff to compete with Saban's Army, but he was reasonable in his demand. In discussing it with his new boss McGarity, Smart told him there were a few highly paid staffers he didn't plan to retain. He would rather use their collective salaries to hire eight or so young, hungry personnel staffers who would only earn about $40,000 annually. Smart explained that it'd keep Georgia budget neutral, a gesture the Georgia AD appreciated.

"Kirby was great about explaining everything and the reason," McGarity said. "He was great with the whys—this is why I need this, this is why I need that. It wasn't just because another school has X and we need that."

After studying under the master of college football for eleven years, Smart would make tweaks rather than wholesale changes to Saban's "Process." He'd regularly reference Saban and Alabama when explaining how and why something should be done, from players to coaches to administrators. When players complained about being tired those first couple of years, he reminded them that's what it took Alabama to reach the mountaintop. Didn't they want the same for themselves? It resonated.

From the type of players Georgia prioritized to staff makeup to practice schedule, it felt like Alabama East. "It's the exact same thing," said former LSU assistant Pete Jenkins, who consulted with both programs. "It's just a different shade of red."

Years after Smart arrived in Athens, his offensive coordinator, Todd Monken, made a similar point when he chatted up Rick Minter, an old friend, before a Georgia-Vanderbilt game. He had a simple explanation for what made Georgia so successful. "You want to know anything about our program? Just call Nick [Saban]," Monken said. "We're total clones of each other."

Smart's and Saban's program arcs remarkably mirrored each other. Just like Saban's first season at Alabama included bumps in the road as he established his new culture, so too did Smart's Georgia program. Georgia struggled in its first home game against FCS opponent Nicholls State, prompting early panic from McGarity before the Bulldogs held on for a 26–24 win. After a loss to Vanderbilt, traditionally an SEC East bottom dweller, dropped Georgia's record to 4-3, Smart calmly told his staff the only way it'd get fixed was through recruiting. Smart finished 8-5 in his first season as a head coach, but there was reason for optimism after signing the nation's No. 3 recruiting class, which included future NFL first-rounders Andrew Thomas, D'Andre Swift, and Isaiah Wilson.

The payoff came in year two—just like it had for Saban in Alabama—when the new talent quickly meshed with the returning players and the program took off. A Week 2 win at Notre Dame showed Georgia was the real deal, like Saban and Alabama's 2008 season-opening win over Clemson nine years earlier. The Bulldogs started the season 9-0, rising to No. 1 in the rankings, before a 40–17 road loss to Auburn. The loss shook Georgia back in focus, a reminder that it hadn't arrived yet, and sent it rolling through the rest of its schedule. The Bulldogs easily handled a rematch against Auburn in the SEC Championship, sending Smart and his team to the College Football Playoff. After surviving a double-overtime Rose Bowl against Baker Mayfield and the Oklahoma Sooners, Georgia had a national championship bout against Saban's Crimson Tide back home in Atlanta.

Smart came about as close as one can to winning a national championship before Saban and Alabama ripped his heart out. It was a blur for Smart and Georgia fans, who watched the Bulldogs enter halftime up 13–0 against an anemic Jalen Hurts–led Tide offense, only to see Saban switch quarterbacks on the way to a stunning 26–23 overtime win. Smart's first game against his mentor ended in a devastating loss.

Somehow, a year later, it followed a similar script. Tua Tagovailoa was the starting quarterback this time, but an injury limited his effectiveness, and Saban switched to Hurts. Despite not playing much that season, Hurts guided Alabama to another comeback win that knocked Georgia out of the College Football Playoff race. In less than twelve months, Smart had lost two heartbreaking games to Saban and Alabama in the Mercedes-Benz Stadium in Atlanta. It created a narrative that as good as Smart had been as Georgia's head coach, as much as he had already accomplished in three years, his imitation of Saban's Alabama could never top the original.

BEHIND NICK SABAN, SCOTT COCHRAN was the face of Alabama football. He became the most famous strength and conditioning coach in college football, making more than $600,000 annually and appearing in commercials, where he let loose his trademark guttural "YEAH, YEAH, YEAH." Cochran was ostensibly in charge of making sure Alabama football players were physically ready for hard-nosed SEC competition—a task he was very good at—but his real value came in understanding people and managing relationships. He had a knack for stopping problems before they made it to Saban's office, explaining to players what the Alabama head coach meant in his brutal assessment on the practice field. When players were considering leaving the organization, whether for the NFL or a rival program, Saban dispatched Cochran to talk them into staying.

By 2020, though, Cochran was considering a change himself. Saban's approach was wearing on him, and he became increasingly interested in switching to an on-field position. That opportunity arose after Lane Kiffin landed at Ole Miss and started talking to Cochran about a special teams coordinator role. Cochran had never coached a position before, but Kiffin was intrigued, knowing Cochran's strong relationship with players and how it would translate on the recruiting trail. The deal ultimately never happened, and Cochran believed that Jimmy Sexton, who represented Kiffin and Saban, stepped in to block it. (Sources close to the situation pushed back on that and said Kiffin just opted to go in a different direction.) Cochran was mad. Saban wasn't thrilled, either, when he found out his valued confidant was considering a jump to a rival SEC West school. Saban told Cochran he wasn't ready to be an on-field coach and would need to start investing more time around special teams, comments that didn't sit well with Cochran and only amplified his desire to leave.

Amid the infighting, Smart saw an opportunity. A month after Cochran's Ole Miss dalliance fizzled out, Georgia had a special teams coordinator opening after Scott Fountain followed Sam Pittman to Arkansas. Smart called Kiffin to pick his brain on how he had planned to use Cochran and why it didn't work out. Smart had tried to hire Cochran when he first got to Georgia, but when Cochran said no, the once close relationship took a hit. After Cochran got wind that Georgia was again a possibility, he made the trip to Smart's lake house in Georgia to sell him in person on why it made sense. It was a risky hire, but the upside was too good for Smart to pass up.

"You're taking Alabama's guy so now when a recruit is down to Alabama and Georgia, you put him in a room with Scott and he says, 'Here's the difference in the programs and here's why I left,'" said a source with knowledge of the situation. "There's a lot of value to that."

After Cochran left, one Alabama insider described Saban as like Michael Corleone at the end of *The Godfather, Part 2*. All the key parts of his family were now gone, and he was alone.

Smart was evolving as a head coach, starting ever so slightly to ease up on the long hours he demanded of his staff and show his appreciation more. Swiping Cochran from Alabama was part of an offseason overhaul to try to get Georgia over that hump it hadn't managed to overcome in forty years. The offense had grown stagnant, prompting a move to bring in Monken from the Cleveland Browns to push Georgia to be more aggressive. It forced out offensive coordinator James Coley, a coach Smart had a lot of respect for, but a step he thought was necessary to get Georgia to the next level.

In a COVID-19–impacted shortened 2020 season, Georgia didn't quite meet expectations, suffering another loss to Saban's Crimson Tide, and missed the College Football Playoff for a third consecutive season. Saban went on to win his seventh national championship that season, surpassing Bear Bryant's record six national titles and reminding everyone he still ruled the sport. Inside the Georgia program, though, there was a feeling the Bulldogs weren't that far off and were very well set up to make a run in 2021.

And then NIL went into effect.

Smart was willing to be more aggressive than Saban when NIL first came into play, but he had similar concerns about its deleterious effects on his carefully manicured culture. He wanted it to reward talented returning players who had already proven themselves, rather than endorse throwing big money around for high school recruits. (Two years after NIL went into effect, Smart told top Georgia boosters he wanted to build a $30 million NIL war chest to be able to retain and recruit top talent, according to a source familiar with the situation.)

Like the LSU and Alabama programs he had been a part of under Saban, Smart demanded maximum effort every single day from his players or they wouldn't play in games on Saturdays. The extreme illustration of that philosophy came during midweek practices known as "Bloody Tuesday," where Georgia players went full pads and full speed to build and test mental and physical toughness. "It's not easy to do, it's hard," Smart said, "but so is winning." No one wanted to look inferior on Bloody Tuesday, building an incredibly physical and competitive environment.

"If you're not doing things right at Georgia at practice, you'll get embarrassed. I'm talking physically," said Georgia offensive line coach Stacy Searels. "You have to have a chip on your shoulder and be ready to compete every day, or it can be really hard."

Geoff Collins, who worked with a young Smart during his first year at Alabama, saw a coach who excelled at blending high expectations with genuine love for the people he demanded it from. As Georgia Tech's head coach, he saw it when he was forced to be on the opposing sideline in an annual rivalry game against the Bulldogs—Smart won both games—and later when he spent time around the Georgia program as he took a year off from coaching during the 2023 season. The blueprint was so similar to what he witnessed at Alabama but he noticed the little ways the younger Smart made tweaks to Saban's successful approach.

"One of Kirby's biggest positive traits is his connection with the players and being able to coach them ridiculously hard because he also loves them hard," Collins said. "The way he runs it is very intense but very enthusiastic. The level of connectivity with everybody in the building is palpable—that comes from Kirby. He's got the 'Process' down but he puts his own personality to it that has made it really good."

An energetic Smart utilized a microphone to bark out winners and losers during drills to let everyone know where they stood. It challenged not only the players but the coaches, who wanted to avoid hearing their groups called out over the loudspeakers. It was a highly pressurized environment, but the challenge to meet Smart's standard raised the bar across the board. Jack Podlesny, Georgia's starting kicker from 2020–22, said Smart was just as tough on him as he was starting quarterback Stetson Bennett. "When we're in field goal period, he's on the microphone screaming at me, trying to get in my head," Podlesny said. "But that's why games go well. I have more pressure on me in practice than I truly do in a game."

That paid off when Podlesny hit the longest field goal of the season, a 49-yarder, in the biggest game of his life, the win over Alabama in the national championship game. Smart was pure joy after the game, celebrating with a Georgia fanbase that had craved a national championship for four decades. It took a Dawg to restore Georgia back to prominence, a man who understood what it took to win at the highest level, and they loved him for it. A sea of red and black celebrated deep into the night. Their prince who was promised finally slayed the Old King.

Of course, as homage to his former boss, Smart was back recruiting the day after the championship game.

AS GEORGIA READIED ITS TITLE defense, Smart pitched his team on being the hunters rather than the hunted. He knew from experience that winning a second national championship would be even harder than the first. He now had to combat complacency, with every program in the country—and especially Alabama—wanting to take down the new champion.

To help prepare his organization for the new challenges, he turned to familiar faces. Muschamp, who had initially come on board as an analyst to spend more time around his son Jackson, got bumped up to an on-field position when Cochran took a personal leave of absence. He joined Searels, who replaced offensive line coach Matt Luke, who was thoroughly burnt out from what college football had become and left the profession.

It was Muschamp's first time working for Smart after serving as his older teammate and helping him get jobs at Valdosta State and LSU. It was a full circle moment for the fiery coach who had survived the hard-charging Saban, only to land with his closest imitator twenty years later. He couldn't help but think of Saban's LSU coaching staffs, which were stacked with future head coaches giving it their all every single day for the greater good. "Our situation at LSU is no different than what Kirby has done here at Georgia," Muschamp said.

The former head coach of two SEC schools ripped off a plethora of platitudes about Smart—extremely intelligent, great work ethic, could be the CEO of a major corporation—but what we really wanted to know was how Kirby's verbal dressing downs compared to Saban's. "There's ass chewings from both of them that I've gotten at a high rate," Muschamp said with a laugh. "I think both of them do a very good job with the ass chewing part of things." Muschamp had mastered the art of the ass chewing, too, but slid into a secondary role nicely.

Georgia wasn't the preseason No. 1 team—that honor went to Saban's Crimson Tide—giving Smart plenty of bulletin-board material to motivate his team. Somehow being picked to finish No. 2 in the country morphed into the outside world saying Georgia would finish 6-7, a narrative that had no basis in reality but clearly worked as players parroted it as another source of motivation. "No one thought we'd win a national championship again, and that's our goal every year at the University of Georgia," said safety Christopher Smith. "That's the expectation for us."

The polls predicted Alabama and Georgia to be on another collision course, but after the Crimson Tide faltered in two games, the path was wide open for a Georgia repeat without having to go through Saban again. Georgia played with its food at times during the 2022 season, experiencing close calls against Missouri during the regular season and Ohio State in a College Football Playoff semifinal, but after fourteen games it was back in the national championship game against an upstart Texas Christian team that had surprised Michigan in the other semifinal.

• • •

ON THE EVE OF THE national championship game, Smart and TCU head coach Sonny Dykes sounded the alarms.

The two men, both sons of coaches, lamented what their beloved sport had become as they put the finishing touches on their title game preparation. It cast a pall—a needed one, according to other coaches—on the sport's premier event.

The pressure was building on college football coaches. The hours were brutal, and the recruiting calendar was getting worse and worse. As *Mad Men*'s Don Draper would say, That's what the money is for, and, yes, the money had never been better. But for those inside the system like Smart and Dykes, the big paycheck didn't wipe away the day-to-day stress or the increasingly worsening work-life balance that made them practically strangers to their families for most of the year. The stakes were so high and the game was full of so many competitive people that no one felt able—or willing—to take a break. If Alabama was bringing recruits on campus, Georgia felt the need to do so, and down the line. Dykes practically begged the NCAA to legislate time off into the schedule, because if it were up to the coaches, they'd never be able to. "You have to protect us from ourselves as college coaches," Dykes said.

Smart agreed. "We're all to blame for kind of eating our own. It's like cannibalizing because you won't stop, and it just keeps going."

Being a college football head coach in 2023 wasn't nearly as glamorous as the outside world believed. Smart, fresh off his first national championship, was one of the game's top coaches, but he was still at the beck and call of talented teenagers he wanted on his team. The life Smart and Dykes had chosen was about recruiting as much as anything, which meant spending Friday nights flying around the country just to be seen at high school football games. Not that they wanted to, but because they knew they had to, because if they weren't, someone else out there would be.

"I tell people all the time we've got to eat a lot of shit sandwiches," Dykes told us. "You have to be willing to do that, and that's part of our job. I tell our coaching staff all the time I'm a college football coach, I better not have an ego, because I'm begging eighteen-year-old kids to come to my school. How can you have any ego? You've got all these guys making all these millions of dollars a year, and you get blown off by a bunch of kids. If you're not comfortable with it, find something else to do."

More and more were considering whether they needed to, that maybe they weren't built to last in college football as long as they expected. Some desired a jump to the NFL, where it was all ball and no recruiting. Smart was the future of the sport and was as talented a recruiter as any coach in the country, but those who knew him well didn't expect him to still be coaching for another twenty years. The toll on the modern coach was growing too big to sustain as long as legends like Bobby Bowden and Joe Paterno, who both coached into their eighties, had. Smart only knew one speed—all out—but even he wondered if it was sustainable.

"It's not the profession that I originally got into in terms of relationships and coaching," Smart said. "It's changed so much." He admitted at a Texas coaches convention that after the first summer of NIL and transfer portal, "I was ready to step down and resign. I was done."

But first, he had history to pursue. Georgia throttled TCU 65–7, the most lopsided result in bowl game history at the time, giving Smart and Co. back-to-back titles. It was clear that Georgia was the new behemoth of college football.

There was little time for celebration before tragedy struck. Twelve hours after a parade to celebrate the school's second straight title, football staffer Chandler LeCroy and football player Devin Willock died in a one-car crash. Police later revealed that LeCroy, who worked in the recruiting department, was drunk and driving more than one hundred miles per hour, allegedly racing star player Jalen Carter, before fatally crashing. The incident raised questions about the organization, and were further amplified when multiple players were arrested for excessive speeding after a crash killed one of their teammates.

It was against that backdrop of swirling questions about the team's culture that Georgia attempted to become the first modern-era school to win three championships in a row. (Minnesota won from 1934 to 1936.) Smart could do something Saban had never done if he kept on his current trajectory. He had diligently replicated college football's most successful blueprint in Athens, and he now had a chance to show his adjustments made it even more successful than the original.

CHAPTER 5

Calling Collectives

AT THE OPULENT OCEAN PRIME restaurant in Washington, D.C., a scene almost too unbelievable to imagine unfolded.

At one table sat the Ole Miss collective brain trust. Walker Jones, a former Under Armour executive, with his team, including William Liston, a Jackson-area lawyer, and Lauren Hoselton, a former Ole Miss track athlete.

Representatives from the Georgia, Tennessee, and Washington collectives sat at another table a few feet away. Georgia and Tennessee, fierce rivals on the field and the recruiting trail, were sharing nineteen-dollar old-fashioneds. In Ocean Prime, there were laughs; there were stories of saving their head coaches' asses. And there was a shared sense of bewilderment at how it had all come to this.

This drink-and-dinner crew was in town to meet with elected officials and lobbyists. They wanted to make sure their voices were heard in the writing of possible NIL legislation. College sports officials, from conference commissioners to high-profile head football coaches, had earned their frequent-flier miles pouring into the nation's capital in 2023 trying to influence Congress, and the money men behind some of the sport's most aggressive collectives didn't want to be left out.

That Ocean Prime group would later make up the backbone of The Collective Association (TCA), an organization intent on representing the collectives and pushing back on the narrative they were to blame for college football's latest problems.

"We're being misrepresented and taking a lot of hits we don't need to," said Russell White, the first president of the TCA. "The NCAA has picked us as the group to point at, and we've got to work together or else we're screwed. Not only will we be blamed for everything but, as things evolve, we won't have an opportunity to be a part of what's going on."

Jones, an ex–Ole Miss football player, had quickly emerged as a leading voice of the movement. The six-foot-four Memphian with a booming baritone voice was fearless in pushing back on anyone he didn't think understood the lay of the land, from recently appointed NCAA president Charlie Baker, the former Massachusetts governor, who he would call a clown on social media, on down.

Jones was trying to educate or, better yet, "work on," his former coach and now U.S. Senator Tommy Tuberville. When the longtime Ole Miss and Auburn head coach first got involved in proposing legislation to fix college football, he believed collectives were at the heart of a problem. Tuberville wasn't willing to go as far as saying collectives should be outright banned, but it was clearly on his mind.

"Everything goes back to the collectives," Tuberville said. "We fought for years to keep boosters out of recruiting, and now they've been asked to come in. They really don't even want to be in the business, but they are afraid if they don't get out there and raise money that it's not really going to work; they'll get behind the eight ball and not be able to get recruits."

Jones, an accomplished businessman, challenged that narrative as lazy. He explained to his former coach how misunderstood he thought collectives had become and how they were trying to help players in a woefully outdated system that generated billions of dollars from their labor. Tuberville went into it planning to target those "rogue groups," only to refocus his proposed legislation with West Virginia senator Joe Manchin away from the collectives and more toward the NCAA's wish list.

"Are there a few bad apples out there? Of course there are, but most of these collectives are run by smart business people that are putting checks and balances in place," Jones said. "They are doing things the right way. Eliminating collectives could actually create more problems."

· · ·

STARTING JULY 1, 2021, COLLEGE athletes could legally capitalize on their name, image, and likeness (NIL) rights. After the long, protracted battle to give athletes those rights, a commonly held belief was that NIL would allow athletes with legitimate marketing value to make money filming commercials, selling T-shirts, and earning appearance fees, among other avenues. Players with big social media followings or notoriety, say a Heisman Trophy winner, could be paid to endorse products like a professional athlete.

What college administrators hadn't anticipated—but should have—was that eager boosters would team up to create investment funds, billed as collectives, to pay athletes, regardless of whether there was any true return on their investment. The front door was thrown open for boosters to come calling under the guise of NIL, and they barreled through it like the Kool-Aid Man.

Of course, as anyone within shouting distance of reality knows, NIL was hardly the beginning of players getting paid. Despite all the talk of "amateurism," money had changed hands under the table since college sports were born. The very first collegiate event, an 1852 rowing regatta between Harvard and Yale, was bankrolled by a railroad baron. The almighty dollar always was and always would be interwoven with college sports.

There had been "collectives," too, albeit informally, that came together to ensure top football players were rewarded for their performance on the field. Sometimes, a booster signed off on a car loan. Other times, golden handshakes were exchanged after games or solid jobs provided to a member of the recruit's family. In one particularly ingenious approach favored in the South, recruiting funds were funneled through local churches—a tax boon for the booster, with the church earning a tidy little "donation." Middlemen known as "handlers" did the deed rather than agents: a high school or 7-on-7 coach, an "uncle" or family friend who could be courted and paid to deliver a specific player to a specific school. According to coaches who lived in both eras, the transactions were supposed to be discreet, far quieter than the world of NIL. Some even wistfully reminisced about the old way of doing things.

"You approached giving a car to a guy in a whole different manner," said a longtime SEC assistant coach. "You didn't want him to feel like he was getting bought. You didn't want him to feel like we were buying and paying for him. And that's the way NIL is."

Boosters, commonly known as "bagmen," worked in the shadows to en-sure the dollars got distributed efficiently. They disliked direct payments, so they devised safer ways to ensure top players were cared for in a way that wouldn't trip any NCAA alarms.

A prominent former SEC coordinator aptly called one such program "Adults Only." Under this system, a hard-core group of boosters would se-cretly gather deep in the bayou or somebody's secluded farm or backyard, and over a casual dinner and drinks they'd put together a master plan and recruiting list for the upcoming season, in the presence of an assistant coach or recruiting staffer sworn to silence. When the time was right, a life-altering offer to employ the parent of a top recruit would be extended, a job offer that technically didn't violate any rules. The parent might not be qualified for the job, but as long as they showed up daily, the job was theirs for life—providing not just a paycheck but coveted health insurance and pension benefits. The lifetime financial value was enormous, and it miti-gated risk. It wasn't a ton of cash up front that could lead to a flashy pur-chase that might draw unwanted attention. Even better, the desired player never had to know what went down. (This practice continued even after NIL, with some boosters more comfortable with their well-worn strategy that had evaded trouble for decades.)

"It may be the local propane company, may be down at the gas com-pany, may be on a barge, but it's got benefits, it's got hours, it's got struc-ture, and it allowed a family to pay their bills," the former SEC coordinator said. "That's where you can really help kids in the South. The family can live—not lavishly, but they can cover their bills. And the kids know nothing about it."

This coach had attended one of those secret meetings. It opened his eyes to how business truly got done in the SEC, where everyone was look-ing for an edge, and the recruiting battles often exceeded anything found on the field come Saturday. He claimed he never directly bought a player, but it didn't take him long to realize when a player had been bought—to his benefit or not.

"There [were] times when, holy smoke, things are working because ev-erything is seemingly way too easy right now," he said. "I could sense when I was getting help I hadn't asked for because it was too easy. I could also sense when I *knew* I was outrecruiting everybody the right way and things weren't quite happening; there was a delay there; I had to figure out who's been bought, how, and why."

When convinced a player was on the market, the coordinator said he went to another staff member and told him that the "old-fashioned way" wouldn't be enough, so if the program wanted him, it'd have to get in the *other game*. And when it did, the program pulled the coordinator off the recruit and assigned a different assistant coach willing to play that game.

Cheating was rampant throughout college football, and for a time, big-time programs suffered severely. In 1987 Southern Methodist received the "death penalty," which wiped out two full seasons after the Mustangs were found guilty of widespread recruiting violations, including maintaining a slush fund that provided cars and cash to players and their families. Alabama came close to receiving the same fate in 2002 after one of its boosters allegedly paid a top defensive lineman recruit from Memphis. Ole Miss received a season-long television ban in 1995 and four years of probation after being accused of its boosters offering cars and cash to recruits. At one point, the SEC even had a former FBI agent on retainer to help investigate cheating claims. That ended when Mike Slive became the SEC's new commissioner in 2002. While Slive made it a priority to curtail cheating, he promoted a culture of keeping problems in-house. SEC schools stopped ratting each other out.

COLLEGE FOOTBALL IS FULL OF colorful characters but you'd be hard-pressed to find one as unique as Jimmy Rane. At seventy-seven years old, Rane is nothing less than a modern-day John Wayne, by *Forbes*'s calculation the only billionaire in the state of Alabama, a ferocious supporter of Auburn athletics, a member of its board of trustees since 1999, as well as the subject of more than his fair share of recruiting rumors and critical SEC message board posts.

A big man with a broad face and engaging manner, Rane is the CEO of Great Southern Wood Holdings, the parent company he started in 1970, and manufacturer of YellaWood, one of the world's leading sellers of pressure-treated pine. If you're from the South, odds are you know Rane from his days as the star of the old ubiquitous YellaWood television commercials featuring the "Yella Fella" himself in a big yellow cowboy hat, riding, without fail, to the rescue.

YellaWood is part of Rane's $2 billion-a-year empire comprising, among other entities, three sawmills, seventeen manufacturing plants, a major trucking company, an import-export business, and a downtown restaurant with relationships and contracts across North America, South America, Asia, Europe, and the Middle East.

But for all his global reach, Rane remains an Abbeville boy through and through. He is the grandson of poor but proud Sicilian immigrants; the son of Anthony J. Rane, affectionately known as Mr. Tony, a pillar of the community who helped bring a major textile plant—sheets and pillowcases—to Abbeville in July 1953 and watched it grow from twenty-five employees to more than fourteen hundred spread out over a 553,000-square-foot factory and fifty-three acres. In the mid-1990s, NAFTA closed the mill down and turned Abbeville into a ghost town, before Rane stepped in.

To travel to Abbeville, tucked into the southeast corner of Alabama, in 2023 is to take a trip back in time. The downtown streets resembled the look and feel of the 1950s, a meticulously crafted renovation seemingly straight off the set of the sitcom *Happy Days*. A Sinclair filling station here, an RX Drugs store there, the single-handed rebuilding of a once-dead textile town by Rane in the manner of his idyllic youth.

A former linebacker and offensive lineman at Abbeville High, Rane never forgot those happy days growing up, days he now calls "just heaven." His corporate office and gleaming adjacent pine-paneled conference room on the outskirts of town are filled with not just Tiger helmets, championship rings, and memorabilia but vintage American and European art and artifacts, each and every piece a testament to Rane's respect and affection for history.

A southern boy's intense love for Auburn football dating back to October 4, 1958, when his high school football coach took the team to witness a 30–8 Tigers win over UT-Chattanooga.

"It was Band Day. I had never seen anything like that in my life," Rane said. "Bands from all over. Cheerleaders. The pageantry. We went down to Coach [Shug] Jordan's office, the mass of people. Coach Tom went in and we just waited outside. I just fell in love with Auburn football that day.

"Auburn had won the national championship the year before, in '57. But I actually didn't have the infection, the virus, until I visited campus. You had to kind of get there and get infected."

The infection. The virus. If there's a better way to describe what football means to millions in the South (and elsewhere), we never heard it. Rane's Auburn infection had lasted sixty-five years and counting as he came to wield unusual power as eventually the senior member of the board of trustees, portrayed in some quarters as the ultimate kingmaker with a controversial hands-on role in the hiring and firing of head football and basketball coaches.

Perhaps more than any university in the country, Auburn had a reputation for being ruled by its wealthiest boosters. In 2006, ESPN identified Bobby Lowder, a longtime trustee and former CEO of Colonial BancGroup, as the most powerful college sports booster. After a series of controversies and the failure of Colonial Bank, Lowder's influence diminished, while others believed Rane's grew. One college sports executive with deep ties to the school referred to the overall infighting as a "shit show" and blamed it partly on Auburn's willingness to cater to its top boosters' wishes.

"They bow down to [business executive and trustee] Raymond Harbert and Jimmy Rane," the person said.

Even the slightest step in the direction of that kind of power met with an unequivocal denial by Rane.

"I am not a big man on campus and I have no intention in portraying myself that way," he told one of the authors of this book back in 2012. "I am not a power broker. I'm trying to do good; I don't need the money. I don't need anything. I'm trying to leave the world in a better place than I found it."

Despite Rane's denial those around Auburn spoke of a man with considerable power and a willingness, when necessary, to wield it. According to a source with knowledge, Rane played a significant role in the ouster of Auburn head coach Gus Malzahn in 2019, and then attempted to exert considerable control over the search process to replace him. One search committee member said Rane was very aggressive in trying to get the committee, which he was not on, to hire his preferred candidate.

Rane has donated millions to Auburn over the years, and his Jimmy

Rane Foundation has awarded 620 college scholarships since 2002 to help "kids in the middle" with his annual fundraising dinner, which attracts a glittering array of SEC royalty, past and present, including coaches like Nick Saban, Kirby Smart, Dabo Swinney, Gene Stallings, and running back George Rogers.

But for as much control as his critics believe Rane has held over Auburn athletics for the last two decades, he has largely stayed away from the area into which other top boosters around the country have dived headfirst to supercharge their favorite teams. While his company has provided some support to Auburn's NIL collective, Rane said he hadn't personally donated to On To Victory.

"My sense—I hear things—all I've seen NIL do is raise the water level for everybody," he said. "So now you have this above the board and on top of that, you still have cash deals that still sway some players. That's cash just like the old days. You just raise the water level for everybody."

Rane knows from experience, harking back to what he witnessed in the late fifties when he first fell in love with the game.

"I remember '58, '59 at Auburn, everybody who wanted could go down on the field," Rane said. "The players would have their helmets and people would just stuff money in their helmets. Pretty common everywhere. So money's been part of the game forever but not to the perversion it is now. I don't know how it sustains itself. My biggest worry is life lessons, character building. How can you build *character* when money is the decider of everything?"

Rane romanticized the good old days before money ruled all, but he had been previously accused of injecting his own cash into the system to pay Auburn players. Former Auburn coach Terry Bowden accused Rane in a 2003 newspaper article of being involved in a system designed to make direct payments to Tiger players. In the article, Bowden claimed he held a ledger of all the payments made to players during his time as head coach, and that fifty to sixty Auburn boosters contributed $5,000 annually, collected by an Auburn assistant coach, that funded the payroll. Bowden implicated Rane as allegedly one of those involved boosters, an accusation Rane vehemently denied.

"The message boards are full of Big Yella, but knock yourself out because I've never been to a meeting anywhere where people were asked to bring cash or give cash," he said. "I've never seen any of that. I've never even been asked to do that."

Bowden didn't just accuse Auburn's wealthiest booster of paying players, though. The former Auburn head coach levied a harsh personal attack, calling Rane "high maintenance, a wannabe, a jock sniffer, a loose cannon," in the 2001 interview that eventually ran as a 2003 *Opelika-Auburn News* story.

When asked about Bowden's comments, Rane took a pregnant pause before reaching back into his love of history and the Duke for his answer.

"All I can tell you is what Winston Churchill said," he began. "'You do your worst, I'll do my best.' I do think Terry should get on his knees every night and thank our board of trustees. I really do. I think the record speaks for itself. I'll tell you this and I think John Wayne said it best: 'I want my family to love me, my friends to respect me, and the rest of them can go straight to hell.'"

IN 2021, SOON AFTER IT was legally permitted, the University of Florida, through the work of attorney Darren Heitner and former Gators' pitcher Eddie Rojas, launched Gator Collective, believed to be the first school to create such a collective. According to Heitner, the initial idea was to connect rabid Florida fans with players for autographs, live Zoom Q&As, and other perks on a digital platform as part of membership. He thought it was a win-win—players would make money, and fans would feel like they were getting to know their favorite stars uniquely.

Other SEC schools quickly followed, with Texas A&M and Tennessee emerging as two of the most aggressive and well-heeled operations. Early on, schools had a big decision to make with the NCAA's increasingly opaque rules. Should we be aggressive and risk potential penalties down the line? Or should we be cautious but risk getting passed on the highway by rivals willing to test the speed limit? The schools that allowed the riskier option typically had proud fan bases desperate for success and relevance. Spending big on NIL was an opportunity to supercharge their favorite football program, which may have fallen on hard times.

On its face, it was a weird dynamic. The top college football programs were raking in money hand over fist but still crying poverty and begging for financial help from outside supporters to pay for facility upgrades, escalating salaries, and everything else. The NCAA's NIL rules at the time prohibited the schools from paying the athletes directly, so they had to turn to common folk to kick in cash to get the players paid rather than cut them a slice of the revenue.

"To me, it's so awkward," Heitner said. "That was not what we ever envisioned."

With schools forced to cede operations to third parties, a wide variety of people tried to come up with solutions. Some were wealthy boosters who were friends with the head coach. That was the case at Alabama, where Nick Saban trusted Larry Morris, a lawyer in his late seventies, to start High Tide Traditions to try to raise money from his wealthy friends. Having a lawyer involved with the operation was a popular choice as the collectives navigated treacherous legal waters beneath the NCAA's confusing rulebook. At Maryland, Harry Geller, an entrepreneur in residence teaching at the university, started the school's first collective, initially focusing on just basketball. Geller started with a nonprofit model—a 501(c)(3)—where fans could donate and get a tax deduction and Maryland players received appearance fees to visit children's hospitals, food banks, and other charitable endeavors.

Geller was using a lifetime of skills learned as a businessman to help his beloved school solve a perplexing problem. But there was a moment a year into the process when he realized he had put himself in an unwanted position. At the Maryland basketball office one day, new head coach Kevin Willard introduced Geller to people as "the most powerful man in Maryland basketball." Geller laughed at first, but then the moniker made him nervous.

"I didn't do this to have power like that," he said. "I love Kevin Willard, and I'm happy to help him, but I really just want to go back to being a fan."

But others relished the power that bankrolling a collective brought. Eighty-six-year-old Phil Knight was a prime example. The cofounder of Nike desperately wanted his beloved Oregon Ducks to win a national championship before he died and took a hands-on role in turning Oregon's Division Street collective into one of the country's most cutting-edge and wealthy operations.

"I had a deal that really needed to get done quickly, really quickly, and we were waiting on Phil to wake up [the morning of the deal], because he has to agree on every contract," said a top NIL agent who has frequently dealt with Division Street.

John Ruiz, a flashy Coral Gables–based lawyer, enjoyed a similar status as a one-person collective who poured millions into his beloved University of Miami football and basketball programs through his MSP Recovery, aka LifeWallet, health care reimbursement company. He turned heads when he announced a two-year, $800,000 deal for basketball player Nijel Pack to transfer to the U. Ruiz relished his role as the new NIL kingpin, bragging on X about his deals, which he believed would restore Miami football to its 1990s heyday. Ruiz's money led to a talent infusion and intense curiosity around the industry, but it created cultural problems too. Incoming freshmen and transfer players were the first to capitalize on the new market, upsetting returning Miami players who had already made a significant impact on the field but made much less in compensation. Josh Gattis, Miami's offensive coordinator in 2022, said it created constant issues for the coaching staff during a season that started with high expectations but devolved into a bitterly disappointing 5-7 record.

"It created problems in the locker room," Gattis said. "These guys were getting contracts to be paid significantly more than the players who were actually playing on the field. When you're eighteen to twenty-two, you're all talk downstairs in that locker room. 'I'm getting this, I'm getting that.' Here comes the knock. 'Hey, coach, we need to meet; I hear so and so is making this.'" According to Gattis, players and their families constantly asked to meet with head coach Mario Cristobal and Miami's NIL people for more money.

Depending on irrational sports fans to bankroll your operation can lead to wild ups and downs. The typical collective had three main tranches: the big-money donors who gave in the six-to-seven-figure range, the middle money boosters who gave five figures to low six-figures, and the average fans who might pay a monthly membership fee of $9.99 for exclusive content. The money was all pooled into one collective pot to be divided according to the program's wishes. If, for instance, a football program desperately wanted a certain player and knew the price tag would be high, it would go to specific donors to pony up more money for that specific deal. This was especially effective during the transfer portal windows, when top talent could pop up out of nowhere and schools had to strike fast if they wanted to be legitimate contenders.

Given the circus nature of NIL, schools increasingly threw up their hands and turned to third parties to help in organizing and operating their collectives. Las Vegas–based Blueprint Sports, backed partly by tennis legend Andre Agassi, represented more than twenty-five collectives including those from Penn State, Maryland, and Arkansas. Altius Sports Partners, cofounded by Oliver Luck, was another. By the end of 2023, Altius boasted partnerships with more than three dozen Power 5 schools, including Michigan, Texas, USC, and Arizona.

Blueprint specialized in working with what CEO Rob Sine called "the kingmakers," megadonors with close ties to an athletic department and its coaches, who believed they could raise millions through their relationships. Moneymen and -women soon realized what any political candidate or fundraiser would tell you, that raising large sums is much harder than it looks. At Alabama, old-school lawyer Larry Morris initially refused to pay for a website for the collective—"Nobody looks at websites," he told one friend—and struggled to attract his booster friends, who told him they were already asked to give significant money for Bryant-Denny Stadium and Coleman Coliseum renovations.

Even when money flowed in, it could be fleeting if the collective didn't have a real business plan to support and capitalize it. When the initial rush of money came in, excitement abounded that boosters could finally pay athletes directly. But over time, especially if the on-field results didn't correlate with the level of investment, the desire to fork over significant sums of money waned. It was like bankrolling a high-end restaurant, buying the chef all the top ingredients he wanted, only to be served gas station sushi. They weren't going to keep throwing good money after bad, prompting concerns of donor fatigue.

"We started to take over people's projects for their collectives because they were hitting the wall," said Sine. "'I can't keep writing these checks. I want to just go to games and be a fan.'"

Blueprint offered what Sine described as a "soup-to-nuts" approach.

Among other things, Blueprint could help fundraise, solicit sponsors and corporate partners, and even hire local staff to work exclusively for a collective to interface with student-athletes on their engagements and make sure they got paid on time each month. It was an early area of struggle for the less organized collectives, leading to deeply frustrated players, and an area where Blueprint made its mark.

"Everything that should be done to run a professional organization in a professional collective is what we focus on," Sine said.

Sine advised his collectives they needed to spend more than $10 million annually if they wanted to compete in the big leagues. It might sound like an enormous number, but the money went fast when you broke it down. More and more programs wanted to "level-set" their roster—i.e., give every player the same base amount—a smart, effective plan that immediately ate up millions.

For instance, if the base amount for every one of your eighty-five scholarship players was $40,000, you were talking $3.4 million before the car was started, let alone left the garage. Your luxury models—starting quarterback, left tackle, edge rusher, wide out, running back, a cornerback—would of course cost even more. That's before you went shopping in the transfer portal and tried to convince an elite athlete pondering a trip to the NFL Draft to return for one more season. Sine believed it took at least $7 million each year to put a program in the conversation for a national championship.

When your dealership happened to be located in the hypercompetitive SEC, those costs quite naturally got higher. According to multiple people with knowledge of the SEC market, a $5 million baseline a year was needed to win enough games (six) to become bowl eligible; $7 million to $8 million for seven or eight wins; $10 million or more to contend for a title.

AT OLE MISS, WALKER JONES dealt with a fan base that historically had fewer fans and less money than many of its SEC peers. The school didn't have the booster financial firepower of newcomer Texas, Tennessee, Florida, or Texas A&M, but it desperately wanted to win, especially over in-state rival Mississippi State.

When Ole Miss head coach Lane Kiffin heavily flirted with taking the

Auburn job, one of the reasons behind his interest was the War Eagle's superior NIL war chest. That put Jones and the rest of his team on the offensive to raise as much money as possible to make Kiffin feel good about the program's future ability to retain and acquire high-level talent. Ahead of Ole Miss's Egg Bowl rivalry game against Mississippi State, a top donor approached Jones and told him he'd contribute $500,000 to the collective if Kiffin stayed in Oxford. (After Ole Miss lost to Mississippi State as part of a three-game losing skid to end the regular season that threw a cold towel on the excitement of an 8-1 start, the donor returned to Jones with an updated offer. "I'll give that fucker five hundred thousand to leave.")

Still, Kiffin's Auburn flirtation helped the Grove Collective raise an astounding $10 million, giving it the bankroll to push the Rebels over the hump. Unlike Miami and Oregon, Ole Miss relied on local businesses and a smaller collection of boosters rather than one big benefactor. The group had come a long way in just a year since Jones joined. Ole Miss's initial collective efforts started slowly, with Kiffin complaining to his agent, Jimmy Sexton, that he would have to leave the school if the money didn't start rolling in. Sexton recommended that Kiffin call Jones, a former coaching agent for him at CAA and a talented sports marketing executive. That's all Kiffin had to hear. He relentlessly pursued Jones until he said yes.

Not long after coming on board with the Grove Collective, Jones and his team faced a tricky situation familiar to virtually every major college coach: a breakout player with suitors galore and dollar signs in his eyes. In this case, the player was Quinshon Judkins, an unexpected revelation as a true freshman running back from Pike Road, Alabama. Kiffin had worked tirelessly to land Judkins, including sitting in the pouring rain alone at his high school state championship game because he believed in his abilities in a way Nick Saban and Auburn head coach Bryan Harsin didn't. Saban never really pursued Judkins; and it was too late by the time Auburn showed sincere interest.

But after Judkins ran through the SEC with 1,567 yards and sixteen touchdowns in his first college football season, he faced a barrage of outside interest curious to see if he'd leave Oxford.

Kiffin's directive was clear: We can't lose him. It was as much about what it would say about Ole Miss as what it said about Judkins's actual roster value. If Ole Miss couldn't keep an underrated player it found and developed, it would be open season on the rest of the roster. They had to keep him to send a message to the rest of the country that Ole Miss wasn't backing down and could be competitive with the sport's heavyweights with top talent.

Negotiations can be more fraught if agents aren't involved, and that was the case with Judkins. Quinshon's mom, Teva, understandably wanted to get every last dollar for her rising star. The back-and-forth was sometimes tense, with the Ole Miss side eventually telling Judkins's camp that if they kept pushing for more money, the program couldn't afford any offensive linemen to block for him up front. There wasn't an unlimited pot just lying around, and every extra dollar that went to one player meant a dollar less for additional talent. The two sides eventually agreed on a deal that would pay Judkins high six figures to return for the 2023 season, according to multiple sources familiar with the negotiations.

The Grove Collective announced Judkins had re-signed as if he were an NFL free agent running back agreeing to a new deal in a rapidly changing college football world. But even as relief washed over everyone involved, there were open questions about whether it was the best use of the collective's resources. In the NFL, organizations increasingly declined to spend big money on running backs, preferring to draft a new one every few years rather than make a sizable investment in a depreciating asset.

"As good as he is, for the amount of money he ate up, you could get five or six really good players," a program source said in spring 2023. "When it rolls around this coming year, is it worth it again? He's a difference maker from a running back standpoint, but running backs get beat up all the time."

Judkins eventually realized this himself. As he struggled early in Ole Miss's season, not breaking sixty rushing yards in a game until Week 5, he questioned whether the school's collective had deployed its limited resources correctly. He told people he thought the collective had spent so much on quarterbacks and defensive players that it didn't have enough left for talented offensive linemen to block for him.

Even so, after the 2023 season, Judkins's camp was looking for a seven-figure payday to return for another season. Ole Miss decided to let him walk—he landed at Ohio State—and spent its money elsewhere. A year earlier, losing Judkins would have represented a crisis. Now, it was an opportunity. Kiffin, who excelled at the dating app–like nature of transfer portal recruiting, put together the nation's top portal recruiting class, according to 247Sports, headlined by Texas A&M defensive lineman Walter Nolen, South Carolina receiver Antwane Wells Jr., and Alabama cornerback Trey Amos.

OLE MISS SHOWED IT COULD punch above its weight class, becoming one of the most prominent collectives in the country, though the top honor still belonged to the group in Knoxville.

Many collectives opted to work in the shadows but not Spyre Sports.

The Tennessee-based sports marketing agency didn't hide its lofty ambitions and how it could help the Tennessee Volunteers football program. In a splashy February 2022 story in *The Athletic*, Spyre's cofounders Hunter Baddour and James Clawson unveiled their strategy. Spyre wanted to raise *$25 million* annually. They also admitted they had direct conversations with seven recruits in the 2022 class (a blatant NCAA violation) and planned to invest millions more into helping Tennessee head coach Josh Heupel sign a star-studded 2023 class. The goal was clear: "If we execute, Tennessee will be able to close the talent gap with teams like Georgia and Alabama a lot quicker than the previous model," Baddour told *The Athletic*. "We're prepared to invest a substantial amount of resources into the 2023 recruiting class. When you add all that together, it's well into the seven-figure category."

A month later, it became clear Baddour wasn't bluffing, when five-star quarterback Nico Iamaleava of Warren High School in Downey, California, and one of the top recruits in the Class of 2023 committed to Tennessee. It didn't take long, either, for many to deduce Iamaleava was the anonymous five-star prospect featured in another *Athletic* story, which detailed an astonishing $8 million deal. The numbers stunned the industry and reset the market for what a top-flight quarterback prospect could command on the open market. The best part? The actual number was $10 million, according to a source with knowledge of the deal.

Heitner, who had created the Florida NIL that set so much in motion, said he wasn't to blame for his creation turning into a monster. To him, Tennessee's deal with Iamaleava was the tipping point.

"If that was happening at Tennessee and *The Athletic* could report on it and there were no consequences whatsoever, with his lawyer outwardly saying we are violating regulations, well, if Tennessee is allowed to do it and get away with it, gosh, every SEC school has to do it too," Heitner said. "And every Big Ten school. I think that's where you had a sea change."

Baddour had learned his lesson. He wouldn't agree to talk specifics about his involvement in recruiting and retaining top players for his beloved Volunteers.

"The NCAA language is so murky on [whether] if you're retaining talent, are you inducing them to stay?" Baddour said. "We've been very out there, more so than a lot, and there's a lot that I'd love to say, but out of respect to our relationship with our athletic department, I want to be much more on the safe side."

In person, Baddour, a Knoxville native, isn't nearly as brash as his spicy quotes implied. Closing in on his fortieth birthday, he still had a boyish look, easy smile, and penchant for wearing sports coats. He was polite, a no-sir, yes-ma'am guy with a strong southern accent to boot. He spent a decade working as a marketing agent at Allegiant Athletic Agency, a sports agency with primarily football and golf clients. In September 2020, he left Allegiant to form Spyre with Clawson. Quickly deducing that the new arms race in college sports would be for NIL money, Spyre created the Volunteer Club as a Tennessee-specific collective. It promptly made waves in the industry and gave Tennessee a leg up on its SEC competition. "They just have way too much money to play with," said one NIL agent who has done deals with Spyre.

Still, the school hesitated to embrace the collective's founders. Tennessee administrators like university chancellor Donde Plowman know Spyre represented risk, and at their core, university presidents are risk averse. Plowman and other top Tennessee leaders weren't lining up to schmooze with Baddour and Clawson when they found themselves in the same room, even if they loved to celebrate the success the football team was having.

Behind the scenes, the NCAA started looking into what Baddour and his group were doing in Tennessee. The splashy stories around Spyre were used as yet another example of the NCAA's enforcement division being unable to do anything to slow down, let alone stop, what detractors thought was blatant pay-for-play. Eventually, the NCAA focused on the collective's deal with Iamaleava.

It zeroed in on Spyre paying to fly Iamaleava on a private plane for meetings in Knoxville. On paper, it looked like an NCAA violation—a booster couldn't pay to fly a recruit into town—but the NCAA's guidance was so ambiguous and left so much wiggle room that Spyre believed the NCAA couldn't prove it did anything wrong.

"Spyre Sports could have rented the space shuttle to fly him from Los Angeles to Knoxville if they wanted to," said Tom Mars, who represented Spyre in its dealings with the university and NCAA enforcement. "We kept saying he had marketing-based meetings when he was in Knoxville, we have evidence of that, but that didn't seem to be their focus. They wanted to talk about airplanes."

Facing pressure from a membership begging it to act on high-profile cases, the NCAA plowed ahead. According to those familiar with the situation, enforcement's goal was to have the Committee on Infractions declare Iamaleava ineligible and have Spyre Sports disassociated from the athletic department. But this time Tennessee wasn't going to play nice. Mars, already a thorn in the NCAA's side, readied a defense. As he got up to speed he quickly surmised the NCAA had made a major mistake.

"They picked the wrong case," Mars said. "They picked the wrong case because they were just incensed that Spyre Sports had not only done this, but kind of bragged about it publicly.

"I think Spyre was the red cape that got the bull to charge." A raging bull that ran straight into a sword could prove fatal.

CHAPTER 6

Raising Arizona

FEBRUARY 2023. ANOTHER CRISP WINTER day in the Sonoran desert. The passion in Jedd Fisch's voice rang out in the desert air as he recalled the personal message he had delivered to his Wildcat football team time after time over the past two-plus years—Family First.

"We say in our program it's personal," he began. "That's our motto, and that has a *million* different meanings. It's *personal* to build a relationship with a kid. It's *personal* how you talk to your players. It's *personal* when people don't give you respect. It's *personal* to win championships.

"There's not a recruit that hasn't been to our house five times. Not a mom my wife doesn't talk to. We're so invested in our players . . . so *invested* in these kids."

An investment, it appeared, that was beginning to pay dividends. Since his arrival in Tucson in late December 2020, Fisch and his staff had spent countless hours retooling a downtrodden program that boasted exactly *one* head coach with a winning record since the turn of the century. This was a precipitous fall. The glory days of revered head coach Dick Tomey (1987–2000, .595 winning percentage) were followed by one recycled "name" coach after another (John Mackovic, Mike Stoops, Rich Rodriguez), and the final straw, the dismal Kevin Sumlin era (2018–20, .310) that mercifully ended after a biblical 70–7 blowout at home by archrival Arizona State.

When vice president and athletic director Dave Heeke started a nationwide search for a new coach he said he needed someone who could change the culture and somehow manage the shifting sands unnerving the sport. Fisch had been among the finalists when Heeke hired Sumlin, and in the process developed a strong personal relationship with university president Bobby Robbins. But the fact that Fisch was even available for an interview was nothing less than a medical miracle.

IN MARCH 2003, JEDD FISCH was in the spring of his twenty-sixth year of life, in his second year as a defensive quality control coach for head coach Dom Capers and the Houston Texans. Standing in the parking lot of his Houston condo, he felt a sharp pain in his back, so sharp he blacked out for a spell. He spent the weekend trying to relax until the pain became so unbearable he was forced to call a Texans' team doctor. Before Fisch could utter more than a few sentences about his symptoms the doctor sensed Fisch was slowly but surely dying. The cause: what's known as an aortic dissection of the ascending aorta (an aneurysm in the largest heart artery), descending at a rate of 1 percent per hour since the parking lot collapse. Fisch was rushed to the hospital, where doctors discovered a softball-size tear necessitating immediate life-threatening surgery. Unfortunately, only a few renowned heart surgeons in the world could perform it. Fortunately, and here's the miracle part, Joseph Coselli happened to live in Houston.

"A very small percentage [live]," Fisch later recalled. "I said it was a fine line between life and death, and [Coselli] said: 'Yeah, like dental floss.'"

Fisch would spend six days hooked up to a ventilator in the ICU, unable to speak. Undergoing follow-up surgery, he remained so focused on football he scribbled a note to Capers: *Do I still have my job?* (He did.) He would eventually spend four weeks in the hospital and six months in rehab, his relentless drive and work ethic tempered by a sudden brush with death.

"I do feel like I handle adversity better now than I did then," Fisch said in 2015, by then the quarterbacks/wide receivers coach and passing game coordinator under Harbaugh at Michigan. "If you lay in a hospital bed and were told there's a thirty percent chance of paralysis, a thirty percent chance of kidney failure and a thirty percent chance of you not waking up and you have to sign your life away, to come out and see a couple incompletions?"

• • •

DESPITE A HIGH-PROFILE RÉSUMÉ AND glowing reputation as an inno-
vator on offense, Fisch had circled several previous college head-coaching
openings without an offer—a situation seen by some as slightly desperate
at this stage of his professional life. That's not how Dave Heeke saw it. In
his eyes, the forty-four-year-old Fisch was a man in full, gregarious and
organized but also not taking one minute for granted.

"His ability to articulate his vision—'this is where I think it's going . . .
this is what I want to do,'" recalled Heeke. "Yet he didn't give up on the
true collegiate experience and model. He also had this keen awareness.
He's a forward-thinking person. He was always thinking ahead and planning while still living in the moment."

Heeke's announcement of the Fisch hire was met with a less-than-
rousing reaction, putting it mildly. Wildcat fans, to quote a local headline,
were "Up in Arms." On paper, a coaching nomad, a career assistant who had
spent the past twenty-one years jumping back and forth between college
and the pros, beginning with his days as a graduate assistant in 1999 under
Steve Spurrier at Florida. Bouncing between five NFL teams and four in
college—Minnesota, Miami, Michigan, and UCLA—before two years as an
assistant offensive coordinator under Sean McVay during the Los Angeles
Rams Super Bowl run, followed by a year as the quarterback coach for Big
Bill in New England.

"That was the challenge," said Heeke. "You're looking at twelve or
thirteen different stops both in college and pros. Bright thinker. Offensive
minded. We had done it traditionally. In conversations with the president
[Robbins], maybe we just need to do something different. Can't be the old
retread coach? It was almost like, Why not? Why wouldn't we hire him?"

The last time Fisch had coached college ball was at UCLA in 2017,
where he had served as offensive coordinator, quarterback coach, and, interim head coach for the final five weeks for the Bruins. Nothing like the
shaky ground he was now walking onto—both in Tucson and in the sport
as a whole.

"Nothing is the same," he said. "Nothing. I would say it's the most dras-
tic of any time frame of any coaching decision you could make. Being gone

for those three years became the most unbelievable difference you could ever imagine."

Unlike virtually every other head coach on the planet, Fisch had never played a single down of high school football, never mind college. Like his father, tennis was the son's early love, and he was good enough to earn All-State honors in New Jersey. But when his mother began dating a local high school football coach, Fisch found himself watching hours and hours of black-and-white game film and loving it.

By the luck of the draw Jedd's freshman-year roommate at the University of Florida turned out to be Howie Roseman, future GM of the Philadelphia Eagles, already meticulously plotting his path to the NFL. Equally bitten by the football bug, Fisch made a complete nuisance of himself around the Gators' offices, going so far as to leave notes—reference letters, annotated coaching manuals, clinic thoughts—on the windshield of Spurrier's Buick every day for 420 straight days. Until the Old Ball Coach finally relented and agreed to a brief sit-down.

The sit-down—all five minutes of it—got Fisch a job, if you want to call it that. Making copies, typing schedules, grunt work. Spurrier wouldn't let the sophomore anywhere near a football field, so Fisch coached at a local high school until one day defensive coordinator Jon Hoke offered him a real job: as a graduate assistant, the beginning of a life's calling.

More than twenty years later, the boss of something for the first time, Fisch asked two of the most influential voices in his life—McVay and Belichick—for advice.

"Sean said it's always about open, honest, and ongoing communication," Fisch said. "I think the ongoing part is critical. I think you can keep players if the communication is ongoing. If you move on and lose the ongoing then there are some questions about your sincerity.

"The beautiful thing about Bill is he makes sure you know where you stand. Know where you stand as a coach, as a player. Your value. I think if I can help our players understand where they *stand*, I think they have a better *understanding* where they stand in this NIL world. It takes away some of the jealousy. That's where Bill is so good. Because he's so honest."

Such honesty proved a hallmark of Fisch's first year, as he plotted and planned ways to raise Arizona into the pantheon of Power 5 programs. Relying on the lessons learned under McVay and Belichick, thinking how to create a winning culture, started with this question: What are our bedrock principles of values and standards?

For Fisch the values were written in stone: respect, accountability, integrity, selflessness, and enthusiasm.

Standards? Standards were different; they changed every year. To define those standards the first year—and every year after—Fisch invited team leaders over to his house for a barbecue, followed by a meeting in the family room that began with another question: What do you want our team to be about?

"We hung them up in the locker room so they can see you *chose* these twelve standards. You decided what you want our culture to be," said Fisch. "This year, they wanted it to be about 'Us' and 'Ours.' Not 'my, my, my.' Standard No. 1. Next, Tell the Truth. No lying. Look each other in the eye and tell the truth."

Fisch's favorite. Be A Pro.

"To me, that was really what I wanted our program to be about," he said. "Very few of our players are going to be NFL players. But that doesn't mean the players can't be *professionals* in their life. We have to help you understand you become a pro in life if you learn etiquette. If you learn respect."

Building trust, a sense of brotherly love, a *family* culture, while at the same time flipping a roster, attracting fresh talent, wining and dining donors, navigating the portal, and, oh yeah, attempting to solve the Rubik's Cube that was name, image, and likeness right out of the box.

"That first year, that first [2021] class was, What is NIL?" said Fisch. "I don't even know what the rules are. What I was saying was, whatever the other teams are saying, if it's legal, we'll do it. That was my pitch.

"Talked to Dave [Heeke] and said whatever NIL thing you want to throw out there, have a website, click on it, but I've got other issues."

Issues that began with an out-of-date football facility Fisch labeled nothing less than "a disaster."

"The building was nothing, I just focused like it was old-school college football," he said. "You've got to get your facilities right or you're never going to win. I spent the first offseason designing, redesigning, picking out carpet. Went old school first. You need facilities to compete. That's still true. That's 101."

By February 2023, the now 162,500-square-foot Lowell-Stevens Football Facility shimmered in the noonday sun, in the latter stages of a massive $14 million upgrade. Inside almost everything was either new or improved—new coaching offices and meeting rooms, expanded weight room, a players' lounge with a pool table, requisite barbershop offering twenty-five-dollar cuts twice a week, and something Arizona's director of player personnel Matt Doherty called "a game changer," a quiet "mind-over-matter" room devoted to developing leadership skills, mental toughness, and confidence. This was known as the Fifth Quarter Room.

Nearby was another room, what Fisch called his "closing room," a serene living room–like area ten steps from his office desk, featuring comfortable couches and shelves lined with NFL team helmets and photos, a not-so-subtle reminder to parents and recruits of a certain professional pedigree.

"A big sell," said Fisch.

IN PERSON, FISCH CHECKS A lot of boxes—handsome, passionate, engaging, whip smart, a storyteller. Like the story with a football twist of how he met his wife, Amber, in a bar in Atlanta, while hanging out at the end of a fun night with University of Oklahoma head coach Bob Stoops, Spurrier, Miami's Dennis Erickson, and a couple of other GAs at the annual American Football Coaches Association Convention.

"Coach Stoops was just honored as Coach of the Year. He pointed her out—'Jeddi, might be a good one to talk to,'" said Fisch with a laugh. "Stoops bought her a drink for me. That's how we met. She was a meeting planner for [AFCA executive director and former Baylor head coach] Grant Teaff. She's been around football now twenty-two years, twelve moves. We hope that it's not NIL that causes another move."

Like virtually every other head coach, Fisch said early on he found himself scrambling for NIL answers and funding. He realized from the get-go he didn't have the likes of Phil Knight's wallet in his back pocket and knew he also had to compete with U of A's monster basketball brand for donor dollars.

When players got around to asking about NIL money, as they invariably did, Fisch said he relied on the Bill Belichick school of Tell It Like It Is.

"I laid it out in a team meeting. 'There's no BS in here, guys. You guys lost twelve games in a row before we got here and you lost seventy to seven in the last game of the year.' There's not a ton of people dying to give money to that group."

Indeed, the football donor well had pretty much run dry, having just coughed up $14 million to upgrade the facility. So what did Fisch do? He became the head of his own development team: Ending an already long off-season day calling donors for two hours, until nine at night, from his office desk after dinner. Flying to California to round up a couple of dozen big spenders. Flying to Connecticut to hit up some rich alums, then New York City, back to Phoenix and Scottsdale, pushing the same financial button.

"I'd say, 'Hey, football pays for twenty sports. Basketball pays for basketball. So if we don't get football right we're going to get annihilated, and so are the other sports you enjoy watching here. So we need your help,'" Fisch said. "I still do it. I was on the road recruiting for thirteen days, and I had nine dinners explaining the importance of NIL."

The entire football facility looked like the result of a similar sell. Every square foot was a testament to Fisch's all-consuming drive to elevate Arizona football while acknowledging the past—honoring Wildcat legends like Ricky Hunley and Chuck Cecil with spots on his coaching staff and naming Tedy Bruschi senior adviser. One entire wall was filled with photos of prominent guest speakers—McVay, Belichick, former Ravens coach Brian Billick, Seattle's Pete Carroll, the Eagles' Roseman, Spurrier, Jay Glazer of FOX Sports.

Inspirational messages were everywhere you turned. Not sappy slogans, but words intended to carry a deeper meaning. Be A Pro. It's Personal. Fisch might as well have piped his voice through speakers preaching *This is Arizona football!*

FISCH AND HIS STAFF HAD known they would need all the help they could get the moment they saw the returning roster.

"The real cold shower was seeing the team for the first time," said

Doherty. "Holy smokes. This is a Pac-12 team? You immediately noticed the body types. They didn't look the part.

"It was more just spitting the bit," he added. "This workout is too hard. A culture of corner-cutting that had festered for years. Guys who didn't take too kindly to being pushed and held accountable."

No surprise then that the Wildcats went 1-11 that first season, losing to San Diego State 38–14 and Northern Arizona by 2 at home. Still, there were signs of the revival to come. Malcontents moving on. Long physical practices, hours in the weight room, an attention to detail paying small but noticeable dividends on both sides of the ball.

In year two, Fisch continued to reshape his roster—either pushing players into the portal or recruiting over them. His stellar Class of 2022 (ranked twenty-second overall by 247Sports and No. 1 in the Pac-12) he sold on little more than an NIL wing and a prayer.

"I said, 'Okay, this is what we're going to do. We're going to make this available, and this available, and this available,' but we had no collective. Had no real money available. So what we'll do is give you an opportunity to do a podcast, an opportunity to sell your jersey. So we signed that class without a dollar. People think we signed that class because we were ahead of the NIL curve; we had not one dollar for one recruit, one player from that signing class."

It was a game-changing class in every sense of the word headlined by quarterback Jayden de Laura, a transfer from Washington State; five-star wide receiver Tetairoa ("T-Mac") McMillan; quarterback Noah Fifita and linebacker Jacob Manu, teammates at powerful Servite High in Anaheim, California. A premium was placed on skill and explosion, every position defined by a specific set of NFL-like criteria.

Take left tackle, for example.

"Athletic ability was huge," said Doherty, "the ability to move, function in space, balance and body control, ability to strike, how fast do they come off the ball with violence and want-to. You're looking for explosive guys everywhere. It doesn't matter."

But the real "game changer" in Fisch's mind was the decision to reach back into the past and embrace what Dick Tomey had started in the late 1980s—building a winning program around the Polynesian community, the influx of Polynesian players adding size, depth, and a warrior spirit to the roster. By 2023, Arizona had two dozen such players and another half dozen coaches on its roster from hotbeds like Hawaii, California, Utah, and Nevada.

"The more I've been around the Polynesian culture, the more family over everything is real," said Fisch. "It's not about going out as much as it is *hanging out*. I think the more these kids hung out together, the more they loved one another, the more they embraced playing for one another. What I did here was study history, and this place hadn't won consistently since Dick Tomey. What did he do? Let's do that."

Hour after hour searching and analyzing potential recruits, extracting, as always, the steepest price at home. Until one day Fisch called a time-out.

"I changed my routine in the middle of year two," he admitted. "Was never seeing my wife, ever, ever, ever. Not seeing the kids."

So Fisch said he made the conscious decision to have coffee and chat with Amber for at least an hour every morning. He encouraged his two youngest daughters, Ashlee and Kendall, already invested in their favorite players, to attend practice. They drew closer to the team, crying after losses.

Thankfully, in 2022, there were fewer tears than the previous season, as the Wildcats improved to 5-7, finishing with wins in two of their last three games, over UCLA and, in a revenge game, Arizona State.

De Laura, the transfer quarterback from WSU, started all twelve games and had a breakout season throwing for 3,685 yards and twenty-five touchdowns, leading the nation's sixth-best passing attack. The six-foot-five, 205-pound freshmen McMillan made an immediate impact with thirty-nine catches for 702 yards and eight touchdowns.

Fisch's frequent flying and dialing for donor dollars was beginning to pay off.

"We were able to say to every scholarship kid on our team, you're going to get eighteen thousand bucks," he said. "And if they're good in school they're going to get another six thousand in Alston money [an education-related award] and a laptop. That was our twenty-four-thousand-dollar baseline. And every walk-on got half that, twelve-five.

"I told them, 'Guys, just like in life, if you're good at something you're going to get paid more. If you're not good at something, you're not.' That was our plan. You needed $1.8 million to execute the plan. If you think about it, some programs are giving that to one player. We're talking about needing that for 112."

Compounding the problem was a donor base that naturally skewed older and more skeptical. Arizona retirees were happy to help fund an expanded weight room or upgraded locker room, but to just randomly pay a kid? Not so much. In response, Fisch turned to one of his team's twelve standards: *Tell the truth.*

"What if I told you that money has now enabled that kid's mom and dad to come watch him play? Now they can fly over from Hawaii. What if I told you that enabled that kid not to drive DoorDash at night so he can pay for diapers for his three-year-old son? I don't want to say we pull on the heartstrings, but we tell the real story here."

And when the Big Boys came calling, sniffing around his stars, tough choices had to be made. All-Pac-12 wide receiver Dorian Singer told Fisch he had a $250,000 offer on the table from USC to transfer. A number that would have not only busted the Wildcats' NIL budget but sent the absolute wrong message to the team.

"I said go," said Fisch, and Singer went to 'SC. At the same time he told his compliance people to keep a close eye on four or five of his best players, especially the ethereal McMillan.

"The saddest part now is the after-game handshakes are a little bit dirtier than they used to be," said Fisch. "When you have players that are pretty special, you question what people's motives are.

"We can sell family and development and NFL contacts as much as we want, but in the end these kids are going to hear things they never heard in their lives before. You're not talking about a tennis team. How they grew up is very, very different. What we may not consider life-changing money is to them. I love T-Mac and his family. I think you have to invest differently. I made sure when I was on the road that I flew out to Hawaii to see his grandma, his family. He was already on our team. I wanted to make sure they understand how important he was to our program. That's what you have to do when you're not playing on the same budget."

As 2023 spring practice was about to begin, 102 of the 112 players on Fisch's roster had never played a single down for Kevin Sumlin.

• • •

IN MANY WAYS THE NUMBERS man for U of A football was Matt Doherty. On most days in his small, sparsely furnished office, the team's director of player personnel was "drinking out of a fire hose." He would scroll through the NCAA's official transfer portal website, filled with 127 pages of names, fifty names per page, of *just football players* looking to transfer schools, 6,350 entries offering little more than a name, position, and school.

"I essentially oversee the identification and evaluation of the talent," Doherty said. "It's my job to oversee the process of getting players in front of position coaches, coordinators, and to an extent, Jedd. He's not going to see these guys until the conversation has accelerated to . . . we want him."

As at most Power 5 schools, Doherty's was a multilevel operation: working with paid subscription services such as National Preps and Tracking Football that regularly updated the portal and offered a deeper dive into a player's history and background—size, speed, number of snaps, other analytics—along with additional information obtained from websites such as 247Sports, On3, and Rivals; cross-referencing, narrowing the potential pool of, say, offensive linemen to around sixty select names before passing those names to position coaches or analysts for further evaluation. An exhausting process, to be sure, made more so by the pool of sharks often circling the same players.

"The obviously aggravating thing about the portal," said Doherty, "is that you can have the best talent evaluator on the planet in your building, telling you how good the players are popping up, but it does absolutely nothing in terms of acquiring the player."

It helped that Doherty and Fisch went back a long way—to 2015–16 and Jim Harbaugh's staff his first two seasons in Ann Arbor, when the Wolverines won twenty games (and lost just six). Doherty's initial "baptism under fire" came in New England in 2009 under Nick Caserio, then the Pats player personnel director, where Doherty said he never left the building from six in the morning until ten at night, seven days a week. Signature stints with Al Golden and Mark Richt in Miami soon followed. Doherty was at North Carolina State when Fisch came calling in late 2020.

Like a hedge fund manager, Doherty spent hours every day trying to determine where the market was headed. Searching for value, for tells.

"A lot of my job is reading the market and being able to tell him when it's going to move a certain way," said Doherty. "What I can at least do for Jedd is say, the word out there is this is the number. The problem is there's absolutely no way to corroborate that. Some of the dollar amounts you're seeing tossed around publicly are completely full of shit."

Whatever the stakes, by the time the 2023 season kicked off Doherty and the coaching staff had more than their fair share of winnings hands—pulling a collection of difference makers out of the portal: quarterback de Laura, speedy wide receiver Jacob Cowing (UTEP), running back D. J. Williams (Florida State), linebacker Justin Flowe (Oregon), nose tackle Bill Norton (Georgia), and defensive tackle Tyler Manoa (UCLA), to name but a few.

Doherty was long since resigned to his year-round fate, living from one dead period and portal window to the next, wrapped around what he deemed an "explosion" of unofficial visits starting in March and April, then thirty to thirty-five official visits already set for June. It was a form of free agency that never seemed to end.

"The time investment is the time investment," he said with a sigh. "What kills you is constantly having to entertain people."

With that, Doherty touched his heart and talked about his infant daughter, Ellie, at home. He had barely seen her for much of her first year.

LATER THAT SAME FEBRUARY DAY, Dave Heeke was sitting around a conference table in his office across the street, quietly and intelligently dissecting the chaotic state of college football. Thanks to his efforts and those of his development and compliance staff, Fisch would soon have a football-only collective in place. Desert Takeover was certainly not Knight and Division Street up in Oregon or John Ruiz down in Miami or whatever the University of Texas was throwing into the kitty, but a solid, reliable, community-based collective offering members a tax deduction and fringe benefits, like exclusive access and private autograph sessions. Heeke walked that fine line between attracting NIL donors with a finite amount of money to give and appeasing coaches demanding more assistants, better facilities, and higher salaries, forget about funding day-to-day operations. One request after another.

"Adult conversations," said Heeke. "They're hard. They can be a little raw. It begins to change the principles and philosophies of the college model and tests how far are you willing to go one way at the expense of leaving others out."

Speaking of which, just two months earlier Heeke had signed Fisch to a five-year contract extension through the 2027 season.

"I think Jedd is on the right track," he said. "I think we are on the right track."

As winter turned to spring, where that track was headed for the Wildcats or the historic Pac-12 Conference, nobody knew. Athletic directors like Heeke, now in his seventh year in the desert, were essentially flying blind with bullets coming from every direction. All he really had was . . .

"The hope is we'll survive," he said. "The power of the Pac-Eight, Pac-Ten, Pac-12 through the years, this great conference in the West, how could you imagine that not existing to a degree? But the landscape has changed, and it's controlled by the networks. That's challenging. We're faced with a big challenge right now on how to hold the group together. Because everyone wants to be together, but out of the corner of your eye you have to think about what if? What if there's something when they start shooting, where does the plane land when everyone starts going down? That's the real challenge."

Little did Heeke know . . . the destruction of a 108-year-old conference was just six months away.

CHAPTER 7

The Summit

ON JUNE 7, 2023, AS smoke from wildfires across Canada covered much of the Northeast, University of Arizona president Robert C. Robbins welcomed dozens of major college power brokers, thought leaders, and so-called stakeholders to a U of A–sponsored Future of College Athletics Summit to be held in our nation's capital. The timing could not have been better. The system was under siege, with no solution in sight.

Dr. Robbins had been the president of U of A since June 2017. Prior to that he was the president and chief executive officer of the Texas Medical Center in Houston and chairman of the department of cardiothoracic surgery at the Stanford University School of Medicine. Known to family and friends as Bobby, Robbins was an internationally recognized cardiac surgeon—so there was no hint of hyperbole when he told the crowd gathered in D.C. that college sports, particularly college football, was "in the ICU." Robbins had used the same phrase twelve hours earlier, during a private interview in the oak-paneled Round Robin Bar inside Washington's historic Willard Hotel.

"Maybe that's a little strong," he said that night, "but there's a whole set of factors, in my opinion, that could really alter college sports for the next twenty-five years."

Robbins was uniquely qualified to offer an opinion. He had grown up in tiny Ellisville, Mississippi, itself a history lesson come to life as the first county seat of Jones County, the "Free State of Jones," and later traces of the Freedom Riders and the KKK. Robbins was raised by his maternal grandparents on the campus of Jones Junior College, where his grandfather taught math for forty-seven years. Their old Victorian home was without central heating or air-conditioning, set hard by the railroad tracks, whites on one side, Blacks on the other.

"I played basketball, football, and baseball with those Black kids, they were my friends," Robbins remembered. "My grandmother and I would go to the Black high school on Friday nights and watch them play football because they were so good."

From the time he was five Robbins ran free on the campus, going to football practice every day, shagging balls, standing behind the huddle listening and calling out plays. A star quarterback in high school, he was headed to Ole Miss to take his shot playing SEC football before tearing up a knee water-skiing ended that dream. He was playing spring ball at Jones J. C. when he realized that the hours devoted to football, practicing until seven at night followed by a shower, dinner, and film study, while majoring in premed were getting him nowhere fast. He wanted to become a doctor, believing his only way out of a one-stoplight town was getting all As. He said goodbye to football, and earned an undergraduate degree in chemistry from a liberal arts college in Jackson, Mississippi, and then a medical degree from Ole Miss.

In the back corner of the bar, Robbins talked sports and medicine for nearly an hour, sprinkling his iced tea with packets of Sweet 'n Low he pulled from the pocket of his sports coat. He was still looking sharp near the end of a fifteen-hour day that began with a 7:30 a.m. SportsCenter interview in Tampa and would eventually end with a 9:45 p.m. West Wing tour at the White House.

Asked if anything in his medical background had prepared him for the college sports spotlight at such a crucial period, Robbins offered a two-word answer. "Never panic," he said.

Later, after a few more sips of iced tea, he added: "I used to tell residents, look, it's not rocket science. It's basically blocking and tackling heart surgery. And I know a lot of famous astronomers. Heart surgery is pretty easy.

"This falls into the category of heart surgery. I was thinking about it when getting ready to do SportsCenter this morning. I remember this heart transplant I did one time at Stanford. The person, their heart, their left ventricle is supposed to be down here but it was up here. So you had to put a regular heart into the chest, but the plumbing was all backward and you had to figure that out. It wasn't *that hard*, but you had to work at it and be committed to it. I think that's one of the reasons [NCAA president] Governor Baker was selected, because he's said to have great political skills. Let's get into Congress and let's get going."

Ah, yes, the U.S. Congress, the citadel of compromise and bipartisanship. Whoops. Sorry. The current House of Representatives and Senate, particularly the House, bitterly divided, consumed with personal and party agendas and no small matter of political acrimony, was the very same dysfunctional body the NCAA, college presidents, and conference commissioners were hoping, praying, pleading to fix what Robbins called "a complex set of problems."

"We're here for a reason, because we think Congress is a key stakeholder," he said. "We need to get something done—even if it's one thing. Something around NIL, because we need a national approach to this."

Whatever optimism Robbins and others may have felt at that point was undermined by the reality of congressional action, or rather *inaction*, on college sports regulations. In 2020, Senator Marco Rubio (R-FL) presented the first NIL bill, and though there had been a flurry since, it took four long years to get even one out of committee when an NCAA-friendly bill made it past the first step in June 2024. College leaders were eager to put all their eggs in a basket that had shown no signs of delivering what they needed. Instead, a series of congressional hearings—one more cringeworthy, self-indulgent, and out of touch than the next—started popping up like cherry blossoms in D.C.

Exhibit A:

A March 29, 2023, hearing held by the House Subcommittee on Innovation, Data, and Commerce called, we kid you not, "Taking the Buzzer Beater to the Bank: Protecting College Athletes' NIL Dealmaking Rights." The first federal hearing chaired by Republicans in the post–Mark Emmert era was described by one reporter who attended as "two and a half hours of congressional grandstanding, State U cheerleading, [and] empty questioning."

The six handpicked panelists, a well-intentioned group, did little to educate anyone on the current state of NIL. Among them, the commissioner of a league with virtually no NIL activity; a football player who graduated in 2014, seven years before NIL went into effect; the president of a D-II school where *total* NIL activity barely reached five figures; and an athletic director with one of the smallest departments in the Power 5 group from a state without an NIL law.

THERE WAS A BUZZ IN the committee room, well before Nick Saban walked in, about the Alabama head coach's attendance. One young female legislative aide from Texas got a heads-up from her high school football coach father that Saban would be on the Hill that night, and she *had* to get a photo with college football's premier coach. She was one of dozens who quickly swarmed the diminutive Saban as soon as he walked into the room shortly after 6:00 p.m. He had a team of people with him, including Alabama athletic director Greg Byrne and system vice chancellor Clay Ryan, but there was not much either could do once the twentysomethings, decked in Brooks Brothers suits, realized the night's biggest celebrity had arrived.

At his heart, Saban was an introvert. A frequent game among reporters and administrators at the SEC's annual spring meetings in Miramar Beach was guessing how long Saban would last at the conference's reception on the beach. A typical over/under was about ten minutes, with Saban looking for someone he knew and engaging him or her in conversation to run out the clock. But there were no familiar faces to save him at this moment as the circle surrounding him got bigger and bigger. He had no choice but to take photo after photo with strangers, unhappily applying a clenched smile as onlookers who knew him well couldn't help but be amused. "I'm sure he just loves this," one knowingly said before cracking up.

Saban was just one of several SEC dignitaries that descended on the Capitol trying to lobby for NIL reform that night. Other heavyweights included SEC commissioner Greg Sankey, Auburn football coach Hugh Freeze, and Kentucky basketball coach John Calipari.

That Saban and other SEC coaches used some of their precious free time to travel to Washington to lobby for a solution spoke to the severity of the situation. Earlier in the day, he had met with Majority Leader Steve Scalise. Saban desperately wanted a fix for what he believed to be an untenable problem plaguing college football and was willing to take photo after photo with admirers if it helped even 1 percent. When it was finally time for Saban to leave, it was like watching the president exit the room. His team surrounded him, strategized the path of least resistance, and ushered him out of the building and into the smoky D.C. night.

IT WAS AGAINST THIS BACKDROP that the next morning a passel of power players, so-called stakeholders, and respected "thought leaders," convened at the University of Arizona's Washington, D.C. Center for Outreach & Collaboration on Pennsylvania Avenue. Among those attending: Charlie Baker, Sankey, ACC commissioner Jim Phillips, Kansas chancellor Doug Girod, respected college sports administrator Oliver Luck, and Missouri athletic director Desirée Reed-Francois.

Microphone in hand, the silver-haired Robbins told the crowd the aspirational goal of the summit was solutions to "very complicated problems."

"I think there's plenty of people in this room who are smart enough to figure out solutions to a desperate problem we have in college sports," he said. Tongue in cheek, he admitted that given the "narrow window," Congress was not exactly "the first place we'd all think about [but] we are desperate for the U.S. Congress to try to help us, to work with us, to try to find some solutions to the enormous problems we are going to be talking about today."

The first panel, moderated by ESPN's Pete Thamel, featured Baker, Robbins, and Knight Commission CEO Amy Privette Perko.

On the 100th day of his presidency, Baker said he had already visited or met with seventy-seven of the NCAA's ninety-seven conferences on a listening tour to understand "what people are talking about and worried about." He explained that his background in health care afforded him the perspective needed to deal with an age-old presidential lament: the unwieldy nature of the NCAA's governance structure: eighteen hundred members and more than one hundred seventy committees.

"Fundamentally," he said, "we have to figure things out."

In person, Baker came across as the kind of leader who didn't suffer fools, the kind of politician who prided himself on preparation. The six-foot-six former Harvard basketball player, with the accompanying Boston accent, was a pragmatist about the challenges. When you were a Republican governor in a Democratic state, you had to be.

When asked about the realities of Congress actually offering an NIL solution, Baker all but brushed aside the question for a five-minute no-notes soliloquy that took previous NCAA leadership to task while offering a path forward for resolving his organization's most pressing problems.

"I think it was a big mistake for the NCAA not to do a framework around NIL when it had the opportunity," he began. "I think there were too many people in college sports who thought no rules would work really well for them. And what everybody discovered is no rules, no accountability, no framework doesn't work well for anybody. Because you do have a situation where it's basically impossible to find anybody—[ticks off on his fingers]—student-athletes, families, coaches, ADs, college presidents, *anybody* who thinks this current system 'works.'"

From there Baker was off and running on what he believed were three basic solutions to the current crisis at hand: a real, transparent registry for NIL deals; a certification process for agents; and a uniform, standard NIL contract. When he finally got around to the original question, he stated that he believed Congress had far more ability than the NCAA to preempt state laws and "more legitimate authority to create a level playing field."

There was a feistiness to Baker, whose youthful energy belied his sixty-six years on Earth. He was only four months into a job his friends warned him not to take, and the frustration over what he inherited was clear. There were fires burning all around him, but he had only one hose and was trying to triage the most pressing issues. He got particularly animated at one point after a fellow panelist brought up the inequity of the NCAA shouldering all the football problems while the College Football Playoff kept all the revenue. He didn't discredit the idea, but in taking over an organization he believed had long been unable to "choose what it wants to focus on when it needs to focus on it," he needed to deal with the five-alarm fires or he risked taking an early credibility hit. He highlighted growing concerns around sports betting, calling it the "next really big challenging issue for student-athletes"; NIL; and a holistic athlete model as the chief concerns he needed to deal with immediately. "I need a whole bunch of people to come to the conclusion I know what I'm doing," Baker growled, his voice rising in tension.

During a question-and-answer period, Brent Chapman stood up to challenge Baker on the idea of having a government agency like the Consumer Financial Protection Bureau (CFPB) to oversee NIL. Chapman happened to be the former chief information officer for three financial services companies, including the largest non-bank mortgage servicer in the country at the time, and knew full well the CFPB, which monitors banks and other financial institutions, answered to no one. Not to the president. Not to Congress. No one. Not exactly a best-case scenario for the NCAA and college sport.

Chapman was now the founder and CEO of myNILpay.com, a Venmo-like platform that allowed fans to directly pay athletes.

"You open up the app and all 500,000 student-athletes are pre-loaded—every school, every athlete, DI to DIII," Chapman said. "You go in and search by team and then name, hit 'pay athlete,' put in your credit card, and it sends an alert to the athlete's email account. If we don't have their email—we have a little under half—our support team goes on Instagram, does some direct messaging, and also reaches out to the coaches and says, 'Hey, they've been paid.'"

When all was said and done—seven and a half hours from start to finish—an outspoken consensus had formed that *something* needed to happen to get the states out of the NIL business and calm the transfer and realignment chaos. Could Baker be the one to deliver it? He earned early praise for his straight-shooter approach and how hard he was working his D.C. connections to try to find a federal solution. "He doesn't have any baggage," said Tom McMillen, the president of LEAD1, which lobbied on behalf of athletic directors. "The NCAA has lots of baggage, but he doesn't personally. He can go in there with goodwill. What that translates to is really hard to say."

Baker's hope was that bills could emerge from committees that summer, make it to a vote in the fall, and be signed into action by President Biden before the calendar turned to 2024. His fear was it would lose significant traction if it butted up against a presidential election year that promised to suck all the oxygen out of the room.

WHATEVER GOODWILL AND OPTIMISM THAT had been generated over two days appeared to fade as the political waters surrounding NIL grew even more muddied. The swirling ash from Canada was still darkening D.C. skies when these events occurred:

- The Texas legislature passed a law effectively eliminating any NCAA control over NIL in the state
- Alabama's Republican senator Tommy Tuberville and Joe Manchin (D-WV) went public with the Protecting Athletes, Schools and Sports Act of 2023, the so-called PASS Act, with regulations seemingly straight out of the NCAA playbook—prohibiting, for example, NIL from being used as an inducement in recruiting and in the transfer portal. It contained one requirement that virtually guaranteed howls of protest: student-athletes must complete their first three years of academic eligibility before they would be allowed to transfer without penalty.
- Following in Baker's footsteps, a NCAA Working Group on NIL presented a series of proposals that would develop a registration process for NIL service providers (such as agents and financial advisers), create a standardized NIL contract or contract terms, and provide greater transparency about NIL activities.
- Sen. Ted Cruz (R-TX), the leading Senate minority lawmaker on the powerful Senate Commerce Committee, introduced draft discussion of another NCAA-friendly bill that would give the association power to oversee NIL, transfer policies, and eligibility, and provide federal protection against legal challenges.
- Senators Richard Blumenthal (D-CT) and Cory Booker (D-NJ) announced a discussion draft of legislation that would "prioritize athletes' health, education, and economic rights." As announced in a press release, the College Athletes Protection & Compensation Act would set national standards for NIL, establish a Medical

Trust Fund to provide care to injured athletes, establish a central oversight agency that would "set, administer and enforce rules and standards to protect athletes who enter into endorsement contracts," and "set national standards to give athletes the economic and educational opportunities they deserve."

SIX DAYS AFTER INTRODUCING THE draft legislation, Dick Blumenthal walked into a coffeehouse in blue-collar Shelton, Connecticut. It was late afternoon on a Tuesday and the place was almost empty, save the senator and a reporter.

The former attorney general for the state of Connecticut for twenty years, Blumenthal had held a Senate seat since 2011. A well-groomed man with a sharp mind (a degree from Harvard and JD from Yale Law), Blumenthal had a keen eye for important issues and was unafraid to take on the likes of Big Tobacco, Microsoft, and Craigslist. Coffee in hand, he said he'd loved being a state AG, because when he made a decision something happened.

"In this job," he said, "I do a lot of votes. It doesn't have the same result."

As for his proposed legislation, the senator offered no predictions about its chances. "As you know, anything in the Congress these days is an uphill battle because of how political everything has become between the House and the Senate," he said. "The House is sort of crazy. Nobody knows what's going to happen with the appropriations because [then House Speaker Kevin] McCarthy is not in control. But the draft is bipartisan. It's the first bipartisan proposal. The idea of an athletes' Bill of Rights, the idea of a trust fund, guarantees on scholarship, mental health, enforcement authority, I think those concepts have legs. Whether it's the next two months, the next two years . . . so I think it's a step forward. That's how I would characterize it. A major step forward given the landscape.

"I have a lot of respect for Charlie Baker. I think his heart is in the right place. He's a very smart guy. We have talked a fair amount before this latest cascade of events. He reached out the day we announced our discussion draft. He expressed support for the kind of concepts we're talking about.

Not to say he endorsed it. He can speak for himself. But he's supportive of the effort. So I find it hugely ironic. But, you know, if you swim with the sharks you better be a shark. The NCAA has always impressed me, at least until Charlie took over, as somewhat maladroit in the way they position themselves resisting the change we've been talking about."

The handwriting had long been on the wall, he said, only the NCAA honchos and the major conference commissioners never really read it. Instead they were electing to spend hundreds of millions of dollars on legal fights to protect their own self-interest. Or better yet, their bank accounts.

"It's clearly been all about the money," said Blumenthal. "And I think that's the lesson."

Asked to put a percentage on any kind of NIL and student-athlete rights bill ever being passed, Blumenthal put the odds at slightly less than fifty-fifty. "I would say four out of ten. Right now, the odds are against anything getting done. The one constant here, according to the title of your book, it's the money."

The senator said he'd spoken with SEC and Big Ten leaders, and what he'd heard was an increasing sense of urgency. "They're riding the tiger and not quite sure where it's going or how to get off," he said. What he'd told them is not to expect his support on antitrust: "They've asked for it. I've resisted it." He thought the Commerce committee was the most likely spot to finally get an NIL-related bill out of committee, but he still put the odds of Senator Chuck Schumer, the majority leader, putting one up for a vote as not great. There were too many other pressing issues around the country to make this a must-pass bill, and too many conflicting viewpoints to rally consensus around one approach. Blumenthal tried to work with colleagues across the aisle, having the most success with Senator Jerry Moran (R-KS). He'd had conversations with Tuberville, too, but didn't offer the slightest hint of optimism. "His Republican colleagues don't know what to do about him," he said.

MEETING TOMMY TUBERVILLE IN AN empty Birmingham-area Marriott lobby, one naturally wants to address him as senator. "Don't curse me with that name," Tuberville said. "Call me Coach."

Now in his late sixties, the slender Tuberville was the senior senator from Alabama but still saw himself as a college football coach. The former Auburn head coach had considered a run for Alabama governor in 2018, going on a monthslong listening tour through the Yellowhammer State, before ultimately deciding he'd rather pursue another coaching job or become an athletic director. "Athletics, especially at the college level, is what I know best," Tuberville told *USA Today* after he pulled out of the race.

But in 2019, Tuberville caught the political bug again and decided to challenge Democratic senator Doug Jones to represent the red state. The real fight was surviving the Republican primary, where Tuberville's strong name recognition carried him past former attorney general Jeff Sessions and Representative Bradley Byrne. Tuberville easily beat Jones in the general election in fall 2020, putting him in a powerful position as one of one hundred senators who could shape the country.

On this day he seemed more interested in gossiping about which coaches might get fired than discussing serious legislative efforts, but NIL legislation was in his wheelhouse. As the former head coach at four schools that cared about football—Auburn, Cincinnati, Ole Miss, and Texas Tech— Tuberville had a deep knowledge of how college football worked and maintained friendships throughout the sport. Saban and Kirby Smart called frequently, he said, giving him an earful about NIL and pushing him to do something. He was hesitant at first.

"I know a heck of a lot more about college football recruiting and all that than the federal government, but I'm learning," Tuberville said. "It didn't take me long to figure out you don't want the federal government in your business."

Tuberville wasn't kidding about his lack of federal government knowledge—he famously flubbed the three branches of the government—and was quickly making an infamous reputation for himself on the Senate floor. His obstinate blocking of military promotions provoked rebuke even from his fellow Republicans. He told us he believed he could deliver every Republican and Manchin every Democrat to an NIL bill, but no one seemed to believe him. He persisted, nevertheless, genuinely believing he was the best-qualified person in Congress to solve college football's problems. He knew he had to have bipartisan support, though he struggled to come up with the name of the New Jersey senator who was also working on a bill—Cory Booker. He knew the stakes, though, back in his home state.

"You can't have Texas A&M out there recruiting high school players and giving them two million dollars to come, and Alabama and Auburn can't do that with freshmen," Tuberville said.

Tuberville knew how to turn on the folksy charm when he wanted something. It might have been a facade, but it offered insight into how he had been a successful college football head coach for years, primarily recruiting young Black men while at the same time saying during a Trump campaign rally that Democrats "want reparations because they think the people that do the crime are owed that. Bullshit!" The comments were widely decried as racist. Whatever he lacked in traditional credentials, his time in college football taught him how successful appealing to the lowest common denominator could be, whether with hard-core SEC football fans or political animals. After winning four straight games against rival Alabama, Tuberville embraced a "fear the thumb" slogan that Auburn fans loved and Alabama hated in equal measure. His flair for theatrics seemed suited to what politics had become, and he had long been opinionated with his staff about topics far beyond Xs and Os.

Now, as a Republican senator from Alabama, he was closely aligned with former president Donald Trump, who had endorsed him in his race, but in our conversation, he didn't always toe the company line. He advocated for universities to pay the players themselves, an idea some of his former coach friends were on board with but that wasn't widely shared among his Republican colleagues. "The university should be paying this, not outside groups," he said. "I'm all for saving education, college sports as we once knew it, and saving Olympic sports."

Consider Tony Franklin, beyond skeptical of Tuberville's intentions. Franklin, a liberal football coach in an industry that trended conservative, worked as Auburn's offensive coordinator during Tuberville's final season, before being fired. Franklin had always been unafraid to speak truth to power, notably calling out what he believed to be inappropriate COVID-19 policies at Middle Tennessee State, which ultimately resulted in his dismissal. Franklin detested everything Tuberville stood for, both the guy he once worked for and the guy he devolved into as a senator.

"For him to be in charge of fixing college football is a nightmare," Franklin said. "If you go back through his history, place after place, event after event, time after time, it's nothing but lie after lie. When he was elected, I said that makes him the perfect politician, because he genuinely cares about nothing except himself—whatever it is that gives him power and makes him feel good."

Franklin compared Tuberville to circus showman P. T. Barnum. He was good at entertaining an audience with what he knew they wanted to hear, but it was rarely genuine. Deep down, Franklin believed, Tuberville just wanted to be able to tell his coaching buddies he was working hard for them in the political swamps of D.C., regardless of whether he ever accomplished anything. "He doesn't give a rat's ass about those kids," Franklin said.

The early assessments of the Tuberville-Manchin PASS Act were that it wouldn't accomplish much. It received endorsements from Baker ("a major step in the right direction") and the collective Power 5 commissioners ("another step forward"), but it never got much traction on the floor. It came off as too one-sided, too friendly to the NCAA, to have much of a chance of getting the liberal side of the aisle on board, even to try to compromise.

As Tuberville learned, being a senator didn't come with the same power he wielded on a college campus as head football coach. Just because he and his famous coaching friends wanted it done wasn't enough to convince his colleagues. His recruiting skills had gotten rusty in retirement, no match for a world that excelled in finding new and creative ways to do nothing.

IN A SPARSELY ATTENDED HEARING, several senators marched in, sat down, pontificated about something they knew little about, and left for some other opportunity at an easy sound bite.

You could have said that about any of the nine congressional hearings since 2020 about the threats facing college athletics. This one, a Senate Judiciary Committee hearing appropriately named the "Hail Mary Hearing," on October 17, 2023, the tenth and final NIL-focused hearing of the year, had higher stakes and bigger names attached, but the results were all the same.

The hearing occurred at a complicated time, with the debt ceiling debate and war between Israel and Hamas dominating the nation's attention. It felt strange seeing prominent senators devoting precious time and energy to name, image, and likeness and antitrust exemptions amid that backdrop.

Senator Lindsey Graham (R-SC) took the microphone to state the obvious: "College football is in chaos," followed by Blumenthal, who said, "College sports are in need of reform. It's in need of reform now."

The obvious aside, throughout the more than two-and-a-half-hour hearing, the majority of the senators seemed more interested in offering rambling monologues that showed scant knowledge of the actual issues rather than questioning the seven assembled witnesses, which included college sports heavyweights like NCAA president Baker, Big Ten commissioner Tony Petitti, Notre Dame athletic director Jack Swarbrick, Ramogi Huma, executive director of the National College Players Association, and Walker Jones, executive director of the Grove Collective at Ole Miss.

Senator Josh Hawley (R-MO) quizzed Baker about transgender swimmer Lia Thomas and female athletes having to share locker rooms with transgender athletes. He wanted to know whether Baker disavowed statements of support for Hamas from student groups on college campuses. Hawley blatantly trying to hijack the hearing felt like it would be the low point, until the senior senator from West Virginia strode onto the dais. Joe Manchin, a former West Virginia football player, *should* get it. He was a close friend of Saban, affectionately referring to him as "Brother Saban," and paid far closer attention to college football than all but a few of his peers in the Senate.

Unfortunately for the athletes, Manchin believed the environment he experienced playing at West Virginia back in the late 1960s was ideal and not worth changing. "He's so strident in his belief that nobody ought to be getting any NIL and it's a good deal to get room, board, and tuition," says former Big 12 commissioner Bob Bowlsby, who has had multiple conversations with Manchin about the topic. "He's dyed in the wool of the old days."

That was abundantly clear in Manchin's out-of-touch comments delivered at the tail end of a hearing that was already careering off the rails. He decried how NIL had destroyed the system he knew, making sure to note that he would have paid West Virginia to let him play, rather than expecting anything in return. Then he said the quiet part out loud.

"It's hard to root for the kids when they're multimillionaires as freshmen and sophomores," Manchin said.

It should be noted Manchin never complained about his friend Saban making more than $11 million a year. He never seemed upset about fellow West Virginian Jimbo Fisher getting a ten-year, $95 million guaranteed contract that aged like sour milk the moment it was signed. No, for Manchin, it seemed that only when the unpaid, largely Black, group of athletes started getting a chance to make some money did alarm bells go off in his head.

Speaking of bells, Senator John N. Kennedy (R-LA) rang a rather loud one at one point in front of Baker and other witnesses. "I'd be real careful inviting Congress to micromanage your business," he said. Whatever the wisdom of that advice, given Congress's dysfunction, that prospect felt distant. Meanwhile, as the calendar turned and a New Year loomed without an NIL bill advancing to the president's desk, an old saying sprung to mind: Desperate times call for desperate measures.

CHAPTER 8

Macy's I

I N MIKE LOCKSLEY'S SPACIOUS OFFICE inside the $149 million Jones-Hill House in College Park, Maryland, a gaggle of championship rings from his time at Alabama sit prominently displayed at the center of the room.

During three seasons as an assistant at Alabama, Locksley was part of a national championship team, two national championship runner-up teams, and two SEC championship teams. The message is unspoken but simple enough: The man leading Maryland's football program has championship pedigree.

Not that he got to enjoy the night he won the biggest of those rings.

To college football fans, the 2017 national championship game may feature the most famous ending to a title game ever. Locksley, as co–offensive coordinator, was part of Saban's brain trust that decided, while down 13–0 to Georgia, to switch from Jalen Hurts, reigning SEC Player of the Year and owner of a 28-2 record as Alabama's starter, to Tua Tagovailoa in the second half.

Tagovailoa, a true freshman, immediately sparked an Alabama offense that seemed stuck in neutral under Hurts. Alabama battled its way back, forced overtime, and ultimately won on a 2nd-and-26 pass from Tagovailoa to DeVonta Smith to win.

When Locksley returned to his hotel, looking to celebrate his first national championship, he was greeted by a familiar albeit unhappy face. Averion Hurts, father of Jalen, was furious that his son got pulled as the starting quarterback in the middle of a national championship game. "This is some bullshit what happened," Hurts told Locksley, who had to calm down the passionate quarterback father for the rest of the night rather than celebrate.

It only got worse when Locksley flew back to Tuscaloosa and had to attend a staff meeting the next day. Despite saying, "I've never been happier in my life," right after winning the game, Saban's tone had drastically changed.

"We got lucky," Saban told his bleary-eyed staff the next morning. "They gave us the game, and we didn't play to our standard."

Then Saban hit the assembled coaches with a sentence that encapsulates everything about who he is as a coach.

"I know you guys want to feel all happy," Saban said, "but that was last year."

In fact, it was less than twenty-four hours after the conclusion of a national championship victory. Less than twenty-four hours after Locksley achieved what he thought would be a career-defining moment, one that he had dreamed about when he first got into coaching. He couldn't believe what he was hearing.

"I remember sitting at the table thinking 'last year'? That was fucking last night, and I didn't get to fucking enjoy it," Locksley said. "The first time I've won a national championship I didn't fucking get to celebrate one iota. But it shows you how he works."

That complete aversion to complacency, that uncanny ability to turn the page immediately, is something Locksley was still grappling with. Maryland was 4-0 after wins over Towson, Charlotte, Virginia, and Michigan State, and Locksley was still trying to figure out the right balance of how to enjoy the victories and not focus solely on all the things that needed improvement. His wife, Kia, calling him a Scrooge after the 31–9 win over Michigan State seems to have resonated. He has seen firsthand how successful that never-ending—and never attainable—pursuit of perfection can be, but he also openly wonders whether it's sustainable. He spent three seasons at Alabama, rising from analyst to co–offensive coordinator and finally offensive coordinator, where he won the Broyles Award as the nation's top assistant coach. He enjoyed his time in Tuscaloosa, a chance to rehabilitate his tattered career in near anonymity under college football's greatest coach. But working for Saban comes with a steep price.

"Imagine every day you go to work, you gotta make a fourth-and-two call to win the game," he said. "That's how that pressure cooker is. Even if you win, you've got to win a certain way. And if you lose, you don't want to be in Tuscaloosa."

Locksley assembled a group of top lieutenants who understand the demands and benefits of Saban's hard-charging style. His offensive coordinator, Josh Gattis, spent a season with him at Alabama. Brian Williams, his defensive coordinator, twice worked for Saban's protégé, Jeremy Pruitt. Lance Thompson, his outside linebackers coach, was a top recruiter for the recruiting-obsessed Saban in three different stints at two schools. Ryan Davis, the program's strength and conditioning coach, studied under Scott Cochran, Saban's longtime right-hand man, during the peak of the Saban Alabama dynasty. They learned the blueprint to dominate college football from the master and have the scars to prove it.

"One of the cheat codes is seeing something like Coach Saban," said Davis, who spent four seasons at Alabama. "When you have coaches that have seen it, that have been in it, they're not surprised by it, but they also understand what it takes to keep driving. We're not satisfied with that."

Davis might lead Maryland's strength and conditioning program, but he's not an old-school strength coach meathead. He references James Clear's *Atomic Habits* and Sisyphus when explaining Saban's famous "Process," and how he and Locksley deploy it at Maryland. Davis's role in guiding the team to be physically ready for a punishing Big Ten season is critically important, but like his mentor Cochran's consigliere role to Saban, Davis's most significant value comes in understanding and monitoring the mental and emotional sides of the football team. Locksley and Davis got an up-close look at how that relationship between Saban and Cochran worked at Alabama, where Cochran acted as part-time psychologist and full-time father figure. They are trying to emulate that approach in College Park.

It comes with an acknowledgment that Davis is around the players more than anyone, including Locksley, and knows their struggles and motivations. Every time Locksley sees Davis, he has one question for him: Where's the team at?

"I know that he knows I'm really the only other one in the program that understands his perspective," Davis said. "I don't have a position group that I make decisions for or guys that I've recruited to make decisions for. The decisions are always for the whole."

Locksley's practice plan is full of what he saw Saban run at Alabama. His in-season schedule for his assistants is the same as it was at Alabama. He even runs out onto the field at home games to the same song, AC/DC's "Thunderstruck." After a disastrous first head-coaching stint at New Mexico, where he went 2-26 and was accused of punching an assistant, Locksley was utilizing the lessons he learned from the most successful and well-run organization he's ever been around.

It's an interesting experiment: Can you take the formula that worked so well under Saban at Alabama and deploy it successfully at a school with a mere sliver of the fan support and passion the Crimson Tide evokes?

LOCKSLEY ARRIVED AT MARYLAND MONTHS after the death of offensive lineman Jordan McNair from heat stroke following an offseason workout, which led to an investigation that found a "toxic culture" around the program and ultimately led to the firing of head coach DJ Durkin and strength coach Rick Court. Locksley not only had to win games on the field but also had to rehabilitate the program's tarnished reputation in the community. Could parents and coaches trust Maryland to care for their young men after what happened to McNair?

No one was better equipped to handle that unenviable situation than Locksley, who grew up going to Maryland games in the 1980s and played football at nearby Towson University. He was one of theirs. A Southwest D.C. native, Locksley had survived a hard life and could empathize with what young Black men and their parents were going through. He had lived through his family getting evicted from their home after his dad walked out on the family and his mom couldn't scrounge up enough money through odd jobs. He had seen his two older brothers, Bryant and Eric, spend most of their adult lives in prison, primarily for selling drugs. In a 1991 interview with the *Baltimore Sun*, he called inner cities a trap and said, "I wanted to get out and coach, but I'd go back to the cities and show the people there is a way out."

And saddest of all, he had lost a child too. Locksley's second oldest, Meiko, was shot and killed in Columbia, Maryland, on September 3, 2017. He would later learn that twenty-five-year-old Meiko, who played football for him at New Mexico, was suffering from chronic traumatic encephalopathy (CTE), a degenerative brain disease, at the time of his death. Locksley and Marty McNair, Jordan's father, shared a trauma bond in the loss of their beloved sons, building a friendship as they grappled with a throbbing pain that never went away.

Locksley might have been the only qualified coach in college football who could say with a straight face that Maryland was his dream job. What he inherited, though, was closer to a nightmare. "It was at rock bottom," he said. "There were a lot of issues, whether trust issues with the players, obviously all the things that went on with Jordan's death and medical and all that stuff. So we started from ground zero."

That first year was challenging, the hardest thing Locksley and his band of Alabama expats had experienced, even more arduous than those years spent in Tuscaloosa. Maryland started that first season hot, including a win over a ranked Syracuse team in Week 2, before the wheels fell off. The foundation wasn't sturdy enough to withstand the adversity that hit when the Terrapins blew a winnable game against Temple. It worsened the following week in a demoralizing 59–0 loss to Penn State. There was talent on the roster, but the best players weren't always the best leaders, and a bad attitude from a top player can poison the well. "They'd make a bunch of yards on game day and then spend all week missing class, positive drug tests, all types of issues that you can't win with," Locksley said.

The turning point came in the season finale against Michigan State. Maryland was limping through the season finish line with a 3-8 record when it traveled to East Lansing. They lost an ugly 19–16 game, but battled hard and something clicked. After the game, Keandre Jones, a linebacker transfer from Ohio State, stood up and told the team that if they had played like that all season, they wouldn't be feeling like they did. Jones, who had seen winning at the highest levels in Columbus, said Maryland had a bright future if the team just bought in.

"With our player-led culture, that was a culture driver," Locksley said. "I think that played a catalyst going into year two, which obviously dealt with a pandemic."

From a pandemic to the tsunami of NIL and the transfer portal hitting at the same time, the changing landscape hasn't been easy for the Terrapins.

The fact is that Maryland is a middle-of-a-pack program with aspirations for more in a conference full of richer and more prestigious football programs. Maryland left the Atlantic Coast Conference in 2012 for the greener pastures of the Big Ten, a controversial move made out of financial desperation. The school's athletic department had spent itself into deep debt, prompting it to ditch its long-standing rivalries with Duke and North Carolina for Iowa and Purdue because of the attached check. People around the University of Maryland have likened that move to the Big Ten to buying the smallest house in the most expensive neighborhood. Yes, you're in the club, but everyone knows you eked in rather than genuinely belong. Maryland's biggest value to the Big Ten was its television market size—no one seemed to really care what it did on the football field.

In many ways, Maryland was in no-man's-land in the college football ecosystem.

Locksley, who enjoys Gucci sunglasses and expensive suits, likens it all to clothing stores.

Just go with him.

Programs like Alabama and Georgia are Saks Fifth Avenue, he said. High-end luxury stores with rich customers (i.e., big boosters) and the sway to get the top clothing lines (players) into their stores. Upstart programs like Charlotte are the Target of college football. They don't have the big money or prestige, but they are popular with a certain clientele.

Maryland, the program's head coach explained, is like Macy's. Not high end but not discount either. And that's not a place you want to be, said the man known as "Locks," who calls Maryland's NIL situation "Anita Locksley" after his mother, because he says he's always trying to make ends meet.

The problem for Maryland, he said, was the Saks Fifth Avenues of college football have the resources—and prestige—to pluck away top talent. After the 2022 season, Maryland lost a starting tight end to Alabama, a starting offensive lineman to LSU, and a rising defensive lineman to Arkansas. On the other side, Charlotte, led by Baltimore native Biff Poggi, raided Maryland's backup depth for nine players in one offseason.

"I'm getting eaten from both ends, and that's why you don't see fucking Macy's very much anymore," Locksley says.

The big question for Maryland, he said, was whether it was willing to pump in the resources to elevate to the Saks Fifth Avenue level. If not, it risked slipping down to Target. And at this moment, that meant raising money.

When you sit across from Locksley, it is easy to see why he has long been regarded as one of the nation's top recruiters. One of only seven Power 5 Black head coaches headed into the 2023 season, Locksley had a relaxed, just-tell-it-like-it-is approach, influenced by the real-life struggles he had overcome, that felt candid and refreshing in an industry full of bullshit and clichés. The man once nicknamed "Manute" as Towson's starting safety after seven-foot-seven rail-thin NBA player Manute Bol, because of his lankiness, was now older, wiser, and more rotund. He joked, "I wouldn't be as fat as I am and I'd probably have more hair if I didn't deal with the stressors that go with an eighteen-to-twenty-two-year-old controlling your livelihood."

Locksley got animated and leaned forward in his chair when talking about how the fans needed to pony up more money rather than complain about lackluster results. Never have fans had more opportunity to directly influence their favorite team, but they must donate big money to compete at the highest levels. Getting them to do that was a Herculean task that Maryland has never excelled at. "How bad do you want to win a championship, Maryland?" Locksley asked. "You want to be 8-5, 7-5? We've shown we've got a recipe for that." In the big picture, Maryland cultivated a few major boosters like Under Armour founder Kevin Plank and Barry Gossett, whose name adorns multiple athletic-related buildings on campus, but never had much success getting the rank and file to invest financially in its football program.

"I talk to some of my colleagues, and they say, 'Oh, we raised such-and-such,' I'm like, shit, it ain't hard to raise money out there in oil country," said athletic director Damon Evans. "There are schools where raising money is not hard, and I've been at one of those schools. It ain't hard to raise money at Georgia. It's been a challenge here to raise money, but we have to find a solution to it."

Evans encouraged top boosters to donate to the school's One Maryland collective, knowing it could mean fewer dollars coming his way to pay for facility upgrades and other athletic department expenses. He explained to them the rising costs of player talent acquisition, and that the school can't get involved in paying players, so it must come from the donors. "It's one thing for facilities," Evans said, "but if you don't have players, it's tough." Maryland already learned that the hard way when it finally opened the sparkling Jones-Hill House, one of the nicest indoor facilities in college football, "ten years too late," according to Locksley. While a facilities arms race once overtook college football, from Alabama installing an ostentatious waterfall to Clemson including a slide and barbershop in its football facility, by the time Maryland finally caught up, NIL became the top shiny new object.

"Maryland people can say I don't like the NIL, but that's not an option," said Hall of Fame basketball coach Gary Williams, who won a national title at the school in 2002. "We have to raise money to be competitive in NIL in football and men's basketball. That's just the way it is. We have to accept it."

Not all Maryland's top boosters have embraced it.

Growing up just a few minutes down the road from Maryland's College Park campus, Barry Gossett first fell in love with the Terrapins in the 1950s heyday of Jim Tatum when, as a Boy Scout, he worked as an usher at football games. As he got older and became a successful businessman, serving as chairman and chief executive officer of two lucrative companies, Gossett invested more and more of his time and energy into his love for Maryland athletics.

On Maryland's campus, Gossett's influence is everywhere.

Evans's job title is Barry P. Gossett Director of Athletics. In early 2023, Maryland broke ground on a $52 million indoor basketball practice facility named the Barry P. Gossett Basketball Performance Center. For years, Maryland football players lived in the Gossett Team House. He and his late wife, Mary, gave $21.25 million in 2018 to create the Barry & Mary Gossett Center for Academic & Personal Excellence. The gregarious Gossett, now retired and living in Florida, had donated more than $50 million to the university's athletic endeavors.

So it wasn't a surprise that Evans turned to Gossett and encouraged him to donate—as he had for so many other things so many times in the past—to Maryland's NIL collective. He agreed to join at the elite level for $2,500 annually but wouldn't pour millions in the way he had for so many other Maryland athletic endeavors.

"They have asked for NIL money, and I've steadfastly said I can't bring myself to pay for play because I think it's the wrong message for these kids," Gossett said. "I'm just an old curmudgeon in that way. I'll support the academic support unit; I'll support whatever we need for facilities, scholarships, and everything else to provide everything we can for the kids. But I ain't going to pay them."

Gossett understood why other donors were willing. He knew the argument was predicated on obtaining and retaining the best talent. The Terrapins had received a strong lesson in the realities of the new world that spring.

MARYLAND FINALLY FOUND WHAT IT believed to be the quarterback who could elevate the program to the next level, but the vultures were circling.

A program that had produced NFL star receivers like Stefon Diggs and D. J. Moore could never quite find the right guy to lead the offense. It had been more than twenty years since a Maryland quarterback (Scott Zolak) had been drafted.

But Taulia Tagovailoa was different.

The younger brother of Miami Dolphins starting quarterback Tua, Taulia didn't have quite the talent of his older brother, but he was significantly better than anything Terrapins fans had seen under center in a long time. With a capable quarterback, Maryland fans were dreaming of bowl game trips after mostly hitting midtier bowls, if any at all, since a 2001 Orange Bowl appearance.

Taulia started his career at Alabama, part of a quarterback room that included three future starting NFL quarterbacks in his older brother Tua, Jalen Hurts, and Mac Jones. He spent a single season in Tuscaloosa before realizing if he wanted to see the field more often than just in mop-up duty at the end of a blowout win, he'd have to seek out greener pastures. He needed to get away from the long shadow Tua cast over him too. Lia was quieter and shyer than his big brother, and seemed so used to being in his shadow at Alabama that he had gotten used to it. He had the talent to be more than just Tua's younger brother though.

For a kid born in Hawaii, Maryland might not have been the most natural fit, but the connection to head coach Mike Locksley was undeniable. Locksley played a big role in the development of older brother Tua, to the point that the family felt comfortable entrusting him with Lia. He also had a clear path to the starting job at a program desperate for consistency at the quarterback position.

Taulia led Maryland to a 2-2 record in the pandemic-shortened 2020 season in his first year as a starter, and followed it up with a 7-6 2021 year that included Maryland's first bowl trip in five years. Maryland entered the 2022 season with loftier expectations and started the season 6-2, including a one-score loss to No. 4 Michigan. As Maryland's on-field play improved, so too did Galu Tagovailoa's influence over his son.

Galu Tagovailoa was the epitome of the quarterback dad. He was an okay athlete himself but seemed to live vicariously through his two sons. When Tua was Alabama's starting quarterback, Galu was a frequent visitor to the Tide's practices, unafraid to let coaches know if he believed they were handling his son incorrectly. He even went toe-to-toe with Nick Saban during Tua's final season in Tuscaloosa, a feat few have achieved and lived to talk about. Galu was so hands-on with Tua that he turned the naturally right-handed boy into a left-handed-throwing quarterback just because he wanted another left-hander in the family.

Taulia was allowed to stay right-handed, but Galu was just as involved in his career. The Maryland starting quarterback wasn't shy about needing more NIL money, pushing the coaching staff to find more opportunities for him to make some. Those around the program believe that though Lia might have been making the ask, the source of the question was Galu. "His dad is a menace," one source around the program said. Before Maryland's Mayo Bowl game appearance against North Carolina State, Tagovailoa and two other players went to Locksley and said they'd need $50,000 each to play in the game, according to sources familiar with the situation. Tagovailoa then threw one touchdown pass in a 16–12 Maryland win over NC State that might be best remembered for Locksley getting a vat of Duke's mayo dumped on his head afterward.

There was a belief that Lia could declare for the NFL Draft after the 2022 season, but after working out an NIL deal, he agreed to return for his final season. The school announced the news in a social media post featuring a goat, a not-so-subtle nod to Tagovailoa's quarterback status for the school.

"My goal when coming to Maryland was to help Coach Locksley turn this program around," Taulia said in a statement. "After winning back-to-back bowl games, I believe we have things going in the right direction. But we're not done yet. I'm not done yet. After careful deliberation, I have decided to return for my senior season."

That statement was intended to put an end to any rumors of Taulia leaving, but it didn't take long before they started cranking up again. Just a month later, the in-demand quarterback met with his head coach and asked him what he could do to keep him at Maryland.

"He's begging me, 'Coach what can you do? I don't want to leave, there's no place I'd rather be than here, but what is it you can do?'" Locksley said. "I'm like 'I'll do the best I can.'"

It turned out that as much as Maryland fans appreciated Taulia's potential, so, too, did fans of quarterback-needy programs across the country. No position was more valuable than quarterback, where starters willing to shop their services in the transfer portal could command upwards of $1 million annually.

That big offer came his way: $1.5 million from an SEC school for a single season, according to the quarterback. Taulia didn't name the school, but according to sources familiar with the situation, Auburn was after Maryland's quarterback. That created a complicated situation for Taulia, who started his career at Alabama and whose brother won a national championship at the school. Could Tagovailoa really leave Maryland to play at Alabama's biggest rival?

At times, the answer looked like yes. Taulia hadn't entered the transfer portal yet, but that hadn't stopped a message from making its way to him and his family that there was a lot of outside interest in his abilities.

He had a chance to make life-changing money and return to the Southeastern Conference if only he jumped in the portal. As enticing as it all was, it was equally stressful for a college student who had a chance to be Maryland's greatest quarterback if he returned to College Park. "Taulia had so much going on that at one point he just needed a full day to decompress and get his mind together," said Maryland offensive coordinator Josh Gattis. "Because of the nature of college football and the quarterback market, you think no one should talk to your kids, but this word 'tampering' is not enforced. There's all different ways that people get in contact with players."

Maryland didn't have anywhere near the powder keg of finances available that an SEC blue blood did, but all the key power players knew the program couldn't afford to lose the player who represented the biggest source of preseason hope for a famously fickle fan base. It was as much about the message it would send that Maryland wasn't serious about competing with the big boys as it was about Tagovailoa's impact on the team.

When Evans heard the rumors about Tagovailoa leaving were real, his instruction to Locksley was simple: We can't let him leave. On the verge of what everyone expected to be a breakout season for Maryland football, the loss of Taulia could be devastating.

"You lose your starting quarterback? *You lose your starting quarterback?* For a school like us that's trying to build, that's harder to overcome," Evans said. "Michigan State lost their starting quarterback Payton Thorne, but Michigan State is a much more established program. Some programs can overcome that, but it would have knocked us back a couple steps and we don't need that right now."

Complicating matters was a belief that Taulia's father, Galu, was pushing him to secure the biggest possible offer. It got serious enough that Tua, now with the Miami Dolphins, got involved. Tua, who won Locksley his first national championship in 2017, couldn't stand to let his younger brother go to Alabama's biggest rival. "We're an Alabama family," Tua told his younger brother. "You're not going to Auburn."

Still, a day before Maryland's spring game on April 29, Taulia was still contemplating entering the transfer portal. Locksley had to work the phones of loyal Maryland football supporters to raise as much money as he could to keep what he thought was one of the nation's best quarterbacks in his program. Ultimately, Tagovailoa got a significant deal in six figures to stay at Maryland, but nowhere near the $1.5 million he publicly claimed to have turned down.

"I got a homeboy discount because we ain't paying him one point five [million]," Locksley said. "Now, down the road, would we? Who knows how this thing's gonna shake out."

When it was all said and done, even Taulia had to stop and acknowledge how wild the entire scenario was. "It was crazy," Tagovailoa said. "I think the people I talked to, telling me like, 'Bro, that's crazy,' but I feel like it's bigger than the money, bigger than anything like that. I'm locked in with Maryland and now I'm going to finish out over here."

LOCATED ABOUT FIFTEEN MILES FROM Washington, D.C., and thirty miles from Baltimore, Maryland competes for attention with professional teams like the Ravens, Commanders, and Orioles, and all the other social things to do in the D.C. area, like museums and shopping every weekend. It's a tough sell, both financially and time wise, to get your family to spend its entire weekend watching football, leaving plenty of fans to stay home on Saturdays and spend their Sundays inside FedEx Field instead. In the SEC, programs like Alabama, Auburn, Ole Miss, and Mississippi State don't have to worry about competing against professional sports teams.

There are open questions, too, about whether the school has the booster base to support its aspirations in both football and basketball. Both programs have won national championships, though the school's 2002 basketball title carries more relevance than what Jim Tatum's group accomplished in 1953. Unlike the SEC, where every program not named Kentucky knows where the money goes first, the truth is that more Maryland fans still care about basketball first over football. In fact, Maryland donors started talking about a basketball-only collective back in August 2020, nearly a year before NIL even went into effect, and eventually launched Turtle NIL, one of the first collectives in the country. It took more than six months for football to get its collective before Maryland, with the help of Blueprint Sports, eventually started combining them in 2023 into one collective.

Regardless of whether Maryland fans would rather have a basketball national championship than a football one—or that it felt more attainable—football drove the financial engine. It was the reason the Big Ten landed a more than $8 billion TV rights deal—Evans estimated football accounted for 80 to 90 percent of that value—and could generate serious money through ticket sales and licensing deals. Locksley and Evans both brought up the pandemic and how if the Big Ten had stuck with its initial plan to cancel the 2020 season, it would have been financially ruinous for a lot of schools, Maryland included. "I sat on these Zooms where ADs and commissioners said we have to play football," Locksley said. "You find out we're a basketball school, but eighty-five percent of our operating revenue comes from football money."

The ten university athletic departments that made the most money in 2023, according to *USA Today*'s database, read like a who's who of football powerhouses: 1. Ohio State, 2. Texas, 3. Alabama, 4. Michigan, 5. Georgia, 6. LSU, 7. Texas A&M, 8. Florida, 9. Penn State, and 10. Oklahoma. If Maryland wanted to close the financial disparity gap, football was the path.

"Basketball makes a lot of money here, but we need to understand what drives what," Evans said. "What drives conference realignment? TV partners, football, and marketplace. You might not like it. No disrespect to Duke, ain't nobody talking about adding Duke. It's about football."

Evans, who previously served as AD at Georgia before resigning after a DUI scandal, talks a big game about what's possible at Maryland. As he explains his big-picture vision, the former Georgia wide receiver still looks like he could run out onto the field and play, with arm muscles bulging out of his T-shirt. He is constantly thinking about Maryland's place in the college football pecking order and ensuring that the school always has a spot with the big boys. He believes there will ultimately be a breakaway where forty to fifty programs start their own league amid NCAA and legal issues. Despite its membership in the Big Ten, Maryland's place in that breakaway league isn't guaranteed. Could it be involved? Yes. Will it be? Maybe.

"I want a seat at the table," Evans says. "I want to have a nice big turkey leg and a goblet of wine and just be sitting there at the table eating with everyone else. We'll figure out a way to be at the table."

The easiest way to get that seat? Be really good at both football and basketball. On this particular Saturday in the fall of 2023 Maryland played Indiana, both looked to be on the upswing. There's a palpable sense of the opportunity this football season possesses. Maryland, annually bestowed with the horror of having to play Ohio State, Penn State, and Michigan, finally had a manageable schedule that had people believing nine or ten regular-season wins were possible.

On a beautiful sunny day in College Park, the D.C. metropolitan area's six million residents mostly found other ways to spend their Saturday. As Locksley and the team ran out onto the field, SECU Stadium was a third full, at best, for a 3:30 kickoff. The fans missed what could be the Terps' best game of the season as star quarterback Taulia Tagovailoa threw for 352 yards and five touchdowns in a 44–17 win over the Hoosiers. A Citrus Bowl rep was there and thought the Terrapins could make the January 1 bowl if they kept winning the games they should.

Maryland was 5-0 for the first time since 2001 and looked ready for a nationally televised game against No. 4 Ohio State the following week. Evans's eyes get big talking about what a standout season could mean not just for the football program's trajectory, but for his entire athletic department's. Maryland could never seem to get over the hump whenever it got off to a good start, but if it could finally put together the season everyone believed possible, more fans would attend games and invest in the program. And when more fans do that, Evans says, maybe stars like Heisman Trophy–winner Caleb Williams, who grew up just ten miles away from Maryland's campus, will stay home rather than flee across the country in search of football glory.

"Is this year a big year? You're damn right it's a big year, and Locks knows that," Evans said. "I'm not afraid to say this year is significant for us. If things don't go our way this year, does that mean we're done? No, not at all. But if we do what I think we're capable of doing, it continues that ascension."

That ascension up the college football mountaintop would prove to be more arduous than Evans expected.

CHAPTER 9

A Brave New World

I T WAS ONLY A LITTLE past lunchtime but downtown Nashville was already awash in a happy hour glow. Music City was more than living up to its name, as 2023 Memorial Day weekend revelers, including more than a fair share of tipsy bachelorettes in white cowboy boots, jammed Lower Broadway and surrounding streets. From one corner to the next, country music bars shook with bands blasting out some Tuesday afternoon honky-tonk tunes.

A few blocks away a different crowd was forming on the second floor of the hipster Thompson hotel. Thirty-one of the top high school football players in the country, truly the class of the Class of 2024, and their parents or guardians were milling around a three-day event hosted by On3, a college sports media and data company trying to capitalize on the booming NIL market.

Top-rated edge rusher Colin Simmons of Duncanville, Texas, three months away from a commitment to Texas, was there. So was quarterback D. J. Lagway of Willis, Texas, a Florida commit; Sammy Brown, a six-two, 225-pound linebacker–running back out of Jefferson, Georgia; and wide receiver Ryan Wingo of St. Louis, who had driven to Nashville straight from a visit at Tennessee. Ryan's father, Ronnie, said his speedy son was being recruited by at least twenty-eight schools and had already made no less than forty-five official or unofficial visits.

"We're a traveling family," he said.

The On3 Elite NIL Series was the brainchild of founder Shannon Terry. The bearded fifty-three-year-old father of four had big plans for his new website, with twenty-seven years in the recruiting and sports media business to back it up. He was known as a hard-charging businessman whose win-at-all-costs methods rubbed no small amount of people in the media industry the wrong way.

In 2000, Terry had taken over Rivals, acquired by Yahoo in 2008. Two years later he founded 247Sports, which he sold to CBS Sports in 2016. Five years later he started On3. He built the business, he said, around several different spokes—a fan subscription site with more than a hundred reporters covering twenty-seven teams; a vertical centered around high school recruiting and who's going where in the transfer portal; and a big bet on covering the booming business of NIL, backed by multiple full-time reporters. Two months shy of On3's two-year anniversary, future plans called for what Terry called "the Holy Grail"—a private LinkedIn-like network for athletes, and a "Wikipedia for Athletes," a super database for fans, media, and athletes. His approach, which included the On3 Elite NIL series, increasingly blurred the lines between journalistic coverage and commercialization.

A former co-captain of the basketball team at Lipscomb University, a faith-based private university in Nashville, Terry had a bit of the southern preacher in him. He was a business evangelist with a cold eye for opportunity.

Before the event began in earnest, On3 ran the elites through a "car wash" of ten-minute video and print interviews with J. D. PicKell and college sports business reporter Pete Nakos. Both asked some routine recruiting questions before shifting to the elephant in the room—how name, image, and likeness money factored into their ultimate decision to commit to a school. Most players were content to defer or offer milquetoast answers to that question.

"Nothing I really worry about," said linebacker Brown. "Everybody thinks it's corrupt and it's not. There's a lot of good out there."

One of the top overall athletes in the country, Brown had racked up more than two hundred tackles and 3,500 rushing yards in three years of varsity play. He told PicKell he had made ten visits to Georgia, "verifying what I already know." (Ten visits or not, Brown would eventually commit to Clemson.) Brown would later become one of the first two high school athletes to land a NIL deal through the company's On3 Elite platform and thanked the company for "helping out the athletes and giving them these great opportunities without the risk of consequences."

Day two of the Elite NIL Series brought out the star power in the form of LSU gymnast and NIL sensation Olivia "Livvy" Dunne, hot off a *Sports Illustrated* swimsuit shoot in Puerto Rico, and Kirk Herbstreit, ESPN's ace college football analyst.

But before they spoke, a hundred or so attendees were treated to a series of presentations designed to not-so-subtly pitch their financial and marketing services and help Gen Z (and their parents) navigate a new world of "Brand Building, Picking the Right Team, Financial Planning and Managing Your Money." And more. Much more.

Terry started things off. His twenty-five-minute PowerPoint presentation took the tone of a sermon intended to educate players (and their loved ones) to the promises and pitfalls of the journey ahead.

He began with a preamble that ended in a prayer.

"I woke up this morning and said to myself, how can I reach you guys, how can I touch you? We need to say a prayer. It's all about community, the people in this room. It's not about right now. It's about the rest of your life.

"Heavenly Father, thank you for this day. This blessing. Father, we pray you take this day and this opportunity to learn as much as we can. But most important we pray for your guidance, we pray for your safety, and we pray for good, solid people."

Terry's opening slide contained what he called Five Key Points.

1. Five Stars Matter

"Eighty-one-point-three percent of five stars were drafted in the past NFL draft," he said. "So the odds are in your favor. You are special. Having character instead of being a character. That's the game you're in, like it or not. It's a blessing and a curse, but that's the responsibility and the opportunity. More is expected of you."

2. Generational Impact

"I come from three generations of farmers. My parents didn't go to school. Everything I got, I earned it, just like you guys. No privilege. I'm fifty-three years old. It took three generations to build equity. You guys can start doing that today."

Another slide showed the current net worth of iconic athletes, all either current or former NFL or NBA stars, from No. 1 Michael Jordan ($2 billion) to No. 4 Peyton Manning ($260 million) to No. 8 Patrick Mahomes ($70 million) to No. 9 Charles Barkley ($40 million). The point being there's a huge difference between "Grow your money" and "Show your money."

3. Play the Long Game

As the slides turned, Terry stressed how the average NFL career lasted just 3.3 years—only 2.5 for running backs.

"What that means, real simple, is that sixty-eight percent of your life is after football. Fifty-three-point-seven years. If you are the elite of the elite you're getting three-point-three years," he said. "The numbers are not in your favor, guys. Be the guy that lives modestly, that learns, that builds relationships. It's just simple math. It's not about the NIL deal. It's about all these other factors that will prepare you for the sixty-eight percent of your life going forward."

That same slide showed NIL money well down the list of reasons for picking a school—number seven behind things like Players Development, Conference, Playing for Titles, Coaches & Relationships, and Education.

4. Understanding Your NIL Value

Terry's penultimate slide revealed the realistic "Roster and Brand Value" for a five star in the summer of 2023. Terry claimed it ranged from $165,000 to $350,000 with up to $375,000 more for a top ten high school quarterback—a far cry from some of the inflated numbers floating around the halls and elevators of the Thompson hotel. On3 developed its own NIL Valuation formula, a tool Terry was fiercely proud of but one that elicited outside criticism surrounding its veracity.

"Roster value is really the definition of the collective and the school," he said. "The brand market is very small. Most of your value is roster value. Put NIL aside. The average school that you're considering provides you with about a hundred and fifty thousand dollars a year in value. So when you get into NIL you're not going into it with zero.

"Don't go in with an attitude. You're already getting an amazing opportunity and amazing value through tuition, room and board, indirect expenses, and other perks, to the tune of six hundred thousand dollars over four years. That's real money."

5. It's All About Relationships

"Right now, that W, that A, that T on your jersey is a once-in-a-lifetime opportunity," said Terry. "Use it. You have the ability now to connect with titans of industry, with leaders, with influential people, that took me thirty years to do. Don't waste it. Connect with them. Ask them questions. You're the smallest person in the room. Use that opportunity to connect with them. That's the No. 1 thing you can get. Don't waste it."

After Terry sat down it was time for Pete Schoenthal, CEO of Athliance, a software company with a focus on facilitating NIL deals and compliance to speak. Athliance, based in Fort Lauderdale, one of dozens, if not hundreds, of start-ups that had jumped into the lucrative NIL space, selling proprietary NIL management and compliance platforms and expertise. It was a gold rush opportunity with lots of money to be made in a largely unregulated new market.

There were established companies like Opendorse, INFLCR, Altius Sports Partners, and Student-Athlete NIL, which all launched before NIL became legal and carved out significant market shares as early adopters. But that didn't stop dizzying amounts of new companies seemingly popping up daily, trying to get a piece of the action. It forced athletes, coaches, and universities to attempt to decipher the intentions behind the companies before partnering with them. Even with the best-intentioned ones, there was still the undercurrent of self-interest and financial opportunities.

"Everyone that is a loud person in NIL, good marketer, or thought leader, all of their predictions or projections are based on helping their own business," said Josh Delander, a NIL expert who had worked at Opendorse and INFLCR.

Coming from a former high school coach and NFL-certified agent, Schoenthal's presentation was a sobering look at the overwhelming task facing families in the room:

"Use the game, don't let the game use you," he said. "NIL is great but remember the end game. Do not make a multimillion-dollar decision over a few thousand dollars. You're going to talk to these schools, talk to these coaches, find out what you're worth. It should be part of your decision. But it should only be part of your decision. NIL is not the end-all be-all. Remember what the goal is."

Schoenthal stressed the need to know what you're signing: the length of deals, time demands, red flags, and the importance of saying no. Collective deals, he said, are legal documents. Contracts are to protect the collective, not the athlete. So work with agents and marketing people who have done NFL deals, who are familiar with the word "perpetuity."

"If you sign something in perpetuity it means *for-ev*-er," said Schoenthal, who now works for WME as a senior manager in its NIL division. "Make sure if you see that word, you understand what you're giving away. Protect your brand at all costs."

The next speakers, Adam Sansiveri and Winston Justice, of the private wealth management firm AllianceBernstein, only added to that burden. Their checklist of things to know and do ran ten deep—everything from paying bills (rent, agencies, trainers) to insurance coordination, to yearly taxes, to building up cash reserves for emergencies. More than once you had to stop and remind yourself these were eighteen-year-old high school seniors in the audience.

The morning's final speaker was a heavyweight: Nick Marquez is the Sports Creator & Emerging Athletes lead at Meta, the parent company of Facebook and all-important Instagram. He was making the rounds pitching the power of his company's platform—he gave a similar presentation at SANIL's NIL Summit in Atlanta a week later—and highlighted the power of building a brand.

His first PowerPoint slide contained these words:

Tell Your Story
Own Your Moments
Build Your Legacy

"How do you define yourself?" he asked. "What makes you, you? Who are you when the lights are off? What are the pieces of your personality? What are your passions, your hobbies?"

From there Marquez was off and running, pitching Meta as the best place for student-athletes to maximize their NIL: 3.46 billion active monthly users, 570 million people who followed athletes on Facebook, another 490 million on Instagram, home of its influential Reels. How 88.5 percent of NIL activities start on social media. This was followed by another list: how to set up an account, build your brand, create content that aligns with your mission, and engage your audience with stories and reels. It was enough to make your head spin, more than one parent looking into their son's eyes and shaking their head. By now the actual reason the assembled were gathered here—extraordinary success on the football field—hovered on a distant planet somewhere. Perhaps a break for lunch couldn't come soon enough.

THE TWENTY-YEAR-OLD GYMNAST LIVVY DUNNE was the unquestioned main, ahem, attraction, particularly if one happened to be an eighteen-year testosterone-fueled high school boy. Accompanied by her mother, sister, and a small retinue of hosts and handlers, Dunne arrived in a form-fitting miniskirt.

In a Q& A session, she charted her rise from an elite gymnast at LSU to social media fame. Dunne was—and remains—the most followed NCAA student-athlete on social, with more than thirteen million total followers on TikTok, Instagram, and other sites. Her estimated NIL value was $3.4 million, another record for a female student-athlete, thanks to endorsement deals with GrubHub, Vuori, BodyArmor, and American Eagle, among others. A month after the On3 session Dunne would reportedly earn $500,000 for a single social media post.

"Take your time to pick your brands and be picky," she said. "There's no problem saying no to brands if it doesn't feel right for you."

You've got to believe it to see it, she said. Be aware of your audience and how you fit in. Use platforms differently. You're more than just your sport. Don't post mindlessly.

"Be authentic to yourself," Dunne added, "because your audience will detect if something is off. And keep some parts of your life private. It's hard. I have security now."

The star of the show turned out to be Herbstreit. The ESPN and NFL analyst mixed an unfiltered view of his personal struggles and professional success with age-old wisdom about the sobering realities of Power 5 football.

"Where you guys are going everyone is going to have equal or better skills than you have," he said at one point. "Hard to imagine, but that's where you're headed. So you have to think about how you can differentiate yourself from the guys you're trying to beat out. Everyone can have ability. The truly elite players—the Peyton Mannings—have a passion for their craft. They never really rest. They outwork their opponents. They become so good at their craft."

Herbstreit was three months shy of his twenty-eighth season on *College GameDay*, but he spoke about his days as a quarterback at Ohio State like it was yesterday. How he came into school just like the five stars in the room—the second-rated QB in the country, with his pick of places. He decided to play where his dad had not only played but captained the team. And immediately faced a cold, hard truth.

"Let's be honest," he said. "The system can play you or you can play the system. I'm a great example. I was overwhelmed. I thought I was ready. Would start for four years. Win three Rose Bowls. I fell flat on my face. I lived that every day. I was embarrassed. Humiliated. Two years of sputtering. Feeling sorry for myself. If the transfer portal existed then I guess I would have felt the need to do that. But I didn't. My dad said to give it one more spring. As a junior I got my feet under me. By the time I was a senior I was a captain of the team. Ended up being voted most inspirational player. What I remember from all that was working through adversity and what it did for me."

Herbstreit said his breakthrough moment occurred when he summoned the courage to see the team's psychologist—an almost unheard-of cry for help back in the early 1990s. "I was terrified," he admitted. "But he became my biggest ally, a game changer. He changed how I approached what I was going through. I had been in the talking-shit group, the most cynical, negative guy. Bunch of us just spitting hate. That's not who I was. I went through the next spring with some hope.

"What I learned is," he said, "when life sucks for a long time the easy thing to do is shut down. The easiest thing is to not try. Maybe you haven't experienced that. You're going to fail. It's okay.

"Life is hard, man. I have four sons. Man, every day is hard. As a husband it's work . . . Learn how to deal with crap. Learn how to fight through things. You're not starting. You feel like you should be starting, and you're not. How do you handle that? I just encourage you guys to learn how to deal with tough times, because they're coming."

In response to a mother's question, Herbstreit spoke of following your passion and not the money, his career at ESPN Exhibit A when the NFL failed to come calling. As a business major at OSU he said he had plenty of post-college opportunities but loved talking sports. So in 1993 he took a local radio job for $12,000 a year, an audition tape he later stitched together landing him a job as a sideline reporter on a fledgling network known as ESPN2 back in 1995. Fifteen games at $875 per game. A nervous, sweaty, Hail Mary audition for *GameDay* that same year leading, out of nowhere, to the dream job he still has today, and where he, too, is coming to grips with this brave new world.

"It's hard for me to relate to NIL," he said. "I've lived with very little money and pretty good money, but I never changed the person I am. Same person today going back to high school and college. I never wanted money. I didn't have that dream. I would encourage you guys to . . . look beyond the numbers. Look for a relationship with a coach. If I was a parent I'd be steering them to education, a good culture, where you're going to grow."

At this point one had to wonder just how much of this wisdom was cutting through the sense of entitlement that bubbled just beneath the surface throughout the event—the way certain five stars walked, talked about all their campus visits, so cocksure nothing mattered except ball. As if trying to pop that bullshit balloon, Herbstreit sent one last message.

"You have to think of a *lifetime* commitment if you play your cards right," he said. "Thinking back on it, Ohio State opened up so many doors for me because I worked the system instead of the system working me. I'd meet people, shake their hand, talk to them. I wouldn't tune them out. Listen to them. Take their number. Stay in touch. And when I got done, it's amazing when you're humble, you're gracious, how much these people want to be with you when you don't matter anymore. Because you'll be replaced, like *that*. They'll be a room like this next year and you won't *matter*. You get hurt or you're a bust, you're *gone*. You're *dust*. Rather than being that guy, have some insurance. Take advantage of the opportunity you're getting."

A conflict in the classroom—a big test or paper due—had kept a couple of five stars and their families away from Nashville, including one special talent, a Southern California kid who could not have cared less about building his brand and everything about becoming the next great quarterback out of the mold of Nick Saban.

CHAPTER 10

The Quarterback

IT WAS A SPARKLING SEPTEMBER night in Carlsbad, California, a beach town north of San Diego. Under glowing Friday Night Lights a raucous high school crowd watched the eighteen-year-old senior quarterback from the local high school perform a special form of surgery on a visiting 6A school from Queen Creek, Arizona.

His name was Julian Sayin. You may want to remember it.

At first glance, the six-foot-one, 190-pound Sayin doesn't overpower physically; he's more Bryce Young than Josh Allen. No matter. On this night, Sayin served notice on what expert eyes had long seen and relished: the textbook release, pinpoint accuracy, uncommon poise and artistry in the pocket, and the ability to *see the game* beyond his years.

Sayin's first pass was a hash-to-hash sideline dart that never so much as flickered in the air. His first touchdown an on-the-run 44-yard dime feathered into the glue-fingered hands of speedy wide receiver Jalen St. Paul, a future D-1 commit to Oregon, in the back corner of the end zone. His second TD, with 2:38 to go in the second quarter, was nothing less than a work of art—a rolling-to-his-left across-the-body toss into a one-foot window that fell between the arms of two defenders and into the outstretched hands of a tight end. By the time the evening ended, Sayin had once again proved why he was the No. 1–rated recruit in California. Playing little more than half the game he completed fifteen of eighteen passes for 248 yards and three touchdowns, powering undefeated Carlsbad High School to an easy 49–9 win over Casteel High. Just the kind of performance that had attracted D-1 offers starting in eighth grade.

By the time the 2023 season ended two months later, the multitalented Lancers, under longtime head coach Thadd MacNeal, had rolled into the CIF San Diego Open Division playoffs with a perfect 10-0 record, before falling to eventual champion Granite Hills on a gutsy two-point conversion, 46–45, in overtime. Sayin had dominated that game from the start as well, completing nineteen of twenty-six for 225 yards and three touchdowns.

His final season stats read more fantasy than football: twenty-four touchdowns against a single interception and a completion rate of 75 percent.

"Julian is the best I've ever had," said Coach MacNeal. "He just has a different skill set. He's a generational talent."

IT SHOULD COME AS NO surprise to serious Sabanologists that a high school quarterback needed to hit certain marks before the head coach signed off on recruiting a future face of his franchise.

Arm strength. Accuracy. Mobility. A specific size. Spatial awareness. Vision. Football IQ. Leadership. Toughness. An appetite for the big stage. The willingness to accept tough coaching. Sayin had all that—and more as a consensus top-three quarterback in the country in the Class of 2024.

"Coach Saban is not trying to sell you on anything," said Sayin the day before the Casteel High game. "He's not going to tell you we need you, we need you . . . you're not guaranteed anything."

In his first public comments, a man not noted for effusive praise, particularly in the case of those yet to play a down for Bama, had this to say about Sayin on National Signing Day, haunting words given the changing tide to come.

"Outstanding player. Ball comes out of his hand really nice. He's accurate, he's smart. He's had a great high school career. Been one of the best players, most productive players in the country on a very consistent basis. We like him a lot."

In person, Sayin had the laid-back So Cal look of a teenage J.Crew or

Abercrombie model, not surprising since he loved the water and hanging out with friends at the beach. Like many people his age, he was into video games, country and rap music, and early Taylor Swift. His response to questions about his recruiting was thoughtful and measured.

"He was very mature in the decision process," said his mother, Karen Brandenburg. "He's just been so even-keeled through the whole thing."

IT'S BEEN SAID THAT QUARTERBACKS are not so much born as bred. Sayin may well be a bit of both. The youngest of four children, he comes from a long line of athletic excellence. His father, Dan Sayin, was a heavyweight boxer at the University of Delaware who finished second in the Eastern Regional Collegiate Tournament in 1984; his oldest sister, Bailey, played soccer at the University of Chicago; younger sister, Jocelyn, starred in field hockey and club beach volleyball in high school; while older brother, Aidan, now a senior at the Ivy League University of Pennsylvania, has been the starting quarterback since midway through his freshman year.

Julian's competitive fire first surfaced around the age of two, when he could be seen shooting foul shot after foul shot with a foam ball at a little hoop in the laundry room. A sales rep then vice president of an East Coast–based printing company, Dan's workday ended about the time his two young boys got home from elementary school. Day after day they would wander over to a local park and toss a football ball around, Julian doing his best to keep up with his older brother.

By the time he turned six, Julian was *really* following in his brother's footsteps, playing quarterback on a flag football team at the local YMCA. Then, at age nine, behind center in a Friday Night Lights (FNL) flag football league boasting twenty-three hundred kids, the largest in the country, followed by Pop Warner tackle football. Dan Sayin coached both teams.

"In flag football, we didn't care so much about defense," he recalled, sitting in the family room of their home with Karen by his side. "Ran spread offense all over the field and ran it with boards at nine years old. Got the whole team around picnic tables and handed out a test. Only had sixteen plays. Perfect scores. Those little kids were smart."

The commissioner of FNL league was Thadd MacNeal. "Coach Mac" was a hometown boy (CHS Class of '89) made good. Fresh off two high school head coaching jobs in L.A., he'd returned to his alma mater in 2011, slowly building Carlsbad into the tough, deeply talented Southern California powerhouse they are today: perennial champions in the fiercely competitive Avocado League, with multiple runs into the finals of the CIF San Diego section playoffs. Along the way, MacNeal earned a reputation as a quarterback guru with a jeweler's eye.

It was the winter of 2014 when Mac got his first good look at the brothers Sayin. Aidan, in seventh grade, was already training with quarterback coach and founder Jose Mohler of Left Coast Athletix, his brother playing the role of wide receiver. Poorly.

"We called him the backstop," said Aidan. "He'd less catch it than bat it down."

Aidan had a world of talent, but Julian, even then, in Coach Mac's words, looked "a little different than everyone else."

"He's a footballaholic, a gym rat," said MacNeal. "Most quarterbacks will do what's required. He's always looking to do more."

It didn't hurt that unlike countless helicopter parents with dollar signs in their eyes, Dan and Karen had their heads screwed on straight right from the start.

"Both parents are so unique in their character traits," said MacNeal. "They're not the normal quarterback parents. Both parents are just really, really humble and not overbearing. Dan, especially, for a guy who's really, really into it, he's very hands off. He's never given me any advice, put on any pressure. He's more, 'These guys are yours. Take care of them. Go do what you do.'"

BY THE TIME SAYIN ENTERED sixth grade, his mind was made up. He wanted to work with a well-known quarterback coach in L.A. He wanted to play tougher L.A. teams. On his own he began texting and DMing coaches, "Can you train me?"

Danny Hernandez eventually said yes.

Thus began what his mother calls the "Karen and Julian show," a true road show, driving from North County to Orange County for twice-a-week workouts with Hernandez. Dan did his part, taking 7-on-7 summer teams north for tournaments against teams from Compton, South Central, and the Inland Empire.

After losing in the finals in one L.A. tournament, Dan found his way across the field to congratulate the opposing head coach.

"I said, 'Hey, you've got a lot of talent on your team,'" said Dan. "He said, 'You've got a good quarterback.' After that, Julian played quarterback on their team."

At age twelve, it was trial by fire against future stars at prep powers Mater Dei, St. John Bosco, and JSerra, and not just on the field. Dan said brawls regularly broke out between rival parents and coaches. Julian never flinched.

Recalled Karen, "He would get pummeled in Compton and then get in the car and say, 'I could have done this better, that better.'"

Back home, Julian followed Aidan yet again and started training with quarterback coach Mohler. "I got a lot stronger and a lot faster," said Julian. "Barbells, free weights, I could feel the velocity coming into my arm. I was always trying to get the same motion, get the stroke down."

At the end of every session the two brothers found yet another way to compete. Throwing a set series of routes against air—digs, outs, rail shots, deep passes down the sideline—grading each and every throw. Points off for a bad toss, bragging rights on the line until the next session started.

"People would leave the session and get in the car in tears," said Aidan. "Mainly him in tears. We've been competing our whole lives. He's not going to compliment you. He thinks he's the best. It's a confidence, not cockiness. He's not going to talk about it but he thinks he's better than you . . . and he'll show it."

Every Saturday and Sunday in the fall Julian's eyes were glued to college and pro football, his favorite quarterbacks running from Brady to Manning to early Russell Wilson to Heisman Trophy–winners Jameis Winston and Marcus Mariota.

You want to know how badly Sayin wanted what those pros achieved? As an eighth grader he told his parents he wanted to leave the comfort of middle school and enroll in Winner Circle Athletics, a human performance prep school seventy miles away in Corona, California. Up at 5:30 a.m. every weekday and out the door by 6:15. Three hours of class in the morning with twenty-five other aspiring athletes. Weights, workouts, practice, and position work in the afternoon. Word began to spread. Some Pop Warner film was exchanged: a white kid with the goods leading an otherwise all-Black team. That year Florida Atlantic offered Julian his first scholarship. It would be far from the last.

Which brings us back to the fall of 2020, when the global pandemic forced the state of California to cancel all prep football games. Older brother Aidan's senior season eventually opened in March 2021 with an abbreviated schedule. He and his Lancers teammates made the most of it, going 5-0, blowing out their opponents 240–32.

After the season Aidan, *The San Diego Union-Tribune* Offensive Player of the Year, committed to Penn. As he had for countless other prospects over the years Coach Mac had sent out hard copies and emails of transcripts and game info on his star players to about one hundred fifty colleges. From there he personally followed up with a select number of Group of 5 and Power 5 coaches with whom he shared long-standing relationships.

With Julian, he cut right to the chase.

Hey, I've got a special one. He's the next one. You've got to see this kid. He's different.

"When I say that they're going to come out and see him," said MacNeal.

Off Julian's freshman tape alone and a few personal throwing sessions, nearly two dozen scholarship offers from the likes of Texas, USC, Notre Dame, Georgia, and Florida rolled in. Brian Kelly and Notre Dame, led by offensive coordinator Tommy Rees, grabbed an early lead, with Steve Sarkisian and Texas looming on the outside.

AFTER THE COVID-19 PANDEMIC SLOWLY came under control, the 2021 California high school football season resumed on schedule.

"We had a senior-heavy class," recalled Julian, then a sophomore. "They all played as juniors. I didn't have to be too much of a leader. I just focused on ball."

And ball out the sophomore did, piloting his team to the Open Division championship game. Still, if there was one game that served notice that he was something special, it was his final drive earlier in the season against archrival Torrey Pines.

"Torrey Pines was a really good team. We played them at home. They were beating us. It's homecoming," said Coach MacNeal. "We crawled back in the fourth quarter to get within five. Get the ball on our own twenty. There was like a minute fifty left. They had a defensive end who's at Stanford now. He was big, a really good player. And he's yelling at us, 'It's over. You guys are done.'"

Not quite. Sayin started chipping away, relying on all those Orange County and Carlsbad training sessions. One clutch throw after another. A scramble for a huge first down. A check down into the perfect play.

"We actually made a clip of it and called it 'The Drive,'" said MacNeal, in homage to John Elway. "Just ice in his veins. The calmness. I remember we had a time-out before we called the winning play. It was like he and I were just discussing plans for the weekend. I've had quarterbacks where the moment is just too big. I'm a veteran guy. This is a sixteen-year-old kid. Literally, I said, 'You like this one, Julian?'"

Yeah, Julian said. That's the one.

In MacNeal's mind it's one thing to be generally calm and have presence, quite another to execute under pressure before a packed house with little or no margin for error. But that's exactly what Sayin did. Delivering a perfect pass to a comeback route in the corner of the end zone for the winning score.

Now the word was *really* getting out. Finding its way into select zip codes in Tuscaloosa and Baton Rouge.

In the spring of 2022, Saban and Sayin had their first chat.

"I was at school. He called my coach. He was very businesslike," remembered Julian. "It's always the same tone. It was definitely exciting, but definitely businesslike."

In May, Alabama made it official, offering a scholarship. Over the summer Bill O'Brien, Bama's offensive coordinator at the time, pressed for a deeper commitment.

"You're on the top of our board," he said.

More pressure arrived during an unofficial visit to T-town in June. Still, the family held firm. Karen, for her part, was really drawn to what Brian Kelly, the newly hired head coach at LSU, was building and selling.

"He took us to his house within a mile from campus," said Karen. "Overlooking the campus. Four hours later we were hooked."

Julian said *his* early list had two-time national champion Georgia on top given his respect for head coach Kirby Smart and his relationship with offensive coordinator Todd Monken. Other major powers—Penn State, in particular—had gone all in, promising a starting spot from the get-go. The word "savior" was tossed around a bit too much for one QB's liking.

"It's weird to hear that," said Sayin. "Notre Dame, we need you. Penn State, we need you. You're the QB. Alabama, it was . . . come compete here."

By this point, the family had made a decision to steer clear of the murky NIL market. Agents, financial advisers, you name it, sometimes three different financial advisers calling on the same day, offering their services. Dan and Karen were in the position where NIL dollars did not impact their son's decision.

"We turned away quite a lot of proposals," said Karen. "People were coming at us all the time."

Instead, with their rising junior as their guide, the family played the long game. A life-altering choice given competition among elite Power 5 programs and their collectives had blown up. For someone with Sayin's skill set potential NIL numbers were in the range of $8 million over four years.

Through word of mouth and friends they trusted, that summer the family made the choice to sign with Athletes First, the largest NFL talent agency, the home to the likes of Aaron Rodgers and Dak Prescott.

The family's message to the agency, just breaking into the burgeoning NIL market, was clear: We're not looking to cash in. We need a gatekeeper to handle the volume of calls and help us understand a rapidly changing landscape. One low-key deal or two, nothing fabricated or unauthentic. Maybe a trading card company or a clothing company Julian likes. And that's it.

ONCE ARCH MANNING VERBALLY COMMITTED to Texas in June 2022, the Longhorns dropped off Julian's list along with Notre Dame. By now he had made two unofficial visits to Athens and offensive coordinator Todd Monken made three trips to Carlsbad. A three-way race between Georgia, LSU, and Alabama was thinning out.

"Georgia was definitely on top for me, the winning culture," said Sayin.

Then, as it nearly always does with five-star recruiting, things got complicated. Dylan Raiola, another five-star quarterback atop the Class of '24, was being heavily recruited by UGA as well, not that it mattered to Sayin.

"Throughout his recruiting process our message was he doesn't care who you're recruiting, who is in the room, he's going to have to compete," said Thadd MacNeal, who acknowledged that because of the Manning name Texas was different.

"Julian's got a chip on his shoulder."

Adding to the equation: according to a Georgia football source with direct knowledge of the situation, an agent from Athletes First, believed to be acting on his own, was pushing the NIL pay envelope a bit too hard, turning off members of Georgia's coaching staff, crossing a fine line between testing the market and testing certain people's patience.

"It got a little aggressive for Julian's liking. And mine, to be honest," Karen said during an interview in July 2023. "We don't want to do anything illegal or jeopardize his eligibility in any way. We're not looking for this huge payout. Am I doing a disservice? Should I be out there shopping him? He's worked so hard and there's not a nest egg."

Meanwhile, Coach Mac and Alabama offensive coordinator O'Brien had connected, having what MacNeal called some "very transparent conversations about who Julian is, what he wants to do." That transparency extended to Saban, who told MacNeal he liked the fact that Julian had high aspirations yet remained grounded.

In October, Sayin made a second visit to Tuscaloosa to watch Bama play Mississippi State. Game day at Bryant-Denny Stadium, the full Bama experience, more time with Saban, talking ball, building a bond, the king slowly but surely grooming what he saw as a future NFL quarterback drafted in the first round.

"That October visit confirmed it for me," said Sayin. "It was pretty surreal. When I took a step back and looked at it, I wanted to play for the best coach. I wanted to develop into a first-round pick. Alabama has proved it with those quarterbacks. You've got Tua, you've got Mac, you've got Jalen Hurts and Bryce Young, those four guys. That's really what made the difference. I wanted to follow those guys.

"When you think of Georgia you think of the defensive guys they've had there. You don't think of the quarterbacks they've had. You think of Alabama, they have everything, and then you start thinking, he went first round, he went first round, he went first round, he went first round."

On November 2, 2022, in the midst of yet another spectacular season in which the Lancers went 10-1 and advanced to the CIF Open Division title game for the third straight season, the junior quarterback went on ESPN during his lunch hour and, in his own understated way, put on a scripted "A" hat and announced his verbal commitment.

Asked by anchor Wendi Nix the deciding factor in his decision, Sayin's answer took just ten seconds: "Alabama is the standard for college football. I wanted to be coached hard by Coach Saban and Coach O'Brien. It's a special place and the highest level of football."

With those words the recruiting waters took on a sense of calm that remained in place even after O'Brien announced in January 2023 he was leaving for the OC job with the New England Patriots.

IF THERE WAS ONE LAST place Julian Sayin wanted to shine it was at the prestigious Elite 11 Finals held in Los Angeles every June. From the time he was thirteen years old, he and his brother had been on their phones trying to figure out how to get an invite. Elite 11 is nothing less than the show of shows for the top-rated QBs in the country. Three days of media madness, on field drills, classroom instruction, and off-field development, highlighted by the crucible: the Day 2 Pro Day competition. Twenty throws—short, long, crossing patterns, rail routes to receivers you barely know. Eight scripted minutes under simulated pressure before every major recruiting service. Handpicked coaches scrutinizing every last throw for accuracy, endurance, pace, and touch.

"I always wanted to be in it," Julian said. "I always saw the TV shows. It was definitely a dream of mine. To get an invite was awesome."

Joining Sayin at Redondo Union High was a who's who of the Class of

'24: his former potential Georgia rival Raiola, who would later commit to Nebraska; Michigan-commit Jadyn Davis; C. J. Carr, Notre Dame; and D. J. Lagway, Florida, among the twenty QBs receiving the coveted invites.

On Pro Day the twenty throws were rated on a sliding scale from three points (highest) to one (lowest). The entire process was designed to see how one handled pressure. All Sayin did that day was hit eighteen out of twenty throws and walk away with the overall MVP award over Raiola and the rest.

"He won every day," said Coach Mac, who attended Pro Day. "And he destroyed Dylan."

If only the NIL waters had remained as predictable.

"It's just been crazy," said Karen Brandenburg a month later. "No one really knows how things are playing out. It's just surreal." So surreal the family made the decision to move on from the aggressive nature of Athletes First and engage with other agencies.

"Julian doesn't want to do a lot of this stuff," said Karen. "I needed an agency that understood that. We talked to big guns that came out of the woodwork."

Arguably the biggest, CAA, made its pitch, having represented Saban for years. William Morris Endeavor brought Joe Burrow's agent into the mix for a three-hour call. Excel Sports Management, the marketing home of Tiger Woods and a dozen other gold-plated professional athletes and announcers, had partner Alan Zucker make its presentation. As the summer went on and the NIL market metastasized, the Sayins watched and waited.

THE FINAL NAIL IN THE coffin of anyone hoping Sayin would change his mind was hammered home during his official visit to Tuscaloosa the weekend of September 23, 2023, a bye week for Carlsbad High football.

"It was pretty cool," he said, in typical low-key Julianspeak. "They rolled out the red carpet pretty good."

Only if one considers this *pretty good*: the *only* official visit by any recruit that weekend; a Friday night photo shoot at the stadium; being golf-carted around to various tailgate parties prior to the Tide's game Saturday afternoon against Ole Miss; a pregame meet with the university president and chat with athletic director Greg Byrne and Coach Saban on the field prior to the game; a postgame dinner and hangout with the team after an impressive 24–10 victory.

The unquestioned capstone of the weekend was a Sunday morning catered breakfast—just Karen, sister Jocelyn, Julian, Tommy Rees and his fiancée, Nick and his wife, Miss Terry—at the Sabans' majestic French Chateau home on the edge of Lake Tuscaloosa.

Afterward, as Saban is wont to do, he and Julian took an off-road ride down to the quiet lake. If ever a moment symbolized what Saban saw in Sayin, well, you'd be hard-pressed to find a better one. The perfectionist worked his magic. Talking about the Process, life in Tuscaloosa, why he and Miss Terry loved it so much, what it meant to be the face of football in a school where giants have walked.

"It was awesome," said Julian.

THIRTY-SIX DAYS AFTER THE LOSS to Granite Hills in the San Diego Open Division semifinals, Julian Sayin arrived on the campus of the University of Alabama as a midyear student, having graduated early from Carlsbad High, and began practicing with the team in preparation for a date against Michigan in the CFP.

By now the family had signed with Excel Sports. It was hard to argue with the choice. Alan Zucker's roster of clients for marketing and sponsorships deals included the entire Manning family, Taylor Swift, Joe Montana, Justin Herbert, and Jim Nantz. Zucker had impressed with his low-key approach and understanding of the family dynamic.

"The driving thing was Alan and his wife flew out from New York," explained Karen. "She's from here. She went to [high] school at Torrey Pines. They were just so interested in our family. It felt like a really nice fit."

And just because the family had been playing the long game didn't mean they'd lost sight of NIL. Yea Alabama, the school's collective, cried poor, but Parker Cain, Excel's vice president of talent marketing and the man in charge of NIL deals, pressed on until the family finally said to Zucker that enough was enough, agreeing to a deal one tenth of what the NIL market could have delivered.

Said Karen: "I said, 'Look, I can negotiate all day long. But I refuse to tell this kid who has wanted to play for Nick Saban since he was little that you lost your position because you asked for [too much] money. Just stop negotiating. It's not worth it.'

"The biggest thing for me was an insurance policy. This kid has worked hard for a long time and he should capitalize to some degree—a nest egg. We talked about that a lot. Financially, having a nest egg for him. Guaranteed. Because I'm the one picking up the puddle of emotions if he gets injured."

Or if something else happened, like a king deciding to vacate his throne.

CHAPTER 11

The Rise and Fall of Jimbo Fisher

A S THE LAST-SECOND THROW INTO the end zone fell incomplete, Jimbo Fisher looked despondent.

As he struggled to process what just occurred in front of him, his sixteen-year-old son, Ethan, wearing a custom hat embroidered "Lil Fish" and a massive diamond chain around his neck, loudly raged against the referees for what he believed to be an uncalled pass interference call. Fisher would later privately advance the same complaint to close associates, thinking he got shafted out of a win. Yet there it was. For all the offseason bluster and hype, Fisher had fallen flat against the man he wanted to beat more than anyone: Nick Saban.

Fisher slowly trudged off the field, under the protection of four state troopers, as 100,077 Alabama fans loudly cheered Fisher's demise, and his wife, Courtney, hurried to catch up to him. As she tried to console him, the proud West Virginian wasn't having it. Just like his former boss, the losses eat Fisher up far more than the wins fill him up. He had wanted this one badly after his former mentor accused him of cheating in what he perceived as a vicious betrayal of the unwritten rules of the Southeastern Conference. He put together his best offensive game plan of the season—critics would later point out that it was his only offensive plan that showed any signs of creativity that year—and couldn't believe it came this close to working, only to fall short. To pour salt into the wound, Alabama cornerback Terrion

Arnold said afterward he read Jimbo's lips saying "Evan, Evan, Evan" and correctly knew the ball was going to A&M receiver Evan Stewart.

As he neared the opposing end zone to head back to the locker room, Fisher turned to his wife and leaned in to say something. Whatever it was he said sent a message. She fell back, letting her husband continue his pissed-off walk to the locker room alone.

Almost beating Alabama in Bryant-Denny Stadium proved to be one of the last real highlights of the Jimbo Fisher era at Texas A&M. The man who arrived with lofty expectations of a national championship finished with a different, more ignominious honor as the recipient of the largest contract buyout in college sports history. Fisher, a West Virginia hillbilly, would get paid $76 million in November 2023 to stop coaching football. Things had gotten that bad in College Station. Life-changing money for a man of simple origins, but it burned his ass nonetheless.

The Fall of the House of Fisher is one of early brilliance corrupted by arrogance and stubbornness. Of a man unwilling to evolve because he believed he knew better.

If ego is the enemy, Fisher's biggest opponent stares at him in the mirror each day.

JOHN JAMES FISHER WAS BORN in Clarksburg, West Virginia, on October 9, 1965. The son of a coal miner, "Big Jim," and a schoolteacher, Gloria, "Jimbo" learned at an early age that hard work was the only way to succeed. At just ten years old, after slacking off in school, Big Jim took little Jimbo into the coal mines and told him to grab a shovel and start digging. It didn't take him long to learn that if he wanted to avoid that life, he better deliver better above ground.

He was intensely competitive, unhealthily so some would say, to the point of getting into fistfights with his brother, Bryan, over board games and cards. Jimbo wasn't the biggest (he stood about five foot ten) or best athlete, but he battled. He always had a chip on his shoulder, with a healthy confidence. He eventually parlayed it into a chance to play quarterback at tiny Salem College in West Virginia for a man named Terry Bowden, a move that changed the trajectory of his life. Bowden, the son of Florida

State head coach Bobby Bowden, took Jimbo to Samford, a small liberal arts school in Birmingham, Alabama, as his quarterback in what became a familiar experience for the young Fisher. Bowden kept bringing Jimbo with him as he started climbing the college football ranks. First as a graduate assistant and offensive coordinator for him at Samford, and then as his quarterbacks coach at Auburn.

When Bowden got fired at Auburn after the 1998 season, Fisher spent a single season as Rick Minter's offensive coordinator at Cincinnati before he hooked up with Nick Saban. Seven seasons and two national championships at LSU later under Saban and then Les Miles, Fisher was one of the hottest head-coaching candidates available. He almost landed his first head-coaching job in 2006 at the University of Alabama at Birmingham, where his first wife, Candi, was from, before university trustees reportedly scuttled the deal. UAB and Fisher had agreed in principle to a deal that would pay him $600,000 annually before the trustees, who typically rubber-stamped whatever was put in front of him, rejected the deal, citing the need for fiscal responsibility. According to multiple stories, their actual reasoning was that they preferred Fisher to team backup with a just-hired Saban in Tuscaloosa instead. When the UAB deal fell apart, Fisher passed on Tuscaloosa in preference to the Bowden family, landing on the patriarch Bobby Bowden's Florida State as his head-coach-in-waiting.

The elder Bowden was nudged out in 2010 to make room for the hard-charging Fisher. It was before the legendary Bowden wanted to go out, and people around the program believed Fisher was growing impatient with waiting any longer. The transition was clunky and awkward—Bowden publicly said he didn't want to retire yet; Fisher denied pushing his mentor out—but he immediately injected some much-needed energy into a proud program that had seen better days.

Fisher won ten games in his first season, the first time Florida State had done so since 2003. He was aggressive on the recruiting trail, signing the nation's second-best class in 2011, headlined by future NFL pros Devonta Freeman, Kelvin Benjamin, and Timmy Jernigan. The Florida State program forever changed—along with Jimbo's life—the following year, when he signed a highly regarded quarterback out of Hueytown, Alabama, named Jameis Winston.

Winston would come to define Fisher in so many ways: Brilliant quarterback play. Winning above all else. When it worked, it worked so well. Winson could withstand Fisher's hard coaching and understood his complex pro-style offense. Fisher loved him and was willing to turn a blind eye to Winston's antics, which included stealing crab legs from a local Publix and yelling offensive comments while standing on top of a table.

Fisher's decision to go all in with Winston and continue playing him, despite sexual assault allegations that came to light in 2013, paid off on the field. (Winston was never prosecuted and later settled two federal lawsuits with the accuser.) In a standout redshirt freshman season, Winston won the Heisman Trophy and guided the Seminoles to a national championship win over Auburn. It was the highlight of Fisher's career, proof that his preferred way of doing things was the best in college football.

There was a cost to the approach.

It didn't take long for Fisher's Florida State culture to start eroding. It'd be too simplistic to blame it all on how Fisher handled the Winston accusations, but there was a pervasive belief around the program that Fisher's favorite players got away with whatever they wanted. Players started taking the success for granted, believing it would never end. Complacency set in.

The 2014 team might have been more talented than the one that won it all the previous season, but the chemistry was off. The team went undefeated in the regular season but started wobbling down the stretch. There were internal issues, including an open question about whether Winston could play in the Rose Bowl against Oregon, according to Florida State University president John Thrasher, though he declined to elaborate on specifics. It all came to a head in California, when a Marcus Mariota–led Oregon team blasted Florida State, 59–20.

"The most unselfish football team I've ever been around in my career was the 2013 team that won a national championship," said Rick Trickett, who spent ten seasons as Florida State offensive line coach. "And the most selfish football team I've ever been around was the 2014 team. It was all about me."

As his grip on the team's culture loosened, Fisher refused to consider his role in the problem. Instead, he was preoccupied with what competing organizations were doing and how that was the cause of Florida State's slow decline. He always wanted more and had an uncanny ability to know when a rival had more than he did. Especially Saban.

He obsessed over the luxurious facilities Saban had at his disposal to sell to recruits. One time he got wind of the Alabama head coach recruiting in Jacksonville using a helicopter to get to three high schools in a day. The next morning, Fisher called John Thrasher.

"I want a damn helicopter," Fisher told Thrasher. He wasn't joking.

Thrasher, who arrived as Florida State's president in 2014, had his hands full with his football coach. Fisher intensely disliked athletic director Stan Wilcox, opting to bypass his direct supervisor in favor of going to the university president. He'd complain to Thrasher about ACC rival Clemson's superior facilities. He'd complain about officiating, once even running over during a game to ensure Thrasher, standing on the sidelines, knew how bad the referees were. He made trip after trip to Thrasher's office demanding this and that, while his boss tried to run an entire university campus.

"He's a very high-strung guy," Thrasher said. "Complex guy with a lot of personal problems. Highly intense and wanted to have everything right there. It just wasn't going to happen overnight."

There are lots of theories as to what caused a change in Jimbo. He always had an edge to him, but he was also funny and enjoyed having a good time. Some point to the national championship in 2013, a crowning achievement for Jimbo that sent his ego through the roof. One former close friend said that after that, Fisher started acting like he invented football. There were personal life stressors too. He had a very publicized divorce from Candi in 2016. A year earlier, his closest confidant at FSU, Monk Bonasorte, had been diagnosed with terminal brain cancer. Monk passed away in 2016, and Jimbo lost the closest thing he had to a stabilizing force. He struggled, at times, under the weight of all the negative attention Winston brought to Tallahassee, all while dealing with his son being diagnosed with Fanconi anemia, a rare, deadly disease. He got frustrated quickly and complained more and more about the things he didn't have. The cracks in the foundation grew.

And when he didn't get his way, he enjoyed flirting with other suitors who promised him more.

LSU was Fisher's most consistent mistress. Each time LSU had an opening—and even when it didn't—Fisher was the name. As much as he clashed at times with Saban, he told people close to him how much he loved his time in Baton Rouge. He admired the fan base's passion and the school's all in approach to football, two critical components to the winning recipe. In 2015 and 2016, Fisher flirted hot and heavy with the idea of replacing Les Miles, his former boss, as the Tigers' next head coach. With the help of Jimmy Sexton, Fisher parlayed the outside interest into getting more money from Florida State.

After back-to-back 10-3 seasons in 2015 and 2016, Fisher's Florida State program rolled into the 2017 season with lofty expectations. The team had a preseason No. 3 ranking and a Week 1 game against No. 1 Alabama in Atlanta, billed as the GOAT—greatest opener of all time. Before the game, Fisher privately lamented to longtime Florida State reporter Ira Schoffel that Saban had an analyst spend the entire summer solely trying to find every trick play Fisher had ever run during his career. Yet again, Fisher was upset about what his former mentor had in Tuscaloosa and what he didn't in Tallahassee.

"You scheduled a game against Alabama, you want me to beat them, they have the best coach in the country, they have the best players in the country, and they have an unlimited budget," Fisher told him.

Deondre Francois, expected to be Fisher's best quarterback since Winston, got hurt in the fourth quarter of a 24–7 loss to Saban's Crimson Tide. Florida State found out later that night that Francois's injury was a season ender for him and, it turned out, for the whole team.

The bottom fell out on Fisher in a disastrous season. Florida State lost five of its first seven games, including to programs like North Carolina State and Boston College. Nothing went right. It got so bad that Florida State rescheduled a previously canceled game against Louisiana Monroe due to Hurricane Irma because the Seminoles found they needed the game to try to become bowl eligible.

And then the Aggies came calling.

TEXAS A&M WANTED A BIG name and set its sights on Jimbo Fisher.

The school's athletic director, Scott Woodward, was known for going big-game hunting when pursuing head coaches. At Washington, Woodward was the one who finally convinced Chris Petersen to leave Boise State. He wasn't afraid to money-whip someone to get it done, and Fisher was the perfect person to pursue, as Woodward knew well his frustration at not getting everything he wanted at Florida State.

Woodward and Fisher had a close relationship, dating back to their time together in Baton Rouge, and he didn't hide his intent to pry Jimbo away from Tallahassee, no matter what it took. And it took a lot—an offer of $75 million over ten years, completely guaranteed. John Sharp, the chancellor of the Texas A&M system, said the only issue was that they actually wanted Fisher for fifteen years.

Thrasher heard the rumors of the Aggies' pursuit of his head coach, and a part of him felt relief. After enduring public relations nightmares involving Winston and other players, it no longer felt worth it. The winning had diminished and the problems were rising. Boosters were frustrated with Jimbo's never-ending demands, and Jimbo was frustrated with the school's slow pace in building facilities to compete against the country's other top programs.

"I just wanted it to be over," the former FSU president said. "I was tired of the rumors, tired of what we were doing, tired of losing. It wasn't a good year. It was pretty obvious that he wasn't investing in the program."

Schoffel, who covered the entire Fisher era in Tallahassee for the *Tallahassee Democrat* and then Warchant, said the program was never able to achieve a cruising altitude once it flew into college football's rarefied air. Fisher expected to be given full control after delivering a national title—he even pushed for oversight of the entire budget at the end—and when it didn't happen, he focused more on winning an endless streak of unwinnable battles rather than on how to get the program back on track.

"It was a rocket ship and it came straight back down," Schoffel said. "It was never built to be maintained."

Still, Thrasher met with Fisher to see what the coach would do to get the program back on track. They talked about making staff changes, and the FSU president told him they'd find a way to make it happen. Looking back on it, Thrasher thinks Fisher was purposefully dragging things out "because had he not, we might have done something differently." He stops short of directly saying Fisher's job security was in question, but the emotional coach had already torched the bridge enough that a return felt increasingly unlikely. When it became clear to Thrasher that Jimbo was leaving for College Station, he called Jimmy Sexton and told him to make sure his client was at his house at noon sharp to finalize the exit because he had a 1:00 p.m. doctor's appointment.

"I never said I was going to release him or fire him or anything like that because I didn't want to be on the hook for anything we would have done, but I knew he was leaving," Thrasher said.

"He came over to my office. He said he was leaving. He was very emotional about it. I think he had invested a lot in the program and certainly understood why. I said that's great. He left."

He left a program in Tallahassee, tired of endless requests, and into the loving arms of College Station that embraced him like a conquering hero.

As Fisher stepped off a private plane in College Station for the first time as the Aggies' head coach, his new adoring fans received him like a king. The school rolled out a maroon carpet for him to walk on from the plane to a waiting GMC Yukon as a band of trumpeters played the school fight song. It was uniquely Texas A&M, a school with traditions it loves and that rivals love to make fun of.

"I think he figured us out pretty quick," said Bowen Loftin, a former Texas A&M president. "He figured out A&M real fast and knew how to address that group, and everything he's done has appealed to the alumni and the current students. A&M is hungry for a national championship, and he wore a ring, so he's the guy."

As Loftin explained, Aggies "crave relevance," and Fisher tapped into that. Whether it's jealousy or indignation, a little brother component is embedded in Texas A&M fans when it comes to in-state rival Texas, a school that seemed to delight in being the big brother and bullying A&M when both were in the Big 12. Texas A&M fans desperately want to see the Aggies succeed and have been more than willing to open their checkbooks to try to make that a reality. "There is a hunger out there for this championship that will never be satiated until we have one again, and maybe several again," Loftin said.

Fisher was just the latest example of spending major money to buy success. Giving Fisher a fully guaranteed contract was unheard of then, but

A&M brass had no qualms about making the $75 million bet on it being a success. Sharp was so sure it would work out that he handed Fisher a national championship plaque with the official date to be added later. Fisher made clear in his introductory press conference that the goal was to win the championship every year, a bold assertion that fired up a school that hadn't won a title since 1939.

"We have to understand that we're not interested in being good," Fisher said on December 4, 2017. "We're interested in being elite. We're interested in being great."

Like his new boss, Fisher enjoyed hunting—in a literal sense, as it was his favorite hobby, and figuratively, as far as getting the best talent on his roster. He was obsessed with securing the top-ranked high school players in the country, the five-star recruits, and paid close attention to how recruiting services like 247Sports and Rivals ranked his top targets. "Recruiting goes on Jimbo's ego," a Florida State staffer told ESPN. "He wants to be known as the baddest motherfucker in the world, whether he's recruiting to Florida State or wherever. That's in Jimbo's DNA."

He wasn't interested in pounding the pavement to convince those top seventeen-year-olds to come to College Station though. Sporting his national championship ring, Fisher believed his résumé and success sold itself.

"He wanted to identify the top talent, but he didn't necessarily care when it came to the active recruitment of players, because his philosophy was, if you win, they will come," said Cody Bellaire, who worked in Texas A&M's personnel department. "That's one hundred percent what he believes. He's like, recruiting will take care of itself. If you're winning games, kids will want to go there."

Bellaire, who had worked for recruiting-obsessed head coaches Ed Orgeron and Les Miles before Fisher, said the Texas A&M head coach was less organized than his previous bosses. While there was a rhythm and structure to what Orgeron and Miles wanted, Fisher would walk into a recruiting staff meeting, pick a position randomly, and watch those recruiting targets. "He might watch four running backs, he might watch forty," Bellaire said. "He was much more loose."

His staff meetings had a similar air of disorganization. When assistant coaches and staffers walked into the morning meeting, they weren't sure if it'd be a twenty-minute or two-hour meeting. There was only one constant: Jimbo eating breakfast as the rest of his staff watched and pretended it was normal. Before the meeting started, an assistant would drop off breakfast for just the head coach—typically McDonald's—that'd be waiting for him as he walked in. As the staff reviewed the latest injuries and recruiting news, Jimbo would dig into bacon or a biscuit.

While his former boss, Nick Saban, was a recruiting-film junkie, breaking down at least three or four recruiting evaluation tapes each day, Fisher preferred to watch the highlights. He had a personnel department capable of doing much more than that, but he told them all he needed were the highlights. He wanted only to see what a player could do, not what he couldn't. Those who had been around him for years said that one bad play could stick in Fisher's head and throw off his entire evaluation. So he'd decided himself he'd rather watch a few good plays then make a call from them.

Saban couldn't have been more different.

Todd Alles, Saban's first director of football operations at Alabama, remembered breaking down film one day with Saban when they got to a player named Mark Barron. Saban kept watching the film when he noticed Alles getting antsy. He asked him if he needed to go to the bathroom. Alles said no but wondered what they were doing still watching the tape.

"What have you seen to make me turn the tape off?" Saban asked Alles.

"Nothing," he replied.

"That's what I'm looking for," Saban said. "I'm looking for a reason to turn it off."

Barron became a unanimous All-American at Alabama and a top ten NFL Draft pick. Saban always wanted to feel like he knew it all—the good and the bad—before he called to offer a scholarship. Fisher just wanted to make sure they were good players and wasn't as concerned about the rest. "We don't need a bunch of choir boys," he'd often tell his staff. He liked kids with an edge and frequently lamented that Texas kids weren't as tough as the Florida kids he had down in Tallahassee. "He hated coaching Texas kids," one former A&M personnel staffer said. At the same time, he didn't mind taking a chance on a kid if the talent was there, which was something that would eventually get him in trouble with his top-rated recruiting class.

He wanted the success Saban had had and tried to model his coaching approach after the Alabama coach's gruff demeanor—he told those close to him he "had to be an asshole because he wanted everyone to understand he meant business"—but it wasn't clear he was willing to put in the corresponding work to accomplish it. His envy paved the way for insecurity and led to peculiar comments meant to diminish Saban's accomplishments. Ahead of his first game against Saban as Texas A&M's head coach in 2018, Fisher had Mike Elko, his defensive coordinator, get on the whiteboard during a staff meeting and give an overview of what the Crimson Tide did well on offense. As Elko started rattling off information about how Alabama succeeded with its Tua Tagovailoa–led offense, Fisher interjected.

"Oh, that's stuff Nick stole from me," Fisher told his staff. "We were doing that back at LSU."

Those in the room looked around at one another, confused. Fisher was certainly not running the type of modern Alabama offense full of run-pass options back in Baton Rouge in the early 2000s. It was well established at that point how much Saban had revamped his offensive philosophy, first with Lane Kiffin and then with Mike Locksley, to move quicker and more pass-heavy after long preferring a more conservative approach. Fisher knew that better than anyone, given how much Saban's shackles on him in Baton Rouge frustrated him to no end. But that was just who Fisher was, especially when it came to his former boss, who was fresh off his sixth national championship.

"You could tell him Nick Saban invented electricity, and he'd say, 'Oh, he stole my blueprints,'" a former Texas A&M staffer said.

IN THE MEANTIME, HE HAD a new boss.

Woodward left Texas A&M to return to his alma mater, LSU, in 2019. A&M hired Ole Miss athletic director Ross Bjork as his replacement. Woodward's timing couldn't have been better, as Ed Orgeron led one of the most talented college football teams ever to an undefeated national championship season, capped off by winning the title game in New Orleans. It was a dream come true for the Mandeville-born Orgeron, who quickly became a cult hero with his "Geaux Tigers" and "We Comin'" phrases.

That euphoria rapidly dissipated. A pandemic-impacted 8-4 2020 season shouldn't have put Orgeron on the hot seat, but there were whispers that if Orgeron didn't have a strong 2021 season, Woodward would make a run at Fisher. It seemed he was ready to go hunting again.

Texas A&M knew this too. Fisher hadn't delivered a national championship, but he capitalized on the pandemic-impacted 2020 season with a 9-1 record and barely missed the College Football Playoff at No. 5 in the final rankings. The cracks beneath the surface were starting to deepen, but outwardly the future looked bright. Texas A&M tried to preempt its former athletic director's pursuit when it gave Fisher a contract extension that bumped him back up to ten years on the contract with $95 million guaranteed. It was again the biggest guaranteed contract in college football history and meant to serve as a wall against Woodward's pursuit.

A&M must have had good intel, because when LSU fired Orgeron that October, of course Woodward set his sights on Fisher. Bypassing Fisher's high-profile agent, Jimmy Sexton, Woodward directly appealed to Jimbo over and over again to come back to Baton Rouge, according to sources. Fisher, who had long flirted with the LSU job, had to think long and hard about what he wanted to do. Woodward was persuasive, and the money was big. Fisher finally told Woodward no for the final time the weekend after the regular season ended after Texas A&M tweaked his contract to add more personal private plane hours. Woodward moved on from Fisher and ultimately hired Notre Dame's Brian Kelly.

"If A&M did not have the year that they had and signed the No. 1 class of all time, Jimbo would have been the LSU head coach," Bellaire said. "I feel very confident that would have been the case."

Instead, Fisher stayed to put the final touches on a recruiting class that rocked the college football world.

A MAN WHO WENT BY the name "SlicedBread" had Jimbo riled up.

It started when Grayson Weir, a reporter for the website called Bro-Bible, noticed a post on an Oklahoma fan site that detailed explosive allegations about Fisher and Texas A&M. The man leveling the claims just so happened to go by the username SlicedBread.

Welcome to the wild world of the SEC.

SlicedBread accused Texas A&M of spending between $25 million and $30 million on its top-ranked recruiting class, largely utilizing LLC shell companies to facilitate NIL payments to desired recruits. Rumors of Texas A&M spending big money on its recruiting class had been the talk of SEC recruiting departments, but no one had laid out the details in quite those terms until the anonymous message board user.

Weir tracked down SlicedBread and learned that he wasn't just a random message board user making shit up, as can frequently be the case. He had a journalism background and was now an Oklahoma booster with knowledge of the NIL recruiting scene. There were details SlicedBread passed along that had Weir believing he was legitimate. After talking it over with his editor, Weir eventually published a story entitled "Texas A&M Boosters Spent Unfathomable Amount of Money to Land No. 1 Recruiting Class, Per Report," with a custom image of Fisher in front of a stack of $100 bills. The story quickly took off, becoming one of the most well-read BroBible stories ever.

"It's objectively one of the funniest things to come out of college football in a long time that a guy named SlicedBread was on the cutting edge of a pretty big story," Weir said.

Fisher didn't find it so funny. In a scene too unbelievable to be true if it didn't happen, Fisher used his National Signing Day press conference to unload. Yes, the head coach was very, very mad at SlicedBread.

"Here's my problem: There is no thirty-million-dollar fund," Fisher said. "This is garbage. It pisses me off. It comes from a site called BroBible by a guy named SlicedBread. Then everybody runs with it. So it's written on the internet; it's gospel. How irresponsible is that?"

He took particular exceptions to the coaches who advanced that narrative, including Ole Miss head coach Lane Kiffin. A day earlier, Kiffin joked, "I didn't know if Texas A&M was going to incur a luxury tax for how much they paid for their signing class." That comment stuck in Fisher's craw.

"To have coaches, in our league and across this league, saying it, clown acts," Fisher said. "Irresponsible as hell. Multiple coaches in this league. The guys griping about NIL and griping about transfer portal are using it the most and bragging about it the most. That's the ironic part. It does piss me off."

Fisher's fiery response kicked off an intense feud between him and Kiffin. The Ole Miss head coach, latching on to Fisher's "clown acts" comment, would frequently refer to Fisher as a clown in private to anyone who would listen. He relished the opportunity to take shots at Jimbo, telling people close to him the Texas A&M coach was a total fraud.

Fisher siccing the hounds on BroBible led to an uncomfortable few days for Weir. Nothing beats the passion of SEC fandom, but it can topple into the dangerous extreme. Recruiting coverage, in particular, appeals to the most fanatic of supporters, and Texas A&M's most ardent fans followed their head coach's lead on the attack.

"I always joke that if I ever go missing, the first place you should look is College Station," Weir said. "They do not like me."

That dislike extended to numerous angry messages that included death threats against both Weir and his mother. "You're going to threaten to kill my mother over a report from BroBible citing SlicedBread?" Weir said. "That's where you're going to draw your line?"

In a preview of his fiery May comments directed at Saban, Fisher vowed to expose dirt on his detractors if they didn't back down. He seemed upset that Saban's comments at the Texas High School Coaches Association convention that his quarterback Bryce Young had earned nearly seven figures in NIL deals before even starting a game were championed, and yet he was getting attacked.

"I'll tell you what: I know how some of those guys recruit too," Fisher said. "Go dig into that. I know the history, I know the tradition, and I know things. Trust me, you don't want to go down that avenue. It's ridiculous, and it's irresponsible, and it's unbelievable. And I ain't just talking about one; multiple people got NIL issues. It's funny when Nick Saban said his quarterback got an $800,000 deal. It was wonderful. Now it ain't wonderful anymore, huh?

"You don't like that we're coming on? Get used to it. We ain't going nowhere."

ASK DIFFERENT PEOPLE, AND YOU'LL get different answers on the inflection point within college football. Darren Heitner, a sports lawyer and one of the best-known NIL experts, pointed to the story in *The Athletic* that detailed Tennessee paying $8 million to a quarterback recruit, later unveiled as Nico Iamaleava, as the moment when everything changed. When no one did anything about Tennessee openly admitting to paying seven figures for a quarterback who had never even thrown a college pass, Heitner said the floodgates opened up.

Others point to Fisher's 2022 recruiting class that featured an absurd eight five stars, according to 247Sports rankings. The crown jewel of the class was Walter Nolen, a six-foot-four, 325-pound defensive lineman who looked ready to make opposing quarterbacks' lives miserable from the moment he arrived on campus. Everyone in the country wanted him before he picked the Aggies. That was a defining characteristic of the 2022 recruiting class: Fisher beat out Saban, Kirby Smart, and Steve Sarkisian for recruits they badly wanted. The Aggies landed the No. 1 wide receiver (Evan Stewart), No. 3 defensive lineman (Shemar Stewart), No. 3 quarterback (Connor Weigman), No. 3 receiver (Chris Marshall), No. 4 defensive lineman (Gabriel Brownlow-Dindy), and No. 6 defensive lineman (LT Overton). It was unbelievable, in the literal sense, to rival coaches that Texas A&M, a program that had always recruited well under Fisher but hadn't previously bested a top-five finish, had just signed the highest-rated recruiting class ever.

That A&M signed five of the top ten defensive linemen and two of the top ten edge rushers especially pissed off rival coaches, who believed in building the foundation of the roster through the trenches. One former SEC assistant, who had coached in the heyday of the wild SEC before Mike Slive cracked down, said defensive linemen were the players that led to the most intense bidding wars from boosters, back when all the money came under the table. Multiple SEC schools, including Alabama, got in trouble in the early 2000s for trying to buy top defensive linemen out of Memphis.

"There's more d-linemen in the south than any other region in the country so they've always had the best d-linemen," the coach said. "If you've got a chance to flip your program, it's going to be with a defensive lineman. Whatever it takes to get them."

A senior sports executive, intimately familiar with the industry and the money involved, said A&M was like Los Alamos in forever-changing college football.

"They were the most aggressive, the most opportunistic, and the most creative," the executive said. "And they executed terribly. Terribly. Created a horrible culture. Created competition that everyone had to go compete against. But to me, this was the first group of an administration, coach, and booster program that was like, 'Hell yeah, this is legal, we're in.'"

Sources around the A&M football program pushed back on that narrative, calling its collective, known as the Fund, not nearly sophisticated enough to merit a comparison to the New Mexico collective of scientists who created the first nuclear bomb. But there was no denying that a combination of a fan base as thirsty for success as if it were stranded in the Sahara Desert and pliable state NIL laws allowed Texas A&M to be aggressive out of the gate.

That approach and its accompanying initial success created a domino effect. Nothing defines college football more than an overwhelming feeling that you must keep up with the Joneses. If Texas A&M could have that much success so quickly, there'd be intense pressure to do the same. A&M's stunning 2022 recruiting class made every Power 5 school, but especially the ones in the SEC, take note. There were concerns from the get-go, however, on the unintended consequences of that aggressiveness. TCU head coach Sonny Dykes, who referenced the power of A&M's huge alumni base compared to his private Dallas-area school, was an early worrier.

"There's a lot of strength in numbers when it comes to NIL. We're not going to be able to go buy a football team like some people are," Dykes said. "That's okay. Like everything in the world, there's a price to be paid for going out and buying a team.

"You do what you believe in and you don't all of a sudden wake up one day and go, 'How did we get here?'"

THAT MOMENT CAME EARLY IN the 2022 season for Fisher. A Week 2 loss to Appalachian State, a school it paid $1.5 million to play to essentially guarantee a win, cranked up the pressure. To lose to a Sun Belt school, months after public feuds with Saban and Kiffin, invoked schadenfreude across the SEC.

It got worse as multiple members of the vaunted 2022 recruiting class started causing internal problems. Fisher had to suspend Stewart, Marshall, Smoke Bouie, and Denver Harris (another five star) for a curfew violation ahead of the following week's game against Miami. Harris and Marshall would be suspended again later in the season, and both five stars transferred out of the program after the season. Fisher knew there were character concerns but bet on their talent, and it quickly blew up in his face. There were major issues with marijuana usage on the team, according to sources, including with players expected to be key contributors and leaders, that led to concerns around an eroding team culture.

Once known as an offensive guru, Fisher's complex pro-style offense now looked anemic. As television cameras panned to him on the sideline, he increasingly looked more like a disheveled mad scientist with papers falling out of a notebook and his glasses hanging off his nose. His look and approach didn't inspire confidence from the fan base. A caller into *The Paul Finebaum Show* said it'd be cheaper to hire a hit man than pay Fisher's nearly $86 million buyout. Police had to investigate that one, but of course nothing is off-limits in the SEC, where the conference's slogan, "It just means more," is as much a threat as it is worth celebrating.

Texas A&M finished the season 5-7, missing a bowl game despite all that talent in College Station. Fisher was now college football's biggest disappointment and a source of a barrage of jokes across college football, where his West Virginia accent and auctioneeresque rapid-fire patter of a speaking style had long made him a transcriber's nightmare and a source of plenty of imitation.

Months after the season ended at the annual SEC spring meetings in Florida, Mark Stoops and Kirby Smart, arm in arm and clearly having a good night, walked past a television and saw Fisher giving an interview. Smart and Stoops started cracking up laughing as Kirby loudly imitated Fisher's high-pitched delivery as they walked off.

Fisher's massive contract hung like an albatross around the football program's neck, but program insiders insisted over and over again that the money would be there should the school ever want to make a head coaching change. Headed into the 2023 season, the school's administration's preference was for Fisher to finally accept making offensive changes, notably giving up play-calling duties. Calling offensive plays was always Jimbo's favorite thing about football, a way to show off the brilliance he knew he possessed but that the outside world now doubted. But with cultural issues around the program, he had to become more of a CEO-style head coach. He initially made a run at Garrett Riley, Dykes's rising star offensive coordinator at TCU, before he hired former Arkansas head coach Bobby Petrino. The hire prompted intrigue across college football, and not simply because Petrino lost his Arkansas job due to a sex scandal with a football department employee that included a motorcycle crash. Petrino had both a brilliant football mind and a reputation for being a jerk. "Bobby's the best football coach I've ever been around, and he's also the biggest asshole I've ever been around," said one source who previously worked with him.

How Fisher and Petrino, two alpha personalities, would mesh became a popular offseason topic. Fisher was notoriously stubborn, the type of person, former staffers said, who had to be convinced it was his own idea before making a change. Minter, who knew both men well, texted Jimbo and told him it was a great hire if he managed it right. "[Bobby] had to run Jimbo's offense and try to make it work," Minter said. "He just couldn't let it go. Jimbo couldn't quite let go and let Bobby run the show."

The pressure ratcheted up with another early season loss. Fisher's Aggies loss to Miami, 48–33, in Week 2 led to an onslaught of angry boosters texting and calling to let their displeasure be known. The big money that ran Texas A&M was restless.

Fisher needed a big win, and here was a wobbly Alabama team coming to College Station in Week 6. The last time the Crimson Tide made the trip to Kyle Field, in 2021, Fisher became the first former Saban assistant to beat the big boss. Texas A&M's 41–38 win on a last-second Seth Small field goal powered a frenzied field rush celebration of overjoyed Aggies fans. On this beautiful Saturday, 108,101 fans—the third-largest crowd in Texas A&M history—were eager to celebrate on the field again. Alabama receiver Jermaine Burton told his teammates before running onto the field, "We have to come out and attack. How bad do you want it? They want to storm the field."

Fisher's insistence on doing things his way, including an overly conservative approach, doomed him against Saban again. Texas A&M led Alabama 17–10 at halftime, but Crimson Tide quarterback Jalen Milroe powered the second-half comeback win for Alabama. The noose around Fisher's neck was tightening.

The whispers about Fisher's impending demise got louder after a road loss to Tennessee. There hadn't been a particularly egregious loss yet, but the displeasure over the poor return on investment was growing among key decision-makers. Texas A&M was the better team in that game, but yet again Fisher couldn't seem to get his team properly prepared to play well on the road. Fisher needed to steady the ship fast.

It was fitting, then, that it all came crashing down against Kiffin. The two traded barbs before the game, as each badly wanted to destroy the other. Lane got the last laugh when his defense blocked a field goal attempt that would have sent the game to overtime, securing a 38–35 win for Ole Miss and signaling the end of Jimbo's time in College Station. With a Board of Regents meeting already scheduled for that week, Texas A&M's administration started working on assembling the necessary money to pay Fisher's mammoth buyout. The outside world largely treated Fisher's $76 million buyout as an impenetrable shield ensuring his survival, but as time passed, it felt more like a sunk cost to Texas A&M decision-makers. The concern was that after another disappointing season, the program would lose top players to the transfer portal and top assistants to other opportunities. Worse, there'd be little reason for fans to have any hope it was going to get better under Fisher. The thinking was that the cost of not making a move and letting the program further deteriorate could be even more expensive long term than the initial shock of paying off Fisher.

While A&M's power players aligned against him, Fisher had no idea of what was brewing. He was excited after a 51–10 win over Mississippi State, still believing he could get the program back on track, before Bjork told him he wanted to meet with him the next day. When Bjork told Fisher on Sunday morning he was out effective immediately, the proud West Virginian was shocked. Not simply because he lost his job, but that Texas A&M would fire him with two games still left in the season. The players were equally shocked. "We came off a real good win . . . and then that next day they came in and said he was gone," said receiver Ainias Smith. "He didn't even have the opportunity to talk to us. It was wild."

Sixteen months after saying his former boss should have been slapped more as a child, Fisher was out of a job. Bjork said the program was stuck in neutral. He no longer believed in Jimbo's ability to get it back on track.

"The assessment that I delivered was that we are not reaching our full potential," Bjork said. "We are not in the championship conversation, and something was not quite right about our direction and the plan.

"We should be relevant on the national scene."

Fisher slunk into the background as Bjork hired Mike Elko, Fisher's former defensive coordinator, away from Duke. Months after his firing, Fisher finally resurfaced as a guest on the popular *Pardon My Take* podcast. In his first public comments about his firing, one man was still on Fisher's mind: SlicedBread.

"College football changed on a lie," Fisher protested. "I'm going to write a book about it one day."

Why couldn't Fisher get over an anonymous message-board poster? It cut to the very core of what he believed about himself. Growing up how he did in West Virginia, the only way out was through hard work, and he prided himself on his intense dedication to football. It didn't matter if it was Nick Saban or SlicedBread, anyone who accused him of buying players was denigrating that work ethic. And he took that personally.

CHAPTER 12

Unrealistic

A LITTLE AFTER SIX ON A picture-perfect Friday evening, University of Arizona president Bobby Robbins took the makeshift stage, the first speaker in the BEAR DOWN pep rally prior to a Wildcats home football game the following night.

Casually dressed in a monogrammed red U of A polo shirt, Robbins looked out at a growing sea of supporters—the band, cheerleaders, students, and fans—still forming in a busy plaza on the edge of campus. This would be Robbins's eighth event of yet another jam-packed day, beginning with a donor update and Hispanic Heritage Month breakfast and ending twelve hours later at a Mexican Independence Day award concert. In between, the sixty-six-year-old Robbins would conduct Zoom calls, meet a half dozen top women's softball recruits, and host a private ninety-minute lunch where the world-class heart surgeon dissected the state of big-time college sports. Three months earlier at the Future of College Athletics Summit Robbins had placed the patient in the intensive care unit. In his view, this time around, the patient had taken a turn for the worse.

"I would say college sports is even more critical than when I made that statement at the summit," he said. "NIL, transfer portal, that's one thing. I'm just talking about the operating budget for athletic departments struggling, almost everyone struggling. One hundred million budgets with twenty-five or thirty-million-dollar deficits."

For example, Robbins said his university had an annual budget of $2.7 billion. Before the recession of 2008, about $1.5 billion of those dollars came from the state. Now, the university received just one fifth of those funds, with the entire $300 million earmarked for financial aid. When the annual budgeting was finished, the difference between profit and loss was razor thin, just $2 million or so every fiscal year. The need to feed the incessant athletic-industrial arms race—expanded stadiums, soaring salaries, finer facilities, more, more, more—added to his headaches. In many ways, Arizona was a classic example of the system gone haywire: football and basketball teams that turned a profit but an overall athletic department deficit that averaged approximately $30 million in recent years.

"We've totally lost control," said Robbins. "We're screwed, and it's a bad place to be."

The frustration in Robbins's voice was palpable. And understandable. Six weeks earlier, he had a ringside seat to the knockout blow of a 108-year-old conference. The Pac-12 "Conference of Champions," the historic home of the Rose Bowl, John Wooden, Kareem Abdul-Jabbar, Bill Walton, Tiger Woods, Jackie Joyner-Kersee, Marcus Allen, and Missy Franklin, to name but a few, went up in smoke in a matter of days. Twelve schools, in his words, "pawns in the proxy war between ESPN and FOX." After pledging their allegiance to keep the conference together, Washington and Oregon had each accepted a $30 million lifeline offered by FOX and followed USC and UCLA into the bosom of the Big Ten.

By the time the latest realignment merry-go-round ended, no less than eleven schools had bolted to the Big 12, Big Ten, or ACC for one reason and one reason only:

Said Robbins: "It's the *love of the almighty dollar*. The love of money did it. There's no other answer."

THE MARRIAGE BETWEEN COLLEGE SPORTS and television will soon celebrate the diamond anniversary of their wedding date. On March 10, 1951, NBC Sports paid a then eye-popping $1.2 million to televise a dozen football games. Nearly forty years later, the NCAA inked its first ten-figure deal when CBS Sports paid $1 billion dollars to televise March Madness for the next seven years, a payout that grew to $10.8 billion over fourteen years, when Turner Broadcasting, now TNT Sports, joined the party in 2010, only to extend their deal six years later to 2032 for an additional $8.8 billion.

While the NCAA kept the lion's share of money to operate the national office and conduct various championships, Division I conferences soon started receiving six- or seven-figure shares depending on how deep their schools went in the Men's Basketball Tournament.

The real money for individual conferences started after the landmark *NCAA v. Board of Regents of the University of Oklahoma* Supreme Court case in 1984. To that point, the NCAA served as a powerful overlord of college sport, exerting complete control over television, limiting the schools shown on TV in an effort that it claimed would protect live attendance. That changed when the Supreme Court ruled 7–2 against the NCAA, declaring that it violated the Sherman Antitrust Act and voided existing television contracts with ABC, CBS, and the cable network WTBS, the forerunner of Turner Sports. It wasn't long before more competition gave way to rampant commercialization.

In 1996, the SEC officially aligned with CBS, giving the conference a weekly football season prime Saturday afternoon time slot that took a regional conference national. The money kept rising, as did the innovation. In 2007, in a game-changing play, the Big Ten launched the first namesake regional network with FOX. The SEC followed suit seven years later, teaming up with ESPN to launch the SEC Network. It gave both conferences another national platform for sporting events plus millions more in annual fees—part of a model where conferences bundled their media rights, so-called Grant of Rights, or GOR, into one big package for one big payout from FOX, CBS, NBC, and ESPN/Disney.

Today the Big Ten and SEC stand alone as the new Power 2, and it's mainly because of lucrative television contracts: seven years and more than $8 billion from ESPN, CBS, and NBC for the Big Ten; a ten-year, $3 billion deal from Disney/ESPN just for SEC's game of the week. Lottery-like winnings for each conference school—$60 to $65 million per school annually in the Big Ten; more than $50 million annually in the SEC. Those numbers were expected to climb to more than $80 million over the next three years, more than double the expected annual payouts for schools from the ACC and Big 12.

IN COLLEGE LARRY SCOTT CAPTAINED the Harvard tennis team and afterward enjoyed a modicum of professional success, mostly playing doubles. Upon retirement he spent a decade as president and chief operating officer of ATP Properties, the marketing arm of the Association of Tennis Professionals. A shrewd negotiator, Scott was the chairman and CEO of the Women's Tennis Association when the Pac-10 came calling in 2009.

Unlike many conference commissioners, Scott hadn't taken the traditional path as a former athletic director or come up through a conference office. He wanted to do things outside the administrative box. And he had big dreams. A year after taking the commissioner's job, Scott very publicly tried to plunder the Big 12 to build a new super conference with Texas, Texas A&M, Texas Tech, Oklahoma, Oklahoma State, and Colorado. As he crisscrossed the country meeting with university leaders on their home turf, folks flew into a frenzy. Scott had underestimated the political pressure he'd face in Texas by leaving Baylor out. Texas governor Rick Perry told his state schools to stand down. Not to be denied, Scott convinced Colorado to break more than sixty years of conference ties to the Big Eight to enlarge the Pac-10 by two, bringing sister-state Utah along for the ride in June 2010. The conference instability raised by his bravado pushed Nebraska to the Big Ten and Missouri and Texas A&M to the SEC the following year. A year after that, Big Ten invited Maryland and Rutgers into its ranks to supercharge its growing regional network with the New York City and Washington, D.C., television markets. With those moves came unintended consequences: the death of long-standing rivalries. The 117-year-old Texas–Texas A&M game? Gone. The Missouri-Kansas Border War that started in 1891? It played out on message boards, not football fields. University presidents needed fans and their money to support their athletic teams, but they determined they needed TV money more. Damn the fans and their silly rivalry games they looked forward to all year if they got in the way of more money.

Despite the failure of the super conference, Scott clearly had impressive influence as a commissioner. In 2011, he negotiated the most lucrative television contract for any conference—a twelve-year $3 billion deal with FOX and ESPN. Mike Aresco, who had worked in ESPN and CBS Sports programming and headed up the Big East (which later became the American Athletic Conference), couldn't believe then ESPN president John Skipper made the deal. It completely skewed the market, he said, and ultimately sent rival conferences to make moves that would generate bigger GOR deals.

With a headshaking linear deal in hand, Scott's grand plan was to launch a Pac-12 stand-alone network. The league had a ton of inventory that wasn't making its way onto TV, including many football and basketball games. In addition, it wanted to tap into its rich Olympic history to further expand its brand. With Utah and Colorado on board, the Pac-12 Networks featured six regional networks, such as Pac-12 Arizona for U of A and ASU fans. In launching the network, the conference decided not to sell any portion to ESPN or FOX and instead partner with a group of digital cable and satellite TV companies, believing a thriving West Coast network boasting the nation's second-largest media market in Los Angeles would prove irresistible to buyers down the road.

Scott was spectacularly wrong.

While the Big Ten and SEC Networks flourished, the Pac-12 Networks elicited constant criticism for poor distribution and minimal additional revenue for the conference schools. That failure, coupled with Scott's lavish spending on a ritzy office rental in San Francisco and propensity for private jets and fancy restaurants, rubbed his bosses the wrong way. His twelve-year tenure officially ended on June 30, 2021.

In stepped George Kliavkoff, previously the president of Entertainment and Sports for MGM Resorts International, a marketing maven who had helped launch Hulu.

Kliavkoff had barely settled in when an earthquake hit—Texas and Oklahoma announced they were ditching the Big 12 for the allure of the SEC. The addition of two athletic powerhouses to the finest football conference in America was the equivalent of a 10.0 on the Richter scale.

Within hours of the Texas-OU exit, Robbins says he got a call from a shaken governor from Big 12 country, telling Robbins he needed to convince his fellow presidents and chancellors to bring the eight remaining teams in his conference into the Pac-12 and make it the Pac-20. It turned out that Robbins had already surveyed the wreckage and was thinking similar things, only bigger.

"When this seismic shift was happening," Robbins recalled, "I was talking to presidents saying if they're [the SEC] going to be that big and that powerful, our only hope is to consolidate the ACC, Big 12 and Pac-12. We need to be a megaconference. I mean a full merger. Big."

Robbins already had a name picked out—the Pacific Atlantic Conference. You wouldn't even need to change the acronym, just the number (along with shifting your conception of what kind of geographical alignments make any sense for college athletics). To gauge the Big 12's interest, Robbins called an old friend, Bob Bowlsby, the conference commissioner, and told him his plan.

"I said, 'Look, man, I want to do this. Problem is we've just hired this new guy. I want you to be commissioner [of the proposed super conference], but we have a problem.' Bob said, 'No, I think we could put this thing together and I want to retire and George can be the commissioner for the Pac-20.'"

For all his positive reinforcement, Bowlsby had been around the realignment block long enough to know that Robbins was more than likely whistling in the wind. Only a week before Texas and Oklahoma's move to the SEC leaked, Bowlsby had told reporters realignment didn't keep him up at night. While Bowlsby slept soundly in Dallas, some of his closest colleagues in the business, particularly Oklahoma vice president and athletic director Joe Castiglione and SEC commissioner Greg Sankey, were secretly negotiating. Bowlsby had worked closely with Sankey for more than a year and a half on a College Football Playoff expansion subcommittee, having no idea that his fellow commissioner was on the verge of swiping his two crown jewels. He couldn't help but be hurt by the betrayal even if he understood its business reasons.

"I would have given *him* a heads up," Bowlsby said. "He had his reasons for not giving me a heads-up. My personal relationships are more important to me than the eventual outcome. I probably would have risked letting him in on it, even if it might have made the deal fall apart. But that's just me."

Bowlsby, who had been in college athletics for more than forty years, knew the truth behind realignment. It didn't give him much faith in a group of school presidents and chancellors with little knowledge or interest in sports, often leaving that land mine in the hands of their athletic directors. When forced to engage, they typically fell back on whatever played best politically with key constituents. When Bowlsby started the process to replace Texas and Oklahoma, he told his board to empower him to make the moves and get out of his way, eschewing consulting presidents or ADs until it was time for a vote.

"It's a very disingenuous process," Bowlsby said. "The AD, the president, the board chair, they are going to do, first and foremost, what's best for their institution. You get in a meeting and everyone is singing 'Kumbaya' and we are going to go forward, and the minute you close the meeting, everyone is on the phone covering their ass and making sure they have a backup plan."

Robbins would soon learn that truth firsthand. But whether out of naivety or optimism, he would not be deterred, spending "hours and hours" on the phone, busting his ass, asking for help. Bowlsby did his part, flying to Montana to meet with Kliavkoff to discuss the Pac-20 idea, offering up his eight remaining schools in a potential merger.

Kliavkoff liked the Pac-20 idea enough to form a subcommittee of six officials—three presidents, including Robbins, and three athletic directors to discuss the idea before bringing it to the entire board. Twelve minutes into a planned ninety-minute call, the idea was all but dead as one school torpedoed all expansion plans.

Two years after that meeting, Robbins's voice held more than a touch of irony as he recalled one of the most outspoken opponents. From the start USC president Carol Folt, a subcommittee member, had been a vocal critic, wondering aloud why the Pac-12 needed to add teams. As Kliavkoff went through a PowerPoint presentation outlining the benefits of adding all eight remaining Big 12 teams, Folt could only stomach three slides before she interjected.

"USC is not agreeing to add a single school to the Pac-12," Folt told the group. "We're not adding any schools. I know it doesn't need to be unanimous, but USC is going to vote against."

Several reasons were cited in advocating against expansion, from concerns over inviting religious schools like Baylor and TCU to rising travel costs. The biggest reason for USC's opposition, according to Pac-12 insiders, was that the school thought it was better than the mostly land-grant collection of Big 12 schools and simply didn't want to be associated with them.

All the while, Robbins believed Folt was already quietly talking to the Big Ten behind her colleagues' backs.

Said Robbins, "The level of hypocrisy was, 'I'm shocked there's any impropriety in this establishment.'"

ON JUNE 30, 2022, USC and UCLA announced they were leaving the Pac-12 for the Big Ten beginning in August 2024. It was what one athletic director called a "holy shit" moment that caught virtually everyone off guard, including Kliavkoff, who happened to be on a Fourth of July weekend vacation in Montana.

"When the L.A. schools moved, that's a bonkers move—to me, it was completely unnecessary," said a high-ranking sports television executive. "Once that happened, it set in motion a series of events I think was inevitable. It had no rationalization. For all the critics who thought it was all about the money—well, guess what? You just confirmed it. There's absolutely no rationale for USC and UCLA in the Big Ten except for money."

Said Bowlsby: "They really sold their fans and their student-athletes down the river for a chance at financial viability."

Shocking as it may have been, in truth it was a moment years in the making. After Scott landed the Pac-12's massive TV contract in 2011, the conference changed its revenue distribution, much to USC's and UCLA's dismay. What had previously been based on how often programs were on television—a major benefit for the L.A. schools—now switched to equal distribution. Pat Haden, USC's athletic director at the time, threatened to look elsewhere if his school didn't get a bigger cut of the financial pie and was called out by his peers in a meeting for bluffing. Chris Hill, who was there as Utah's athletic director when Haden made his threat, said not taking USC's dissatisfaction seriously proved a fatal mistake.

"We should have woken up and said this is unique," Hill said. "We have one market that dominates and we need to recognize that and give them more money since we're all making a lot more money and accept that. We didn't do that. At the end of the day, that was a big mistake."

The man ready to capitalize on the Los Angeles schools' uneasiness was Kevin Warren. Only eighteen months into his new role as commissioner of the Big Ten, Warren wasn't cut in the traditional mold of Jim Delany, his shrewd, visionary predecessor, or other old-school commissioners like Mike Slive (SEC) and John Swofford (ACC). A lawyer with a background in sports law, Warren's stock in trade with three teams in the NFL was as general counsel and chief operating officer. Early into his Big Ten tenure, he let a proverbial FOX into his henhouse, allowing its media partner with a controlling stake in the Big Ten Network to sit in and advise on rival negotiations with ESPN, NBC, and CBS. It was an unprecedented move, according to multiple TV executives who have negotiated rights deals, and left many of the non-FOX networks incredibly uncomfortable to have to make their pitches in front of a rival network. "[FOX is] embedded with the Big Ten in a way that I can't think of any other property that is so intertwined with its media partner," said one television rights expert familiar with the situation. The relationship between Warren and FOX wasn't always rosy—there was friction on both sides, according to sources, in what, at times, amounted to a power struggle. Ultimately, FOX made a compelling argument in favor of future Big Ten expansion at the expense of a fabled conference.

"The wrong guy at the wrong time," said the high-ranking sports television executive of Warren. "FOX took advantage of the position they had negotiated, not inappropriately, relative to their control of Big Ten assets, and they convinced a guy who, you know, it sounded like a good idea to him. Who wouldn't want those two big brands? Who wouldn't want the second-biggest media market in the country? They convinced him to pursue something that, frankly, was going to be really, really damaging."

Sources inside the Big Ten pushed back on that narrative, saying it wasn't the Big Ten that fired the first shot, but the SEC's and ESPN's poaching of Texas and Oklahoma. There were a finite number of marquee brands left after that, and the Big Ten couldn't risk rival conferences scooping the top ones remaining. In fact, Big Ten commissioner Warren strongly recommended to his presidents to add Washington and Oregon in addition to USC and UCLA, according to sources, believing it would strengthen a national coast-to-coast conference. "Everyone knew Oregon and Washington were a good fit, they made sense," said a Big Ten source directly involved in the realignment process. "They didn't really up the money too much—they kept it stable—but they also denied other conferences the ability to grab them."

The Big Ten presidents opted to invite just USC and UCLA, with some believing they did so because they didn't want to cause the Pac-12's demise. Those good intentions, if true, wouldn't last long.

Two weeks after that USC-UCLA bomb went off, the Pac-12 hired Connecticut-based Sports Media Advisors to help mastermind their suddenly muddled media-rights negotiations. Owner Doug Perlman had attended law school with Kliavkoff and quickly became part of a tight-knit negotiations team.

Perlman and Kliavkoff presented Pac-12 presidents and chancellors with extensive data detailing where they stood in the marketplace—particularly TV ratings versus other conferences. The bottom line being that if everything fell into place, they were looking at around $40 million per school, the most likely landing spot somewhere in the low-to-mid-thirties. The Pac-12 presidents and chancellors refused to accept that number, saying if the number wasn't at least $40 million, then not to bother bringing it to them. The Pac-12 leaders were obsessed with what the Big Ten had and expected to be at the same level, despite reams of data that showed the Pac-12 didn't measure up in that way.

"They were laser focused on it," said one source directly involved in the discussions. "They kept saying, 'Oh, we need to be where the Big Ten is. We can't afford to compete. We can't afford to keep coaches.' They would say it over and over again."

In the fall of 2022, after FOX's three-month exclusive negotiating window closed, ESPN put its initial offer on the table: $30 million per school per year. According to one ESPN insider with knowledge of the meeting, the network's offer "got laughed out of the room."

Far and away the most significant reason: Utah president Taylor Randall, who held a doctorate in operations and information management and once ran the university's business school, and one of his business school professors, with little or no experience in sports or media, built their own media rights model that spit out a breathtaking number: $50 million per school per year.

Based on that number, Randall suddenly owned the room, advisers be damned. The Pac-12 presidents' and chancellors' eyes got as big as saucers, dreaming of what $50 million per school would mean, deciding that was where they needed to be, not some measly $30 million. The Pac-12 board told their commissioner and his advisers they needed to go back to ESPN and ask for at least $50 million. "I've been in this business a long time. I've never been on the other side of the table from a professor when I was negotiating rights deals," said Bob Thompson, who negotiated hundreds of deals as FOX Sports Networks president.

The model was deeply flawed, according to those familiar with its methodology, and when pressed, Randall and his business professor couldn't explain how they arrived at that number. Kliavkoff and Doug Perlman stressed to the Pac-12 presidents and chancellors it wouldn't pass the smell test with ESPN and recommended they start negotiating at $40 million per school. A recommendation that went nowhere, as they refused to believe they didn't belong in the same financial neighborhood as the Big Ten and SEC despite little proof other than their own misguided conviction to justify that notion.

"Not a lot of presidents know a whole lot about business because a lot of them come from the academic side," said Thompson, who worked closely with former Big Ten commissioner Jim Delany on the launch of the Big Ten Network. "Not a lot of them know about sports because they aren't necessarily sports fans. Even fewer of them know about sports business because it's a niche inside another niche. That makes it tough to explain to them a couple of worlds they don't feel comfortable walking in, and can lead to some disastrous results."

Reluctantly, Kliavkoff took his bosses' $50 million demand to ESPN. Now it was the network's turn to laugh.

"To lay this at the [Pac-12] presidents' feet, they started keying off the Big Ten money," said an ESPN insider with direct knowledge of the negotiations.

"Money as some kind of barometer of what their expectations were. Which is *insane*. They didn't realize the market had moved and the Big Ten and SEC had separated themselves. But these guys refused to believe that and thought everyone was the same. 'We're just as good as the Big Ten.' Well, maybe on the soccer field or volleyball court but not in terms of market value."

After *New York Post* sports media columnist Andrew Marchand reported ESPN and the Pac-12 were "hundreds of millions apart," negotiations stalled out. Sensing an opportunity, new Big 12 commissioner Brett Yormark, a deeply experienced businessman with an aggressive mindset and diverse sports and entertainment background, including a stint as chief operating officer of Jay-Z's Roc Nation, jumped over the Pac-12 to secure a new deal with FOX and ESPN. The total money was in line with what ESPN offered the Pac-12, ensuring the Big 12's future stability and denying the Pac-12 what could have been its best linear option. Once on the verge of extinction, the Big 12 had showed what acting quickly and decisively meant—from Bowlsby adding BYU, Central Florida, Cincinnati, and Houston as his final major act as commissioner to Yormark outmaneuvering Kliavkoff to secure a seat at the big kids' table.

By the time the calendar turned to the summer of 2023, Kliavkoff was losing control, frustration building over his tendency to keep his circle small, lagging talks, and inability to deliver the big offer. The league flirted with adding San Diego State and SMU to replace USC and UCLA, but waited to make any official move until a TV deal could be finished. Kliavkoff had a July 31 deadline to present final media rights offers. In his first public comments in months about the situation, Kliavkoff claimed at Pac-12 Media Day on July 21 that the conference's situation was improving despite mounting evidence that said otherwise.

"I will tell you what we've seen is that the longer we wait for our media deal, the better our options get," Kliavkoff said. "I think our board realizes that."

On July 26, five days after those comments and five days before the deadline, the University of Colorado, driven by its media darling head football coach Deion Sanders, had seen and heard enough. Chancellor Phil DiStefano texted Kliavkoff that morning, saying, George, our board will vote this afternoon at 3 p.m. to join the Big 12. It was not an easy decision and

I realize its impact on the other members. Kliavkoff would later lament it wasn't even a breakup call, just a text. The Buffaloes preferred an awkward return to the Big 12, the conference it left in 2011, rather than trust Kliavkoff to come up with a viable solution. It was well known within the industry that Colorado was heavily flirting with the Big 12 and the most likely of the Pac-12 schools to bail, prompting Pac-12 administrators to work hard to placate the school's leaders while preaching patience. When Colorado finally proved the Pac-12's worst fears true, it had a devastating effect.

Kliavkoff and his group were working on two primary options. A traditional linear rights deal broken into tiers, with ESPN on top, followed by NBC or Amazon, FOX, and CBS, in that order. The other tier was an all-streaming partnership with Apple. For recruiting and exposure reasons, landing a linear component was critically important for Pac-12 leaders, but there was now considerable skepticism Kliavkoff would deliver one.

The same day Colorado decided to U-turn back to the Big 12, Robbins received a call from Nike shoe god Phil Knight, the personal ATM machine for Oregon athletics and its powerful Division Street collective. Robbins wasn't surprised. He and Knight had spoken several times in the past. Knight had one doozy of a demand this time, insisting Kliavkoff needed to up the ante on the media rights even further into La-La Land.

"You guys really need to push George hard," Knight told Robbins. "Sixty-five is our number. Sixty-five. Sixty-five."

"With all due respect, Mr. Knight, there's no way we're getting to sixty-five," Robbins told him. "If we get a base of forty and we've got CFP money and the Rose Bowl and all the other, our basketball units, we'll get to fifty. We'll be all right."

"No," Knight said, "you've got to get sixty-five in the media deal."

In the same breath as he laid out these demands, Knight talked up the Apple deal and how Oregon was completely into it. Buying time, Robbins thought, in hopes of getting the lucrative Big Ten offer he craved.

On August 1, after taking negotiations right down to the wire, Kliavkoff delivered the bad news: There would be no linear partner as Colorado's departure ended all hopes of delivering the four-tier linear option with ESPN, FOX, NBC, and CBS. Leaving Apple as the lone suitor, with a less than thrilling offer: $23 million per school plus potential additional revenue based on subscriptions that could push the overall per-school payout to $30 million or more.

Kliavkoff pitched it as a compelling deal with significant upside as the industry moved more toward streaming. There was even hope there could be a linear component to the deal, the way Apple did with MLS and a weekly game on FOX. The Pac-12 presidents and chancellors didn't see it that way.

A hard $30 million was a number Bobby Robbins could accept (what choice did he have, really?), but $23 . . . that was hard to swallow. He did the math and figured the league would somehow have to convince at least three million households a year to pay a hundred dollars for an annual subscription, knowing full well the entire alumni base for the Pac-12, now that USC and UCLA were gone, was only about two million. Robbins later likened the need to drum up subscribers every year to "selling candy bars for Little League or Girl Scout cookies."

"If every one of them signed up, we still can't make this work," he said.

More Zoom and phone calls ensued, hundreds of them, he said, the final Zoom the night before the fateful morning of August 4. Eddy Cue, a senior vice president at Apple and direct report to CEO Tim Cook, was holding firm. Twenty-three was the number. Robbins and Washington president Ana Mari Cauce pushed, and eventually Cue ever so slightly relented, willing to go up to $25 million a school. With so much at stake, Robbins was not a fan of negotiating in a virtual world.

"You can't get a read on people," he said, "but I was looking into Ana Mari's eyes and listening to what she said and I just said [to myself] things are going south."

His gut impulse, Robbins said, was that Washington and Oregon were a package deal.

A chief concern for Washington, according to sources, was that head football coach Kalen DeBoer was not on board with a streaming-only option, feeling it would hurt recruiting and the Huskies' chances at competing at the national level. Jen Cohen, Washington's athletic director, believed accepting the Apple deal to stay in the Pac-12 would diminish the school's chances of keeping DeBoer in Seattle long term.

When Cue, who was gung ho to get the deal across the finish line, heard about DeBoer's concerns, he offered to clear his entire schedule that Thursday (August 3) and fly first to Eugene to meet with Oregon head coach Dan Lanning and then Seattle with DeBoer to alleviate any lingering concerns. Cue felt if he got face time with both, he'd be able to get them comfortable with what Apple's unique platform could do for their programs. Lanning and Oregon were willing to meet with the Apple senior vice president, but Washington ultimately declined the offer. It was a telltale sign that, despite her public posture to her fellow presidents and chancellors, Cauce didn't fully support the Apple deal amid rumors that Washington could soon bail for the Big Ten. Cue never made the trip.

In the past, for self-protection purposes, Robbins had held a series of informal conversations with the Big 12. This time, he took formal action, contacting the conference and asking specifically about the process for admission. Told all it took was an email requesting an application, he had a university lawyer send it in.

"We needed an insurance policy," Robbins said. "We wanted to apply just in case. I didn't want to be Washington State or Oregon State."

By 10:00 p.m. on the evening of August 3, self-interest had finally taken a backseat, a consensus forming that the only way to avert Armageddon was to stick together. At seven the next morning, Robbins later explained that the entire group had agreed to sign their Grant of Rights "in blood," damn the blowback from critics back home.

At 6:55 a.m. Robbins's phone rang. Oregon president John Karl Scholz, just a month into his tenure, was on the line. From the first words out of Scholz's mouth, Robbins knew what it was about.

"This is the hardest . . ."

"Stop. You're leaving, right?"

Yes, first Washington and then Oregon were out, official members of the Big Ten beginning with the 2024 football season. The Big Ten's existing members didn't want to dilute their revenue shares, creating a temporary hurdle, before FOX agreed to pay $30 million each, with the promise of $80 million or more a year down the line in the Big Ten's next media rights deal. "The natural expectation was that Cal and Stanford would be before Oregon and Washington to the Big Ten," Thompson said. "When it turned out the other way, it was an indication FOX was funding it and FOX went for the football brands."

Robbins immediately called Michael Crow, his longtime colleague and confidant at Arizona State, and told him to rush ASU's application in to the Big 12. "We need a Plan B," he told Crow. That same night the Big 12 board of directors voted unanimously to admit Arizona, Arizona State, and Utah, bringing the conference total to sixteen, not-so-innocent riders on a merry-go-round of realignment entirely out of control. The four remaining Pac-12 schools were suddenly in need of life preservers, Stanford and Cal finding theirs twenty-seven hundred miles away in, of all places, the ACC. Washington State and Oregon State were left dead in the water, and a revered conference in ruin in a matter of seventy-two hours, victims of a proxy war and, beyond a doubt, the most unrealistic of expectations.

"I don't think people completely comprehend what's happening here, not yet," said the high-ranking sports television executive. "I always say the beauty of college sports and college football in particular, you have regional confederations who through the game of football have acquired a national appeal yet, at their essence, were still regional. Their brands attached to that region. SEC is Southeast. Big 12 is Southwest. Big Ten is Midwest. Pac-12 is West Coast.

"The destruction of the Pac-12 blew that sky high. It destroyed all of these traditions almost overnight. All of that is gone, and it's stunning to me."

In wake of the demise, Oregon State and Washington State hired Oliver Luck, the former West Virginia athletic director and NCAA vice president, as a consultant to help guide them through what he described as a "series of unfortunate events," the treacherous path ahead. There weren't many, if any, good options available to the leftovers—an alliance with the Mountain West was the most likely—but Luck urged before doing anything that OSU and WSU do everything possible to keep the conference alive until the stroke of midnight on August 1, 2024, when all Pac-12 rights and property would revert to the two remaining schools. Luck saw great value in the Pac-12 brand, its history, archives, and most importantly its $30 million state-of-the-art studio in San Ramon, California. His advice: "Keep the conference open. There may be some money in it. The whole point is to buy time to figure out what the new iteration should and could look like."

• • •

SAFELY SHELTERED UNDER THE BIG 12 umbrella, Robbins and his AD, Dave Heeke, held a press conference in Tucson, Heeke doing his best to eulogize a dead body—"Great people, great rivalries, great colleagues." The decision, he said, was about the future, about stability both financially and competitively. Robbins added right off the bat how excited he was about the move.

What else could they say? Neither man used the word "survival," but as Robbins told parts of the backstory to the local media—the all-streaming part, the failed blood oath, Oregon and Washington's fatal one-two punch—nobody would have blamed him. Speaking of which, one reporter asked the appropriate question: Who was to blame? Was it the networks, the schools, or, simply, complete chaos consuming college sport?

Robbins took a deep breath before he answered. Anger, frustration, and some cold, hard truths spiced his words.

"That's a long, long conversation," he began. "We want to get into the whole media-industrial complex here? We want to open that up? If people want to start blaming people they're plenty of people to blame. You can make your own narrative. But I think, no question, that the media companies had a big influence on this.

"I would love to see the day when the university presidents and chancellors, we're pretty smart here, we're in control. I don't see that happening for a while. That would be the goal, right? We would be the ones engaging with the media companies to sell them something of value, other than getting whipsawed around, getting moved here. I'm hoping we're going to be part of the Big 12 for a long time, but we might be part of Mega Conference United next. So I don't think there's blame. I think everyone is doing what they think is in the best interest of their university."

Those who had to manage university presidents through the realignment process were deeply doubtful much would change. That the Big Ten accepted Washington and Oregon but told Stanford and Cal, two of the country's top universities and perfect fits in the conference's research consortium, to take a hike said it all.

"We're all academics. Every damn president talks about it like it's some Gold Card, like you really care about academics," a high-ranking Big Ten source said. "No, you don't. That's why the Big Ten didn't take Stanford, why they didn't take Berkeley, because you don't give a shit about academics; you literally only care about how much TV revenue is going to be there.

"The reason we added USC, UCLA is because it added more inventory and it gave more money to the institutions for their athletic departments. Can we make money or can we not make money? Oh, we can make money? Great. And that's it."

ESPN is now all snuggled in with the SEC and ACC, and to a lesser extent the Big 12. FOX has made its big bet with the Big Ten and the Big 12. CBS lost its SEC Game of the Week after twenty-eight years and is now in the Big Ten business. NBC also has a piece of that pie, though its major cash cow is still Notre Dame. The destruction of the Pac-12 dropped the power conference ranks to a Power 4, though the SEC and the Big Ten were the clear rulers of the sport, with schools nationwide eager to join their ranks, Florida State chief among them.

Deeply frustrated by the ACC's lagging TV revenue compared to the SEC and Big Ten, FSU had openly lobbed bombs at the conference's league office, setting up a potentially historic legal battle over the legitimacy of what boiled down to pieces of paper. Until Florida State filed suit, no school had tested the legal legitimacy of a conference's Grant of Rights, believed to be ironclad. (Clemson would later join the club in trying to legally fight its way out of the ACC, too.) The idea behind the GOR was that even if Florida State left, its TV rights would remain with the ACC, a move that would cost Florida State hundreds of millions in lost revenue. Florida State wanted to leave and take its TV rights with it. Where the Seminoles' case would go was unclear, though the desire to join a richer neighborhood was anything but.

There was a time when the ACC's annual TV payout of $39 million seemed like a dream—third best of any conference—but now it provoked righteous anger. The cause? As former president Theodore Roosevelt once said, "Comparison is the thief of joy." It's not that the money isn't extraordinary because it is, but still less than others, and that's enough to stoke anxiety and relocation desires. The need for that next dollar had slowly but surely eaten away at what was left of the soul of college sports.

CHAPTER 13

Trying Times

TUCKED INTO WHITE RIVER STATE Park on the edge of downtown Indianapolis, the headquarters of the National Collegiate Athletics Association spans approximately 300,000 square feet of glass-lined buildings, including the adjacent Hall of Champions museum. The newest four-story structure opened in 2012, a state-of-the-art facility holding a ballroom big enough to house the NCAA's entire staff of nearly five hundred people. The original four-story monolith had opened in 1999 after a fierce multicity competition resulted in the organization's move from Overland Park to Indianapolis. As one passed through that main entrance it was impossible to miss the messaging outlined alongside the right-hand wall.

> 90 Championships
> 500,000 Student-Athletes
> 1,100 Members
> 3 Divisions
> 1 Association

Standing there, aware of all of college athletics' challenges, one had to wonder if one association was enough.

• • •

ON THIS DAY INSIDE THE adjacent 35,000-square-foot Hall of Champions, the NCAA's enforcement group gathered for its final meeting of the year. About fifty investigators and support personnel were seated around circular tables in a second-floor conference room, another twenty or so additional staffers plugged in via video chat, a diverse mix of male and female, young and old, Black and white.

Standing before the group was Jon Duncan, the association's vice president of enforcement for going on ten years. If Duncan had been before an audience of athletic directors, coaches, conference commissioners, stakeholders, and others who crossed paths with enforcement, the mood would have been a little different. Words like "incapable," "incompetent" "arbitrary," "dictatorial," and "inflexible" are often used by these types to describe the monitoring group they feel has long outlived its usefulness as the sheriff in the Dodge City of revenue-generating sports.

Texas Christian University head football coach Sonny Dykes, who guided his program to the national championship game in January 2023, was among the critics.

"Let's not have a bunch of rules if they aren't going to be enforced," Dykes said. "All it does is cheapen the game and our profession, quite frankly. You better have someone to write tickets to enforce those rules, and right now, there's nobody doing that."

Duncan was trying to meet that demand. A lawyer by training, he started as the interim vice president of enforcement in March 2013 after spending the previous fifteen years working in private practice in Kansas City, consulting with the association on various working groups and task forces. His first task had been restoring the broken confidence from a calamitous investigation into the University of Miami football program that had cost his predecessor her job (more on this later).

"Dedicated, committed, passionate," Duncan answered when asked about the current state of enforcement. "I feel good about our role in protecting compliant programs. But maybe also frustrated if you want both sides of the coin, because there are things that slow us down, things that prevent us from getting the information we need."

The overriding mission, he maintained, was ferreting out misconduct and protecting the sanctity of college sports. He was uninterested, he said, in targeting a specific coach or school, unsavory or otherwise.

"I don't think like that," Duncan said. "We apply facts as we understand them to bylaws as we understand them. I'm kind of clinical like that. What I won't do is intentionally make an example of somebody to send a bigger message. But I'm absolutely mindful that members want to see activity in these kinds of cases."

Sitting in a first-floor conference room inside national headquarters, Duncan spoke about the elephant in the room—the mind-bending matrix known as name, image, and likeness.

The latest interim NIL policy had been issued six months earlier, a June 2023 guidance memo based on five questions routinely posed by membership. The answers boiled down to one no after another:

- Institutions may not use NIL transactions to compensate a student-athlete for athletics participation or achievement or as an improper inducement.
- Any entity closely aligned with an institution—such as a booster group—is subject to the same NIL scrutiny and must adhere to NCAA rules and policy.
- A booster or collection of boosters is not permitted to engage in recruiting activities, including recruiting conversations.
- NIL compensation may not be contingent upon enrollment at a particular school.
- Athletics department staff members are prohibited from representing enrolled student-athletes for NIL deals.

Day in and day out enforcement lived in that netherworld of no. Knowing full well there was a band of outlaws out there in the badlands playing in the gray; using NIL money as an inducement to sign or transfer; collectives doing the dirty work for the recruiting coordinator; paper trails as rare as Spanish gold doubloons; the beating heart of every enforcement case—people with firsthand knowledge of violations—reluctant to come forward for a whole host of reasons.

"Coaches have their reasons, student-athletes have their reasons, and the ADs have their reasons," said Duncan. "The coach, for example, may not have clean hands himself or herself. Or coaching is a small community and many of these coaches used to work together with somebody or may in the future work together with somebody. They don't want to get their friends in trouble or they don't want to be known as a rat. Snitches get stitches.

"For student-athletes, we could interview them, force them to provide materials. If they lie to us or they don't sit for an interview, then we're in the position of penalizing, significantly penalizing a student-athlete who didn't do anything wrong, necessarily, who just received an offer or an inducement or a contact outside of the portal. Didn't do a blessed thing wrong but then gets in trouble from us for not wanting to talk about it. They, too, don't want to be seen as a mole, a snitch, a tattletale, or a rat."

IN NOVEMBER 2010 THE NCAA'S newly elected president Mark Emmert had arrived in Indianapolis from the University of Washington with an agenda to show that cheaters would not profit. He found what he was looking for in the Nevin Shapiro case.

"It was a pivotal moment in a lot of ways," Emmert said. "I had come in, kind of guns blazing, trying to get a lot of things done early, using the assumption you've got more juice to get things done early rather than later.

"The blame I'll certainly take for the Shapiro case was I was pounding on the table to close some cases, to get some things done. I'm sure people felt the pressure. I created this environment where we've got to move."

In September 2011, Shapiro, then serving twenty-two years in prison for his role in a $930 million Ponzi scheme involving a fake grocery-distribution business, contacted the NCAA with a story straight out of *Lifestyles of the Rich and Famous*. In a series of jailhouse interviews he told investigators that between 2002 and 2010 he had personally provided hundreds of thousands of dollars in "extra benefits" to at least seventy-two University of Miami football players, paying cash for big hits against opposing teams, cover charges at nightclubs, entertainment at strip clubs, and champagne-soaked nights on his multimillion-dollar yacht with the knowledge or direct participation of more than a half dozen Hurricane coaches.

But, as so often happened, six months in, the investigation stalled out. People identified by Shapiro as involved in the scandal refused to cooperate or otherwise suddenly suffered from amnesia when confronted by investigators.

In an effort to appease Emmert, Ameen Najjar, the senior supervising investigator assigned to the Miami case, went rogue. When Shapiro's bankruptcy attorney suggested using that case as a means to leverage sworn testimony from at least a half dozen uncooperative witnesses in the Miami investigation, Najjar went all in—despite being told in no uncertain terms by the association's in-house counsel that the bankruptcy attorney could not take depositions on the association's behalf, as any information obtained would "be subject to significant scrutiny," and likely circumvented the NCAA's legal authority to compel people to testify.

It would take two more years—until August 2012—before the NCAA discovered Najjar's backdoor play. It arrived in the form of an invoice submitted by the bankruptcy attorney for $57,112 for billable hours between October 2011 and July 2012. By then the bankruptcy attorney had already taken depositions from two alleged eyewitnesses to Shapiro's payouts.

By the time the NCAA finally got to the bottom of the rot, Miami's president and boosters were screaming bloody murder. Emmert was forced to offer an unprecedented mea culpa in a conference call with the media.

"This is obviously a shocking affair," he told reporters. "It's stunning this has transpired."

The fallout could not have come at a worse time for enforcement. The damage proved incalculable, both inside and outside the office walls in Indy. Whatever trust between membership and the national office disappeared into darkness; enforcement morale bottomed out. Najjar was fired and the vice president of enforcement dismissed despite a review that determined she "never knowingly took any steps that were inconsistent with legal advice."

That's when Duncan stepped in.

In many ways he was the right man for the job—midwestern, courteous, steadfast, earnest, and principled to a fault. Those who have known Duncan for years speak of his quiet strength and tough-minded yet kind and considerate nature. His insistence is always on doing *the right thing* whatever that thing may be or how often the rules changed.

"The biggest upside [of the Miami case] is it led to Jon Duncan being in charge of enforcement," recalled Emmert. "Jon brought a very different approach, trying to bring a much more collaborative, cooperative approach to working with the schools."

These qualities were on full display as Duncan began the final staff meeting of 2023. He started with a series of shout-outs—anniversaries, birthdays, pats on the back—before beginning the year in review.

"It's been a trying year for a lot of us," he said, "but we're staying the course."

He admitted there were "more questions than answers" about the trial balloons floated in Charlie Baker's recent letter to student-athletes stressing the need to modernize college sports. Duncan stated how "refreshing" it was to have a president who was proactive and not reactive. Baker's letter, a NCAA spokesperson later said, had created more than one billion impressions on social media, 80 percent positive, "a unicorn kind of day" given the usual popularity of the NCAA.

As Duncan flashed a series of PowerPoint slides, he noted the staff had opened 91 cases during the year, closed 76, done more than 500 hours of interviews, talked to nearly 1,900 different people, and suspended 136 coaches for minor violations.

"Did we get better this year?" Duncan asked. "Personally, I do believe we got better, particularly in understanding and enforcing NIL. Although I don't think we can say with confidence that our members are safer than last year."

The coming year, he said, the staff would be spending more time focused on NIL in the face of "complicated, unnerving, and likely divisive" reforms. He stressed to those in the room and engaged on the video call the need to be strong and work together in an effort "to advance the interests of this department for the good of intercollegiate athletics."

If that charge sounded like a quixotic quest, that was fine and dandy to Duncan. Even if the job seemed impossible at times, balancing conflicting demands and misperceived public perceptions, Duncan said his conscience was clear believing his department could rest its head on a collective pillow knowing they did their best with the resources at hand.

"Even on a tough day," their leader said, "we're in a very special place."

• • •

DURING AN OPEN GIVE-AND-TAKE WITH staff that was part of the year in review, one senior investigator whose province was football said the name of the game was still recruiting. Three days later, that same investigator, afforded anonymity by the authors in order to speak freely, offered rare on-the-ground insight into the difficulty of policing the netherworld of NIL.

His most difficult task: determining whether the promise or delivery of NIL money was used an inducement for the players to sign with a particular school.

"The paper trails are not necessarily accessible," he said. "A lot of institutions will say we have nothing to do with this [NIL] agreement. The young man will say I'm bound by this nondisclosure agreement. And the third party [e.g., the collective] does not necessarily have to subject themselves to our process."

The investigator had been around long enough to have a clear picture of the going rates. For a high-end recruit, he said, the bonus to sign with a Power 4 school backed by a serious collective was around $150,000 up front and at least another $150,000 per year for impact players. NIL dollars for an official visit—a growing trend—tended to run anywhere from $5,000 to $20,000, depending on demand. For the cream of the crop, meaning five-star quarterbacks with huge upside potential, a million or more a year in NIL money was on the table. The deals were proffered by agents, financial advisers, parents, the high school coach, all of the above.

"It is wide open," said the investigator. "You have everyone from NFLPA-certified contract advisers to an individual the kids trust. It really comes down to this: who has access to and influence over the kid?"

It sounded like the "cesspool" of AAU summer-league basketball all over again.

"Exactly. We were kidding the other day. We have to have a grand opening saying we are now AAU basketball. We have arrived."

Some of the money might have looked like AAU money, but not when it came to one exclusive category—call it the Tiffany's of NIL. Say you had a proven starting quarterback from a Power 4 conference with one year of eligibility remaining. He was weighing the NFL draft against an open NIL market. Then take a deep, playoff-caliber team missing that one critical component desperate for a shot at a national championship. Multiplied by an equally hungry collective or, better yet, a secret booster network with money to burn that wanted to avoid public scrutiny.

"So what we're hearing for some of your top end quarterbacks is around the lower end, a million point five," the investigator said. "At the high end, depending if certain individuals return [to college] and because they're graduate students, it could be close to eight million."

Eight million dollars? For one year?

"For one year."

WHEN WALTER BYERS TOOK COMMAND of the NCAA in 1951, enforcement was little more than an afterthought. The advent of television and increased commercialization of college sport soon prioritized the need to police the membership—but only slightly. The staff was small and operated on a slim budget. Its work largely consisted of holding educational seminars and producing brochures to help athletic departments identify problems before they proliferated.

It wasn't until the early 1970s that enforcement made major headlines for its investigation of UNLV basketball coach Jerry Tarkanian. "Tark the Shark" had turned the Runnin' Rebels into the hottest show in town with a Gucci Row of casino moguls and, much to the NCAA's dismay, associates of a mob-controlled city supporting the team. Back-to-back twenty-nine-win seasons culminated with a trip to the 1977 Final Four. A year earlier, the NCAA had pressured UNLV to suspend Tarkanian for a variety of "questionable practices." In response, Tark sued the association, touching off a bitter legal battle that made it all the way to the Supreme Court. UNLV was eventually placed on two years' probation and banned from postseason play, setting the stage for a series of congressional hearings.

In February 1978, John E. Moss, chairman of the House Committee on Oversight and Investigation, opened one such hearing with a statement that seemed to summarize a growing antipathy toward enforcement.

I was approached by the gentlemen from Nevada, Mr. Santini, and fully seventy of our colleagues, who requested that we examine the NCAA's enforcement procedures. They were prompted by allegations of unfairness, arbitrariness, inequality, secrecy, and other abuses of excessive power which they and I felt deserved scrutiny in an official and public forum for the first time. For after all, this is a private organization, responsible to no one outside itself, with powers normally reserved to governments.

Over time, the organization's enforcement arm became more known for ineffectiveness than abuse of power. Never was that more evident than in a college basketball scandal that shook the sport in September 2017. In an operation FBI investigators dubbed "Ballerz," the federal government arrested ten individuals, including assistant coaches from Arizona, Auburn, Oklahoma State, and USC, for a pay-for-play scheme to funnel top players to certain schools and, later, to specific sports agencies.

At a much-ballyhooed press conference in New York, William Sweeney, the assistant director in charge of the FBI's field office, proudly proclaimed, "We have your playbook." Prosecutors in the case deemed it "arguably the biggest and most significant federal investigation and prosecution of corruption in college athletics."

More than six years later, though, little had changed. The five assistant coaches involved—all Black—were fired, and some went to prison. But some of the biggest names in the sport caught up in the scandal, including Kansas head coach Bill Self, received little more than a slap on the wrist. Even with the FBI's assistance, the NCAA was no match for what was the real playbook, which was: *Say nothing.*

"The shortcoming in the enforcement environment today and always has been enforcement doesn't have the power of subpoena or the weight of perjury," former Big 12 commissioner Bob Bowlsby said. "Everybody lawyers up. The coach lawyers up, the university lawyers up, you go through a long, protracted process, and you end up penalizing somebody with a slap on the fingers after spending millions for lawyers and millions for the run of the infractions process. If you can't defend yourself in the infractions process, you get hammered. If you can, more often than not, you walk."

Duncan was constantly speaking with athletic directors, conference commissioners, coaches, anyone and everyone, trying to impress upon them the importance of cooperating before adding a caveat: "If you can't help me there's nothing I can do for you. I'm tired of you, Mr. AD, or your coaches, or your student-athletes talking to the media about how bad enforcement is then refusing to cooperate with us. So if you want to be part of the solution, I'll take it. If not, shut up."

WADING INTO UNQUESTIONABLY MURKY WATERS, the NCAA had issued memo after memo offering NIL guidance or guardrails, knowing full well that without concrete proof of a payment or a concrete promise prior to signing, any such dictums were effectively meaningless.

"What's going to be substantial, in my opinion, to be that one case from the NCAA and the NCAA actually has teeth to investigate and enforce some of the guidelines they've issued because some of the guidelines are pretty simple," said Cody Gambler, Maryland's associate AD for compliance. "But until a coach, until an administrator, an AD, or someone of that caliber, sees the enforceability, until they see the negative impact of this, you'll have a lot of people assuming there's just no rules right now."

"I don't know why we're calling it NIL anymore," said Mike Aresco, the American Athletic Conference commissioner who announced his retirement in December 2023. "It's pay-to-play. It's pay-to-recruit. It's pay-to-retain."

In October 2022, acting upon a recommendation from the NIL Working Group, the powerful Division I board of directors voted unanimously to further clarify and tighten "interim" NIL guidelines. The board essentially said, "You want rules? Well, here's one": It approved a proposal that said the enforcement staff and Committee on Infractions "will presume a violation occurred" unless the school "clearly demonstrates the behaviors in question were in line with existing NCAA rules."

Loose translation: Guilty until *you* prove yourself innocent.

Under the proposal—approved as a bylaw at the NCAA's annual convention three months later—investigators would no longer be hamstrung with uncooperative witnesses and could use circumstantial evidence to presume a school violated the rules.

"If it looks like a duck and quacks like a duck, it's a duck," Duncan told a crowd of administrators at the 2023 convention in San Antonio. "Instead of putting the burden on the enforcement staff to always come up with a smoking gun, which we don't always have, there is a presumption. It puts the presumption on the school. It's a really powerful tool."

In an NCAA conference room, Duncan stressed the need to consider what the offended school is alleging against a flood of denials pouring in from the other side, no documented proof in sight.

"The kid lies to us. The dad lies to us. The agent lies to us. The uncle lies to us. The coach who told him [to enter the portal] is going to lie to us," Duncan said. "All the third parties involved are going to lie to us. None of them have a phone with any record on it. The only people willing to cooperate with us are the losing school and they don't have any proof. All they knew is the kid was here and now he's there."

In that case, said Duncan, there is no case.

"Everybody wants instant justice, complete transparency, and draconian penalties when it's somebody else," he said. "'Go get them. They're cheating.' They don't necessarily feel that same way when it's their own school."

As difficult as it was to prove, Duncan said a third party striking a deal with a player before he or she signed with a school would be treated more aggressively than ever. And despite the absence of announced penalties at that time, Duncan said enforcement had opened investigations; some had been closed without penalties while others remained active.

Still, without any major NIL-related investigations, there was skepticism that enforcement would actually do anything without cops on the highway to slow down programs speeding faster and faster in pursuit of football glory. That finally changed on the Thursday of the 2024 NCAA convention in Phoenix, when word leaked out of the first fully completed and resolved NIL case. The penalties, stiffer than anyone imagined, sent a strong message to college football: You might have thought we disappeared, but we were just biding our time.

In the most serious NIL-related penalties yet, Florida State was fined 1 percent (nearly $1.7 million) of its athletic department budget, forced to disassociate from a collective, and offensive coordinator Alex Atkins was suspended three games and given a two-year show-cause penalty. The penalties, a result of a negotiated resolution between the school and the NCAA, derived from an alleged meeting between Rising Spear, an FSU-tied NIL collective, and a recruit. In that meeting, which Atkins allegedly drove the prospect to, the collective offered the player $180,000 his first year to enroll at Florida State.

In some corners of the college sports world, the penalties provoked criticism, highlighting the challenge Duncan and his team faced. They got yelled at for doing nothing and they got yelled at for doing something. The hope within the NCAA was that the Florida State case would slow the speeders down for at least a few miles. The enforcement team knew it had to keep pushing cases to set some boundaries. Which is exactly what they did.

Eight days after the Florida State case, it was publicly revealed that enforcement was investigating the University of Florida for possible violations in the recruitment of a high school quarterback named Jaden Rashada. Two days later, the NCAA poked the proverbial bear, notifying the University of Tennessee it was investigating its NIL collective for "pay-for-play" inducements.

In our December 2023 interview, Duncan had presaged the moment. With various state laws allowing a patchwork of NIL-related rules, it was only a matter of time before some states rose up in an effort to supersede NCAA bylaws. Until that time, Duncan's team had to operate under the rules adopted by member schools—state laws be damned.

"Well, somebody's going to have to sue us or we're going to sue somebody," Duncan told us. "We just can't have states saying you can't do enforcement here."

But, oh, they would say that.

After receiving notice of an investigative inquiry, the University of Tennessee readied for war. The school had previously cooperated with the NCAA in its investigation into Jeremy Pruitt's football program, which included allegedly paying players' parents using money stashed in Chick-fil-A bags. There was self-interest in the cooperation, though: Tennessee would get out of paying Pruitt's nearly $13 million buyout if it fired him for cause, which it later did.

It was different this time around. Tennessee fans liked third-year head coach Josh Heupel, and the program seemed to be in a good place. A little more than a year earlier, Heupel and the Volunteers beat Alabama for the first time in fifteen years. The win led to an immediate spike in undergraduate applications. There was a ton of money to be made in Tennessee football. The school couldn't afford to get hammered by the NCAA again, not with the Vols finally rolling. In an email response to the inquiry, Donde Plowman, the University of Tennessee chancellor, tore into NCAA president Charlie Baker.

"Two and a half years of vague and contradictory NCAA memos, emails and 'guidance' about name, image and likeness (NIL) has created extraordinary chaos that student-athletes and institutions are struggling to navigate," she wrote. "In short, the NCAA is failing."

Emmert, who knew Plowman well, wasn't surprised by her strategy, this time around aimed at his successor. "She has been, in many cases, extremely supportive and cooperative," he said. "She's a very good person, with good values, but she's got this fan base out there. They want the kid to play no matter what, they want the coach to coach no matter what. They assume the NCAA are these bad guys who make up the rules."

Spyre Sports, the Tennessee-related collective at the heart of the matter, enlisted the help of Jim Harbaugh's attorney Tom Mars, who took to X to accuse the NCAA of "new heights of absurdity." Tennessee attorney general Jonathan Skrmetti teamed up with Virginia attorney general Jason Miyares and filed a blistering federal antitrust lawsuit that resulted in a preliminary injunction granted by U.S. District Judge Clifton L. Corker. In his ruling Judge Corker wrote, "It is hereby ordered that, effective immediately, Defendant NCAA; its servants, agents, and employees . . . are restrained and enjoined from enforcing the NCAA Interim NIL Policy" and the bylaw applied to inducements. A week later the NCAA's Division I board of directors instructed its enforcement staff to pause investigations into third-party participation into NIL-related activities.

"I agree with this decision, while the progress toward long-term solutions is under way and while we await discussions with the attorney general,"

Baker said in a letter. "In circumstances that are less than ideal, this at least gives membership notice of the board's direction related to enforcement."

The combination of Corker's decision and the NCAA's subsequent pause on investigations allowed collectives to finally speak more openly without fear of penalty. Collective leaders believed it was absurd they couldn't have honest conversations with players about NIL compensation during the recruiting process and believed the lack of clarity actually led to more bad decisions. The argument was, essentially, why deprive recruits of a critical piece of information and then act surprised when things didn't work out and that player subsequently hopped in the portal?

"I think the temporary restraining order in that case was the turning point," said Russell White, the president of the Collectives Association (TCA). "Before that, it was a lot of 'everyone knows what's happening, but we're not going to say it.' Even in meetings with athletic departments, collectives were sitting with coaching staffs deciding tiered systems, who makes what based off position or what was important to them.

"They'd always say the coaches make suggestions. You literally get a list sent over sometimes to pay this kid this much. Prior to that, people were still being very quiet about it."

The Tennessee case represented a watershed moment, celebrated by one side and likened by the other to an asteroid crashing into the NCAA rule book.

"I think this will be one more brick in the wall that is the end of the NCAA," said attorney Tom Mars, who represented Spyre Sports in the case.

If the courts eventually decided in Tennessee's favor, the Duncan group could basically pack up shop, take a nice long walk around White River State Park, and not bother to return to the office.

CHAPTER 14

Michigan Man II

T HE FIRST TIME JIM HARBAUGH spoke with NCAA investigators about impermissible recruiting contact he did so without counsel. By the time Michigan submitted a ten-page memorandum, double-spaced, in 11-point font, as to why neither the school nor its coaches should face serious charges, Tom Mars was at his side negotiating with the association.

"We had some conversations," Mars said in a September 2023 interview. "We worked out an agreement in principle that would not have been of any significance whatsoever."

That sentiment changed in June 2022. That's when the NCAA notified the university and Mars it had come into possession of some new information and wanted to interview Harbaugh again. With Mars in attendance, the two senior investigators assigned to the case, a male and a female, asked some general questions about whether Harbaugh remembered meeting with a couple of prospects and their parents in Ann Arbor on two occasions during a "dead period," when no contact was allowed. Based on past experiences with the NCAA, Mars's internal Geiger counter began to tick.

They don't ask these kinds of questions unless they have some credible reason to believe you were there, he told Harbaugh.

"Well," Harbaugh said, "I would remember that, but I don't."

On October 4, 2022, the investigators were back for yet another video interview, eighteen months after the purported meeting. Mars, on high alert now, cautioned Harbaugh to be nothing but honest. *If you don't remember, say you don't remember. If you do remember, say you do remember and answer their questions.*

This time when the investigators came calling, they had specifics: Benny's, the famous Ann Arbor diner, on such and such a Saturday in February; Benny's diner, on this or that Saturday in March. A thirty-four-page transcript of the interview showed Harbaugh never wavered. *I don't remember any of those meetings.* One investigator, attempting to trip Harbaugh up, spun what Mars later termed a "word salad" question he was forced to interpret.

"She's asking if you're lying," said Mars.

"No, I'm not lying," replied Harbaugh.

Lacking subpoena power, NCAA investigators are forced to use other tactics—teasing out information or evidence, withholding it, holding the possible loss of eligibility over a player's head, threatening a coaching suspension, playing cat and mouse.

"If you were in a civil case, taking a deposition, they would show you something, let's see if this helps your recollection. They didn't do that," said Mars.

Funny thing was, as Mars discovered, the investigators had done essentially that on the same case with Grant Newsome, a U of M graduate assistant. In a July 13, 2022, interview with investigators, Newsome had twice denied any knowledge of being at a dinner meeting at the Brown Jug, a campus pub, in February 2021 with a prospect and his father during the forbidden pandemic dead period.

"No, I don't—I don't recall that," Newsome told investigators.

In response, an investigator refreshed Newsome's memory with a veiled threat:

Okay, Coach—so we've had multiple interviews where it's been reported that you were at that dinner and there are expense reports—for that weekend for the [prospect and his father] being in town. So I need you to think very seriously about whether maybe you recall that dinner because we have very specific information from multiple individuals about your presence occurring at that dinner. So I don't know if you want to take a minute to think about that or you feel very secure in that answer that it didn't happen.

At that point, according to a transcript, Newsome abruptly ended the interview saying maybe he should retain "personal counsel." Twelve days later Newsome returned with a lawyer to say, yes, he had a "vague" recollection of having met at the Brown Jug with the prospect and his dad. Despite his attempts to mislead an investigator, Newsome later received little more than a slap on the wrist from the Committee on Infractions. (When Mars asked why Newsome basically walked away scot-free, Mars said he was told such decisions were at the discretion of enforcement in terms of what or who to charge.)

Hoping to break a logjam, Mars asked one of the investigators if they would provide evidence similar to what they presented Newsome. A small mountain of material—receipts, telephone records, an eyewitness account of Harbaugh and his daughter coming into Benny's for takeout, chatting with a prospect and his father—soon landed in Mars's lap, hundreds of pages of transcripts he condensed and sent to Harbaugh. The smoking gun, ah, bun, as it were, a breakfast receipt from Benny's noting the purchase of, of all things, a cheeseburger.

"When I showed Jim the receipt," Mars recalled, he said, 'I guess I was there. You know anybody else that has hamburgers for breakfast? That's what I order for breakfast. It's obvious I was there. You can tell them I was there. I still don't remember anything about being there.'"

Admission in hand, Mars went to work on a settlement, in NCAA-speak, a "negotiated resolution," otherwise known as a NR. "You're talking about a guy fifty-nine years old," Mars told the investigators. "Been bumped in the head a lot. You're asking him to remember something that happened eighteen months ago. He meets hundreds of prospects a year. How do you know he's lying, given the fact he promptly acknowledged he was there?"

The negotiations went on for months. Enforcement insisted Harbaugh admit he lied or was deceptive during interviews. In a video conference call with Duncan and his team on January 18, Mars had drawn an indelible line against any such admission. As Mars recalled, this was his response: "We'll never agree to any NR that involves Jim Harbaugh saying he lied to anybody, he was deceptive, that he intended to mislead anybody. If that's a requirement of the staff, as I'm hearing you suggest it is, then we have nothing to talk about."

The next day Yahoo Sports national columnist Dan Wetzel wrote a story that said negotiations had "broken down" over Harbaugh's refusal to admit he lied to investigators. The word "impasse" was used in the headline, which accurately described the current state of the talks. But Jon Duncan and his staff didn't much cotton to reading the news in a national story written by a columnist with ties to Mars.

Duncan dashed off an email to Mars saying such leaks were totally unacceptable, and in response, the NCAA was going to make a sweeping request for his phone records.

In an attempt to cool the waters, Mars sent Duncan and his team a text he had received from Wetzel two and a half hours before the story was posted basically informing Mars the story was running.

"Dan didn't ask for comment," Mars said. "I think he was just trying to make sure he wasn't off base. I was actually on a long phone call so I really didn't have much time or interest in texting Dan about it."

Duncan wasn't buying it. Enforcement wanted images of Mars's cell phone records. At which point Mars said he went into a version of Dean Smith's famous "Four Corners" offense, slowing things down, circling back from time to time with language in which Harbaugh would admit he didn't remember the dead-period Benny's meetings until his memory was refreshed, searching for legal language that would satisfy both sides.

"It was like dancing on the head of a pin," said Mars. "The minutiae involved in the discussions were unlike anything I'd ever seen. Spending months asking ourselves are we going to blow this deal up over whether we use this word or that word?"

Finally, after six torturous months, in July 2023 a negotiated resolution between Michigan, the NCAA, and Jim Harbaugh was submitted to the Committee on Infractions. In it, Harbaugh would serve a four-game suspension to start the upcoming season. Case closed, or so Mars, the university, and enforcement thought. Until Ross Dellenger of Yahoo Sports, as wired in as any college football writer in the country, reported that the Committee on Infractions had rejected the resolution as too lenient, and it was later discovered, "not in the best interest in the Association." The COI claimed Harbaugh "was not truthful" during the investigation.

Dellenger's story set off an entirely new round of fireworks in Indy. The enforcement staff was livid over yet another leak, suspecting Mars had once again been the source. Back came a demand for cell phone and text records.

That's when things got ugly.

"I got so bowed up and pissed off about it, I wrote them a letter and basically said I'm not going to give you that information," Mars said. "And if you push me, you take any more action that might [affect] Coach Harbaugh, I'll sue you for tortious interference in Benton County, Arkansas. It got very personal and they backed off."

Two weeks later, as the subsequent Harbaugh cheeseburger backlash spilled out publicly on the pages of Yahoo, ESPN, and *Sports Illustrated*, the NCAA decided to play a trump card: a statement from its vice president of hearing operations.

"The Michigan infractions case is related to impermissible on and off-campus recruiting during the COVID-19 dead period, not a cheeseburger," the statement from Derrick Crawford began. "It is not uncommon for the COI to seek clarification on key facts prior to accepting. The COI may also reject a NR if it determines that the agreement is not in the best interests of the Association or the penalties are not reasonable."

Mars was livid and not just about the spigot of leaks. In a post on the social media platform X he wrote: "Pursuant to the NCAA's internal operating procedures, and under threat of penalties, Michigan, the involved coaches and their lawyers are prohibited from uttering a word about this ongoing case. Yet the NCAA can issue a public statement putting its spin on the case? Unreal."

This dispute eventually led to the question: Do you believe Enforcement is attempting to make an example of Harbaugh?

"I do. I really do. I do," Mars replied. "There's really no other explanation for the disparity between [Harbaugh and] Grant Newsome."

In a subsequent letter to the NCAA, Mars said he took pains to point out that exact disparity—only to get a response that he said read pretty much like this: "We think there are circumstances that support our decision. Go pound sand."

(The NCAA would later deny any attempt to single out Harbaugh or send a larger message. "It's just not what moves us," said a high-ranking official.)

• • •

AS IF THE NCAA NEEDED any more ammunition against Harbaugh, he decided to launch another rocket in its direction at Big Ten Media Days. Without prompting, he delivered an impassioned speech in favor of paying players, this at the very time the association was lobbying Congress for a limited antitrust exemption that would prevent players being classified as employees.

Then, in a press conference prior to the season opener against East Carolina, Harbaugh was back on his soapbox offering a six-minute soliloquy on the state of college football.

"I don't understand how the NCAA, TV networks, conferences, and schools can continue to pull in millions off the efforts of college students across the country without sharing ever-increasing revenue," he said. "We have to try to make it better, and right now the current status quo is unacceptable and won't survive."

In the wake of the news that the Committee on Infractions had nixed a deal, attention turned to Michigan athletic director Warde Manuel. What would he do? In an earlier meeting in Manuel's office, Harbaugh had owned the entire "impermissible" episode—telling his AD he should have known about coaches watching player workouts on Zoom, analysts coaching on the field, the breakfast and dinner meetings—while holding the line on one thing: he had never lied.

Manuel later said after the COI sent the negotiated resolution back that he had conversations with both in-house and outside counsel on how to move forward. "We had agreed the violations occurred—head coach, [graduate] assistant coach—what would we put forward?" he said. "The recommendation was to suspend Jim for three games. That's where I said okay."

WITH HARBAUGH WATCHING FROM HOME, the Wolverines blasted outmanned East Carolina 30-3. More importantly, they sent a direct message to the NCAA. Before the game they had stepped off the team bus at the Big House in T-shirts bearing their head coach's last name and familiar number 4, Harbaugh's old number. Quarterback J.J. McCarthy, the unquestioned star and spokesman of the team, added the word "FREE" in marker on white tape above the word "HARBAUGH." Then, on their first play from scrimmage, Michigan's offense huddle broke in single file—eleven hands extending four fingers to the sky.

ON ANY GIVEN DAY, NCAA Enforcement receives tips from whistleblowers in all shapes and sizes: current or former coaches and players, scouts, administrators, angry ex-wives, the media, bloggers, and meathead bullshit artists claiming wrongdoing at ol' State U. With each and every tip cataloged by a member of its development team for real-time access, the investigative staff focused on corroboration and that knotty problem called . . . proof.

In mid-October 2023, an "independent third party" traveled to the national office in Indianapolis to present what NCAA president Charlie Baker later called "very comprehensive" evidence of impermissible activity under Harbaugh's watch. Baker later told a select group of reporters at the NCAA convention in January 2024 that the evidence provided was so compelling as to require immediate action. So it was late on the afternoon on October 18, within days of the presentation to the NCAA, that both the Big Ten and Michigan were notified the association was "investigating allegations of sign-stealing by the University of Michigan football program."

"We had to make a decision at that point," Baker said later. "Because it was the kind of thing that had consequences for the outcome of games, we made the unusual decision to simultaneously call the Big Ten and Michigan and tell them about this."

At 12:17 p.m. Eastern time the next day Yahoo Sports published a story by Dellenger and Wetzel that tapped into what had become a gushing faucet of leaks, reporting that the NCAA was investigating the Michigan football program for alleged sign-stealing, a violation of Bylaw 11.6.1., which reads, "Off-campus, in-person scouting of future opponents [in the same season] is prohibited."

Observing and attempting to decipher an opponent's offensive and defensive signs communicated by personnel on the field during or after a game by coaches and analysts had long been as much a part of the sport as pigskin. Scouting opponents in person, however, had been prohibited since 1994, in what was originally a cost-cutting measure.

In what was quickly looking like a well-orchestrated campaign to put Harbaugh out to pasture, ESPN's Pete Thamel and Mark Schlabach, citing sources, dropped a bomb at 12:47 a.m. the following day. They identified the low-level Michigan staffer with a military background at the center of what the NCAA called "a vast off campus, in person advance scouting scheme involving a network of individuals."

The man in the middle: a twenty-eight-year-old with the comic book character name of Connor Stalions.

Stalions, who was immediately suspended with pay following the Yahoo report, was a 2017 graduate of the U.S. Naval Academy, where he worked as a student-assistant in the football program, gaining a reputation as a super-fan, "obsessed" with Michigan football. He attended U of M games when the Midshipmen were on the road, deciphered opponent's signals from TV footage—not illegal—and constantly worked on his "Michigan Manifesto," a nearly six-hundred-page Google document, part of his long-term plan to one day run Michigan football.

A retired captain in the Marine Corps, Stalions had parlayed his Navy connection with Michigan's then director of player personnel Sean Magee and linebackers coach Chris Partridge into a position as an unpaid volunteer, before being hired in May 2022 as a recruiting analyst at a salary of $55,000 a year. (Stalions was also accused of running a side business from the front porch of his home restoring old vacuum cleaners and selling an unusual amount of refurbished goods on Amazon, according to a Homeowners' Association lawsuit. Stalions disputed the charges.)

Over time Stalions reportedly set up an elaborate scouting system, paying as many as sixty-five friends and associates through his personal Venmo account to travel to more than thirty games and using their smartphones to record sideline play-calling signals of future Michigan opponents. Stalions reportedly also went so far as to dress in disguise—sunglasses, a Central Michigan polo and hat, complete with a visitor's bench pass—to attend Michigan State's home opener against the Chippewas.

As detailed in *Sports Illustrated*, in January and February 2021 Stalions was said to have exchanged a lengthy series of texts with a student at a Power 5 school trying to break into big-time college football. In these texts, Stalions outlined his grand vision along two tracks—the long-term Michigan Manifesto plus short-term "products" that he believed altered head coaches' thinking.

You can't ask them what they need, he reportedly texted the Power 5 student. You have to tell them what they need. But it can't be up for interpretation. It has to be very straightforward, unique and useful. If not one of those three things, it's pointless.

TOM MARS WAS NOT ABOUT to shut up. On October 21, two days after Harbaugh issued a statement stating he and his staff would fully cooperate in the sign-stealing investigation and disavowed knowledge of any wrongdoing, Mars took to X to argue that "head coaches are presumed guilty the minute the NCAA leaks information about the investigation, which then prohibits coaches from defending themselves in the court of public opinion. What's fair about that?"

One answer arrived five days later in a two-page "Letter of Reprimand" from Committee on Infractions chairman Dave Roberts. In short, shut up. Or else.

"Dear Mr. Mars," it began, "this is a letter of admonition addressing recent comments made by you on social media platforms, directly or implicitly concerning the University of Michigan and your client." The letter went on to say if Mars didn't zip his lip regarding comments "unhelpful to the process and frankly inappropriate under NCAA bylaws," there would be consequences, including "potential penalties for you and your client . . . including the immediate suspension of your client."

"Fuck you, Dave Roberts, is what I should have said," Mars said. "There's no NCAA bylaw that would punish me or Jim."

The closest thing the Big Ten had in terms of ticketing a scheme one high-ranking NCAA official later likened to "going 110 miles an hour when everyone else is going 75 or 80" was a sportsmanship and integrity policy containing two distinct categories of disciplinary action. A so-called standard action fell under the powers of the commissioner and included "admonishment, reprimand, fines that do not exceed $10,000 and suspensions for no more than two contests." Major punishments required approval of the conference's Joint Group Executive Committee composed of university chancellors and presidents. Either way, a very hot potato was now in the hands of first-year Big Ten commissioner Tony Petitti.

A former high-ranking CBS Sports and Major League Baseball executive Petitti was a Harvard-trained lawyer and longtime consigliere to CBS Sports chairman Sean McManus and Major League Baseball commissioner Rob Manfred. Just eight months earlier he had been hired to replace Kevin Warren, who had hastily departed to run the Chicago Bears.

As Petitti was getting up to speed, Harbaugh issued a statement saying he and his staff would fully cooperate in the matter, declaring he had no knowledge of his program illegally stealing signals nor had he directed any staff member or others to participate in off-campus scouting assignments.

None of which satisfied a legion of full-throated high-profile television critics, led by ESPN's Stephen A. Smith, Christopher "Mad Dog" Russo, and Paul Finebaum, each of them calling for Harbaugh's head. With the outside criticism hitting a fever pitch, Harbaugh told his team to embrace the hate. "I've always been a good man, a good guy," Harbaugh said, according to those present, "but right now we're being painted as the bad guy, so why don't we just be the bad guy?"

On his weekly radio show prior to Purdue's November 4 game in Ann Arbor, Boilermakers' head coach Ryan Walters wasted no time piling on. "What's crazy is these aren't allegations," he said. "It happened. There's video evidence. There [are] ticket purchases and sales that you can track back. We know for a fact that they were at a number of our games."

By now the sign-stealing controversy had officially captivated college football. In an effort to calm the growing storm during the first two days of November, Petitti held a series of conference calls updating Big Ten coaches and ADs.

"There were a bunch of people upset," said Maryland head coach Mike Locksley. "I was part of the calls and there were a bunch of people upset. But I always say I'm going to worry about my own shit."

Locksley's Maryland program got indirectly pulled into the scandal because the program's offensive coordinator, Josh Gattis, was Michigan's offensive coordinator in 2021. Locksley said he confronted Gattis and directly asked him, "Were y'all doing this?" He didn't obsess over the specifics like some of his peers—when he looked back on previous losses to Michigan, he was much more upset about mistakes his team made than anything untoward happening—but he understood why other coaches were angry.

"It hurt the integrity of the game," he said. "It made everybody go back and question."

U of M president Santa Ono immediately responded with a letter supporting Harbaugh, urging fairness in any investigation, and warning that taking any action before "any meaningful investigation" would violate conference rules.

"The best course of action, the one far more likely to ascertain the facts, is to await the results of the NCAA investigation," Ono wrote Petitti, adding, "but if you refuse to let the NCAA investigative process play out, the Big 10 may not take any action against the University or its players or coaches without commencing its own investigation and offering us the opportunity to provide our position. That is not just required by conference rules; it's a matter of basic fairness.

"To be clear, oral updates from NCAA enforcement staff do not and cannot constitute evidence, nor do we think the NCAA would ever intend for an oral update to be given that meaning or weight."

In words and action Michigan was moving into battle stations, influential alums texting Ono, begging for war. Said one Ono adviser to another in a text, Those fuckers. They haven't seen a fight like this one now with Ono on board. Past UM Presidents all made the base feel ashamed. No more.

To absolutely no one's surprise, on Friday, November 3, Connor Stalions resigned. A statement from his attorney distanced the football program from any wrongdoing. "Connor also wants to make clear that, to his knowledge, neither Coach Harbaugh, nor any other coach or staff member, told anyone to break any rules or were aware of improper conduct regarding the recent allegations of advanced scouting."

The same day Stalions resigned, Ono was set to meet in Ann Arbor with Petitti. He was wondering how to respond if the commissioner decided to heed the roar from the opposing crowd and unilaterally suspend his head coach.

Conspiracy theorists were meanwhile having a field "Day," as in Ryan Day, speculating that the head coach at archrival Ohio State might somehow be involved. But that message board patter proved a red herring. When Michigan started searching, we were told, the third-party trail eventually led much closer to home—the most logical leaker being someone having legitimate access to the kind of "very comprehensive" evidence presented to the Enforcement staff, meaning likely a former football staffer or assistant coach with a grudge to bear.

As Big Ten coaches and officials pushed for a season-long sign-stealing suspension, advisers to Ono suggested he enlist former interim athletic director Jim Hackett, known for his unique ability to budge Harbaugh's "iron will." Turns out, Hackett had planned on asking Harbaugh to consider a compromise two-game suspension—Penn State and Maryland—if the Big Ten and NCAA would agree to drop any further investigation.

So it was at the end of a torturous week prior to the home game against Purdue that Ono made the point of seeking out Hackett and giving him a very public hug at a pregame tailgate. On Monday, Hackett said he woke up to a text from Ono asking Hackett to give him a call. Ono asked Hackett if he would engage with the school's vice president of communications. Later that day, Hackett and the VP spoke on the phone for the better part of two hours.

By now things were getting weird on multiple fronts. How weird? The Associated Press reported a former employee at a rival Big Ten football program said it had been his job to steal signs, adding he had recently shared those documents—which showed the Wolverines signs and corresponding plays, as well as screenshots of text-message exchanges with staffers of other Big Ten schools—with Michigan in an effort to help Harbaugh and his embattled program. This was followed by a bit of news revealing that staff members at Ohio State and Rutgers had shared information with Purdue prior to its Big Ten title game against Michigan in 2022.

By Thursday, November 9, the legal tide appeared to be turning in Michigan's favor. University attorneys were making powerful arguments against suspension, charging any action would be a "breach" of the Big Ten rule book and exceed Petitti's power under the Sportsmanship Policy.

Friday was Veterans Day, the day before an away game at Penn State.

Media speculation had reached a fever pitch. Reports were ranging from a three-game suspension to a $10,000 fine and public reprimand, but Mars put a pin in those trial balloons when he issued a statement that he was "confident Jim will be on the team flight to PA this afternoon one way or the other," adding, "we're prepared for every scenario."

But perhaps not *this* scenario: around 3:30 p.m., twenty hours before the PSU game, Harbaugh seemingly safe on the team plane to Happy Valley, ESPN's Thamel dropped another bomb. He reported that the Big Ten would prohibit Harbaugh from being on the sidelines during the final three regular-season games but would allow him to coach and attend team activities during the week. Within minutes of Thamel's story on ESPN, Petitti released a thirteen-page letter outlining evidence that the sign-stealing "scheme" was not isolated or haphazard in nature but rather "pervasive, systemic" to the degree it "compromised the integrity of the competition and violates one of the most fundamental elements of sportsmanship."

Petitti also noted that Michigan's November 8 response did not deny the "impermissible scheme occurred" but instead offered what it called "procedural and technical arguments designed to delay accountability." Petitti's letter contained this caveat: it was a sanction of Michigan, not Jim Harbaugh, who the conference said it had no proof was aware of the scheme, noting, however, that Michigan was the university that Harbaugh "embodies." In effect, guilt by association.

Michigan immediately punched back. In its own statement, the university argued Petitti's "hasty" action "violated basic tenets of due process, and sets an untenable precedent of assessing penalties" before an investigation has proven anyone guilty. In essence, the Big Ten was saying you're guilty when we say you're guilty, damn that thing called due process. The statement included a shot at the conference for issuing the sanctions on Veterans Day—a court holiday—thwarting the university's ability to get immediate injunctive relief. It was clear that Michigan intended to seek a court order preventing any disciplinary action from taking effect.

With Harbaugh cooling his heels in a State College hotel, lawyers representing the Board of Regents and James J. Harbaugh had filed a lawsuit seeking a temporary restraining order in Circuit Court in Washtenaw

County, home of Ann Arbor, pointing out, among other issues, the lack of due process and "irreparable harm" done to Harbaugh's character and reputation.

You could almost feel the balance tilting—thirteen current Big Ten schools on one side, the vaunted University of Michigan holding firm on the other, and athletic director Manuel releasing a statement denigrating the investigation and fully supporting Harbaugh. He all but sneered at rival head coaches and ADs calling for Harbaugh's head, saying they should be worried about the new standard of judgment that had been unleashed on the conference.

In something of a surprise, two hours before kickoff on Saturday, a local Circuit Court judge with ties to the university declined to issue a temporary restraining order and instead set a court hearing the following Friday at 9:00 a.m., leaving Harbaugh back at the hotel while his Wolverines faced a packed house of more than 106,000 opposing fans wearing white and shaking pom-poms like their lives depended on it.

So what did the Wolverines do under the interim head coach, offensive coordinator Sherrone Moore, in such a hostile environment? How about throttle the home team, 24–15, a picture-perfect tribute to their old school coach, punctuated by twenty-six carries for 145 yards and two touchdowns from star running back Blake Corum. Behind a ferocious offensive line they finished off the Nittany Lions with thirty-two straight runs and not a single forward pass after 7:41 of the second quarter.

In an emotional postgame interview with FOX Sports Jenny Taft, a tearful Moore left no doubt about his feelings.

"I want to thank the Lord. I want to thank coach Harbaugh. I fucking love you, man. I love the shit out of you, man. This is for you. For this university, the president, the AD. We got the best players, the best university, the best alumni in the country. Love you guys."

Moore then turned and put his arm around Corum, standing just off-camera, and brought him in for a huge hug. "This fucking guy right here. These guys did it. These guys did it." And then he walked away.

"We did it for Coach Harbaugh," said Corum, his nose and face a bloodied badge of honor.

At a conference on Monday, Harbaugh sounded raspy but insisted he was not sick. Waxing poetic about his "iron wall that viruses bash against and shatter," the respect he had come to have for chickens, which back in 2018 he'd said he refused to eat because they were a "nervous bird" but was now raising in his backyard.

"I was dead wrong," Harbaugh said. "I stand corrected. These chickens are low maintenance and high production."

Dispensing with the chicken salute he offered one to his team.

"They've got to be America's team, just got to be America's team," he said. "America loves, loves a team that beats the odds, beats the adversity, overcomes what the naysayers, critics, so-called experts think. That's my favorite kind of team. Yeah, watching from that view on television, finally people get to see what I see every day from the players and coaches. The perseverance, just the stalwartness of these guys."

A collective will undoubtedly tested that week when the NCAA dropped another hammer, presenting evidence to the school that a booster nicknamed—you can't make this stuff up—"Uncle T" had partially funded Stalions's scheme and that linebackers coach Chris Partridge had interfered with the investigation or violated NCAA Bylaw 19.2.1 by failing to cooperate with investigators.

From the moment the first scandal broke, Harbaugh had been facing serious NCAA sanctions—up to the most serious "show-cause" penalty that could ban him from coaching for a specific period of time, under a new bylaw approved in January 2023. The rule significantly altered language from a head coach "*presumed* to be held responsible for the actions of all institutional staff members" to one that read "*shall* be held responsible for their actions and the actions of all institutional staff members."

This left Harbaugh vulnerable, given the ongoing investigations, to a career-ending suspension.

No sooner had the latest NCAA news landed than Michigan fired Chris Partridge. Michigan alum Tim Smith, a member of the Champions Circle collective and a familiar face around Schembechler Hall, denied to Yahoo Sports he was the now-infamous Uncle T, insisting he was being targeted as a "fall guy" by the NCAA.

"I'm not Uncle T," said Smith. "But Uncle T is better than being Asshole T."

The Wednesday before the Maryland game former AD Hackett was back in Ann Arbor, seated in Harbaugh's office alongside Jim Minick. Known as "the Colonel," Minick not only had served a half dozen combat tours as a Marine in the Middle East, but since 2015 he had been Harbaugh's closest confidant, a dear friend since third grade, acting as a liaison between the head coach and the athletic department. Both men were among the few Harbaugh trusted and listened to.

That afternoon they found a man on edge, questioning why Michigan attorneys were suddenly looking to settle the case. Given his phone call with the university's VP of communications, Hackett figured university attorneys were weighing their options, privy to some potentially damaging information. He suggested Harbaugh consider taking his medicine and not fight any suspension.

Hackett's intuition proved right.

That very night, at 9:55 p.m., sensing a slowdown on the university side, Tom Mars had sent a text to Timothy G. Lynch, a Michigan vice president and its general counsel. Mars had not heard a word from Lynch all day—unusual since the court hearing was two days away.

In his text Mars wrote, FYI, if Michigan is even considering withdrawing its lawsuit or doing anything that may deprive Jim of his day in court on Friday we would expect the courtesy of knowing Michigan's intentions ASAP.

At five minutes after midnight Mars said his cell phone rang. It was Lynch, telling Mars he'd been quietly thinking before making the call. In so many words, Lynch informed Mars that Michigan had reached a settlement with the Big Ten and was withdrawing its lawsuit. It was just about the last thing Mars, bracing for a legal battle, wanted or needed to hear.

The next morning on a conference call, Mars, Jeff Klein, Harbaugh's longtime contract lawyer, and a local counsel in Ann Arbor tried to make sense of an eleventh-hour move. Michigan had encouraged Harbaugh to join the lawsuit as a plaintiff and agreed to pay his legal fees. The fact that Michigan had failed to inform its head football coach, his personal attorneys, or outside counsel of its decision only added to the confusion and anger. Bottom line, Michigan didn't have the legal right to dismiss the lawsuit without Harbaugh's consent.

Later that morning Mars said he reached out again to Tim Lynch and asked, for clarity's sake, if Michigan wanted to dismiss the lawsuit on Harbaugh's behalf as well.

"Absolutely," Lynch said.

"You can't do that," Mars said.

And that's when things got heated.

Lynch told Mars in no uncertain terms this was not a negotiation. He needed Harbaugh's consent, and if he didn't get it, Michigan's wasn't paying his attorney's fees.

You already signed an indemnification agreement, Mars fired back.

"This isn't negotiable, Tom," Lynch repeated, according to Mars. "If you screw up this deal or Jim Harbaugh screws this up, we will rain fire down on Jim Harbaugh."

"When do you need answer?" Mars asked.

"Right fucking now," he was told.

"Tim," said Mars, "we're both lawyers. I need to get my client's consent. I can't consent to dismiss the lawsuit."

"Well, you better fucking hurry up and get it."

"How much time do I have."

"Eighteen minutes."

At 1:15 p.m., eighteen minutes later on the dot, Mars called back. He had spoken with Harbaugh, who had provided his consent, reluctantly.

"Not because he agrees with it," Mars told Lynch, "but because you said he doesn't have any choice."

To add one more icy layer to an already frosted cake, that same afternoon the university formally announced it had ended its pending legal dispute with the Big Ten, and here's the frosting: the language of the statement made it appear the decision was Harbaugh's idea—not Michigan's.

"The Conference agreed to close its investigation, and the University and Coach Harbaugh agreed to accept the three-game suspension," the pivotal paragraph began. "Coach Harbaugh, with the University's support, decided to accept this sanction to return the focus to our student-athletes and their performance on the field."

"Big fucking lie," said Mars.

If anything marked the beginning of the end of Jim Harbaugh's time in Ann Arbor, one would be hard-pressed to find a more salient moment.

(Lynch did not respond to multiple requests for comments about his exchange with Mars.)

TWO LONG DAYS LATER MICHIGAN outlasted Maryland on the road 31–24 for football win one thousand, the most by any program. Then, a week later, the Wolverines first overpowered, then sealed a 30–24 win over Ohio State with a last-minute interception for the third straight win over their bitter rivals. If one word described that victory, it might well have been "resilient." All day the brotherhood made plays when they were needed the most. No less a Michigan authority than John U. Bacon called it the "most important win in The Game, ever—and the ripples will run for years."

Mobbed by joyous fans after the game, senior running back Blake Corum celebrated his twenty-third birthday by shouting, "This is what we came back for!"

Corum, who ran for 88 tough yards and two touchdowns, could well have been speaking for Harbaugh, starting right guard Zak Zinter, who suffered a gruesome leg injury during the game (broken tibia and fibula, requiring surgery), and a half dozen of his teammates who had returned to A2 for one more year, one last shot at redemption.

"This being my last game in the Big House, my last four years," Corum said. "I will look back and just pray I left a legacy. I stamped my mark here. I made a difference on and off the field. But looking back at this game, I feel like this is why I came back."

As the postseason playoffs loomed, the big question around the Big House was this: after a scandal- and suspension-soaked regular season, would the only Big Ten coach to win three straight conference titles outright come back? Would the Michigan Man return?

CHAPTER 15

The Power Broker

LANE KIFFIN WAS ON THE phone.

For Jimmy Sexton, this was an almost daily occurrence from 2014 to 2016. The Memphis-based Sexton, a partner at CAA and the closest thing the world of college football had resembling CAA cofounder and Hollywood power player Michael Ovitz, had paired his most famous client, Nick Saban, with his most controversial, Lane Kiffin. Saban needed to revolutionize his offense, and Kiffin needed to rehabilitate his career, and thus an arranged marriage was born. Kiffin, now Alabama's offensive coordinator, was once a wunderkind in the coaching profession, landing the Oakland Raiders head coaching job when he was only thirty-one years old. But as talented as he was at calling plays in the field he was equally talented at pissing off his superiors. He bounced from the Raiders to the University of Tennessee for a single season to his dream job at Southern Cal in a four-year span. He was young, brash, and smart—and didn't mind letting people know it—but it all finally came crashing down when USC athletic director Pat Haden fired him at the Los Angeles airport in 2013. He was radioactive before Saban, at Sexton's encouragement, extended a lifeline. Almost immediately it felt like an arranged marriage on the verge of imploding.

One thing about the job of an agent. When things aren't going well, you hear about it. Often. In Sexton's case, almost every afternoon, it followed a familiar script.

Kiffin called Sexton and told him, "You're going to get a phone call from Nick."

"What'd you do?" Sexton asked him.

"I told him in the meeting he didn't know what he was talking about," Kiffin said.

Sexton braced for what was coming. Five minutes later, Saban called.

"That son of a bitch," Saban snarled over the phone. "I'm going to fire you, Jimmy, for ever talking me into hiring that narcissistic prick."

Sexton would then have to talk down college football's most powerful coach and remind him that the arrangement was a necessary evil for both sides. On other days, Sexton had to remind Kiffin why he was in Tuscaloosa and what was needed to work for Saban. When Kiffin called Sexton one Saturday morning in late November 2015, inquiring about a head coaching job opportunity as the coaching carousel started to take shape, the super-agent unloaded on him. Kiffin couldn't be thinking about other jobs just hours before a home game, he counseled him in no uncertain terms.

"I was screaming at him," Sexton said. "'Let's go play the game today. Let's win the game today. If you win games, you'll get a job. People don't hire guys who are losing; they hire guys who are winning.'"

The Saban-Kiffin nuptials ultimately resulted in a national championship for both men before Saban finally got sick of Lane's antics and fired him right before the 2017 national championship game. Saban never worried about handling egos, fully trusting his hard-charging style would either force a coach to conform or seek opportunities elsewhere. But he met his match in Kiffin, who constantly questioned Saban on the why but refused to adopt Saban's preferred approach. It wore on Saban. "I ain't ever had a fucking coach I can't control, but I can't get him to do shit my way," Saban lamented to one assistant coach about Kiffin. "Goddamnit, this son of a bitch has to listen to me." It came to a head when Saban felt that Kiffin couldn't properly manage two jobs, the way Kirby Smart had the year before, after Kiffin accepted the Florida Atlantic job. As the agent for both, Sexton was predictably caught in the middle.

Such was the life of what many believe to be the most powerful man in college sports (short of, possibly, Southeastern Conference commissioner Greg Sankey). Part psychologist, part ruthless negotiator, part southern gentleman, part mob boss, and full-time power broker, Sexton had his hands on everything of significance in college football with a client stable of the best-known and highest-paid head coaches—a combination that gave Sexton tremendous negotiating power and leverage, which he wielded widely and without quarter to an athletic department's bottom line.

"Jimmy's a genius," said NCAA president Mark Emmert. "Nobody gets to negotiate with himself more than Jimmy."

THE FIRST TIME YOU SEE Jimmy Sexton, he's the polar opposite of what you'd expect, 180 degrees different in looks and style from, say, NFL super-agent Drew Rosenhaus. Despite the CAA pedigree, there's no slicked-back hair, no tailored suit, not a hint of Hollywood style. His portly figure looks like a cardiologist's wet dream, often accented by too-tight sweaters and pants that didn't fit right. At first glance, the divorced father of three looks like your average early sixties southern man who has made one (or two or three) too many visits to Waffle House.

But beneath the rumpled exterior stands a brilliant, cutthroat businessman. "Jimmy, when he wins, he wins, and when he loses, he wins," said former Florida State University president John Thrasher, who dealt with him on numerous deals.

Thrasher was right. Part of Sexton's magic was that he had cornered the market on marquee coaches. Fire one, and odds are he was representing the other coach you were thinking of hiring, time and time again. Tennessee was famous for it, to the point that Sexton, an alumnus of the school, had to publicly deny he was hiring coaches as the school's de facto athletic director. A masterful operator, playing one school off the others, he convinced athletic directors and university presidents to do his bidding, deftly working media relationships on his terms—always on his terms—to ensure only the information he wanted out was published. Ever wonder how those early coaching candidates lists come together? Or sudden contract extensions? That's Sexton.

By and large, Sexton preferred to work in the shadows and was damn good at it. Unlike many of his peers, he shunned the spotlight—he's rarely done interviews. Google the man and only a few photos pop up, with the top result not even about him. "Jimmy's a ghost," said Maryland head coach Mike Locksley, one of Sexton's clients.

But he can be found. Look for Jimmy Sexton at any serious congregation of high-profile coaches and athletic directors. Take the Fiesta Frolic in Scottsdale, Arizona, featuring a mix of conference commissioners, athletic directors, and football coaches from the Big Ten, Big 12, and Pac-12. Sexton mostly hung in the background, appearing occasionally to talk to a client or reporter. He never wanted to be the center of attention, even if his mere presence stole your gaze. A few weeks after Scottsdale, he made his annual trek to the SEC spring meetings in Florida, where he could see many of his clients and then hit their bosses up for more money, a literal one-stop shop.

At the Hilton Sandestin Beach Golf Resort and Spa, Sexton, in a teal polo shirt, posted up at an off-lobby table. A who's who of the SEC made a pilgrimage to see him, from Auburn football coach Hugh Freeze to Tennessee basketball coach Rick Barnes. Sexton never moved, letting his highly paid clients come to him. His list ran coast to coast, from Penn State's James Franklin to Oregon's Dan Lanning, but his highest-profile clients generally resided in the south. In the SEC alone, Sexton represented ten of the fourteen coaches heading into the 2023 season. In addition to still repping Saban and Kiffin, he had big names like Texas A&M's Jimbo Fisher, Georgia's Kirby Smart, and Kentucky's Mark Stoops on his roster.

"I have coaches in every conference," Sexton said. "But it just means a little more to the people of the south, I think."

Sexton told us a story of going to the annual "Big Game" rivalry between Michigan and Ohio State, considered one of the fiercest rivalries in college football, and left thinking it didn't compare to the high stakes he dealt with in the SEC, first as a Tennessee equipment manager and later as the counselor to many of the conference's top coaches. "The Michigan fans were going back to their executive jobs at General Motors," he said. "But the people in the south, when their teams lose on Saturday, they probably call in sick to work on Monday and Tuesday."

No one was better at weaponizing that passion for their clients' benefit than Sexton. He understood the pressure college administrators were under from boosters and trustees to win big, and he held the most coveted commodity: proven winning head coaches. He'd play one school against the other, driving up the contracts for one coach after another. It was brilliant negotiating, though the competition wasn't exactly fair. Sexton knew the market better than anyone and was often paired with a university general counsel or even a president who, facing intense pressure to land a top coach, routinely gave in to his demands. He was the Leonardo da Vinci of negotiating, and the Jimbo Fisher $95 million guaranteed contract, his *Mona Lisa*.

"If I were a college coach today, the first person I'd go to hire would be Jimmy Sexton," Thrasher said. "I promise you that. He set Jimbo up financially for the rest of his life, no matter what he does."

The question was whether that was good for anyone other than Jimbo Fisher. And Jimmy Sexton.

SEXTON, THE SON OF A Memphis-area dentist, started his unlikely rise in the Tennessee football locker room as a manager, picking up players' jockstraps and towels. In doing so, he built a friendship with Tennessee star Reggie White and eventually became suitemates with the thirteen-time NFL Pro Bowl defensive lineman.

One day in 1983, Robert Fraley, a former Alabama quarterback for Bear Bryant turned top agent, approached Sexton, knowing his close friendship with the Tennessee star, with a massive offer for White to eschew the NFL draft and play for the Memphis Showboats of the United States Football League (USFL). When Sexton told White of the offer, the Tennessee defensive end asked him if he'd be interested in representing him. Sexton was only twenty years old but already on his way.

After graduating from Tennessee the following year, he got his first official job at a sports agency, making five hundred dollars a month and working for two former professional athletes turned sports agents, Don Kessinger and Kyle Rote Jr. He signed Chicago Bulls star Scottie Pippen and slowly started building out his client list. His most significant career break came again because of Fraley, though this time out of tragedy.

By 1999, Fraley was one of the biggest coaching agents in the business, representing marquee head coaches like Bill Parcells, Bill Cowher, and Joe Gibbs. In October of that same year, Fraley died in the plane crash that also killed golfer Payne Stewart. Suddenly, without an agent, Parcells turned to Sexton, respecting how he had handled negotiations while the "Big Tuna" was with the New York Jets. Not only did Parcells immediately become Sexton's biggest client, but he became something of a mentor to him. Parcells unlocked a crucial revelation for Sexton, one that would define his career, when he observed to him, "The players business is great, but the coaching side is where nobody is and there's a huge need for it."

Ole Miss head coach Tommy Tuberville became his first college coaching client, but the man who would best define Sexton came later in 1999: Nick Saban.

Dissatisfied with how his then agent handled NFL interest, Saban switched to Sexton ahead of a career-changing move from Michigan State to LSU. Sexton landed Saban a $1.2 million contract that provoked national think pieces and outrage for then LSU chancellor Mark Emmert on his Baton Rouge campus. Emmert defended the contract then, telling his faculty senate that he needed football to carry out his broader academic goals. When Saban won a national championship three years later and Emmert wrote an op-ed for the *New York Times* entitled, "Beyond a Stereotype of Southern Universities," he felt vindicated.

Outside of his wife, Terry, there was no one Saban trusted more than Sexton. He helped him navigate every significant decision, including what he wanted his legacy to be when he was weighing leaving the Miami Dolphins for Alabama. The two weren't afraid to give it back to each other, especially during the Kiffin era, but they built a close friendship that other coaches noticed and wanted to emulate. Over the years, Sexton signed many of Saban's acolytes and helped them get head coaching opportunities. In turn, Sexton always had recommendations for Saban when he had staff openings, knowing the type of personality that could withstand the coach's demanding style.

"I think it's been a fabulous partnership for Nick and a fabulous partnership for Jimmy," said former LSU trustee Charlie Weems, who helped hire Saban. "Jimmy is a very talented and personable guy. He's loyal. He's a guy who doesn't make you feel like he's got his hand in your pocket, even though he really might."

Sexton's influence exploded from there. Sexton continued to represent

NFL players, too, including Carolina Panthers quarterback Bryce Young and New York Jets linebacker C. J. Mosley, both ex-Bama stars, but as one former CAA agent put it, "He might make more money on QBs, but his energy is devoted to SEC coaches." The rapidly increasing value of coaching contracts across the entire landscape proved Sexton's influence.

When he didn't have an SEC coach he wanted, he wasn't shy in his poaching efforts. He went hard after Sam Pittman, who at the time had a local lawyer named Judy Henry representing him. Henry had organized a grassroots campaign to drum up interest in Pittman, then Georgia's offensive line coach, for the job of Arkansas head coach. At the start of a search, he wasn't on any candidates list and wasn't a serious option to replace Chad Morris, but Henry quickly contacted Arkansas athletic director Hunter Yurachek with her pitch on why Pittman was the perfect guy to lead the Razorbacks. At the end of a roller-coaster coaching search, Pittman, who had never been a head coach at the Division I level before, was the surprise winner, a fifty-eight-year-old first-time SEC head coach. Pittman would later say, "To be perfectly one hundred percent honest, without Judy Henry, I don't believe there's any way in the world I would have got this job."

Two years later, with Pittman's stock rising, Sexton started circling. Pittman had taken over one of the worst situations in college football, a program that hadn't won an SEC game in more than two years, and had somehow built it into a winner almost immediately. In year two, Pittman managed a miraculous 9-4 record, the best since 2011. Sexton smelled opportunity.

His pitch was unsophisticated yet admittedly enticing: Did you want to be in the same league as Saban, Smart, and others on Team Sexton? Or continue working with a little-known lawyer who didn't have the cachet or connections that Sexton did? Pittman dumped Henry and hired Sexton. When Pittman made the switch, he made $3 million annually, good for twelfth out of the thirteen SEC public institutions. Sexton helped more than double that number in less than three years together, setting Pittman up with a $6.35 million base salary heading into the 2023 season.

Pittman's story illustrated what many inside college football knew to be true. When a coach ditched another agent for Sexton, it usually meant one of two things, if not both: He wanted a new job and/or more money. Locksley, as Alabama's offensive coordinator, switched from Trace Armstrong to Sexton in 2019, believing he needed some extra firepower to land his dream job at Maryland. Moving to Sexton was also insurance in Locksley's mind that if he stayed in Tuscaloosa, Sexton was the man he needed to negotiate with Saban and Alabama.

"If I was going to be a lifetime coordinator and be at Bama until [Nick] retired, I wanted the person who would be able to get me the most money to do it and be able to negotiate the best deal for me," Locksley said. "There's not a better guy doing it than what Jimmy has done, if you just look at the production."

Sexton and Armstrong had once worked together, but as with other times Sexton had teamed up with agents over the years, the relationships almost always eventually ended poorly. He seemed best suited as a lone wolf.

First, it was with Pat Dye Jr., son of the former Auburn head coach, when the two merged their sports agencies in 2010. It quickly fell apart in a year. As alleged in a lawsuit, Dye believed Sexton stole former Alabama wide receiver Julio Jones from him and then used Jones's influence to sign Trent Richardson and Mark Barron. Dye sued Sexton, who by then had left for Creative Artists Agency, for breach of contract, fraud, violation of trade secrets, and tortious interference.

Arriving at CAA in 2011, Sexton served as the cohead of its football division. He teamed up with Armstrong, a former Chicago Bears defensive lineman, and the duo built the dominant college coaches agency, but hardly spoke to each other at the end. Armstrong left for Athletes First, where he is still one of the top agents in the game, representing heavyweights like LSU's Brian Kelly, Ohio State's Ryan Day, and USC's Lincoln Riley. Sexton later helped groom Clint Dowdle, who spent seven years as his right-hand man before leaving in July 2023 to become rival WME's head of football. Under Sexton's tutelage, Dowdle became a rising star in the business and built close relationships with top coaches, a development some believe Sexton eventually felt threatened by. When Dowdle opted to get out of Sexton's orbit, the CAA agent fought hard to keep as many of his clients as possible. Dowdle took some of his biggest names, including Philadelphia Eagles head coach Nick Sirianni and Notre Dame head coach Marcus Freeman, but Sexton won his share of battles. The most prominent were Oregon head coach Dan Lanning and Florida State head coach Mike Norvell.

When you looked over Sexton's entire client list, it was clear he held so many cards that he controlled the high-stakes poker game.

"The agents have so much control right now, and the deals that are struck are so one-sided," said Kansas State athletic director Gene Taylor. "It flies in the face of people looking at what are you guys doing? We are paying coaches millions and millions of dollars *not to coach*, and the public sees that."

Nick Saban making $1.2 million a year in 1999 was one thing; making $11.7 million in 2023, as the highest-paid coach in college football but with others not far behind, was quite another. In 2023, Sexton represented five of the ten highest-paid coaches, every last one making at least $9 million a year. It can be argued that it was the contrast between these spectacular salaries and the unpaid workforce of largely Black players that shifted public perception, pushing what was once a taboo subject of college football players making money into a mainstream idea.

Call it the Sexton Effect.

"I respect Jimmy. He's a brilliant guy," said one athletic director. "I disagree with the results because it's messed up our industry." The AD detailed what Sexton had turned the coaching industry into: Almost no coach lived out his contract. He was always either renegotiating for more money or negotiating a buyout after each season. "There's no in-between anymore," the AD lamented. "You get your bonuses and then Jimmy is coming and saying, 'He went to a bowl so you've got to give him a raise.' No, I gave him a bonus—that was the raise."

Good luck trying to find anyone to speak out more forcefully against Sexton though. College administrators and rival agents loved to complain about him, but worried about revenge if they spoke out against him with their names attached. Sexton was too powerful and too good at his job to risk getting on his wrong side.

Utah's longtime athletic director Chris Hill knew he was overmatched but determined to hold the line. A Jersey-born, no-nonsense guy, Hill disliked being bullied and wanted to steward his athletic department's resources well. When a coaching agent (not Sexton) pushed him hard for more money for one of his coaches and Hill initially refused, the agent leaked to the media that Utah was dragging its feet and the coach could go elsewhere. "I held the line and got booed at a basketball game," Hill said. "It was just the right thing to do. After that, I said, what's my motivation for holding the line? What's the upside for me as an AD? Well, there is no upside."

It all made sense when you realized everyone was just operating out of self-survival. As Hill surveyed the scene, he discovered no athletic director or university president was losing their job for giving a successful football or basketball coach more money. That coach may have had no real leverage—typically a key component to negotiations—but it didn't matter. Fans thought it was all Monopoly money anyway, so just give the guy more money and move on. No one was hanging championship banners for running the best athletic department profit margin. Until there was a revenue share with the players, it was almost like the school was laundering its massive profits through coaching salaries. "I think we all made more money than maybe we should have," Hill conceded.

"There are some ridiculous amounts of money being paid for people who are frankly not that good," said Bob Bowlsby, who negotiated coaching contracts as AD at Iowa and Stanford before becoming Big 12 commissioner. "When you have money being generated that is so enormous, I think you delude yourself into building things you don't need and paying people that just make it an easy negotiation. You find yourself in a wildly inflationary environment, and I think we're in that right now."

The rare times schools tried to push back against Sexton, often they paid a price. When he secured a $49 million extension for Gus Malzahn at Auburn, primarily negotiating with school president Steven Leath, it left a bad taste in the mouth of Auburn's most influential boosters. They thought Sexton played them, drumming up alleged Arkansas interest in Malzahn to secure the most lucrative deal possible. When Auburn finally moved on from Malzahn in 2019 and owed him $21.5 million—in those pre-Jimbo days, the biggest college football buyout—because of that extension, they wanted nothing to do with another round of Sexton. They quickly hired Boise State head coach Bryan Harsin, who was not a Sexton client.

But just two years later, Harsin spectacularly flamed out, and Auburn hired a Sexton client, Hugh Freeze. This was the power of the Most Powerful; even when you wanted to avoid him, you rarely could for more than one job cycle. An emotional Freeze thanked his agent at his opening press conference, with Sexton in attendance. Years earlier, before his time at Ole Miss ended over calls to escort services, Freeze raved about the impact Sexton, whom he talked to daily, had on his career. "Besides God and the players, Jimmy would be next," Freeze said. "It would be in that order."

Sexton was always working—his number one skill was his availability to his clients—but his time to shine was coaching carousel season. Starting around Halloween, though increasingly earlier and earlier as universities became more trigger-happy, Sexton navigated the complicated world of handling his clients getting fired and hired. It was 24-7 for Sexton as he stayed up all night, taking phone calls to best position his clients. It was a tricky balance for him as he had close bonds with many of his top guys, and one's bad news could mean good news for another.

When the hot-seat talk started cranking up in November, he got hundreds of phone calls daily. From coaches, athletic directors, search firm consultants, journalists, and everyone else with a personal stake in college football. Because he represented so many top coaches, he had the most information and could bend the market to reflect that. "Jimmy was so prepared," said former Georgia AD Greg McGarity. "He had reams of data to justify what he was proposing." Was a coach actually willing to move, or did he just want a raise? Only Sexton and the coach truly knew. Dealing with Sexton was like handling a rattlesnake, even if he promised he wouldn't bite.

The tricky part for Sexton was when multiple clients wanted the same job. He could present their collective interest to an AD or search firm, but he still had to prioritize specific candidates to push to decision-makers. It prompted annual frustration from coaches who realized they weren't as high on Sexton's totem pole as they might have thought when they heard what candidates were getting the most traction.

"Jimmy has done a great job for a lot of people a lot of times, but he's fucked a lot of people, too, by pushing one guy," said a Power 4 coach who, you guessed it, insisted on anonymity for fear of retribution. "Think of all his guys. He's had a lot more guys fail and get fired in three or four years than he has the Nick Sabans and Kirby Smarts of the world."

In November, the coaching carousel again set up nicely for Sexton. Texas oil money made Jimbo Fisher go away, but the bad news for one client created opportunity for others. A big job like A&M had the power to create a cascade of dominoes, and Sexton again had the supply of top coaches. At the end of the regular season, Sexton represented the coaches of eight of the top ten–ranked programs. They'd all be attractive options for programs desperate to win and willing to throw gobs of money at a coach to deliver.

The day after his former head coach Fisher lost his latest job, John Thrasher contacted the current one, Mike Norvell. His message? Don't take any phone calls from Jimmy Sexton. It wasn't a knock on Norvell's agent, but rather an appreciation of his skills. After dealing with Sexton and Fisher, Willie Taggart, and Norvell in Tallahassee, Thrasher knew how good he was at getting more money for his clients. And if Norvell, who led the Seminoles to a perfect 12-0 regular season, allowed him to, Thrasher knew Sexton could get his beloved football coach an offer elsewhere.

Thrasher's fears proved prophetic, but the Texas A&M opening was just the start. In the wildest coaching cycle in memory, the Power Broker was right in the middle, quietly pulling the strings behind the scenes.

CHAPTER 16

Macy's II

ABRUTAL TWO-DAY STRETCH LEFT MIKE Locksley feeling empty and doubting his life's calling.

Maryland football was on the upswing, winning two of its last three games to get to seven regular season wins with a Music City Bowl trip to Nashville on deck later that month. He should have felt optimistic about the future, but instead he was thinking about walking away from it all.

As Locksley sat in his office, one Maryland player after another, young men he promised to take care of and develop in College Park, came to him with one request: more money.

"I literally sat here for forty-eight hours and just got the shit kicked out of me," Locksley said. "And I'm a guy that has relationships with players."

It didn't matter whether it was a star player or a third-string running back. Everyone wanted a cut of the action days ahead of the transfer portal window opening on December 5. The asking price was typically the same, too: $100,000.

Locksley, who made his name recruiting young men from the DMV area—District of Columbia, Maryland, and Virginia—was hurt. He looked at many of his players like sons, and what should have been a familiar relationship had turned coldly transactional. It put him in the uncomfortable position of telling players, no, your NIL is absolutely not worth six figures despite what you might believe. In those situations, Locksley tried to explain the market to the player, but he knew it'd likely just end in the player seeking greener pastures through the transfer portal.

This is what life was like as the CEO of football's Macy's, and Locksley was questioning whether it was worth it anymore.

"It was the first time in thirty-three years that I second-guessed whether or not I wanted to keep doing this, or should I just do TV?" Locksley said. "I'm going to be on TV—I promise you that's what I'm going to do. I'll be one hell of an analyst . . . I was closer to doing that."

It marked a challenging year for a head coach who faced the financial realities of the new NIL world headfirst.

A WEEK AFTER THE EARLY season home victory over Indiana, Maryland strode into Ohio Stadium and gave the Buckeyes all they could handle for three quarters, even leading 17–10 early in the second half. The talent and depth of Ohio State, a full-time tenant in the Saks Fifth Avenue neighborhood, eventually overwhelmed the Terrapins, 37–17, to give Maryland its first loss of the season. A win would have launched Maryland's season into the stratosphere, but with a much-needed bye coming up and winnable games against Illinois and Northwestern the following two weeks, there was still a belief that if Locksley and Co. just took care of business, Maryland would be ranked and 7-1 when Penn State came to town.

But Maryland always struggled with just taking care of the business part of the equation. During the bye week, associate head coach and co-offensive coordinator Kevin Sumlin was arrested for driving under the influence while recruiting in Florida. Just two weeks earlier, a gaunt-looking Sumlin had spent an hour in his office reflecting on his career and where college football was headed. It was jarring seeing him in Maryland gear, both for the unlikeliness of it and for how much time had passed since a youthful Sumlin took the college football world by storm in 2012 as coach of Texas A&M, with Johnny Manziel as his Heisman Trophy–winning quarterback.

When explaining the pressure he had faced as a head coach, he relayed a recent conversation with a surgeon friend. Imagine, he said to his friend, if after a weekend of performing surgeries, a newspaper story on Sunday detailed how many patients survived and how many died. The person who wrote the story wasn't a doctor and didn't know the specifics of the preparation or any underlying conditions patients might have had, but only detailed the final results. His friend briefly pondered it and said, "That would not only hurt my credibility but also shape people's opinions about me."

"No shit," Sumlin told him back.

Sumlin hopped out of his chair as he finished the story and walked over to the whiteboard. He wrote on the board: 12 x 3 = 365.

That, he said, explained everything. Twelve weeks for three hours was what his entire year was judged on. "That's my life," he said. "That's it." Three hours of football for twelve weeks in the fall can power generational wealth and pressure, unlike anything you've ever experienced. Sumlin didn't talk about drinking in the office that day, but for those in and around college football, it was another price to pay in the high-stakes world of the sport. The pressure and the hours are so crazy that coaches look for outlets to relieve it. Steve Sarkisian was famously fired from USC because of reported alcohol problems, including allegedly going on a drunken rant at a booster event before the 2015 season started. Ole Miss head coach Lane Kiffin, who tried to focus his energy on hot yoga and working out rather than alcohol to relieve the stress of the job, celebrated three years of sobriety in 2024.

Offensive coordinator Josh Gattis, winner of the Broyles Award in 2021, worried most about how the hours and stress affected his profession's health. Coaches could be so laser focused on doing what they needed to succeed, particularly when recruiting was in full swing, that many neglected annual checkups, dentist appointments, and other regular health-care visits. Gattis, a father of two, saw his industry wearing down under the stress and long hours required and wondered if more would either leave for the NFL or just quit the profession altogether.

"I spend more time with my players than I ever do with my own kids," Gattis said. "There's a lot of remorse that goes into that. There's a lot that we sacrifice as coaches. I've missed funerals, I've missed weddings, I've missed a lot of important events in life to be a college football coach and to be here for other people's kids. I think there's ways that we can continue to eliminate the stress on this profession as coaches, and you're starting to see some of that stress affect coaches."

Gattis, who had previously worked under notoriously hard-charging coaches like Nick Saban and Jim Harbaugh, appreciated Locksley's approach. The Maryland head coach was understanding if you needed to take your kids to school or deal with a personal life situation. He let his coaches leave right after practice on Wednesday and Thursday nights, giving them at least a couple of nights during the season when they could get home at 6:00 p.m. and be normal adults who could have dinner and do activities with their families. "When I get to Wednesday night, I don't take any stress from football home with me," he said. "I take my keys, get in the car, and I just worry about my problems Thursday morning. It allows me to decompress a little bit and get an appreciation for life."

One thing not good for decompressing? A losing streak.

Coming off its bye week, Maryland lost to Illinois, 27–24, on a last-second field goal. Maryland entered the game as a 14-point favorite, but the loss took the wind out of the team's sails.

Maryland lost again the following week to a Northwestern team led by an interim head coach after Pat Fitzgerald's summer dismissal over a hazing scandal, and then got blown out 51–15 by James Franklin's Nittany Lions. Franklin had once been Maryland's head-coach-in-waiting under Ralph Friedgen. Things came to a head in 2010 when Friedgen went 9-4 and Franklin's contract dictated he had to become the head coach by 2012. Kevin Anderson, in his first year as Maryland's athletic director, decided he didn't want to move forward with either man. Anderson fired Friedgen, told Franklin to go ahead and pursue opportunities elsewhere, and hired Randy Edsall away from Connecticut, fresh off a Fiesta Bowl appearance. Edsall went 22-34 as Maryland's coach before being fired in 2015. Franklin first went to Vanderbilt, where he went 24-15 in three seasons, which included two nine-win seasons at the traditional SEC doormat, before landing the Penn State job. In his first decade as Penn State's coach, Franklin went 8-2 against the Maryland program once promised to him, winning by an average margin of more than thirty-three points.

After losing four consecutive games, any positive momentum Maryland built with a 5-0 start had evaporated. "Same old Maryland" was the refrain from a fan base constantly wary of going all in on a football program that even Locksley admitted thrashed around between sparse periods of success. "You hit a four-game losing streak, and you've got your fans on your ass, and everybody's like, we can't win the big one," Locksley said. "We ain't coming until you win the big one." There was a belief around the program that Maryland could win nine or ten games in 2023 and finally prove it belonged in the neighborhood. But for a pessimistic fan base, the future felt even more bleak with the arrivals of Oregon, UCLA, USC, and Washington in 2024. Behind a fifth-year quarterback, Locksley believed that Maryland had real Big Ten championship aspirations and called it a "critical" season for Maryland football's future.

The rebound came against Matt Rhule in his first year at Nebraska. In a game only football diehards could appreciate, Maryland slugged its way to an ugly 13–10 win to get to six wins and clinch the program's third consecutive bowl game. The win turned the season around, with Locksley's Terrapins playing noticeably better in the final two weeks.

Maryland gave a Jim Harbaugh-less Michigan team—he was serving his suspension for the sign-stealing scandal that occurred under his watch—a real scare before the Wolverines prevailed 31–24. In its regular-season finale, Maryland beat up Rutgers, the school poised to be its top rival in the Big Ten, to get to seven regular season wins. The season felt like a disappointment to some, given what could have been, but when viewed through a historical lens, it guaranteed a third consecutive bowl appearance for the first time since a 2006–2008 stretch under Friedgen.

That's not insignificant for a football program still trying to find its footing. Beyond giving the team and its supporters an excuse to visit the Broadway bars in Nashville, it provided the football program three extra weeks of practice to further develop its younger players. Ryan Davis, the program's strength and conditioning coach, hadn't realized how big a deal that was until Maryland didn't make a bowl game in his first season, which meant players were gone from late November until mid-January. By the time they got back into the weight room, it felt to Davis like the team was starting from zero in many ways.

"What you learn is that cumulative effect is why programs like Alabama are so far ahead. Why are programs like Georgia so far ahead?" Davis asked. "Well, look at it. Their calendar year has been totally different from yours for a very long time. When was the last time Alabama missed a bowl game?

"Think about how that affects development in a four-year plan. If you're playing in the [national championship], it's like four extra weeks you're still sharp. You have athletes that are getting four more weeks of training every year. You wonder why some players are so much more developed than other programs? Holistically, they've got more exposure."

Of course it's not just the extra practices that have Maryland far behind the Alabamas and Georgias of the college football ecosystem. The Saks Fifth Avenue programs will always have more advantages and better access to players than schools like Maryland, stuck in the Macy's neighborhood.

For Maryland to level up, it had to do things differently.

IN AN OFFICE ACROSS THE hallway from Locksley's, Brian Griffin excitedly explained his Maryland model for success. Griffin joined the program in June from the Atlanta Falcons, where he spent three years learning the inner workings of the NFL. As Maryland football's chief of staff, he wore several hats, but perhaps most importantly he was the program's "salary cap guy," as Locksley put it.

Wearing a Music City Bowl zip-up hoodie and olive-green pants, Griffin laid out what he called Maryland's version of the "Moneyball" strategy immortalized in Michael Lewis's book about Billy Beane and the Oakland Athletics. Through various sources—from coaching friends to agents to players and their parents—Griffin built out what he believed to be an accurate survey of the current player value market. He learned early on that, unlike the NFL, where all thirty-two teams operate under the same $242 million salary cap, the money at each program's disposal varied wildly even within the Big Ten conference, let alone the entire country. The bigger and more passionate the fan base, the more money that typically flowed into the collective's coffers. Locksley told us the high-end in the Big Ten was between $10 million and $15 million per year. The low end $2.5 million. Maryland was closer to the low end than the high end of that range.

As Griffin unveiled his model, he plugged in $2.5 million as the salary cap number. "I don't scoff at this number," he said. "It pains me to try to raise it, but it's a realistic number for the University of Maryland versus the $15 million guys out there. I'm not sure any of them are managing it the way we are. I'm not sure they have as much insight as we do."

Maryland's model labeled players at five different levels—All-American, All-Conference, Starter, Two-Deep, and Depth. The projected roster value range for a player differed at each range. Maryland tried to stick to the NFL salary-cap model percentages. For instance, if Maryland devoted 12 percent of a $2.5 million salary cap to the quarterback position, that gave it $300,000 to play with. It's not nearly enough to get in the game for the top available quarterbacks, but that's the reality of the Terrapins' situation. With a $15 million salary cap, though, that would mean $1.8 million for the quarterbacks. "If you don't have a quarterback," Griffin said, "you can't win."

To determine what bucket a QB prospect fell into, Locksley and Griffin looked at the NFL Combine results over the last five years to build prototypes. They looked at measurables and on-field critical factors, among other criteria. They ultimately were looking for players who could fit their team motto plastered throughout the building:

Toughness. Effort. Relentless. Pride. Success.

MARYLAND HAD TO BE SMART with every investment it made. It couldn't afford to have a sizable chunk of its limited salary cap sitting on the bench and not contributing to the team's success. It was why Locksley and Co. primarily didn't get in the mix for top recruits who commanded big numbers but didn't have a track record of production to back them up. Frankly, it wasn't new terrain for a Maryland program that typically punched above its weight class under Locksley but, even before NIL, regularly finished behind more traditional programs like Ohio State, Michigan, and Penn State. Beyond residing smack-dab in the middle of a talent-rich area full of top prospects, Maryland never had the usual advantages to sell to recruits, like a storied history or a stadium packed with a hundred thousand fans each Saturday. What it did have was a track record of developing under-the-radar players for the NFL. Receiver D. J. Moore, and cornerbacks Darnell Savage Jr., and Deonte Banks all arrived in College Park as three-star recruits and left as first-round NFL draft picks.

Maryland focused on developing more talent like that and hoped more players like Taulia Tagovailoa would take the "homeboy discount" to stay and learn under Locksley. Sometimes it worked; sometimes it didn't. You must sell something else when you don't have the most money. For Maryland, that pitch centered on Locksley's strong résumé in the DMV area and his connections throughout the sports and business worlds. He started an investment club and a mentorship program, where a couple of billionaires served as mentors to his football players. He believed those experiences and connections would be worth more overall than the up-front money other programs offered.

Locksley was also actively trying to help young Black men who weren't his players. He launched the National Coalition of Minority Football Coaches to help minority coaching candidates get more opportunities. He walked the walk, too, with Davis, Gattis, and defensive coordinator Brian Williams, all Black and employed in powerful positions within the program. Maryland was the only Power 4 program with a Black university president, athletic director, head football coach, and offensive and defensive coordinators. Locksley would tell prospective players he had been in their shoes once, and now look at him: guiding a Big Ten program and earning nearly $6 million in salary.

"I tell kids I've walked the same path you walked," Locksley said. "These kids who grew up in tough neighborhoods, who grew up without two parents in the home, who had childhood trauma of family members dying, being killed, growing up in the hood. I didn't play in the NFL, and I've still been able to change the lineage of my family because of my degree. I'm the cheat code for a guy like you because you don't have to make the mistakes I made to get here."

Even with that approach, Locksley knew he'd lose 15 to 20 percent of his roster annually. Before the transfer portal windows opened, he and Davis focused on getting the middle part of the roster invested and working like their top performers. If the middle 50 percent could get closer to the top 10 to 15 percent, it made the culture much stronger and limited the desire of players to pop into the portal.

Maryland kept receipts on every player that left the program and how they fared elsewhere. It wasn't to prove Locksley was right, but to build a defense against other programs stealing his players. On this day, C. J. Dippre was on the Maryland head coach's mind. Locksley found Dippre as a two-star quarterback recruit out of Scranton, Pennsylvania, whose only other offer was from Miami of Ohio. Locksley saw a tight end in the six-foot-five Dippre, and over three years, he developed him into one of the Big Ten's best, capped by a thirty-catch, three-touchdown 2022 season. He had a chance to be a key component in one of the nation's top offenses but instead jumped in the portal and joined Locksley's former mentor Nick Saban down at Alabama. In his first season in Tuscaloosa, Dippre had only eleven catches and zero touchdowns.

"Was the extra twenty-five thousand dollars, hundred thousand dollars that you made worth [it]?" Locksley asked. "Maybe, because if you don't go to the league and if you're stacking your money, maybe it's worth it. That's what being Macy's does to you."

Being Macy's also limited Maryland's depth. The program was very bullish on its top players and their ability to play anywhere, but it took more work to retain the nonstarters needed to step in when injuries cropped up. It was simple, according to Locksley: the teams with money could afford depth, and those without couldn't.

That didn't stop Griffin from trying to alleviate that issue. His analytical view and NFL experience were a nice complement to Locksley's burning passion. It was like one big Rubik's Cube to him as he drilled into the data to find Maryland an edge. He loved the challenge of it, genuinely believing it was more fun than work. In the December transfer window, Maryland's salary-cap model pushed the Terrapins to go shopping in the offensive linemen aisle. A good offensive lineman was hard to come by because every program was always in need of one, but Maryland had a strong need with a young group of linemen and targeted market inefficiencies. The Terps grabbed six-foot-five center Josh Kaltenberger (Purdue), six-foot-five guard Aliou Bah (Georgia), and, most interestingly, six-foot-five offensive tackle Alan Herron out of Division II Shorter University.

Maryland lost its share of players to the portal, too, notably sophomore linebacker Jaishawn Barham to Michigan. The former four-star recruit had thirty-seven tackles, three sacks, and an interception for the Terrapins in 2023, and if he put it all together, had the talent to play at the next level. Losing a player like Barham could hurt, but Griffin was desensitized to it at that point. After three years in the NFL, he knew what a professional model did to the coach and player relationship. One minute a coach loved a player; the next he cut him and sent him out into the unemployed world. It could be a cold, ruthless business. Griffin didn't have to like it, but he recognized that if college football kept going down the NFL path, he'd be ready for it.

"It's either a window of opportunity, or you can bitch and moan about it and it's going to be a detriment to your team," he said. "So you've just gotta figure it out, and I think that's what winners do."

THE MUSIC CITY BOWL PAIRED Maryland up against Auburn, the school that months earlier was extremely interested in the Terrapins' top quarterback. It could have been a full circle moment for Taulia Tagovailoa, except he opted out of the bowl game.

Despite already using up his five years of eligibility, Taulia wanted to keep playing at the college level. Except he didn't want to do it at Maryland. Instead, he wanted Maryland and Alabama to sign off on a waiver appeal so he could pick a third school. The belief around college football was that the likely destination was Miami, a Galu Tagovailoa–influenced move to put his two quarterback sons back in the same city.

The Tagovailoa camp called on ESPN's Pete Thamel to advance their argument for the waiver publicly. Lia had played in five games in 2019, one more than was allowed to a redshirt, but in two games, he only played a few snaps. The rules were clear that he had no remaining eligibility, but with everyone suing the NCAA these days, Tagovailoa opted to test the rules.

College administrators and coaches watched the situation closely. It could open a Pandora's box if a player who had used all his eligibility could keep playing college football. What was stopping a player without any legitimate excuses, like injury-influenced waivers, from playing six, seven, eight, maybe even nine years of college football? The NCAA granting Taulia's appeal could open those doors.

Instead, the NCAA denied the appeal and let Taulia know right before the deadline to enter the NFL Draft. He would have no choice but to start preparing for the NFL if he wanted to keep playing football.

It ended Tagovailoa's tenure at Maryland on a bittersweet note. In his four years in College Park, Tagovailoa became the Big Ten's all-time leading passer, surpassing players like Drew Brees. He guided Maryland to three consecutive bowl games, a rare feat for a school that thrashed around. But rather than one last hurrah in a bowl game, he had wanted to head elsewhere, only to get shut down.

Locksley, who signed off on Taulia's waiver, tried to be reasonable about it all, taking the emotion out of it and acknowledging this was the world he lived in now.

"As the head coach here, my job is to do what's best for Maryland," he said. "We have to do what's best for Maryland, he has to do what's best for Lia. We're starting to see this is the business side of college football. This is what NIL has created, the portal has created. I can't be mad at Lia for making a decision like that, but he can't call me selfish, either, if I decided, why would I write a waiver?

"One of the things that I have always tried to do and anybody who knows me will say this: I can be Petty Pendergrass sometimes, but I always try to reverse engineer at least and look at it from that perspective. He took a pay cut this year and stayed here at Maryland. He had better offers to go to other places, but he chose to stay here. That's huge on his part, and it helped us, it helped me, it helped our program. So, when I reverse engineered, I saw that it was kind of selfish, but I also knew that I probably wouldn't be able to afford what he was going to be offered by somebody else. And so, how can I be mad at the kid? It's business."

There was an upside to it too: Locksley could see what he had at the quarterback position heading into the following season. Maryland had already grabbed M. J. Morris, who started five games for North Carolina State that season, and had Billy Edwards and Cameron Edge returning. It's why when Tagovailoa again inquired about receiving extra NIL money to play in a bowl game, the request was quickly turned down.

Maryland looked fantastic against Auburn, racing out to a 21–0 first-quarter lead that showed the country what the Terrapins could do against an SEC opponent that should have beaten Alabama in the Iron Bowl. It was a youth movement, with Maryland players fired up and flying around the field. "Maryland has put an infomercial for 2024 on ABC," play-by-play announcer Taylor Zarzour exclaimed.

Maryland finished strong and beat Auburn, 31–13. After the game, Auburn head coach Hugh Freeze claimed he was too busy with recruiting to be involved much in the game planning ahead of the loss. It was another sign of the times.

The Music City Bowl win gave Maryland back-to-back eight-win seasons for the first time since 2002–2003. Locksley, ever the Saban acolyte, had mixed feelings about it. He knew winning ten games was there for the taking, and it was hard not to be upset about the close losses in the middle of the season. He also knew what he was up against every day in a league full of Saks Fifth Avenues. Maryland had a lead over the Buckeyes and came as close as any program to beating the Wolverines in the regular season, but playing top opponents closely didn't change the final record. Locksley realized Maryland took a step forward in 2023, even if it was a smaller one than he had hoped.

"People don't understand eight wins at Maryland is hard," Locksley said. "It's like winning eleven or twelve at Bama. It's hard. It ain't a championship, but it's hard."

Said Griffin: "What I think Coach is building here is the realization it's really hard to win, but we can beat anyone. At the same time, we can lose to anyone."

There was hope, too, in other programs' successes. When Griffin ran the numbers, he saw a program having success with what looked like a similar Moneyball-type approach: Washington. Led by head coach Kalen De-Boer, the Huskies started the season 13-0, including a Pac-12 championship, and made the four-team playoff largely off the backs of some four-stars and a lot of three-star prospects. They didn't depend on five-stars like the blue bloods. It left Griffin and others around the program feeling encouraged that if Maryland could finally get over the hump, the opportunity was there. "*This close* is the hardest part," he said. "We have to break through to get to that next step in the equation."

Maryland athletic director Damon Evans, who once lorded over a Saks Fifth Avenue program at Georgia, believed it was possible. The man who loved to dream big was as bullish as ever about Maryland's future despite living in the same world that had his head football coach debating whether to give it all up.

"We're coming," Evans said. "This change, to me, will give us an opportunity to do something great. We'll be sitting back, five or six years from now, talking about remember all that chaos?

"And I'll be like, 'That chaos was good.'"

CHAPTER 17

The Agent

IT'S FINALS WEEK AT SOUTHERN Methodist University and Jackson Zager is trying to cram in studying for his functional biomechanics exam that afternoon.

Zager is a twenty-year-old sophomore at SMU in Dallas, a ritzy private school full of students driving Range Rovers and Mercedes-Benz G Wagons. Decked in athleisure wear and drinking a Starbucks cold brew drink, Zager is holed up in a conference room in his luxury apartment building, less than a ten-minute walk from SMU's manicured campus, looking over his notes when an important email pops up in his inbox.

Rusty Hardin, the famous Houston-area litigator, wants him to review the latest complaint draft before filing it. Hardin is Texas law royalty and has represented everyone from Roger Clemens to Scottie Pippen. Why is the eighty-two-year-old Hardin asking a twenty-year-old to review legal documents?

Zager isn't just a regular college student. He's also the NIL sports agent representing Arizona State quarterback Jaden Rashada.

Does that name ring a bell? It should. Rashada is the highly regarded quarterback prospect offered a four-year, $13.85 million NIL deal to play for the Florida Gators, only for the well-heeled boosters who promised to pay those millions to renege at the last minute. Yes, Florida boosters were actually willing to pay Rashada, an eighteen-year-old who had never thrown a single pass in college football, more money than NFL starting quarterback

Brock Purdy. The news hit college football like a meteor, proof to some that NIL was entirely out of control. It was both completely believable and utterly incomprehensible that a fan base, even one as desperate as Florida, would spend *that* much money on a quarterback it felt could change the trajectory of a downtrodden program.

And then it all blew up when Florida's two collectives, the Gator Guard and Gator Collective, couldn't come up with the money and voided the deal. As the details started leaking out, it became a major story in newspapers and websites nationwide. Rashada's life changed that day, but so did Zager's. The young agent was in the eye of a shitstorm of bad publicity, with detractors attacking his age and inexperience. In the middle of it, it felt like every college football reporter in the country was texting or calling Zager about what happened. He stayed quiet, preferring to wait for the right time to share his experience.

"There's a lot of that story that has not yet been told and may never be told," said attorney Darren Heitner, who has worked closely with him. "Ultimately, everyone will realize he did nothing wrong and, in fact, was an amazing advocate for his client."

That moment is coming for Zager, as Hardin prepares to sue Florida head coach Billy Napier, top booster Hugh Hathcock, and football staffer Marcus Castro-Walker in what would be the most significant NIL-related lawsuit since NIL became legal on July 1, 2021.

As Zager looks over the Hardin-prepared lawsuit, his eyes get big and he starts reading a detail he knows could turn his world upside down. "Defendant Billy Napier fraudulently induces Jaden into signing national letter of intent," Zager read aloud.

He stopped himself for a moment, considering what that statement alone meant. It was a declaration of war against an SEC head coach. "I think that'll be the whoa," he said. "Calling Napier out for fraud."

As he keeps reading the lawsuit, the father of a four-star recruit calls Zager and asks for advice. The recruit is already committed to a high-profile school, but another school is pursuing hard ahead of signing day and talking a big game about the money available for his son. Jackson tells the father his standard advice, "Don't make a decision off money," but also says he knows the key people at both schools and is happy to reach out and handle the situation. He promises transparency and offers a buffer for father and son. Rather than a recruit having to awkwardly ask a coach for money, a major no-no in the pre-NIL world, Jackson advises the father to tell the coaches his son has a guy who handles all the NIL stuff and redirect them to him. He estimates this player could likely fetch $150,000 per season.

He knows with the Florida lawsuit looming that his world is about to change again, but until then, business is business.

ZAGER AND RASHADA FIRST MET while both attended prep school powerhouse IMG Academy in Bradenton, Florida. Zager was two grades older, and Rashada had only attended the school for about a month, but the two quarterbacks quickly hit it off.

The six-foot-one, broad-chested Zager was a talented football player in his own right, but on a team that included future Michigan star quarterback J.J. McCarthy, he realized his future wasn't on the football field. But, he believed, it could be representing those on the field. Growing up in a family of lawyers, Zager had long been interested in becoming a sports agent one day. NFL uberagent Drew Rosenhaus, who became an agent at twenty-two, was his North Star. He would jokingly tell an IMG locker room full of future NFL pros he would represent them one day.

That wouldn't have been possible until after he graduated college because of NFL Players Association rules, which require agents to be certified, until the birth of NIL opened a new path for him. He was young and personable and believed he could better serve college athletes his age than older, more accomplished agents who viewed NIL as more of a nuisance than anything. He thought there was an opening in the marketplace for a young NIL agent and quickly began developing a business plan to make his dream a reality.

His first client, Illinois State quarterback Zack Annexstad, was a former IMG teammate. Zager launched his own company, JTM Sports, with another former IMG quarterback, Tommy Thomsen. Early on, it was tough sledding for the college freshman, who desperately wanted to succeed and was willing to sacrifice his social life to make it happen.

He pledged a fraternity, Phi Delt, for a day before realizing that his lifestyle of flying around the country to meet with current and prospective clients didn't exactly align with the fraternity's pledge process. He says he's still friends with many of the guys today.

Nothing mattered more to him than trying to turn his new business into a real career. When he stayed up late, he was on the phone with clients, not enjoying the usual college rites of passage of partying and drinking out of Red Solo cups. As he started building out JTM Sports, he worked as a DoorDash delivery driver to pay for his growing business expenses. It was early mornings and late nights for Zager as he pursued his dream. He eventually stopped after a Dallas SWAT team showed up at the same apartment he was delivering to and told him to drop the food and get out of there.

He'd wake up no later than 6:00 each morning—usually more like 5:30—and start his day with a forty-five-minute weighted backpack walk to get some early exercise and get the endorphins going before jumping into work. He needed to get his mind right before work, already trying to avoid burnout in a career that could be 24-7. From there, he'd work before class, go to class for a couple of hours, and then spend the next eight or nine hours making phone calls, checking in on clients, and setting up potential deals. He told his clients to call him at any time, always leaving the ringer on his cell phone, just in case one of them had a late-night emergency.

"I'm not the type of guy who goes out from ten p.m. to three a.m. I just don't do it," Zager said. "I'll work until midnight. It's fun for me. If I'm in class for two hours, there's still twenty-two other hours."

At the start of the semester, he had to explain to his professors that he'd occasionally have to step out to take phone calls. He says most of them got it.

Zager was slowly growing his client base when Rashada sent him a message in January 2022. Now a four-star quarterback with a rising national profile, Rashada had heard Zager was involved in collective deals and wondered if he could help him. As a California native, Rashada could secure NIL deals while still in high school.

Zager agreed to represent Rashada, a decision that would change both their lives.

• • •

WHEN NIL LAUNCHED, IT HAD been thirteen years since Florida had last won a national championship. After Urban Meyer walked away in 2010, Florida languished in the desert, frequently mistaking Saban disciples for an oasis. First it was Will Muschamp, who worked with Saban at LSU and lasted four years before athletic director Jeremy Foley had seen enough. He then turned to Colorado State's Jim McElwain, winner of two national championships at Alabama with Saban. McElwain won the SEC East his first two seasons—he lost to Saban in both SEC Championship games—before a bizarre situation led to his firing midway through year three: McElwain publicly alluded to him and his players receiving death threats but hadn't provided any details or reported it to school officials.

Florida AD Scott Stricklin then turned to a man he knew well, for better and worse: Mississippi State head coach Dan Mullen. The two hadn't always gotten along in Starkville, but Stricklin badly needed a winner and knew Mullen fit the bill. An offensive coordinator under Meyer during the Florida glory years, Mullen knew the place well and injected his own brand of confidence into the program. It paid off with top ten finishes his first two seasons at Florida, but Mullen didn't love recruiting and would simply never be obsessed with destroying the competition in that arena like Saban and Georgia's Kirby Smart.

Once Mullen was out, Louisiana head coach Billy Napier, another Saban acolyte, walked in.

At this point, Florida was desperate for success, as it had a front-row seat to the college football powerhouse Smart was building in Athens. Eddie Rojas, a former Florida pitcher, had big dreams about what NIL could do for his beloved Florida football program. Along with lawyer Darren Heitner, Rojas launched Gator Collective, believed to be one of, if not the, first collective, and became its chief executive officer.

"I'm about the confetti," Rojas told CBS Sports. "I want to create an environment where Florida becomes NIL-U."

In words that would come back to bite him, he also said that April: "I would venture to say the Gator Collective is paying more guaranteed money than any group in the country. When I write a contract, I want to make sure that we actually have the money in our account."

Florida set its sights on Rashada, one of the nation's top ten quarterback prospects. Mirroring the NFL, where the fifteen highest-paid players were all quarterbacks, a top-flight quarterback became the hottest commodity in college football. The demand far outstripped the supply, sending their value into the seven-figure range. "Those dudes are going to make the most cash," said Cody Bellaire, who worked in the personnel departments at multiple Power 4 schools. "They are the faces of the team. They'll get taken care of more than other positions."

Miami, backed by NIL kingpin John Ruiz, badly wanted Rashada too. Making things even more complicated, Rashada had two agents working on his behalf, unbeknownst to each other. Jaden wanted Zager to handle the deal, while his father, Harlen, hired Michael Caspino, a California-based lawyer who had quickly made a name for himself as the rainmaker for huge NIL deals.

An intense bidding war soon broke out between Miami's and Florida's money big shots. On Miami's side was Ruiz, the CEO of LifeWallet and the early face of spending big money on college athletes. On Florida's side was a man named Hugh Hathcock, who had allegedly made hundreds of millions in car sales. Earlier that year, Hathcock committed to donating $12.6 million to Florida athletics and then launched the Gator Guard, a second Florida collective intended to secure donations from Florida's wealthiest boosters. Florida kept trying to raise the ante, insisting it had ample money to spend on Rashada. Still, Ruiz, a man whose company faced a Securities and Exchange Commission investigation in 2023, felt like the more trustworthy option. Florida offered $11 million, but with Rashada's brain trust skeptical of the money behind it, Jaden instead accepted Miami's $9.5 million deal. (Ruiz later denied that it was that much money but never specified the actual amount.) Rashada officially committed to the Hurricanes on June 26, the early crown jewel of new head coach Mario Cristobal's recruiting class.

No one outside the key participants would ever have known about the money involved had the numbers not been leaked to the media.

Zager was coming out of a hibachi dinner with friends and had left his phone in his car, needing a momentary break from all the business drama. As he picked it up, he saw nine missed calls from Jaden. He quickly called him back, and Jaden unloaded on him, alternating between screaming and crying. Initially confused about what was happening, Zager asked him to slow down and explain why he was so upset.

"You know exactly what I'm talking about," Jaden told him. "You're telling me you didn't release those numbers to On3?"

Zager put him on speaker and frantically searched on his phone for what Jaden was talking about, finding a story from On3's Jeremy Crabtree that detailed the $9.5 million number from Miami, citing sources. Zager told Jaden he didn't even know the Miami number because he had only been dealing with Florida.

"Caspino released those," he told him. "He was the only one who knew both numbers."

Caspino was even quoted in the story, saying, "Jaden left millions on the table. Millions. He did not pick the highest offer. He went there because he loves Miami, the coaches, and the opportunity." Caspino did not respond to multiple requests for comment about leaking the numbers.

That $9.5 million number followed Jaden around like the Scarlet Letter. It changed how everyone saw the high school senior. He was now Jaden Rashada, the $9.5 million quarterback. It ratcheted up the expectations and pressure on a good kid who just wanted to play football. There were early signs it was getting to him, including a lackluster performance at the Elite 11 camp. Two days after the numbers leaked, he didn't look anywhere close to the nation's top quarterback in that event, certainly not one worth several multiples more than the rest of the QBs in attendance.

Those close to Rashada believe he was never excited about going to Miami. "I remember watching his commitment and thinking, this is the most uncomfortable commitment I've ever seen in my life," said Heitner, a Gator alum who helped the Gator Collective with its contracts.

Florida was where Jaden wanted to be. Fortunately for him, Florida's megaboosters hadn't given up hope of reeling him to Gainesville.

Florida's two collectives reengaged with Zager to see if Jaden would be interested in the $11 million offer again. They told him they needed him in orange and blue and would do what was necessary to make it happen. "Hugh Hathcock is calling me and saying, 'Shit, I would have paid eighteen million for that kid,'" Zager said. Knowing their leverage, the young college student said Rashada's price had gone up. The new number was $13 million, with $8 million coming from Hathcock's Gator Guard. The deal also included a $500,000 signing bonus paid to Rashada on December 5. After thinking it over, Hathcock agreed.

"They could have said no," Zager said. "I don't know what they were thinking. I think they thought we were young and [Jaden's] poor. What's he going to do?"

The two sides agreed on November 10. Rashada made his announcement the next day, excited that it worked out for him to play for Florida. Just the cut for JTM Sports, which typically charged 10 percent, would be seven figures.

Zager soon worried it was all too easy and might be too good to be true, even with a signed contract. Florida was saying all the right things, but he had a gnawing feeling the school's collectives didn't truly have the money they had promised. Zager was nervous when December 5 came and went without the $500,000 wire. The next day, December 6, Heitner advised him to at least give them another day. Zager woke up on December 7 to a termination letter that had been sent in the middle of the night. His mind started racing, wondering how it was even possible. His dominant thought was, "Are we fucked?" It spiked Zager's stress through the roof as he wondered how he would break the news to Rashada. Consulting with his business partner, Tommy, they decided to devise a plan before telling their client, taking a few days to prepare themselves for what increasingly felt like a disaster waiting to happen.

That week, Heitner helped set up a call between Zager and Marcus Castro-Walker, Florida's director of player engagement and NIL. Castro-Walker promised that the termination letter would be rescinded and that Hathcock would assume the cost of the entire contract. "I just talked to Hugh, and he said it's all good," he told Zager. According to multiple sources familiar with the deal, Billy Napier was aware of the calls with Hathcock and said, "Scared money don't make money."

One person who was not aware? Florida athletic director Scott Stricklin had no clue what was happening within his own football program until Heitner notified him after the termination letter.

Two weeks passed, and still no money. An important deadline promised to spur action. Everyone expected Rashada to officially sign with Florida on December 21, the start of college football's early signing period. Zager strongly encouraged him not to do so until he received the signing bonus. Rashada initially listened to his agent's advice, refusing to sign a national letter of intent as curiosity piqued about what was going on with the quarterback prospect around college football. Napier had a 4:00 p.m. press conference scheduled to detail his new recruiting class, but as the seconds ticked closer and closer to that time, Rashada still hadn't signed with the Gators. Napier was nervous and decided he needed to get involved personally.

Napier called Rashada and offered a lucrative incentive if he followed his directive. "I need you to sign the letter of intent," Napier told his top prospect. "We'll get you a million bucks, but you have to sign it." Napier directly offering money to Rashada was a major no-no in the NCAA's eyes, the type of move that could get him banned from the sport for years. That Napier would make the pitch himself, according to the lawsuit—and not use an underling to insulate himself—spoke to the desperation of the situation.

Against the advice of his agent, Rashada agreed to Napier's plea and signed a letter of intent.

Finally, sixty-seven minutes after the press conference was scheduled to start, Napier strode behind the podium with news that Rashada was on board. "Can't compliment Jaden enough relative to who he is as a person, as a leader, his character," Napier said that day.

Rashada planned to enroll early at Florida, on January 10, but the signing bonus hung around his neck like an albatross. He loved Florida and dreamed of being the Gators' starting quarterback, but its most prominent supporters had made big promises to him, and he eagerly waited for them to deliver.

Zager reached out to Hardin, a friend of his father's, in late December to gauge his interest in helping if everything blew up. Hardin was on board after an introductory call in which Zager laid out the case details. The priority was still to get Rashada his money at Florida.

As it got closer to Rashada's enrollment date, Jose Costa, who would later emerge as the face of a third Florida NIL collective called Florida

Victorious, set up a January 8 Zoom call with Rashada and Zager. The meeting quickly went south when Costa, who claims to be the owner of the world's largest ornamental plant supplier, started detailing all the money he made during a successful business career, only to tell Rashada he wasn't going to honor the initial deal and instead could only offer $1 million. Oh, and he had a stipulation: Rashada would have to sign away his right to sue if he took the deal.

Florida's wealthy boosters had the power and were putting the screws on an eighteen-year-old. As they debated the limited options, Zager told him the easiest thing to do would be to still go to Florida. He had gotten screwed, but it was still a sizable amount of money, and sticking with the Gators would ensure the whole story would never come out.

Rashada said no.

It was a matter of principle for him. He was devastated about the loss of life-changing money, but he wouldn't just go along with a group of men who had lied and tried to take advantage of him. How could he trust Florida, from Napier to the top boosters, when they willingly negotiated a deal with him, he agreed, and then, at the last minute, they tried to shaft him? If they'd do that before he was even a team member, what would they do once he was in Gainesville full time?

"You dangle life-changing, generation-changing money in front of a nineteen-year-old kid, who grew up without it; you can't expect that young person to not be affected by it," said Rusty Hardin, his attorney.

Rashada asked for his release from Florida on January 17, which was granted. Soon, stories about the behind-the-scenes drama involving Florida and Rashada started popping up. *The Athletic* obtained a copy of Rashada's $13.85 million contract, a bombshell story that sent shock waves through the college football industry. A high school quarterback was being paid WHAT?!

Florida was thrust into PR spin mode, explaining it as rogue boosters making offers they shouldn't and an inexperienced agent who was over his head. Zager is mostly easygoing and has a quick laugh, but he gets fired up when that accusation is thrown his way. He heard through clients and other industry sources that behind the scenes Florida was putting all the blame on him. His clients even relayed that Florida claimed he had fraudulently entered the compensation numbers into the contract.

Rashada now had to find a new home quickly. The options were limited late in the cycle, when most programs already had their quarterback of the future coming to campus.

"People thought the kid's a pariah," said one source with knowledge of the situation. "Jumping from nine million dollars to thirteen million and all the things that surrounded that and then jumping to another school really hurt the kid a lot. There was just zero interest."

The SEC powerhouses were out of the picture now. Eventually, two main options emerged: Arizona State, his father's alma mater, and Texas Christian. Neither was offering NIL money. Family connection won out over a program that played in the national championship game weeks earlier. Rashada would follow in his father's footsteps and play football for Arizona State and first-year head coach Kenny Dillingham. Even after missing out on him, TCU head coach Sonny Dykes couldn't help but feel bad for Rashada.

"It's very sad. The whole thing was sad," Dykes said. "The biggest takeaway is sometimes you get too many people involved in the process that don't have the young person's best interests at heart, and I think that's a slippery slope."

Zager himself spiraled after the Rashada deal blew up. Deep down, he believed he had done nothing wrong, but he couldn't help but blame himself. He had his client on the verge of the biggest NIL deal in college football history, only for it to blow up and get nothing. Worse, he and Rashada were getting trashed in public, becoming the early poster children for NIL gone wrong.

SEC Network analyst Chris Doering, a Gator alum, was one of many who seemed to revel in Rashada's misfortune. "This kid does not deserve thirteen million dollars, and I am so glad to hear that Florida will not be paying him that," he said on SiriusXM. "And happy to hear he will not be attending the University of Florida."

It broke Zager's heart that the Rashadas, counting on that Florida deal to go through, suffered financially and, at one point, risked being evicted. The college student gave them as much as he could—essentially all his NIL earnings—to ameliorate a situation that left him feeling guilty.

"It pissed me off for people [to say] I'm trying to screw the kid over," he said. "I basically made no money [representing] this kid. I feel good for doing it; I'd do it again."

Rashada and Zager were financially poorer but bonded like brothers through the trauma. In time, Rashada was ready to fight back.

THREE MONTHS LATER, AT THE posh Sadelle's in Dallas's Highland Park neighborhood, Zager vented about the deal that turned his life upside down. Before Rashada, he preferred to keep a low profile, not interested in revealing specifics about his clients' deals or landing media coverage. After the Rashada situation, he doubled down, becoming a hermit as he privately tried to pick up the pieces. He refused to let the negative publicity kill his business, but he knew it hurt his ability to sign other quarterback clients. He had been informally helping five-star quarterback D. J. Lagway early in the recruiting process, but Zager bowed out when Lagway indicated he was likely headed to Florida. There was too much bad blood, still too fresh, for him to be able to negotiate across the table from Florida again.

Especially not with what he had planned.

As nearby diners sipped on Americanos and obliviously picked at their eggs, Zager dropped two bombshells: Rashada was cooperating with the NCAA in an investigation and he planned on suing Florida for fraud. Combined, it was a Category 5 hurricane headed straight for Florida.

There had been plenty of horror stories whispered behind the scenes about recruits not getting the NIL money promised to them. But what could they really do about it? It was against NCAA rules to induce a recruit to attend a school via NIL compensation. Admitting you received money to attend a school but hadn't gotten the full payment opened up a can of problems. It'd be like calling the cops to report a robber stole your stolen property. It's why recruits stayed silent, opting to take less money rather than pick a fight with a collective.

Rashada was different. Through no choice of his own, his numbers were already very public. Everyone knew what had happened to him, so there was limited risk. He wanted to turn a negative into a positive for players who didn't have the same platform as he did. "I just don't want this to happen to anyone else," Rashada told his agent.

As Rusty Hardin prepared a possible lawsuit, Zager tried to do some reputational damage control. As he connected with collectives, he'd preemptively address the elephant in the room. "He said all the right things," said one Power 4 collective operator. "He brought up Rashada and said, 'Look, I don't expect you to take my side on that, but I hope over time we can work together and build trust.'"

Hardin, who has known Zager since the agent was a teenager, described him as "forty years ahead of his age" with great judgment in how he handled the tricky situation.

Zager's honest and direct approach certainly worked with Zabien Brown. A five-star cornerback out of Santa Ana, California, Brown was quiet, intensely focused on bettering himself to one day make the NFL and not particularly interested in anyone trying to sell him bullshit. He and his mom, Courtney, were naturally distrusting of others' intentions and weren't quite sure what to expect when they met with Zager and Thomsen for the first time. They went in with their guard up, bracing for possible disappointment. It was striking then for Courtney Brown to see the way her phenom son interacted with Zager over lunch. "I'm watching Zabien open up a little, laugh, and be chattier than he normally would," Courtney Brown said. "I thought, 'Okay, this is interesting.'"

Zager wasn't pushy like other agents they had talked to and impressed the Browns with his informative approach. As they started recapping how things went, Courtney asked Zabien what he thought.

"I was surprised," he told her.

Zabien liked that Zager was close to his age and thought he understood the marketplace well. "I'd feel comfortable attaching my brand to them," he concluded. For Courtney, who knew how monumental it was to hear her son say those words, that was all it took. She had high hopes of what her son, who later committed to play for Nick Saban at Alabama, and Zager could accomplish together.

"God willing, Zabien will hopefully play on Sundays and I think it's important from the get-go to have people in place from a younger age who will have his back, make introductions, and support him throughout the way," Courtney said. "Especially because the NIL space was so new, it wasn't something I felt like I could become a master in."

. . .

THE NCAA INFORMED FLORIDA ON June 9 that it was investigating the Rashada situation. The inquiry stemmed from the fact that Marcus Castro-Walker introduced Rashada to super booster Hugh Hathcock on the school's campus, an NCAA violation. The NCAA interviewed Castro-Walker, who promptly informed other Florida staffers and interested parties what the NCAA had asked and told them that they shouldn't comply, according to sources familiar with the situation, which was another NCAA violation. He wasn't the smartest rules violator and was later fired. Zager and Harlen Rashada, Jaden's father, initially declined the NCAA's meeting request. As did Caspino, who initially represented Jaden in the Miami deal.

Rusty Hardin targeted filing the lawsuit before the 2023 season, but it kept getting delayed for one reason after another. The state of Texas hired him as part of the impeachment trial of Attorney General Ken Paxton, which stretched into late September. By late October, Hardin was eyeing a November file date, and Zager was nervous about what was coming down the pike. He put his professional responsibilities as Rashada's agent over his personal interest in not getting dragged through the mud again in public as an inexperienced college student masquerading as an agent. As the son of a prominent Houston-area attorney, he knew the toll a trial would take. Given the stakes, he believed Napier and Florida would do whatever it took to win, even if it meant attacking an SMU sophomore. He tried to keep those feelings to himself before they eventually spilled out one day on the phone with Jaden.

"To be honest with you," he told him, "if I could have it my way where nobody else is affected, I wouldn't do anything. I'd rather have you not sue them, but that's not what I'm here to do. I'm here to make the best decision for you."

November came and went, and still there was no lawsuit. Hardin oscillated between filing in federal or state court, doing as much research as possible to determine which terrain better suited the case. Zager had remained silent on Hardin's orders. Explaining the strategy, Hardin said, "Don't throw jabs; throw the knockout punch all at once."

After advising Zager not to talk to the NCAA, Hardin reversed course and believed it could benefit their case. A meeting between Zager and NCAA investigators was set for Friday, March 1, at Hardin's Houston-based law offices. A few days before that meeting took place, the NCAA canceled. Following the landmark *Tennessee v. NCAA* lawsuit, the NCAA was vacating any active enforcement of NIL-related rules violations. If Rashada and Zager wanted justice, it'd have to come from the legal system now.

As Hardin and his team put the finishing touches on the lawsuit, Rashada decided to leave Arizona State and transfer to Georgia. After all the drama during his recruitment process, Rashada liked the idea of spending a year behind entrenched starting quarterback Carson Beck and trying to win a national championship playing for Kirby Smart. The move only amplified the interest in a potential lawsuit, now pitting an SEC quarterback against a rival SEC head coach.

Finally, on May 21, days before the Memorial Day weekend, Hardin filed the lawsuit in the Pensacola Division of the U.S. District Court for the Northern District of Florida. The bombshell lawsuit, the first of its kind in the NIL era, named Napier, Hathcock, and Castro-Walker as defendants and accused the trio of fraudulently inducing Rashada to attend the University of Florida with no intention of following through on their financial promises. Specifically, the lawsuit claimed fraudulent misrepresentation and inducement, aiding and abetting fraud, civil conspiracy to commit fraud, negligent misrepresentation, tortious interference with a business relationship or contract, and aiding and abetting tortious interference.

(A week later, in his first public comments about the lawsuit, Napier said he was "comfortable with my actions" and declined to go into specifics about ongoing litigation.)

It had been more than a year since Zager and Rashada saw their names besmirched all over the internet. Now they were ready for their day in court.

"Every lie they tell incurs a debt to the truth," Zager said. "Sooner or later, that debt must be paid."

CHAPTER 18

One Last Ride

TWENTY-FOUR HOURS BEFORE ARIZONA WAS set to square off against the University of Oklahoma in the Valero Alamo Bowl, the lobby of the San Antonio Marriott Riverwalk was awash in blue and red. The atmosphere was part pep rally, part tailgate, as a couple of hundred U of A fans were nestled into a boozy postholiday embrace of a city known for the Alamo, its scenic River Walk, and warm hospitality.

The Arizona faithful were partying hard, and rightly so. Their football team was riding some kind of high: a 9-3 record, six straight wins, the longest such streak in a season since 1998, the most regular-season victories in nearly a decade, the first bowl appearance in six years, and a No. 14 national ranking. Their opponent was a serious test of that ranking, football royalty in the form of the big bad Sooners from the Big 12 sporting a 10-2 record and No. 12 ranking themselves.

Two floors up from the din downstairs a quiet conference room was packed with players and coaches eager to take a final test. From the moment the team arrived in the home of the Alamo, its postseason experience had been uniquely San Antonio: a mariachi band greeting at the airport; a volunteer visit to a local food bank; a trip to SeaWorld, a River Walk boat cruise, the Cats feeling so free as to drop the Haka, the traditional Polynesian war dance, at an Alamo Bowl lunch.

But that was over now. The third-floor conference room was silent and attentive, a team ready to write the final chapter of an inspiring story that had raised Arizona football to heights not seen in thirty years, while show-casing its explosive talent, brotherly love, and most of all belief in the man now standing before them.

"You guys have done more than we could ever ask of a football team," Jedd Fisch began. "Tomorrow is the last time this team is playing together. The beautiful thing about sports is there is a start and there is a stop. There is an ending. The ending is tomorrow night. At the end of the game I would expect tears, tears for what you've accomplished, because regardless of the outcome is the courage of what you've done together, the outcome of the last eleven and a half months is victory."

You could have heard a proverbial pin drop as Fisch looked down and paused before raising his head and coming to a close.

"If you would have told anybody outside of this room we're going to take on Oklahoma, people would have thought we were fucking crazy. This doesn't happen. Yet it happened. It happened. And it happened because of the people in this room. All of us. So tomorrow night is the end of an *a-mazing* eleven months together. Let's not go into tomorrow night thinking I'll fix that the next game. Or I'll block better the next game. Or I'll run that route better *the next game*. Or I'll make that tackle *the next game*.

"Tomorrow night is the last game, and tomorrow night you leave it all out there, you leave it *all out there. Everything you got.*"

FOUR MONTHS EARLIER THE WILDCATS had opened their season at home thumping the University of Northern Arizona before suffering what seemed at the time a debilitating defeat on the road at Mississippi State, where they tied the game with five seconds remaining on a 36-yard field goal, only to lose 31–24 in overtime, ultimately outdone by five turnovers on a big SEC stage.

Two games, Fisch later said, that served as "measuring sticks," an objective way to mark the progress of the program.

"I look at comparisons," he said. "Two years ago we played Northern Arizona and lose twenty-one–nineteen at home. This year we beat them thirty-eight–three. Last year, we lost to Mississippi State at our place thirty-nine–nineteen. This year we go to their place and take them into overtime. I can see we're bigger, stronger, faster. I hear what NFL scouts are telling me—you've got four or five guys that are going to be drafted in the first six rounds. So that's where I see the difference."

In Tucson in mid-September 2023, it was clear what a difference a few months, a football-only collective, and ten additions via the transfer portal can make. The Wildcats looked every bit like a serious Power 5 team—300-plus pound road graders anchoring the offensive and defensive lines, speed and explosiveness at every skill position, playmakers all over the field.

After yet another long, fast, physical practice, Fisch stood on the sidelines of the indoor facility—it was pouring rain outside—and put the progress into perspective. His season-long message was drawn from a bestselling book on leadership by legendary San Francisco 49ers coach Bill Walsh titled *The Score Takes Care of Itself*. Fisch took great pains to show his team the book. He talked about it in meetings, delivering a PowerPoint presentation detailing the road map of how to achieve success.

"That was truly our whole thing," he said. "The score will take care of itself. Regardless of a quarterback injury, a third-down play stopped, whatever happens, just come together as a team."

Indeed, ten days later, after Arizona blew out UTEP 31–10 at home, Fisch's QB de Laura suffered a serious injury to his right ankle late in the third quarter against Stanford. Before he went down, the junior had been playing at an all-conference rate, throwing nine touchdowns while completing 70 percent of his passes. With de Laura sidelined for several weeks the football would now be in the hands of backup quarterback Noah Fifita.

From practice and limited game action Fisch knew the redshirt freshman was a really good player, great in his commitment and game prep. What he didn't know was how he would handle adversity, a moment of crisis, when he took center stage and the game was no longer high school football.

Fisch got a glimpse when Fifita stepped up and led the Wildcats on a nine-play touchdown drive that sealed a 21–20 win over the Cardinal. In his first career start the next week at home against undefeated Washington, Fifita threw for 232 yards and three touchdowns, but the team had no real answer for quarterback Michael Penix Jr., who picked apart Arizona's defense with short passes, the Wildcats closing to 31–24 with 1:11 left, only to see the Huskies recover an onside kick. The following Saturday in a showcase game against undefeated and ninth-ranked USC on ESPN, Fifita threw for 303 yards and five touchdowns, four to wide receiver Jacob Cowing, before the 'Cats fell 43–41 in three overtimes, evening their record at 3-3.

Fisch was impressed by what he saw in the five-eleven, 195-pound Fifita, proving not just dangerous but elusive, with a strong, accurate arm. All the same, Fisch refused to get drawn into any kind of quarterback controversy.

"I got asked and I said, 'There's no change in our plans. Jayden will be our starting quarterback when he's healthy,'" said Fisch. "He has to be one hundred percent but he'll be our starting quarterback."

Fisch never said it out loud—at least not to the press—but he believed the next game on the road against 19th-ranked Washington State was critical. If the team struggled or failed to win he would turn to a healthy de Laura.

"No question about it," said Fisch.

And then Arizona traveled up to Pullman and blew out WSU 44–6. Fifita put on some kind of show, completing thirty-four of forty-three passes for 342 yards; the team rushed for 174 yards; and the defense forced three turnovers. Arizona was 4-3 and hitting on all cylinders headed into a bye week.

During the season Fisch had a weekly lunch with de Laura every Wednesday and Fifita every Thursday. It was time to have a different conversation.

"I talked to Jayden and said, 'How do you want to handle this?' he recalled. "What do you think we should do?"

De Laura told Fisch he should probably start Noah and he'd be ready to go.

Arizona's next two opponents were both nationally ranked—Oregon State at No. 11 and UCLA at No. 20. The Wildcats won both at home to run their season record to 6-3, leading to another conversation with de Laura, this one much harder than the last.

There was no way Fisch could pull Fifita now, so together he and de Laura watched some old Drew Bledsoe and Tom Brady interviews. In September 2001, the untested Brady had replaced the All-Pro after Bledsoe suffered a life-threatening chest injury following a hard but clean tackle by New York Jets linebacker Mo Lewis. When he returned, Bledsoe wasn't happy warming the bench, but he had to make the decision to support Brady because, he said at the time, he had a *C* on his chest—meaning Bledsoe was a team captain.

Now de Laura, a team leader, faced a similar fate.

"We tried to talk through it rationally," said Fisch. "What are you going to do? How are we going to handle this?"

To ease the pain Fisch spoke about the NFL scouts that attended every Arizona practice to see senior wide receiver Cowing and offensive tackle Jordan Morgan. Why wouldn't they say, Hey, this kid started thirty-two games in the Pac-12 and got hurt . . . He's the perfect guy to bring in as our No. 2 or No. 3 quarterback.

"Why don't you show them how good a backup you are?" asked Fisch.

To his credit that is exactly what de Laura did. Becoming what his head coach called an "elite" teammate to Fifita—taking as many practice reps as needed to give Noah's arm a rest, watching tape together, playing big brother to a little brother. In the end, he helped Fifita blossom into a breakout star.

Fifita's own love for the game could be traced to a familiar source. "The thing about football was it was part of my family," Noah told Justin Spears of the *Arizona Daily Star* in a revealing profile prior to the OU game. "In my mind, that was a way to make them proud."

Fifita's bloodlines drew from the defensive side of the ball. His father, Les, played linebacker; his uncle Steve was a first-team All-Mountain West defensive tackle at Utah under Urban Meyer. His other uncle, Kelly Talavou, played defensive tackle for the Baltimore Ravens.

A descendant of Tongan and Filipino immigrants who had long settled in Orange County, California, Noah started playing football at the age of four, a linebacker and offensive tackle quickly turned quarterback when, on a ride home after practice, his head coach—who happened to be his father—asked, "Hey, do you think you could take a snap and put your hand under the center's actual butt?"

"Yeah," responded Noah, "I think I could do that."

Thanks to his father and his extended family, Fifita fell in love with football, first memorizing the names of NFL quarterbacks then their top receivers growing up. Like another Southern California quarterback with the last name of Sayin, Fifita harbored big dreams, attending Winner Circle Athletics in Corona, riding an hour each way with an aunt as she poured the same message into his ears day after day—how every member of a family, no matter how young or old, had a specific role to play.

In his final year of youth league football, Fifita led an Orange County U14 team to a national championship. The team that included Tetairoa McMillan, a recent transplant from Hawaii. The beginning of a bond destined to run from Servite High in Anaheim to the Sonoran desert, where Fifita, T-Mac, and fellow high school teammates linebacker Jacob Manu and tight end Keyan Burnett were among the crown jewels of Fisch's stellar 2022 recruiting class.

By the time Fifita arrived in Tucson his OCD nature had long since been established—Gatorade and water bottles lined up like tiny soldiers in the refrigerator, shoes, sneakers, and towels aligned just so in his bedroom closet and bathroom, a pursuit of perfection that spilled over to six hours of film study a week in high school, and even more at Arizona.

"He's not only somebody who does everything right off the field," said Fisch, "he does everything right on the field."

ARIZONA WOULD END THE REGULAR season on a six-game roll, the final win a 59–23 blowout of Arizona State, Fifita throwing for a school record of 527 yards and five touchdowns. Overall, he completed an astonishing 73.6 percent of his passes (4th nationally, No. 1 for freshmen) for 2,517 yards and twenty-three touchdowns against just five interceptions, earning Pac-12 Freshman Offensive Player of the Year honors.

For his part, the sophomore McMillan would conclude the regular season with eleven catches for 266 yards against ASU. Overall, he ranked 8th in the country in receiving yards (1,242), more than Ohio State's Marvin Harrison, the Biletnikoff Award winner honoring the nation's best wide receiver.

T-Mac's sensational season had unquestionably added a few more gray hairs to Fisch's head beginning December 5 with the opening of the thirty-day transfer portal. Offers of seven-figure money to leave for the SEC or Big Ten were on the table.

"Was I worried? I was worried every day for four weeks," said Fisch.

Knowing there was no way Arizona could match a million-dollar deal, Fisch proposed an alternative focusing on NFL numbers instead. He said he asked T-Mac where he thought he would be drafted.

Top ten, said McMillan.

When? Fisch asked.

After next season.

Okay, said Fisch, let's look up the contracts for the top ten wide receivers coming out of college. The likes of Drake London, Garrett Wilson, Ja'Marr Chase, Jaylen Waddle, DeVonta Smith.

The average, it turned out, was around $28 million over four years for a top ten pick.

"So when I tell you you're going to make twenty-nine million over five years or twenty-eight over four, would you care?" Fisch asked McMillan. "What if I told you [you] had to move twice? What if you had to be in another offense?"

To Fisch that was the argument. And it worked. In the face of collective kingmakers at Ohio State throwing million-dollar NIL offers around, McMillan stayed in with his football family in Tucson and out of the portal for far less than he could have made.

OVER THE THANKSGIVING HOLIDAY WEEKEND Fisch was sitting in a somewhat similar place, his name popping up on Coach of the Year lists and being tossed around as a candidate at various head-coaching vacancies, most notably in a Zoom call with folks at Texas A&M.

"Job opportunities in different places, most of them not intriguing," he told us the first week in December, admitting the only school he really listened to was A&M, a job that eventually went to Duke's Mike Elko. "Most of them I was able to use when talking to our kids. 'Hey, I turned down more money to be with you. Why wouldn't *you* turn down more money to be with *me*?'"

In a text the Sunday after Thanksgiving Heeke indicated the school, now officially on its way to the Big 12, was more than willing to up the ante on Fisch and, as his head coach insisted, pour more money into his assistant coaches' pockets.

We can make it good for him financially and he has most everything else in place in a great place, including NIL, Heeke wrote. President and AD fully in. Doesn't need to jump to a mediocre job just for the money. He could be a hero here.

Twenty-four hours later it was reported that Heeke and Fisch were in talks that would make him the highest-paid football coach in school history.

THE ALAMO BOWL GAME AGAINST Oklahoma landed on the calendar exactly three years and five days after Fisch was officially hired. Asked to reflect on the rise from 1-11 his first year, to 5-7 his second season, then to 9-3, the talk turned to the price of putting a true *team* together, to first grow then sustain a culture of "we" not "me."

"I think our time and our energy that went into team building far outweighed the money that other team's put into their players," Fisch said. "And I would say the price of sacrifice—my wife talks to players' moms, grandmoms, aunts, those things have dollar value."

With pride in his voice Fisch noted how his youngest daughter, Kendall, had a swim meet the previous Saturday and there were Jayden and Noah sitting in the front row for all four of her races. More than a thousand people in the stands could barely believe their eyes. The two star quarterbacks of Arizona football—who could have been anywhere else, and who in another version of the story would have hated each other's guts—sitting there cheering for an eleven-year-old girl.

"That doesn't happen if you don't pay the price of time and investment in these kids," said Fisch. "That's the price that we've all paid. I think that's what really helped our program get going again."

THE VALERO ALAMO BOWL FEATURED the highest-ranked matchup outside the CFP and the so-called New Year's Six Bowls. To be sure, Oklahoma presented a multitude of problems, particularly on offense, averaging 502 yards per game (fifth in the nation) and 43 points (third). In five of its ten victories the Sooners had scored more than 50 points.

Before a boisterous pro-Sooners crowd the Wildcats took the fight to OU right from the start. They jumped out to a 13–0 second quarter lead on two field goals and a 35-yard touchdown pass to Cowing, his record-setting twelfth of the season before Oklahoma put together a 75-yard drive to draw

within six, 13–7. After its initial offensive burst Arizona found itself struggling to maintain possession against the physical nature of OU's offensive
and defensive lines, trailing 14–13 at halftime.

A crowd of more than fifty-five thousand had barely sat down when
thirty-one seconds into the second half the Sooners struck again, this time
on a 63-yard touchdown pass by freshman quarterback Jackson Arnold,
the 2022 Gatorade National Player of the Year. Oklahoma's next possession—a twelve-play 84-yard drive—resulted in a 22-yard field goal, making
it twenty-four straight points for OU and a growing feeling in the stands
that Arizona had more than met its match—a feeling that only grew worse
with less than a minute left in the third quarter.

The Sooners were knocking on the door once more, first and ten on
the Arizona 23. A touchdown here and the scoreboard would read 31–13,
the game essentially over. One could almost hear the impassioned words
of Brian Kight, the motivational speaker who had addressed the team the
night before, echoing in the air.

> Here's the thing: Not everybody wants to do what you guys did to
> get here. Each of you had your own journey, a shared journey. Re-
> flecting on this one last ride, this one last ride together. You will be
> on other teams but you will never be on *this* team again. So think
> about this *one last ride.* Don't waste it. Honor it. How do you honor
> something? You fight for it . . .

With time ticking away, Arnold completed a short pass over the middle down to the 3-yard line. Flying in from the secondary, Wildcat safety
Dalton Johnson blasted wide receiver Jalil Farooq, forcing a midair fumble
that was picked off by free safety Gunner Maldonado and returned 87 yards
down the sideline for a touchdown. A trick play pass added the 2-point conversion. A potential 14-point swing on a single *How do you honor something?
You fight for it* play.

Oklahoma 24, Arizona 21.

On the first play of the final quarter Arizona's defense rose up and
picked off another pass—its fifth turnover of the night—setting up a 37-
yard field goal to tie the score at 24. Then, with less than ten minutes to go

and the ball on the Arizona 5-yard line, Fifita and McMillan took over. In typical T-Mac fashion he made three straight clutch catches to move the ball to near midfield. Then, with 5:46 left on the clock, Fifita scrambled out of the pocket, rolled right, and threw a strike that Cowing caught on the run, sprinting into the end zone for a 57-yard touchdown, his second score of the night.

Seventeen straight points, 31–24 Arizona.

But the Wildcats weren't finished fighting. Not yet.

A blistering quarterback sack/fumble by defensive lineman Isaiah Ward and recovered by fellow defensive lineman Jacob Kongaika—the sixth turnover of the night for Arizona—set up a 19-yard touchdown burst by running back D. J. Williams.

Final score: Arizona 38, Oklahoma 24.

In the end, as gutsy a performance as one would see during the entire bowl season. And only the second ten-win season in the last twenty-five years of Wildcat football.

One last ride.

On the field after the game, with balloons and confetti filling the air, Fisch praised his 'Cats resilience and courage.

"The way our team played tonight I thought was pretty amazing," he said.

The next day, the impact of what millions had witnessed in prime time on ESPN was still reverberating around the college football world. Responding to a text praising his team's effort, Fisch offered these words:

What a moment—I love my kids and they love each other. That's the difference. They play hard for one another . . .

After a long dark winter, it seemed, the turnaround in Tucson under a once nomadic coach had captured college football's heart, at least for a few precious hours.

The Wildcats would finish the season ranked eleventh in the country. In many ways, it was truly a fairy tale come true. But a cold hard reality was waiting right around the corner.

CHAPTER 19

The Old King II

TYLER BOOKER, ALABAMA'S STAR OFFENSIVE lineman, was sitting at home January 9, 2023, watching the national championship game, already disappointed he wasn't playing in it, when a tiny moment sparked both ire and inspiration.

It wasn't something that happened on the field, but rather something that was said near it.

ESPN analyst David Pollack, a Georgia alumnus, felt good about Georgia's 35–7 halftime lead over TCU. It was clear to anyone watching that the Bulldogs were in another stratosphere compared to the Big 12's Horned Frogs and were well on their way to a second consecutive national championship. Pollack used the halftime show to proclaim Georgia the new king of college football.

"Obviously you've seen the last couple of seasons now really they've taken ahold of college football," he said.

Sitting next to Pollack on the set, Saban didn't say anything, but his face told it all as he solemnly nodded his head. In the rare years Saban's team was out of the national championship race, he typically appeared as part of ESPN's coverage, which served the dual purpose of getting his program national airtime and strengthening a burgeoning relationship with the sports TV network. Those appearances had always gone well, with Saban displaying a gift for communicating complicated topics in an easily digestible manner. When he signed up for another year of it, he couldn't have known he'd be told to his face that his protégé had surpassed him.

The brief Pollack-Saban encounter spawned reactions all over the sport. As if Saban needed any more motivation, Pollack had given him a hefty heaping. Marcus Spears, who won a title with Saban at LSU, predicted his former coach would show the clip "a thousand times next year in his locker room and during preseason."

At home, as Booker watched Pollack declare Georgia the new ruler of the sport, he had only one thought: "We'll see."

NICK SABAN WAS ON A mission to restore Alabama football as the sport's top dog. The dynasty's outside walls were crumbling, and Saban was desperately trying to prevent the fall of Rome. Alabama had missed the playoffs in 2022, perhaps the most disappointing season in more than a decade in Tuscaloosa, and the Crimson Tide looked like a worse team in 2023. The Old King knew his army wasn't as ferocious as it once was, and the mystique had dissipated. There was a time when Alabama seemed to win before the game was even played, its physically imposing team intimidating opponents just by walking off the bus. Opposing coaches moved away from what they did best, concerned they had no chance of succeeding against Saban's legion. But those days seemed to be a long time ago now.

To make matters worse, it was Saban's most talented disciple, Kirby Smart, who had a burgeoning dynasty in Athens that had a chance to become the first college football program to win three consecutive national championships in the modern era. Saban had never accomplished that, and, over seventy now, he probably never would. But he sure as hell wouldn't let his protégé, using his blueprint, be the one to do it.

Ahead of the 2023 season, Saban was "very aware" of what Smart had built at Georgia and what it meant for his place in the pecking order. "He has a lot of pride in himself and his work," said Todd Grantham, a defensive analyst at Alabama, "and he wanted to reestablish himself."

Saban largely eschewed using external factors as motivational source material, but this time he leaned into the disrespect angle. The outside world no longer viewed Alabama as the dominant presence in college football, and Saban made sure every one of his players knew that. "For this program being in that spot for so long and then hearing so much about how this is the new team on the block, this is the new Alabama," tight end coach Joe Cox said, "I think they took it to heart."

Quarterback Jalen Milroe and cornerback Terrion Arnold teamed up to create a motto to encapsulate the team's 2023 desires. They settled on LANK—Let All Naysayers Know.

A SEVENTY-ONE-YEAR-OLD NICK SABAN FACED another offseason of significant staff upheaval and had to replace offensive coordinator Bill O'Brien, who left for the New England Patriots, and defensive coordinator Pete Golding, who decided to team up with Lane Kiffin in Oxford as Ole Miss's defensive coordinator. No college coach handled the near constant staff turnover Alabama has experienced better than Saban. Rarely did Saban have any semblance of staff continuity as rival programs annually plundered his top assistants, hoping to steal a recipe so good it'd make Gordon Ramsay jealous. He forever changed the game when he invented what became known as the analyst position, a spot where he scooped up fired head coaches to help for limited money in a behind-the-scenes role. Over time, Saban became known for his rehabilitative prowess after helping coaches such as Steve Sarkisian, Mike Locksley, and Billy Napier, who originally came in as analysts, to go on and become Power 4 head coaches.

"It was almost like when professors go on sabbatical, and they go to research or write," Locksley said. "When I took the job, I knew I was just going there for one season to figure out what this man does to have built this dynasty that he built, take the things I liked, and then try to rebrand myself as a coach."

So many of the coaches Saban still knew personally were either retiring or already on staff with one of his former coaches. He no longer had a long list of options to tap into when he had staff openings. He primarily relied on Jimmy Sexton for recommendations—that's how Golding ended up in Tuscaloosa in the first place—but it was still a major source of frustration for him.

His first choice to replace Golding was Grantham, who had previously worked with Saban at Michigan State and been an SEC defensive coordinator at Georgia, Florida, and Mississippi State. Grantham was flattered, but the unrelenting hours and now having to deal with extra recruiting headaches with NIL and the transfer portal led him to take a job with the New Orleans Saints instead. According to sources, the looming potential presence of Jeremy Pruitt was also a deterrent for prospective candidates. Saban loved Pruitt, who worked as his defensive coordinator from 2016–17, and had complete confidence in the former Tennessee head coach's ability to run his defense. He wanted him back on his staff. The problem was Pruitt's disastrous tenure at Tennessee had long-lasting ramifications after the school received harsh NCAA penalties, and the expectation was Pruitt would receive a show-cause penalty. That became a no-go in SEC commissioner Greg Sankey's eyes—he had previously discouraged Saban from hiring Hugh Freeze while Ole Miss was still under NCAA penalties—and indeed Pruitt later received a six-year show cause, eliminating any chance he had of being Saban's defensive coordinator. Eventually, Saban turned to Kevin Steele, lately of Miami, whom he knew well after employing him on two of his previous Alabama staffs.

Finding an offensive coordinator replacement was a bigger challenge. He talked to former Cleveland Browns head coach Freddie Kitchens, former Tennessee head coach Derek Dooley, Akron head coach Joe Moorhead, and Washington offensive coordinator Ryan Grubb, before finally hiring Notre Dame offensive coordinator Tommy Rees. The struggle to fill two highly valuable staff positions raised alarms in Saban's mind.

Saban was self-aware and knew he had a reputation for a demanding environment in which not everyone was built to last. One program insider described working for Saban this way: "It's the grind of all grinds and it beats the hell out of people. He can still dangle national championship fruit in front of people all year round, and it keeps them going." After a playoff-less 2022 and Saban's age becoming more of a talking point, he couldn't quite promise that anymore. It hurt his ability to attract the best of the best he knew he needed to populate his organization.

When one job candidate dropped Pete Jenkins's name—the former defensive line coach at LSU and now a consultant for Alabama—Saban called Jenkins with an important question about the candidate in question.

"Can he work for me?" Saban asked. "Or is he going to come, stay six months, and then spend the rest of his life saying what a son of a bitch I am?"

Jenkins, perhaps the greatest defensive line coach in SEC history, had seen Saban's transformation up close over the last twenty years—from the brutal working conditions in Baton Rouge, where no one dared ask for a day off, to the man in Tuscaloosa who smiled more often and had mellowed considerably. He saw a man who was finally starting to appreciate his unprecedented run of accomplishments. The seven national championships. All the young men he brought in as recruits and developed into NFL players. Coaches like Sarkisian, Locksley, and Lane Kiffin came in damaged and left as top coaching prospects.

Jenkins adored Saban and would always be allegiant to him for what he did for his career, but understood that the Alabama head coach could sometimes be misunderstood. Saban would tell his players and staffers to focus on the message behind his words, not simply the words themselves, which frequently included profanity that would make New York cabbies blush. Still, it could make for hurt feelings and guys feeling underappreciated. Jenkins tried to serve as a Saban interpreter to offer the true meaning behind his actions and words. He always believed his former boss had good intentions, even if he could be coarse and rough around the edges. As Saban aged and finally started showing his personality to the world, including a hilarious affinity for immature "deez nuts" jokes, Jenkins saw more of the man he always believed to be hidden under the tough exterior. Ahead of the 2023 season, Jenkins assessed the state of college football's greatest coach.

"He wants number eight bad. *Bad*," Jenkins said with as much emphasis as he could on the word. "It's in no way taking away from his desire or his hunger to be successful. But nobody has ever, ever accomplished what he's accomplished. Seven national championships? The greatest on Earth, Coach [Paul] Bryant, had six. That's why Coach Saban smiles a little more. He's a little more human than he was."

• • •

THE 2023 CAMPAIGN TO TAKE down Georgia on the journey for an eighth title would take everything Saban had.

The man who had stockpiled talent better than anyone in college football history was now dealing with an attrition problem.

Saban had long been the master at getting talented players to come to Tuscaloosa, promise them nothing, and convince them to wait their turn, sometimes for three or four years. From running back Derrick Henry to defensive end Jonathan Allen to linebacker Rashaan Evans, there are countless examples of talented players waiting years to get their chance before becoming excellent NFL players. It was all part of the ubercompetitive environment Saban built and everyone believed in. Locksley, who spent three seasons at Alabama, said Saban's ability to develop the backups—the twos, threes, and fours—was "the secret sauce for Bama."

The new landscape made that increasingly difficult. With NIL deals and the transfer portal giving every player one free move, it became harder to convince those players to come in the first place let alone stay for an undetermined role when guarantees beckoned elsewhere. The 2023 team looked great on paper, but a closer examination revealed it didn't have near the depth of the marquee Saban teams from earlier in his run. The talent was more spread out now, with former assistants Kirby Smart and Steve Sarkisian scooping up more than their fair share of top recruits.

Grantham, who had to go against Saban's Alabama behemoths year after year while at Mississippi State, was always blown away by how much talent in Tuscaloosa was willing to sit and wait. When he got to Alabama in 2022, he noticed that advantage was gone.

"The model went away," Grantham said. "Now, it's about instant gratification, and guys want to play now as a true freshman, which if you can, is great, but there's nothing wrong with developing. I always thought they did a great job at getting the organization to buy into if I bust my tail, I work, and I trust the process, I'm going to get rewarded at the end of my tenure here. The portal really took that away."

Gone, too, were Alabama's top two players from the previous season. Heisman Trophy–winner Bryce Young and Bednarik Award–winner Will Anderson went Nos. 1 and 3 in the NFL Draft, taking away the program's top-end talent. While defense figured to be better, the offense had question marks throughout, especially at the quarterback position. For the first time since 2015, Alabama had a wide-open quarterback competition. Jalen Milroe had the most experience after starting against Arkansas the previous year when Young was injured, while Ty Simpson, a former five-star recruit, had the best pedigree. After an up-and-down spring where neither won the job, Alabama brought in Notre Dame transfer Tyler Buchner, who was very familiar with new offensive coordinator Tommy Rees, his former quarterback coach in South Bend. Saban told those close to him that the quarterback he liked best was actually true freshman Dylan Lonergan, who had impressed during fall camp, but was resigned to going with a more experienced veteran option.

What Alabama's offensive identity would look like dominated the Alabama airwaves all offseason. It typically ended in a familiar conclusion: Saban and Co. would just need to have it figured out by the time Texas rolled into town in Week 2.

ENERGY PULSATED THROUGH THE STRIP on a beautiful Friday night before the heavily anticipated Week 2 game against No. 11 Texas. The Longhorns, set to join the SEC the following season, had come oh-so-close to knocking off Alabama in Austin in 2022. A huge contingent of Texas fans made the trip to Tuscaloosa to get their first taste of what a game inside Bryant-Denny Stadium felt like.

The most monied of the fans ended up at the Roll Call rooftop bar of the Alamite Hotel, partially owned by Saban. Texas governor Greg Abbott held court at a long table of Longhorns backers as university president Jay Hartzell and athletic director Chris Del Conte eventually made their way to the bar. However, the bar patron with the highest approval rating was ESPN personality Paul Finebaum. If you didn't know any better, you might have thought the "Mouth of the South" was the politician rather than the governor. Finebaum, who chatted up Abbott as he walked in, shook hands and took photos for hours as Texas and Alabama fans flocked to the man who had become the face of the SEC Network. In Tuscaloosa that night, they treated him like a modern-day Elvis, desperate to get his take on the game and be in his presence if only for a moment. Not known for staying out late, Finebaum seemed faintly bemused by the scene.

Under Sarkisian, Texas had amassed a talented group of offensive and defensive weapons that looked like they could give Alabama problems. Saban thought very highly of Sark, to the point that he even told him he'd have a chance to succeed him at Alabama before he took the Texas job. With an already-banged-up secondary, Saban worried about what Sark's brilliant offensive mind would come up with to attack his defense. In a message to a friend the morning of the game, Terry Saban said it was a mix of excitement and tension hours before the biggest game of the young season. She and her husband had recognized, as Grantham did when he got to Alabama, that the game's changes had a deleterious effect on their dynasty.

"The new rules [portal] have made our team thin," Terry Saban said. "Good players are not willing to sit on the bench any longer when they can go play elsewhere immediately, so we get picked apart just like our coaching staff. Therefore, injuries are more significant than ever with no second string on the bench! It's crazy what college football has become."

Those concerns proved prophetic when Sark and the Texas Longhorns beat Alabama 34–24, the worst home loss in Saban's seventeen years in Tuscaloosa. Before that Saturday night, no team had ever defeated a Saban-led Alabama team by more than seven points in Bryant-Denny Stadium. Alabama finished the game down two turnovers after Milroe threw two interceptions—a major source of frustration for its coach, who detested mental errors—and allowed Texas quarterback Quinn Ewers to have all day in the pocket to attack downfield. When it was over, as Texas superfan Matthew McConaughey celebrated on the field, the questions were building on whether this Alabama team had the right stuff. The path to even the SEC Championship, let alone another playoff trip, looked as unlikely as ever.

Somehow, the Texas loss wasn't the nadir of Alabama's regular season. That came the following week on a trip to Tampa to play South Florida. It was a bizarre matchup even before the game started, a result of a two-for-one scheduling arrangement that sent Saban and Alabama on the road to a non–Power 5 team for the first time.

Following Milroe's two-turnover performance against the Longhorns, Saban opted for a quarterback change and picked Buchner to start against USF. It did not go well. Under brutal weather conditions, Buchner couldn't

do anything against a USF team that entered the game as a 33-point under-
dog. Saban eventually yanked Buchner at the half in favor of Simpson, who
was good enough to beat the Bulls 17–3. As much concern as an Alabama
loss can create in the Yellowhammer State, the near loss to South Florida
had the panic billowing out everywhere. There was talk that this could be
a three- or four-loss Alabama team, an absolute disaster in the Saban reign.

It dimmed the spirit of even the most optimistic Alabama fan, but Saban and the team's leaders knew it had to be a wake-up call. The team
couldn't perform like that again if it hoped to meet its preseason goals.
Booker asked his teammates, "How do we want this season to end?"

"We were at the bottom," Booker said. "How are we going to rise? What
are we going to do in order to rise, to get where we want to get to?"

Saban had an idea. Two days after the game, he proclaimed the quarterback competition was over and that he was returning to Milroe as his
starter. Alabama had tried something different against South Florida, and
Saban realized it failed miserably. Milroe wasn't perfect, and his penchant
for costly mistakes unnerved Saban, but the Alabama head coach realized
he was the best option this team had.

"We were still trying to figure ourselves out, going through a couple
quarterbacks and figuring out if those guys would give us a spark," said
Alabama assistant head coach Holmon Wiggins. "After that, we realized
here's who we are and here's who gives us the best chance to win."

THE WOBBLES DIDN'T END AGAINST South Florida. Each week on *The
Paul Finebaum Show*, there was a discussion about what another loss might
mean for Saban and Alabama. The proclamations of the dynasty's demise
cropped up again.

Saban had yet to lose two games before November in a single season
since 2004, but here was Lane Kiffin and a talented Ole Miss team coming to
town. Kiffin desperately wanted a win over a man he admired and whose skin
he enjoyed getting under. Like a gnat, Kiffin always had something up his
sleeve to try to annoy his former boss. This year, Kiffin revealed to the world
that his coaches believed defensive coordinator Kevin Steele wasn't the one
calling the defensive play calls but, instead, co-defensive coordinator Trava-

ris Robinson had taken over the duties. Kiffin wasn't lying—staff members would later confirm the accuracy—but it was meant to create controversy in Tuscaloosa and force Saban to address it. It was perfectly Lane, whose mom used to call him "Helicopter" because he always liked to stir shit up.

Kiffin believed this was his year to get Saban, that Alabama was vulnerable and there for the taking. With Alabama not on the schedule the following year because of SEC expansion, he also didn't know if he'd ever get a shot at joining the former Saban assistants club who beat the master. It devastated Kiffin to know he blew his best chance to beat him when the Crimson Tide held off the Rebels 24–10.

After the Ole Miss win, Alabama began to develop an identity. The offense started clicking, and the defense started meeting preseason expectations. It became clear that Alabama no longer had the talent to overpower opponents, but it kept finding ways to win games. Milroe and Rees weren't a perfect marriage, but Rees started adjusting his plan to better suit Milroe's skill set. He may have preferred to use Simpson or Buchner, but it was readily apparent that Milroe was the only answer as long as the Tide's offensive line continued to struggle up front.

"I remember early in the season saying who we want to be and who we are, are two different things," Rees said. "Who we thought we were going to be or who we can be are going to be two different things, and that's okay. Let's just work to find ways to build who we are and what we can do and build around it."

Tight wins against Arkansas and Texas A&M put Alabama back on track with a 6-1 record as it entered the back half of its schedule. Meanwhile No. 1 Georgia continued to steamroll its opponents and comfortably sat at a perfect 7-0.

As Alabama started to evolve on the field, so had its NIL efforts off it. Alabama athletic director Greg Byrne struck a big deal with Learfield, a third-party rights holder, believed to be in eight figures, to give Alabama a baseline for its football players. Saban wanted everyone on the roster to all receive the same base salary—$25,000 to start as a freshman—and then each player could earn more depending on their true brand value. Bryce Young, who starred in a national Dr Pepper commercial, earned seven figures from endorsement deals.

After the Learfield deal, Alabama folded its High Tide collective into Yea Alabama, the new university-endorsed entity. Alabama hired Aaron Suttles, a longtime beat reporter, away from *The Athletic* to run Yea Alabama's content as part of a subscription model for fans. There was also the creation of the Walk of Champions foundation, a 501(c)(3) charitable group, to raise tax-deductible money to supplement Yea Alabama's subscription funds.

Elliot Maisel, the chairman of Walk of Champions, was no stranger to Alabama football. Maisel was the chairman of Gulf Distributing, a wildly successful beer distributing company that primarily served Alabama and Florida but stretched into Texas and Colorado, and the older brother of beloved college football writer Ivan Maisel. Maisel was at one of Saban's early meetings with top Alabama boosters when he'd first arrived in town. It was an important get-to-know-you for the new leader and his benefactors. While many were eager to shake Saban's hand and offer help, Maisel had hung back. Finally, he approached.

"You were kinda slow coming up here," Saban said. "You must be one of those guys who didn't want to hire me."

Maisel protested that wasn't the case but all the same he did have a point to make. "I didn't give a shit whether you came here or not. I'm here for ya, but we'll make a coach out of anybody. [Dennis] Franchione won ten games. Mike fucking Shula won ten games. We're Alabama."

"Do you have a card?" Saban asked.

"I don't have a card," Maisel replied. "I'm from Mobile."

"We got to win Mobile in recruiting," Saban said.

"WE WERE BUDDIES FROM THAT point forward," Maisel said later.

In the offseason, Maisel and Saban would talk as much as three times a week. The offseason also became the time when Saban and Byrne later made trips to four booster-heavy hot spots to raise awareness and money for Alabama's NIL efforts. Saban would use his stature to help secure NIL deals for his top players too. Maisel knew from his many conversations with Alabama's head coach that deep down he was still uncomfortable with NIL but realized it wasn't going away.

"Nick's a winner and he wants to stay a winner," Maisel said. "I think his biggest difficulty is penetrating the mindset of the kids. You've got high school kids saying they won't come for a visit unless you pay me five thousand dollars. Nick's response is, 'Well, I guess you're not coming.'"

Maisel's Walk of Champions, which eventually hired former Tide quarterback John Parker Wilson as its president, was originally built around raising tax-deductible donations, only for the Internal Revenue Service to issue a guidance warning that foundations could lose tax-exempt status if their primary focus was paying players. Essentially, the IRS said, no, you don't deserve a tax deduction for paying a young man to play for your favorite college football team. It disrupted Walk of Champion's plan and exposed a key part of the bizarreness of the whole situation: wealthy boosters had long benefited from a quid pro quo for their athletic financial generosity, from tax deductions to better seats at football games. Donating money to a for-profit collective like Yea Alabama offered the most direct way of ensuring your favorite team had good players but didn't come with the other usual perks. This turned off a portion of the donor base.

Alabama's NIL coffers were in a much better place more than a year after Saban publicly went after Jimbo Fisher for buying every player of Texas A&M's recruiting class, but still paled in comparison to some of its biggest rivals. Alabama didn't have a billionaire superfan like Oregon's Phil Knight or Tennessee's Jimmy Haslam, the Cleveland Browns owner. Its core donor base was aging and slow to embrace pouring in major money while the on-field results still met their lofty expectations.

"Georgia is going to have more money," Maisel said. "Texas is going to have more money. Texas A&M will have more money. LSU, those people are nutso, they're going to have more money. So is Ohio State. It doesn't matter; we'll have enough to be competitive."

Maisel believed in the power of the Alabama brand above all else. What he'd soon learn was how much the Saban brand exceeded even that.

SABAN CAUGHT THE ALABAMA STATE troopers assigned to protect him off guard. The most famous man in the state of Alabama had broken from his routine and was now running over to an exuberant Alabama student section as his security detail struggled to keep up.

After a raucous crowd inside Bryant-Denny Stadium seemed to power Alabama to its seventh win on a come-from-behind 34–20 score over Tennessee in the Third Saturday in October rivalry, Saban wanted to personally thank the fans for their impact on the game. The rowdy Alabama students were overjoyed by the surprise visit from their fearless leader.

"I've never seen him run like that," quarterback Jalen Milroe said. "He must be happy."

The run to the students illustrated how far Saban had come in seventeen years. The nomadic coach made Alabama his home and loved his adopted fans. There were hiccups along the way, times of feeling unappreciated and struggling under the self-inflicted weight of title-or-bust standards, but what felt like a business relationship at first grew into one of mutual admiration. It was different than the fan base's feelings for the Bear—less reverence and more hard-earned appreciation—but Crimson Tide fans learned to adopt all Saban's quirks. They embraced his preferred style of football they deemed "joyless murderball," of running the damn ball and a swarming, powerful defense. Above all, they loved how much he won.

No one did a better job of bonding Nick to the Tuscaloosa community than his wife, Terry. Nick long joked that Terry was the cohead coach of the football program, and she was in on every major decision he made. She was intimately familiar with every nook and cranny of her husband's organization, and it was well-known that no assistant coach was hired until he got her stamp of approval. More than anything, though, she softened some of those rough edges. When she heard through other coaches' wives that Nick was keeping the staff too late at the office, she'd implore him to give them a little more time off to spend with their families. She helped him navigate social settings where he could be awkward and standoffish.

Saban loved to preach the power of the cumulative effect to his coaching staff. Putting in hard work day after day wouldn't make you great overnight, but the cumulative effect of that daily effort would pay off. For Lance Thompson, who first worked with Saban in 2002 at LSU and then again twice at Alabama, that was the best way to describe his marriage too.

"Miss Terry is the model coach's wife," Thompson said. "She's softened Nick through the years. The cumulative effect of Miss Terry on Nick was the most beneficial thing in making him the man and the coach he is today. It was Terry and how she managed him."

Thompson, the lead recruiter on Julio Jones, can still remember Terry asking him every time she saw him that year about how things were going with the five-star receiver out of Foley, Alabama. "How's Julio? How's [his mother] Queen doing?" After Lance gave the latest update, the response was almost always the same. "We've got to get him," she told him.

She was the Queen of Tuscaloosa. Without Terry, Nick never would have been Alabama's head coach. Even more importantly, without Terry being happy in Tuscaloosa, Nick never would have made it to the seventeenth year of ruling one kingdom the way he had in 2023. On this October Saturday, a man frequently accused of being a robot early in his tenure needed to show appreciation to a fervent group that had given him so much.

"I wanted to thank them because of what a great job they did, the impact that they had on the game, the atmosphere of the game," Saban said. "I think they kept the energy level up for our team and kept the momentum rolling in the second half for us. It was fantastic.

"I wish I could thank each one of them personally."

ON THE MONDAY OF THE bye week, Saban was in Birmingham for his annual appearance at the Monday Morning Quarterback Club. It was the lone speaking engagement he'd make during the season, long baked into his schedule, and a chance for him to tell some stories and give updates on his 7-1 team to a room full of wealthy Birmingham businessmen and lawyers.

Before meeting with the club, he briefly met with local media. He talked about using Catapult, a GPS-like system embedded in players' shoulder pads, to analyze each player during the bye week to better understand whether they are more psychologically or physically tired, using benchmarks from earlier in the season to interpret the data. It was a smart, analytical way of understanding, beyond just the look test, whether players were maximizing their performance and what might be the cause if they weren't.

The answer prompted us to ask whether Saban did the same for his assistant coaches. Was there an analytical way for the Alabama head coach, who was always looking for ways to improve, to gauge whether his coaches were performing at their peak or might need a break?

Saban, who would turn seventy-two the following week, paused to ponder the question before delivering his answer.

"I don't know, is there an analytical way for anybody to know whether I need a break?" Saban said. "Did you ever think of that? We've got all these young bucks out there coaching, I know they don't make them like they used to, but you ought to be worried about me, not them."

After answering, Saban smiled and started laughing, but the season was already wearing him out. He desperately tried to wring every last ounce of talent out of a group he knew wasn't nearly as talented as his previous title teams. He was still the engine that powered the massive Alabama locomotive and was doing everything he could to hide any signs of slowing down. "I don't know if he's ever gone to the bathroom, I don't know if he's ever stopped to get anything to eat," said Joe Cox, who arrived at Alabama in 2022. "He grinds for sure, and that's why he's the best at what he does."

The effects of fifty-plus years of a relentless pursuit of perfection with the hours to match the intention were taking their toll on him. He wore hearing aids, though he tried to hide them in public settings, lest risking anyone using them against him in recruiting. Those who had known him for decades said he wasn't quite as sharp as he used to be, though not for lack of effort. He had become the game's elder statesman, unafraid to speak out on the issues he believed plagued it, but some of his recent passions didn't resonate as well. His arguments about the need for college football to have parity rang hollow for opposing coaches, as no coach had benefited more from the lack of parity than him.

The Saban retirement rumors always lingered beneath the surface, largely due to his age, but the whispers grew louder around Alabama's bye week. More and more informed insiders worried this could be the end for college football's greatest coach. The fourteen-hour days hit harder than they used to. Father Time remained undefeated.

"When I was young, I could work 'til two in the morning, get up at six, and be there the next day and be full of energy and go for it," Saban said. "When you get a little older, that gets a little tougher."

• • •

NO MATTER WHAT HE DID or how much better he was at appreciating his accomplishments more as he aged, the losses always stuck with Saban more than the wins. Sure, he had seven national championship victories, but he also had three national championship defeats.

Despite all he had achieved, he was still driven by doubt and insecurities. The losses powered him to do more, to not let a previous mistake doom him again. He'd frequently tell his team to "never waste a failing," and he lived that to the extreme.

Outside the title game losses, no losses ate him up more than the ones against Auburn in Jordan-Hare Stadium. Saban was never the type of coach to really dial up the rivalry-game theatrics—there were no veiled references or refusal to say the school's name like other coaches—but he understood the importance of the Iron Bowl to his program and its fan base. No program rankled Saban as often as the one on the Loveliest Village on the Plains.

There was the improbable and historic Kick Six last-second loss in 2013 that left him crying and at a loss for words in the postgame locker room. Four years later, a team that went on to win the national championship got its butt kicked inside Jordan-Hare Stadium, 26–14. Fast-forward two years, another loss to the Tigers, this time after future NFL first-round draft pick Mac Jones threw two pick-six interceptions. No matter what he did, Jordan-Hare Stadium was a House of Horrors for the legendary coach. Former Auburn head coach Gus Malzahn had been a formidable opponent, dialing up exotic play calls that gave Saban's defense fits.

He knew he'd get more of the same from first-year head coach Hugh Freeze, who had a similar background to Malzahn and was known for his offensive prowess. Auburn looked awful the previous week, losing to New Mexico State, 31–10, at home. The Tigers had nothing left to play for except pride, while Alabama was one week away from playing Georgia in the SEC Championship. It couldn't have been a more dangerous combination.

Alabama looked sloppy and uninspired throughout a slugfest with the Tigers. Freeze called plays that Alabama hadn't seen on tape in its film review, frustrating the Crimson Tide. As the minutes ticked off, it looked increasingly hopeless for Alabama. Saban had willed this roller coaster of a team to improbable win after improbable win, but the magic looked like it had finally run out. For the second year in a row, Alabama would finish with two regular season losses and miss the playoffs. The revenge tour would end meekly.

Until Alabama dug itself out of what turned out to be a shallow grave.

Facing 4th-and-31 with forty-three seconds left in the game, Alabama called the play "Gravedigger." Auburn only rushed two defenders, giving Milroe time to hang back in the pocket to survey his options downfield. He took six seconds that felt more like six minutes before finally unleashing a dart to the back corner of the end zone. Isaiah Bond caught it, setting off pandemonium, and gave famed Alabama painter Daniel Moore his newest inspiration. Finally, Saban had the miraculous, no-way-it-should-have-happened win in Jordan-Hare that he had been on the receiving end of far too many times. "I guess if you're in this long enough, sometimes it goes against you on the last play," Nick Saban said, "and sometimes you're fortunate and it goes forward."

The "Nightmare in Jordan-Hare" made Alabama 11-1 on the season and raised the stakes for the game it wanted all year.

THE NIGHT BEFORE THE SEC Championship kicked off in Atlanta on December 2, Saban and Smart sat down for a joint SEC Network interview. At one point, Smart told his former boss, "I won't be doing this when I'm your age, I promise you that."

Saban quickly deadpanned, "That's because you're smarter than me."

The next afternoon, as they readied for the most important game of the season, the pair shared a heartfelt moment. For as much as each wanted to destroy the other on the field, their hard-earned love and admiration meant they knew what the other was putting himself through every day to be the best. It was respect for the all-out commitment to the Process. Looking back on their conversation, it's hard not to think both might have known something was up.

"You're about to be right about one thing, I'm too old for this," Saban said with a laugh.

"No, you ain't," Smart said. "You did a great job this year."

"Nobody's done as good a job as you have," Saban said. "This long to be this good."

"Try to enjoy it, man," Smart said. "Helluva coach. Appreciate all you did for me."

The moment over, it was game on.

It was a decidedly Georgia-heavy crowd inside Mercedes-Benz Stadium, but Alabama fans were loud and fired up. They wanted a chance to knock off big, bad Georgia just as much as the Alabama players did. The stakes were huge. If Alabama had any shot at making the four-team playoff, it had to beat No. 1 Georgia. The undefeated Bulldogs, which hadn't had a loss in twenty-nine games, were in the pole position, but a loss threatened to knock them out too. For both teams, it was likely win or go home.

It looked like a heavyweight fight from the moment the game kicked off. The two monsters of the sport threw haymakers at each other, one after another. The Old King and the Young Prince coaching their asses off, trying to will their young men to victory. When you watch teams like Alabama and Georgia, they look physically different, hit differently, and play differently than your average team. It's no surprise how many go on to play professionally.

Georgia looked brilliant on a seamless eight-play, 83-yard opening drive to go up 7–0 early. Alabama adjusted, changing its base defensive formation to force different looks. It worked marvelously, as Saban showed that he still had a few tricks. The defense clamped down while Alabama's running game got going. Milroe, Roydell Williams, and Jam Miller all had success against the Bulldogs, and before you knew it, Alabama built a 17–7 halftime lead.

Georgia wasn't going to fold, not in this game. The Bulldogs added an early third-quarter field goal to cut it to 17–10 and then hung around headed into the fourth quarter. The Georgia faithful came alive when Carson Beck had a 1-yard touchdown run to make it 20–17 with 10:16 left in the game.

Could Alabama hold on to the lead? Or would its preseason dreams go up in flames to the new king of the sport? With the game on the line, Alabama again tapped into the Milroe to Bond dynamic. First, it was a 21-yard pass to Bond. Then a 12-yard pass. Then a 13-yard pass. And finally, an 11-yard pass as Bond raced toward the end zone. Alabama athletic director

Greg Byrne let out a huge fist pump after it looked like Bond got in for a touchdown, only to be ruled down a yard short. Bond, who had four catches for 57 yards on the drive, looked exhausted as he came off the field. As teammates celebrated him, Bond needed oxygen after leaving it all out on the field. A play later, Roydell Williams punched it in to put Alabama up 27–17.

Georgia marched down the field again to cut the lead to 27–24, but the Bulldogs couldn't get a stop to give it one last chance. A nine-yard Milroe run secured the result. Final: Alabama 27, Georgia 24.

As Alabama began to celebrate, a staffer loudly yelled, "Somebody forgot to tell them this is Bryant-Denny East. We don't lose in this stadium!"

The win gave Saban a 5-1 record against his most successful student. He was especially successful against Smart in his Atlanta backyard, beating him in three SEC Championships and a national championship in Georgia's capital. Kirby was gracious in defeat, going up to multiple Alabama players to congratulate them after the game. He found Alabama star safety Caleb Downs (a Georgia native), center Seth McLaughlin (another Georgia native), and cornerback Kool-Aid McKinstry. Just like his boss had been when it was his turn, Kirby was calm and already processing the loss in the moments right after.

As Nick made his way off the field, his wife, Terry, overcome with emotion, told him, "This team deserves it. You deserve it."

"It was awesome to see the team realize [Georgia] can imitate, but they can't replicate what we have," said tight end C. J. Dippre. "They're not the standard, we are."

Booker, who had privately used it as his motivation all season, let loose a WWE-type rant at the man who doubted Alabama's place atop college football.

"I came to Alabama to further the dynasty," he said. "To hear somebody challenge my coach to his face like that? I take that personally. I feel like everybody who saw it did, and then we responded to that."

Alabama had let the naysayers know. Saban, facing challenges from every direction, reminded the SEC who was still king. Deep down, he knew he couldn't fend off Kirby Smart's flourishing Georgia program forever. But that night, for one last stand, he could.

CHAPTER 20

Michigan Man III

ABLIZZARD OF MAIZE-AND-BLUE CONFETTI RAINED down from the rafters inside NRG Stadium in Houston. As one true-blue Michigan Man saw it, each and every piece telling a story of his undefeated, unbowed football team, the very last *team* standing at the end of a tumultuous 2023–24 season that had shaken a sport to its core. A final, resounding Michigan vs. Everybody one-finger salute to the media cynics and chorus of critics, the doubters who had denigrated the head coach and members of his staff as cheaters, dismissing the grinding, the sweating, the *believing* by a band of brothers paying the ultimate price day after day, week after week, month after month, inside the hallowed ground known as Schembechler Hall.

"A glorious feeling," Jim Harbaugh told ESPN sideline reporter Holly Rowe moments after his Wolverines had pummeled 2nd-ranked (and previously undefeated) University of Washington, 34–13, to cap a historic 15-0 campaign, earning arguably college football's most storied program its first national title in twenty-six years.

Five weeks earlier, shortly after the Wolverines blanked anemic Iowa 26–0 in the Big Ten Championship game, the CFP Selection Committee had rewarded the nation's No. 1-ranked team with its top seed and a matchup against surprising fourth-seeded Alabama, outraging a Seminole nation of undefeated Florida State fans. Harbaugh sidestepped any personal acclaim, giving all glory to God, Jesus Christ our Savior, during a post-selection interview on ESPN, deflecting every last question from Rece to Booger to Herbie—back to a team "that played for each other."

A brotherhood not so much motivated, he said, as "galvanized" by the witch's brew of controversy, suspensions, and here-today-gone-tomorrow reports that had Harbaugh at odds with Manuel one day, on the verge of signing a ten-year $110 million contract extension the next, and interviewing with NFL teams the next. A convulsive regular season capped by the news Michigan had received an official Notice of Allegations from the NCAA related to the alleged COVID-19 dead-period infractions.

Bad news that, frankly, paled in comparison to what Sarah and Jim Harbaugh learned just hours before his sixtieth birthday celebration on December 23.

Knox Jack Anson, the eight-month-old grandson of longtime friend Todd Anson, had been diagnosed with stage 4 metastatic childhood cancer and was facing a dangerously grim prognosis.

"You want to know who the Harbaughs really are, this is from them both," Todd forwarded a text to a friend. "This is who they are."

From Jim: Our Hearts are breaking and profoundly saddened, abundant prayers on the way for Knox and the entire family and mercy for Kristin and Chris—love you guys so much and praying for a miracle to ease your pain . . .

From Sarah: Bless ur hearts . . . Lord have mercy . . . I'm so sorry Todd. Let's go attack this neuroblastoma with an enthusiasm unknown to mankind . . .

But that was hardly the end of the love and prayers. Not by a long shot. Soon Anson was hearing from Jack and Jackie Harbaugh and players on the team—quarterbacks J.J. McCarthy and Davis Warren, a cancer survivor, in particular. Harbaugh telling his good friend the team would dedicate the Alabama game to Knox, about to undergo his first round of chemo treatment.

We have a shot too and that's all we can ask, Harbaugh had written at the end of his text. Hang in their pal, proud of how strong you are!

Trailing the Tide 20–13 with less than five minutes left in their semifinal matchup, the Wolverines proved their mettle, going 85 gritty yards on eight plays in 3:07 to send the game into overtime, only the second such occurrence in the 110-year history of the Rose Bowl. In OT it only took two plays for Michigan to forge ahead, the second, a determined 17-yard scamper by Corum into the end zone. With Bama facing a fourth-and-goal from the 3-yard-line, the nation's No. 1-rated defense rose up and made the play of the day, swallowing up quarterback Jalen Milroe's draw up the middle, a game-ending goal-line stand that stood as a testament to toughness and will. Alabama offensive lineman Tyler Booker tried to console a despondent Milroe, who hit himself in the head and ripped off his helmet and came within inches of spiking it into the ground. Other visibly angry Alabama players didn't show the same restraint to the point a disappointed Saban later lamented "showing your ass and being frustrated and throwing helmets and doing that stuff . . . that's not who we are and what we've promoted in our program."

"First it was Penn State, Penn State were stronger than us. We had to take care of business," said star defensive tackle Kris Jenkins afterward. "And then it was Ohio State, we had to take care of business. Then it was Bama. Time and time again, people doubted us. It didn't matter the situation. We had to prove to the world, we had to remind the world what this Block M means, man. Who we are."

True to his word, inside a jubilant locker room Harbaugh presented a Game Ball to eight-month-old Knox Jack Anson.

In the tunnel just outside, Manuel relived the triumph with one proud Pop. Whatever animosity existing between an athletic director and Jack Harbaugh's youngest son washed away in postgame bliss. Austin Meek of The Athletic was on hand to chronicle the scene.

"He's everything that you want in a leader of a group of young men and staff," Manuel said. "I love him. He's just awesome."

So about that contract extension, Meek inquired. How's that coming along?

"Hey, brother, I'm working on it. Believe me."

It was a funereal scene in the opposing locker room as Alabama players and coaches came to grips with a dream season that had suddenly gone up in smoke. Another trip to the national championship was within Alabama's grasp only for McCarthy and Corum to rip it away. Moments after the loss, with confusion and anger still billowing out of the Crimson Tide locker room, Aaron Suttles, the school collective Yea Alabama's director of media, had a message for Alabama fans.

"In the disappointment, we need to take action," Suttles said in a video posted on social media. "We need to help build Alabama's NIL entity into the biggest in the country. Yea Alabama needs your support. We need to keep the train rolling, keep this thing moving forward."

The video was at the direction of Alabama athletic director Greg Byrne, who told members of his team that raising NIL money needed to be the top priority for the next few weeks. Alabama's brain trust was deeply concerned about what was lurking around the corner if fans didn't start giving in significantly larger numbers, believing that top players were going to start leaving for bigger financial opportunities elsewhere. The reckoning was coming.

BEFORE A BOISTEROUS SOLD-OUT CROWD of 72,808 the Wolverines' defense had dominated Washington from the start, holding the Pac-12 champs to just 46 yards on the ground, their longest run of the night a grand total of 9 yards. Michigan's battering ram offense took care of business, *averaging* 8 yards per carry on its way to 303 total yards rushing; Corum and running back Donovan Edwards alone combined for 238 yards and four touchdowns.

The relentless Corum summed up a sparkling career with words deserving a place of honor in the school's Football Hall of Fame:

"I just want to be remembered as a Michigan Man. Someone who did good on the field, but also did good in the community, did good in the classroom, and laid a foundation for the next generation. That's honestly how I want to be remembered."

For his part, Harbaugh, ever the odd duck, promised to commemorate the night by inking his otherwise pristine Dad Bod with a 15-0 tattoo below a Block M to signify the milestone win achieved earlier in the season—a promise he kept on the day of Michigan's 2024 spring game. Another solemn promise following the dismal 2020 season—"We're gonna to do it or we're gonna die trying"—now achieved, in threes:

40-3 overall

A record three straight CFP berths

Three straight wins over Ohio State and Penn State

The next morning Paul Finebaum, arguably Harbaugh's most vociferous critic, willingly ate some crow: "This is truly remarkable," he said on ESPN's *Get Up*. "I don't want to be wrong about something—you never want to be wrong—but if you're going to be epically wrong, out of this constellation, out of this universe wrong, I'll take it. I think Jim Harbaugh has silenced all those who doubted him in the early days."

NO SOONER HAD HARBAUGH HOISTED the national championship trophy than members of his inner circle were advising him to ride off into the sunset.

With good reason. As it turned out, Harbaugh had found himself getting squeezed from both sides—by a process he hated and a place he loved.

In the wake of the Stalions investigation, enforcement had made yet another sweeping request for Harbaugh's school-issued and personal cellphone records dating back eighteen months. In response, Mars wrote another stinging email, saying he would need to review 6,199 emails plus the texts, and oh by the way, your request is illegal under Michigan employment and privacy laws, "outrageous and offensive and without probable cause." (And it wasn't just Harbaugh. The NCAA had demanded similar records from the entire coaching staff, only to drop that request.)

In the end, Mars knew Harbaugh would eventually face two Committee on Infractions hearings before what he deemed a hostile crowd and a certain suspension that could cost him half a season—or more.

"I WILL TELL YOU THIS," said Mars, "I told [Harbaugh agent] Don Yee and Jim as clearly as I could, more than once, more than twice, that in my opinion if he stayed at Michigan . . . the COI is going to punish Jim under the vicarious coaches' responsibility legislation, and he's dealing with a COI that's clearly manifested bias against him. He's going to sit out four games, maybe six, and whatever we do the COI is going to find him guilty."

On the other side, by this time, Michigan had offered to make Harbaugh the highest-paid coach in college football—a rollover five-year contract worth north of $11 million per year plus additional performance-based bonuses. In exchange, it pressed for termination language that would protect the university in the event of an unforeseen turn in the sign-stealing investigation.

"I think where the stumbling block came was trying to find the best way to handle any additional information from the second case we didn't know at the time of [the contract] signing," Manuel said.

"So to your question did this affect Jim's decision to go to the NFL? I don't know," said Mars. "But I know I told him under the circumstances I could not imagine *any* reason why he would not take the opportunity to go to the NFL if it presented itself."

IN THE HOURS AND DAYS after the national championship game, Harbaugh swatted away every last query about his future—"I just want to enjoy this," he said. "I hope you can give me that. Can a guy have that?"—choosing instead to bang a familiar drum, suggesting slashing 5 to 10 percent off coaching salaries and the television deals to create a pot to pay players.

"There used to be an old saying: Old coaches—my dad's used it, my brother's used it—we're all robbing the same train here," he said. "Like coaches, administrators, media, television stations, conferences, NCAA. And the ones that are really robbing the train, the ones that could easily get hurt, are getting a very small piece."

Back in A2, Harbaugh and the team had returned to a hero's welcome. At the end of a raucous National Championship Parade before tens of thousands of adoring fans, Harbaugh, true to his quirky, inquisitive nature, invoked, from memory, part of the St. Crispin's Day speech by King Henry V, as written by William Shakespeare, from memory, inserting a few of his stars at the top.

J.J. McCarthy, the MVP. Corum and Sainristil. Keegan and Zinter. Jenkins and Barnett.

In their flowing cups freshly remember'd. This story shall the good man teach his son; and Crispin Crispian shall ne'er go by. From this day to the ending of the world, but we in it will be remember'd; we few, we happy few, we band of brothers; for he to-day that sheds his blood with me shall be my brother; be he ne'er so vile. This day shall gentle his condition.

And gentlemen in England now a-bed shall think themselves accursed they were not here, and hold their manhood cheap whiles any speaks that fought with us upon Saint Crispin's day.

Team One-Forty-Four. We salute you: A band of brothers.

Thank you.

HE LEFT WARDE MANUEL TO answer *the* question the athletic director said he had only heard about five hundred times that day riding alone in the back of a pickup truck—take that for what it's worth—on the parade route that day: "I am working on getting this man a new contract."

DURING A TWO-DAY GETAWAY WITH Sarah on Coronado Island off the coast of San Diego, Harbaugh had unloaded to Todd Anson. He told Anson he wanted to remain at Michigan but believed Manuel—no matter his public pronouncements—was not the advocate he needed in his corner. He also raged against Petitti, who before the three-game Big Ten suspension had promised to meet Harbaugh in Ann Arbor and brief him on what the conference was doing, only to stand him up. (Through a spokesperson, Petitti declined an interview request.)

The day after his outburst to Anson, Harbaugh had an initial interview with the Los Angeles Chargers. Afterward, his tone had softened. Leaning toward taking the NFL job, if offered, he dialed down the Manuel rhetoric, no longer interested in a potential legal battle and fighting people he later said were "gunning for me." It suggested in attitude and tone that his days in Ann Arbor were numbered.

Indeed they were.

On Wednesday, January 24, news broke that Harbaugh had agreed to a five-year contract to be the next head coach of the Chargers at a reported $16 million per year. Done with the NCAA, frustrating U of M contract jabber, thrilled to be *wanted by the Spanos family*, intrigued by the prospect of taking Justin Herbert, the team's dynamic young quarterback, to another level.

Manuel told Meek of *The Athletic* he was "at peace" with the effort to retain Harbaugh, despite a torrent of criticism circulating on U of M blogs and websites.

"I hear about what was happening on social media, some of the language and things that people directed my way," Manuel said. "That doesn't take away from the effort we put into it. They have no idea what communication and conversations we had."

Was Manuel surprised at the news? "I don't want to use the word 'surprised,'" he replied. "This was the third year Jim had spoken to NFL teams. I can see where people would be interested.

"As I told Jim, 'I'm sad for us, happy for you,' if that's what you want to do."

With his head coach out the door, Manuel made the smartest and most obvious move and immediately elevated offensive coordinator Sherrone Moore, who had excelled as interim head coach against Penn State and Ohio State. Moore had already received full-throated support from Harbaugh and the players, but Manuel wanted more.

"I want to hear *your* plan," Manuel said, according to *The Athletic*. "I don't want to know what Jim's plans were, and every answer to the question is, 'I'm going to do what Jim did.' I want to know what Sherrone thinks."

Two and a half hours later, what Sherrone thought was *more than* good enough. Not that Moore was about to walk into college football's version of the Presidential Suite. Many of Michigan's best players were either out of eligibility or headed to the NFL Draft, and the looming NCAA investigations were dark clouds on the horizon.

Still, Michigan had their new man. The right man, it appeared, to lead during the difficult months ahead. And for all those questioning whether Big Blue deserved to stand atop college football's mountain, let no less an authority than Charlie Baker be your guide.

In his meeting with reporters at the association's annual convention, the NCAA president pointed out that Michigan had won eight straight games after the sign-stealing scheme was revealed. The Wolverines, in his mind, had erased all doubt.

"At the end of the day," he said, "no one believes at this point Michigan didn't win the national title fair and square."

CHAPTER 21

Dominoes

FTER A GUT-PUNCH ROSE BOWL loss, Nick Saban was exhausted. A grueling season that took every ounce of his energy and experience had come up seven points short in overtime. For a man who always thought more about the losses than any big win, it ate him up that a season many of his coaching peers called perhaps his best failed to climax in a national championship.

Saban, a man who religiously stuck to his routines, was so tired after the Rose Bowl that he even gave his staff a few days off. He himself headed to his $17.5 million oceanfront estate on Jupiter Island in Florida to recuperate and consider his place in college football moving forward.

Returning from Jupiter Island a few days later, Saban arrived to find his football house on fire. He knew he had to replace wide receivers coach Holmon Wiggins and special teams coordinator Coleman Hutzler; now he had to deal with longtime friend and defensive coordinator Kevin Steele retiring. In addition, co–defensive coordinator Travaris Robinson, who played an important defensive play-calling role during the season, wanted to be bumped up to full-time coordinator, but Saban didn't think he was ready, according to multiple sources familiar with his thinking. Hurt by Saban's refusal to promote him, Robinson left to join—who else?—Kirby Smart in Athens. Everywhere he turned, it seemed, Saban felt heat. He'd had to be more hands on with the defense than ever in 2023, with it becoming clear early on that Steele wasn't up to the task, leaving him drained and longing for the days of Smart and Jeremy Pruitt. He eyed former Maryland head coach D. J. Durkin for a defensive assistant role, but there were concerns that Saban's beloved defense would never be what it once was.

"The people inside who were close to him, they told him you need your guys in here because he kept getting further and further away from people who knew him and that system the way it was created and evolved," said former Alabama assistant Lance Thompson.

As Alabama assistants sought opportunities elsewhere, so did Alabama players. Seventeen left. Isaiah Bond, the hero of 4th-and-31, threatened to go into the portal, unhappy with his below-market-average NIL compensation, and it took everything Saban had to keep him on the roster. (Bond's comments a week earlier at the Rose Bowl presaged the situation: "We work so many hours of the week. So I feel like, honestly, the least they could do is pay us a little bit for how many hours you're putting in. At the end of the day . . . we're walking around some days like we're eighty-five and we're nineteen, twenty years old. It's a lot of tax on our body. The money definitely helps a little bit.")

Saban and his closest confidante, Miss Terry, bemoaned what college football had become and wondered whether another year was worth it.

"We were met with coaches leaving, players leaving or asking for money," Terry Saban told a longtime friend. "Another year of rebuilding the staff and the team . . . these rules are murder!"

The buzz that Saban was considering walking away grew, but the Alabama head coach held firm to his routine. At the time, he was actively interviewing coaches for open positions and was close to making hires for many of them. He called Maryland head coach Mike Locksley, his former offensive coordinator, Tuesday afternoon to talk through prospective minority candidates for those jobs. But later that night, Saban called Jimmy Sexton and told him he was likely going to retire.

That next morning, however, Saban appeared on the SEC head coaches' teleconference and seemed as fiery as ever. As other coaches lamented what the sport had become, with one even using the word "extortion" to describe dealing with players who threatened to go into the portal if they didn't get more money, Saban got heated during a discussion related to the NFL. When talking about using helmets that had microphones in them, a hot topic in light of the Michigan sign-stealing scandal, an animated Saban said if they wanted to adopt NFL rules, they should also do player contracts to stop what had turned into free agency.

No one on that call had any idea what Saban was weighing internally. As the seconds ticked on his office clock, he was still debating what he was going to do. Was he really ready to retire from the game he had ruled with an iron fist and that had given a boy from tiny Monongah, West Virginia, generational wealth? Even the idea of walking away had long scared him. He had been part of organized sports since he was nine years old and had once admitted, "I'm scared to death of what it's going to be like if I'm not part of a team."

He compared a post-football life to growing up fearing the monster he believed was hiding in his bedroom closet.

"You never know what's behind the door," he said.

At 3:55 p.m., having finished his last prospective assistant coach interview of the day, Saban sat in his office chair wondering what speech he was going to give to his team in five minutes. He called Miss Terry one last time as he weighed his decision. She gave him her blessing to do what he thought best.

When he walked into the team room at 4:00 p.m., he started explaining the need to be 100 percent all in to be able to truly be the best. Players had heard this talk before and nodded along. But then came the anvil: Saban said he could no longer give that 100 percent and was retiring. The price was simply too much for him to keep paying. The bottom fell out of the room.

Julian Sayin, the five-star quarterback who looked like the future of the program, quickly texted his mom. By now Karen and Dan had made the dramatic decision to support their son's dream as a family. Together they had driven across the country from Carlsbad to a new home and new life with daughter, Jocelyn—now enrolled in UA graduate school—in Tuscaloosa.

"OMG, Saban is retiring," Julian told his mom. "I'm not lying."

ESPN senior writer Chris Low, who was as close to Saban as any journalist, broke the news minutes later, at 4:06 p.m., with a simple tweet, "Nick Saban is retiring, sources tell ESPN. He won six national titles at Alabama."

Saban's stunning decision sent a shock wave through his sport, setting off a series of dominos that, one after another, impacted programs, coaches, and players, seemingly at the speed of light, one by one—the unrelenting force of the transfer portal, the imperial power of the Big Ten and SEC, the seductive appeal of NIL, to the greatest force of all: self-interest.

Saban's bombshell hit mere hours ahead of NCAA president Charlie Baker's big "State of College Sports" speech at the NCAA convention in Phoenix. In the hallways and meeting rooms inside the Phoenix convention center, all anyone could talk about was Saban this, Saban that. Any chance of Baker earning any major headlines evaporated the minute Low sent his tweet. Back in T-town, the aftereffects were just beginning to hit.

At seven the next morning, a Thursday, Ellis Ponder, Saban's right-hand man and the program's chief operating officer, called Julian Sayin.

"Can we talk to you, Julian?" Ponder asked.

Inside the football facility, Ponder wanted to know if Sayin wanted to speak with Saban. More sad than mad, Julian told him, "No, I don't think I need to." That Friday morning, though, following the encouragement of a wellness staffer to talk things out, Sayin and Saban spent a few moments together. Saban said all the right things—you're going to have a successful career, a really good chance to start next year—before offering a hug and a pat on the back.

And that was that.

THE MORNING AFTER SABAN'S DECISION, Jimmy Sexton walked into Alabama's football facility. He was allegedly there to meet with his most famous client, but those around college football couldn't help but shake their heads knowingly at what was brewing. It was Sexton's time to shine, an opportunity to enrich multiple clients through a blue-blood coaching search, and what better place to kick off those efforts than in Tuscaloosa. It was a classic Sexton high-wire act as he leveraged Alabama interest into raises for coaches while still making sure one of his clients landed a job that had been especially lucrative for Sexton. "Jimmy needs the Alabama job in his portfolio," said one high-ranking Power 4 administrator.

The early names mentioned for the job in media reports were practically all Sexton clients: Oregon head coach Dan Lanning, Texas head coach Steve Sarkisian, Ole Miss head coach Lane Kiffin, Florida State head coach Mike Norvell, and Washington head coach Kalen DeBoer. Alabama athletic director Greg Byrne had no choice but to engage with the Power Broker. With a collection of the top available coaches, the game ran through Sexton.

Lanning, who spent a season as a graduate assistant under Saban at Alabama, was the early hot name, with some reporters even erroneously saying he was in Tuscaloosa the night of Saban's retirement. It turned out he was at his home in Eugene watching a Jason Bourne movie with his family.

There was skepticism that Sarkisian would leave his great situation in Austin, coming off a playoff appearance, even if he had deep personal ties to Saban and an Alabama program that had resuscitated his career. There was communication between the two sides, but even with it never looking particularly realistic, Alabama's interest in Sark helped Sexton parlay it into a $10.3 million annual salary, a nearly 84 percent raise from what the Texas head coach made ($5.6 million) in 2023, along with a country club membership and personal use of a private plane.

That left Kiffin, Norvell, and DeBoer. Kiffin badly wanted the Alabama job—he even told people he turned down the Auburn job the prior year to have a chance to replace Saban, but he could never get real traction in the search. Kiffin hoped Sexton could push hard to slide him into the job if Norvell and DeBoer bowed out, but Byrne wasn't going there.

Byrne zeroed in on Norvell and DeBoer, two of the hottest coaching candidates in the country. Norvell guided Florida State to a 13-1 record—Alabama had made the playoffs at the Seminoles' expense—and had southern recruiting ties. DeBoer didn't have those ties but only days earlier had led Washington to the national championship game against Harbaugh's Wolverines. What happened next showed the brilliance of Sexton. Florida State believed Norvell was leaving for Alabama and was fighting to do everything it could to prevent that from happening. There was so much concern in Tallahassee that FSU officials had preliminary contact with Kiffin's camp and made clear the Ole Miss coach would be the school's top target to replace Norvell, according to sources familiar with the situation. Washington also believed DeBoer was leaving for Alabama and was fighting to do everything it could to prevent that from happening. No matter what happened at that point, both were cashing in big time.

It wasn't until midmorning on Friday that Florida State felt confident Norvell was staying in Tallahassee. The two sides agreed to an eight-year deal that will pay Norvell more than $10 million annually, a raise of $2.5 million a year.

Later that day, Byrne made Washington head coach Kalen DeBoer his official pick to inherit Saban's throne. Only a year earlier, Ponder, Saban's chief of staff, was asked what the post-Saban succession plan looked like, and he admitted there wasn't one. There was no natural successor, no hand-picked prince to keep the Process going once Saban made the decision to hang it up. Saban had successfully groomed Smart and Sarkisian and given them the blueprint to dominate the sport, but they had become too successful in their own right, too entrenched at Texas and Georgia, to leave.

Before the season, no one could have predicted a forty-nine-year-old man from South Dakota with zero ties to Saban would be the heir apparent. DeBoer almost surely knew the old adage that you never want to replace the legend, you want to replace the guy who tried to replace the legend. If he didn't know that before accepting the job, he faced the stark realization on his first official day *on* the job.

When a college unveils its new football coach, it is typically one big celebration full of platitudes and hopes for what the new guy can accomplish. It is the dawn of a new era.

Saturday was DeBoer's turn for a coronation, but Alabama's power players were far more interested in their outgoing king. All eyes were on Saban as he and Terry walked into a Bryant-Denny Stadium event space minutes before DeBoer's scheduled press conference. The cameras focused on the Saban royalty and not on DeBoer and his wife, Nicole, as they slid past to find their spots on the dais. Saban faced a receiving line of university trustees and boosters who wanted to offer well wishes as he embarked on a retirement that, rather oddly, included still coming into the office every day.

When it finally came time to announce DeBoer as the new coach, a single moment encapsulated the awkwardness of the transition. As Byrne began to introduce the most important hire he'd ever make, multiple trustees leaned forward and turned and craned their heads to get a better look at

Saban to see how he would react. Only after the Old King started clapping did his court follow suit.

DeBoer said all the right things about following Saban that day, but it didn't take long for Alabama to be forced to grapple with the ramifications of a post-Saban world.

TROY DANNEN, THE NEWLY HIRED athletic director at Washington, went from watching his football program play in a national championship on Monday to needing a new coach by Friday. The dominoes were falling that fast.

Dannen put together a list of a half dozen or so qualities his next coach must have. First and foremost, he needed to be a "maniacal" recruiter, then a developer, someone with Big Ten experience, a passionate and energetic coach, and, finally, a winner. As he went down his checklist, he became intrigued by the man who just engineered the biggest turnaround in college football: Jedd Fisch.

Eight days earlier, Fisch said on *The Jim Rome Show* that he had no interest in leaving Arizona. "I have a lot of interest in seeing if we can get to that CFP," he said. He had a five-year, $25.5 million contract on the table through the 2028–29 season. Both Heeke and Robbins confirmed any dollar difference from the previous extension would be privately funded by donors. Fisch was content in Tucson, but without a signed extension, he was willing to listen to the right kind of suitor. On Saturday afternoon, Dannen made a call to the most popular man in Tucson to gauge his interest.

"It was an intriguing job," Fisch said. "That's for sure."

By the time Fisch finished talking, Dannen was far more than intrigued. He believed he had found someone who checked every last box.

"After that phone call, you talk about blowing your socks off, blowing the doors off, whatever it was, I hung up the phone and said, 'We found the guy. This is the guy that matches everything we wanted,'" Dannen later said. "Then it became can we get him?"

At ten o'clock that Saturday night Dannen called back and offered Fisch the Huskies' job: an average of $7.75 million per year for seven years. Now Fisch had a decision to make. He weighed a return to Arizona, where he was already dealing with the loss of top assistant coaches and key players looking to cash in on the portal; a contract extension accepted but not officially approved by the Arizona Board of Regents. As he considered the brighter lights, the bigger Big Ten stage, more resources, and far more money—critically, he said, an average of $3 million more per year in the assistant coaches salary pool—he knew the answer. The next morning, Dannen, roughly thirty hours after his first call, was on a private plane, a guaranteed $54.25 million contract in hand.

On Sunday Fisch called a 4:30 p.m. team meeting to inform his now former players he was taking another job. The meeting lasted a grand total of three minutes. Heeke had concerns that the NCAA would view any specific references—a better job, team performance—as tampering, an attempt to induce Arizona players to follow Fisch to Seattle. So Fisch offered a generic goodbye, telling the team how appreciative he was of their time together, that he loved them, and that the Washington job was a once-in-a-lifetime opportunity for his family and every assistant on staff.

The reaction was what you would expect it to be.

"Lots of distraught faces," Fisch said. "You could hear a bit of mumbling, disappointment."

"Family" is a funny word. Heartwarming when everyone is huddled around a roaring fire on Christmas Eve. Heartbreaking when, in a matter of hours, the man who sold the word "family" from the moment he set foot in Tucson moved *his* to the Pacific Northwest virtually overnight. Given the constant talk of *family* and *family culture*, could Fisch understand a fractured feeling of outright betrayal?

"Oh yeah, it was brutal," he said. "Absolutely brutal. That's where it got a bit salty, where people got disappointed. I just kind of walked but it was the only thing I was allowed to do. If I had done anything else other than that, I would have gotten nailed. The NCAA needs to figure out a way when you commit your whole life to a kid for three years you should at least be able to give him a hug and say goodbye."

Fisch said the move had been hard on his family as well, with his wife, Amber, and two youngest daughters, Ashlee and Kendall, emotionally undone by the whole "no contact" command.

"Amber was hysterical, the girls were hysterical," Fisch said. "They couldn't talk to T-Mac, Noah, Jacob Manu, some of the other guys we had enormously close relationships with. The girls were really sad. They can't say goodbye, they can't hug and text their big brothers. It's very hard for them because they *loved* Noah, *loved* T-Mac. Hopefully one day, when everybody's eligibility is over, there can be a real good family dinner again."

In many ways, a New Age NCAA—NIL and the portal—had long since set that departure price. Not that many in Tucson beyond the Fisch family cared. A close-knit community seethed with anger at the astonishing speed at which a man they had embraced had shed one program's colors for another.

Management at one brew pub near campus was so pissed off they taped photos of Fisch's smiling face wearing a purple UW hat across their urinals.

"This is a small town and people love this place," said Heeke, "and when you rip their soul out a little bit or cut them open, they will never forgive you."

Humberto "Bert" Lopez was one of those people. He and his wife, Czarina, had been major U of A donors for more than forty years, one of only four "Legends" who stepped up and funded Desert Takeover at the highest level, well beyond the $100,000 minimum required at the Founders level. He had taken a particular interest in the 2023 team, doing a number of NIL deals through his various businesses. Lopez told the *Arizona Daily Star* that Fisch's departure "upset me to no end."

Lopez, so upset over how it all unfolded, texted Fisch upon his departure: You could have been a legend here at Arizona had you stayed. I [will go] out of my way to make sure you didn't get the best players. I don't ever wish anyone bad luck and you are the first one. You disappointed me. I thought we were friends.

Like many other donors Lopez doubled down on the football collective and became a driving force in making sure McMillan and Fifita didn't flee to the SEC or, worse, follow Fisch to Washington.

Lopez had no need to worry. The day after Fisch's departure Bobby Robbins had flown to Los Angeles and met with Les Fifita at an airport hotel near LAX. The Arizona president expected to hear that Noah, T-Mac, and the Servite High crew were history, following their coach up north. Robbins told Fifita he'd find T-Mac and Noah more NIL money, but there was no way

Arizona could compete with Washington, USC, or Ohio State, which, Robbins learned, had offered a combo package worth $2 million to lure Noah and T-Mac to Columbus in the summer of 2023. For Robbins, the meeting was personal. Even when Noah wasn't playing, the university president had made sure to stop by the bench before each game, give Noah a hug, and tell him, "Be ready, Noah, be ready, God may have a plan for you today."

Les Fifita had witnessed those moments and later heard more from his son, who said he had found a sign from God in, of all things, a fortune cookie that read: "You don't have to travel far to find the satisfaction you're looking for." Now his father had something to say that shocked Robbins.

"It's not about the money," Fifita said. "This is about unfinished business. Commitment. Family. We're staying here."

The day after Fisch and twenty-one assistant coaches and staff members relocated to Seattle, Heeke made a smart, fast move and signed San Jose State head coach Brent Brennan to a five-year deal. Speaking of boxes, Brennan checked more than his fair share—he was a former graduate assistant and assistant coach under Dick Tomey, and a finalist for the job that went to Fisch before becoming the head coach at San Jose State, where he turned the lowly Spartans into two-time Mountain West regular-season champions.

"Coach Tomey was my mentor, my friend, he was kind of my football dad . . . such a critical part of my process," Brennan said at the press conference announcing his hiring. "He was the guy I always called when things got hard for me professionally, personally. He was incredible for me that way."

At virtually the same time, Fisch delivered his opening remarks to a crowd of UW faithful. Talking about a "new beginning" and how excited Ashlee and Kendall were to be part of a vibrant community.

"We are in this thing together for hopefully a very, very long time," he said.

ONCE SABAN RETIRED, A THIRTY-DAY transfer window opened up for every Alabama player. With the regular transfer windows closed for all other schools, it put new head coach DeBoer on the defensive as rival programs looked to pick apart the Crimson Tide's talented roster.

The problem was Alabama didn't have the financial artillery to fight back against top suitors. Insiders detailed a fan base that had grown complacent under Saban and didn't feel a burning pressure to kick in major money the way Tennessee and Texas boosters had. They believed the name on the front of the jersey and its storied history trumped all else and would always serve as a siren song to top recruits regardless of who was coaching. And, to their point, Alabama was still succeeding at a very high level despite not having one of the top NIL operations, so something had to still be working.

What the average Alabama fan didn't realize, but what those intimately familiar with the NIL market did, was Alabama had greatly benefited from a Saban discount. The Crimson Tide was able to get players below market value who wanted to learn under Saban and willingly eschewed short-term money in the belief that he could best prepare them to cash in down the line with the bigger NFL payday. That was the case with five-star cornerback Zabien Brown, who graduated early from historic Mater Dei High School, to start the process of learning as soon as possible from the defensive backs guru.

"Could Zabien have gotten a lot more money? Absolutely," said Courtney Brown, Zabien's mother. "But if that's not what matters to him, that's not what matters to me. He chose the school based off the coaches, based off Nick."

For every Zabien Brown, Saban knew that he was still losing recruits he badly wanted for bigger dollars elsewhere, and had tried to sound the alarm multiple times, most aggressively in his comments directed at Jimbo Fisher, but Alabama's NIL war chest still lagged behind rivals.

"People didn't want to give when Saban was there because they got lazy," said a source with knowledge of the situation. "Fuck it, Saban's going to take care of it. People don't make change until the pain is too great. They were not willing to change because there was no pain with Nick Saban as their coach."

The NIL source, who more than a year earlier called Alabama's NIL operation a "house of cards," was predictably concerned about what was to come. "We're fucked," the source said. "It's not tenable without Saban."

With Saban gone, so too was the Saban discount.

Isaiah Bond, the hero of the Iron Bowl, was the first to jump ship. He entered the transfer portal and practically everyone in the sport knew he was headed to play for Sarkisian at Texas. At Alabama, Bond made less than six figures in NIL compensation despite being the Tide's leading receiver. While visiting Texas, Bond was pictured in a Lamborghini.

The levees really broke on January 17.

Freshman Caleb Downs, who had the potential to be the best defensive player ever under Saban, entered the transfer portal. Saban loved Downs and had admitted that he and Malachi Moore were the two players he had the hardest time telling he was retiring. Downs did practically everything right during an All-American season that made clear he had a very bright NFL future. The former five-star recruit should have been the foundation of the DeBoer era, but was already out the door. He came to Alabama to learn under Saban, the defensive wizard, and when the offensive-minded DeBoer couldn't convince Travaris Robinson to come back to Tuscaloosa, Downs had seen enough.

Brown was considering doing the same. Saban's retirement came as a complete shock as Alabama had stressed during the recruiting process that the legendary head coach wasn't going anywhere anytime soon. When Courtney Brown asked Tide receivers coach Holmon Wiggins about the Saban retirement rumors earlier that year, he emphatically shut them down. "He'll basically die on the field," Wiggins told her. "He has more energy. He's still keeping us out 'til midnight."

After all he had gone through—the summer classes, skipping social activities, giving up the last half of his high school senior year, diligently trying to memorize the Alabama playbook ahead of spring practice—Brown was angry that on his very first day of classes, Saban bailed on him. He wondered whether any of it was even worth it.

"I think he felt burned," Courtney Brown said. "He was immediately like, 'I'm not going to stay here.'"

Brown called Jackson Zager, Zabien's agent, to talk through the possible options. Zabien hadn't entered the portal, but there would be considerable interest if he did. Brown and Zager talked several times that first week, with the young agent impressing the recruit's mother with his calm in the face of chaos.

Brown didn't care at all about how much NIL money he made at Alabama—it was all about the long-term benefits of playing under Saban to make his NFL dreams come true—but after Saban's shocking decision, that would change. "I knew if we went elsewhere we'd be leaning in and negotiating for a much higher NIL deal," Brown said.

Alabama had no interest in letting it get to that point. Not long after leaving his job as Buffalo's head coach to take an assistant job at Alabama, Mo Linguist jumped on a plane to meet with Brown and other parents out in California to sell the vision of the new regime. Ultimately, it was enough to convince the Cali five-star to stay put in Tuscaloosa.

And then there was Sayin, a quarterback already so good that Terry Saban told a friend back in September before the Texas game that she wished they had him for the 2023 season. Now, on his very first day of college classes, the real reason he came to Alabama had walked out the door. His head spinning, Sayin was devastated but didn't want to make any rash decisions. Unfortunately, Sayin and DeBoer's new staff got off on the wrong foot right from the start.

It started when general manager Courtney Morgan, who had joined De-Boer on the private plane from Seattle to Tuscaloosa, immediately began throwing his weight around. Morgan took a combative attitude with Parker Cain, the family's NIL contact at Excel Sports, accusing Sayin, who took a far-below-market value deal to play for Saban, of being all about the money. Morgan had also promised to call Sayin's mom to discuss the situation, but never followed through.

The heartbreaking moment came during Sayin's first (and only) meeting with DeBoer. He had already waited some ninety minutes outside Saban's old office when DeBoer finally brought him in. He told Julian to hang in there, and how he was going to like the explosive new offense, before asking a curious question to arguably the most coveted high school quarterback in the country.

"How do you spell your last name again?"

"A two-minute meeting with DeBoer," his mother, Karen, later said, in tears on the phone. "Two minutes. Asked him how to spell his last name. The kid is devastated, and not because he needs attention. He wants to play on Sunday. How's he going to get there when he came to play for Nick Saban and the program, and now he's watching this. It's incredible."

When DeBoer added Washington redshirt freshman Austin Mack, who had four years of eligibility remaining to an already-crowded quarterback room, the writing was on the wall. The move prompted a flood of calls to the Sayins from every corner of the head-coaching universe, including USC's Lincoln Riley and Ohio State's Ryan Day.

Sayin wasn't afraid to compete with Mack, but he told his mom the loss of structure under Saban had taken a toll, although he refused to point a single finger at the man who brought him to Alabama.

"Julian will not listen to a negative thing about Nick Saban right now," said his mother. "He won't listen to it."

On the morning of January 19, exactly seven days after DeBoer and the UW crowd first set foot in town, Sayin entered the transfer portal.

That very same morning, Karen was sitting alone in an airport on her way home from an ill-timed business trip, choking back more tears on the phone.

"I know people are going to attack him, but he shouldn't have to go through that," she said. "He's been loyal to them from the beginning. Never took any other official visits. Always recruiting for them. This was his dream and it blew up. He has to think about himself at this point."

I'll play for free, Julian had said to his mom. *I'll play for free. I don't care. I just want to be developed.*

Two days later, on January 21, Sayin made it official: he was transferring to Ohio State, reuniting with a familiar face in the Buckeyes' new offensive coordinator Bill O'Brien. Later that day, Karen Brandenburg sent a text to a friend who had traveled a long, winding year with the family.

Crazy ride for sure but this feels right and so good to him!
I have a happy kid back!

Less than three weeks later, on Friday, February 9, O'Brien returned to his New England roots as the new head coach at Boston College. The same day, in yet another head-spinning move, UCLA head coach Chip Kelly resigned to replace O'Brien in Columbus, the best possible alternative, a coach who had made a big play for Sayin at UCLA.

• • •

A DAY AFTER SAYIN PICKED his new home, Arizona president Bobby Robbins made a shocking announcement: AD Dave Heeke was out in what the university deemed a "transition in the leadership of the department of athletics."

In their statements, Robbins and Heeke played nice. The president thanked his former AD for "his outstanding efforts in leading our athletics program through a period of significant change." Heeke responded in kind, thanking Robbins and others for their partnership, saying how "it has been an honor and privilege to have served the University of Arizona for the last seven years."

"It was out of the blue, that's for sure," said Heeke, the next day. "I never thought in my career I'd get fired. . . . I didn't get fired. Asked to step aside. It's a crazy world, really crazy."

For those playing the political blame game there was no shortage of targets. The university had initially revealed a shocking $240 million budget shortfall. Robbins took to the editorial pages of the *Arizona Republic* to outline an austerity program, including what were described as "draconian" cuts and a hiring freeze.

In an interview at the Alamo Bowl, Robbins had drawn a direct line to years of uncontrolled accounting by the school's admissions office in passing out full scholarships like party favors to thousands of out-of-state students a year carrying 4.0 averages, leading to about $200 million of the $240 million shortfall. Robbins later said the accounting model had miscalculated and the annual structural deficit was closer to $177 million. No matter. By then everyone from Governor Katie Hobbs to the Board of Regents to the chair of the faculty senate to the head of the campus workers union were questioning Robbins's leadership, ringing up a series of no-confidence votes, calling for someone's head on a platter, and not some anonymous chief financial officer who had previously resigned. No, they wanted a *public* figure.

They got Heeke.

"I became a casualty of that," he said. "I didn't get fired for mismanagement. If that, they would have fired me for cause. They're honoring my full contract."

Heeke said his conversation with Robbins Sunday night was neither nasty nor confrontational. A source with knowledge of the decision said Robbins had been taking a lot of heat from a few disgruntled donors, senior administrators, and certain regents questioning issues inside the athletic department, including the time it took Heeke to make big decisions. Robbins would later explain his decision as "simply the right time to have new leadership," modernize the athletic department, and ease the transition into the Big 12.

Heeke had been what he called a "loyal soldier" to Robbins, helping raise money to rebuild the football program, weathering one storm after another—Title IX issues, reported gang rapes by U of A football players, sexual harassment claims, an NCAA investigation into the basketball program. But in the end somebody had to go.

"Bobby's good at compartmentalizing things," said Heeke, whose seven-figure-a-year contract was guaranteed through March 2025. "It wasn't easy for him to do. It hurts me. It hurts me inside that he did it. I think I'm a fall guy."

Less than a month after parting ways with Heeke, the university introduced Desirée Reed-Francois as its new director of athletics. The first female full-time AD in school history, Reed-Francois had graduated from U of A law school and served in leadership roles in collegiate athletics for more than a decade, most recently as Missouri's athletic director since 2021.

Reed-Francois's three references, he said, had been the University of Missouri chancellor, SEC commissioner Greg Sankey, and a former head football coach by the last name of Saban.

"She's unbelievable, just unbelievable," said Robbins.

Asked if he was looking long-term at the SEC and his new AD's valued connections to that conference Robbins offered a one-word answer.

"Yes."

THE TEXT CAME IN UNSOLICITED on the last Sunday night in February from a now familiar contact. Jedd Fisch, referencing a phone interview two days earlier, expressed gratitude for getting a chance to tell his side of the story. He was aware of the brutal beating he had taken leaving Arizona for Washington, casting a pall over a decision that dramatically improved his family's finances and those of his ten assistants, every last one of whom had received a $200,000-a-year raise.

It probably has been the worst month of my life, even though it should have been the best of my life as I achieved something 99.9 percent of the world said wouldn't be possible, Fisch wrote. First time I ever left anywhere without a proper and appropriate goodbye.

THE DAY AFTER APRIL FOOLS' Day 2024 another bombshell hit in Tucson—and it was no practical joke. In a letter addressed to "Students and Colleagues," Robert C. Robbins announced that he had informed the Arizona Board of Regents that he would step down as university president at the end of his current contract, through June 2026, or earlier if a new president was selected by the board.

Just minutes before the official announcement, a source close to Robbins said the president had "pulled the ejection handle" following a recent "interaction" with the regents. In his letter, Robbins described the decision as "difficult" but "the right decision for me and for the university that I love so dearly."

The move by Robbins marked the final domino to fall at a university that, in a span of less than three months, had seen its head football coach, athletic director, and president head for the exits.

According to the source with direct knowledge, Robbins was the victim of power-hungry faculty senate leaders looking for the past four years for something, *anything*, to oust Robbins—beginning with his decision to furlough most of the university's workforce for up to four months during the COVID-19 pandemic in the summer and fall of 2020; then the October 2022 fatal on-campus shooting of Professor Thomas Meixner, chair of the department of hydrology and atmospheric sciences, by a former grad student with a history of threats of violence, resulting in a $9 million wrongful death claim against the university (settled in January 2024) followed by the $177 million financial structural deficit debacle and news the athletic department was running in the red by $30 million a year—money, the faculty believed, that could be better spent on their salaries and academic units.

"They want the university run by the faculty," said the source. "Not by administrators. Not by boards. They want to run the university the way they want to run it."

• • •

WHEN JIM HARBAUGH WAS GROWING up, his favorite television show was *The Rockford Files*, a seventies detective drama whose star, James Garner, played a private investigator who lived in a mobile home in a parking lot on a beach in Malibu. After signing with the Chargers, Harbaugh asked his brother-in-law and two friends to drive his thirty-one-foot Quantum Thor Motor Coach across the country to an RV camping spot he had rented right across from the Pacific in scenic Huntington Beach for $2,700 a month, an effort to decompress after a stress-filled season that had forced a Michigan Man out of the arms of a university he loved.

"I'm just trying to be happy," Harbaugh told Jim Hackett.

Nine days after speaking those words, the NCAA announced the COVID-19 dead-period penalties in agreement with Michigan: three years' probation, a fine, and recruiting restrictions. The Committee on Infractions noted one "former coach" did not participate in the agreement, and any potential future penalties were pending.

Nearly three thousand miles away, seventy-two-year-old Nick Saban was staring out at a different ocean from his beachfront estate. A man who had managed his day down to the minute every single day three hundred sixty-five days a year—who ate the same lunch and wore the same pair of shoes to practice for a decade—suddenly unmoored from the anchor in his coaching life for the first time in fifty years. Passing his time playing golf, doting over his grandchildren, working as an analyst for ESPN, and making an uneasy transition into the *real world* without a coterie of reliable help.

In the end, the unremitting chaos hammering a sport for three long years had taken arguably its heaviest toll on its singular stars. For anyone looking at the price of the new era of college football, two older men walking the beach, one on the East Coast, the other out west, would have been a prescient place to start.

Afterword: A New Model

ROM HIS HOME ON THE West Coast, the soon-to-be eighty-five-year-old Sonny Vaccaro had kept a watchful eye on a historic day, fielding a flurry of congratulatory calls from the likes of Ken Feinberg and Michael Hausfeld on what many had started to see as the dying days of the NCAA, certainly as Walter Byers first constructed it.

On the eve of Memorial Day weekend 2024, the specter of another thunderous legal defeat had spurred a landmark $2.8 billion settlement—pending approval by U.S. District Court judge Claudia Wilken—in *House vs. NCAA* and two other critical cases, opening the door to compensating Division I college athletes for the first time to the tune of some $20 million a year per Power 4 school through revenue sharing. As feisty and passionate as ever, Vaccaro expressed not a single ounce of regret for helping construct the O'Bannon bomb that threatened to destroy the system.

"My personal feeling from watching it close, this instant, it's over," Vaccaro said. "Their greed. They ate themselves. Eventually, righteousness, being right, overturned the greed."

The House settlement toppled the NCAA's more than one-hundred-year insistence on an amateurism model and finally set the stage for schools to directly pay their athletes. But as one legal scholar put it, the settlement "closes one Pandora's box and opens four or five others," in the form of its impact on Title IX, the future of non-revenue sports, and congressional action (or inaction) on an antitrust exemption. Add in the insanity of the transfer portal, NIL, and other wild cards, and the need for a new collegiate model remained paramount.

In his first month as governor of Massachusetts in 2015, Charlie Baker faced a record-breaking snowstorm. The transportation system he inherited wasn't ready for it.

Parts of the New England area were hit with up to three feet of snow—Boston alone experienced a historic twenty-two inches of snow—as Baker and his new executive staff rushed to buy every snow shovel available and utilized every measure at their disposal, including a travel ban and paying prisoners to shovel off subway tracks, in order to keep the citizens of Massachusetts safe. Amid the emergency, Baker earned top reviews for his methodical approach and strong communication, with one headline declaring BAKER PASSES FIRST BIG POLITICAL TEST. A year later, realizing he had been lucky beyond belief, Baker loaded up on snowplows and other equipment in a very public "we are ready" message.

Eight years later, what Baker inherited in the first month of his time as president of the NCAA looked more like a shitstorm.

"Our issues are a betting scandal, congressmen and -women who think we don't give a shit about student-athletes, their health and wellness, or their academics," said Tim Buckley, the NCAA's senior vice president of external affairs.

Recognizing the need to be proactive instead of the NCAA's usual penchant to be reactive, Baker, Buckley, and other key members of the NCAA's senior staff began working on what they believed could be a radical solution in the face of mounting threats coming from seemingly every direction.

"He could end up being the best president of the NCAA or the last president of the NCAA," said University of Michigan regent Jordan B. Acker. "I'm not sure there's a third option there."

Baker, with deep political ties, made frequent trips to Washington, D.C., his first year, pitching key legislators on a federal solution to critical issues like NIL and the rising threat of athletes becoming employees. But it didn't take long to realize it was a long shot and that the NCAA's solution to the madcap craziness would have to come from within. Starting in August 2023, Baker and his senior staff met weekly to develop an ambitious plan they eventually titled "Project DI."

After five months of intense work behind the scenes, Baker finally unveiled the plan before the National Football Foundation dinner in early

December: a new subdivision of Division I that would allow universities to directly pay their athletes through name, image, and likeness, and required schools to invest at least $30,000 per athlete for at least half of their athletes, a figure averaging about $6 million. It was a bold idea from a staid organization that had long fought against anything other than the amateurism model.

Baker privately worried it might not be big enough. For weeks, the plan was debated internally, with the majority believing the time had long since passed to take a stand.

"We've let things happen to us," said a senior NCAA administrator. "Had we taken baby steps, let the pressure out of an overinflated tire, it would have made a difference. All along the way we could have done something different, but we failed. We failed."

Buckley, who served as Baker's chief of staff at the end of his tenure as governor, compared it to what they had done in Massachusetts. As a Republican governor in a state dominated by Democrats, Baker had repeatedly pushed legislation knowing that the initial idea had no chance in passing.

"We would file legislation all the time, fully knowing what we got back from the legislature would be radically different," Buckley said. "Smashed into two other ideas, stripped of all but its essentials, totally part of the game. That's what made him a good governor. He never drew a line that said I will not sign a bill that doesn't have this. He was very disciplined in his public messaging to say, 'We're open to it, we're open to it.'"

If the NCAA process was even more opaque, more frustrating, than a legislative process, the hope remained that one might move the needle in the right direction.

For Baker, the biggest issue with his Project DI idea wasn't its scale but rather whether the organization was too far gone to rally support around it. As the association's influence waned over the last decade, conferences, television networks, and outside figures gobbled up more territory and power and were reluctant to give it up. SEC commissioner Greg Sankey for one was publicly upset that he hadn't been consulted ahead of Baker's Project DI release. (NCAA sources strongly pushed back on this claim and said conference commissioners were informed ahead of time.)

As time passed, Sankey's displays of indignation took on a different tone, more like they were a red herring. The wheels were already in motion for the SEC and rival-turned-partner Big Ten to make their own power play.

As older commissioner stalwarts like John Swofford and Jim Delany accepted their gold watches and left college athletics, Sankey, who had succeeded Mike Slive as SEC commissioner in 2015, became increasingly emboldened to take charge as the dominant voice of college athletics.

The COVID-19 pandemic was the major turning point. He was deeply frustrated with how leaders like then NCAA president Mark Emmert and Big Ten commissioner Kevin Warren handled the situation, believing they rushed into bad decisions while he preached patience to his conference. Without Sankey's steadfast belief that college football was possible in 2020, there was a good chance a season never would have been played. After that success, Sankey, who at his core is a policy wonk, became more strident, confident, and willing to speak out about issues plaguing the sport. After the stunning coup of luring Texas and Oklahoma from the Big 12, *Sports Illustrated* declared Sankey the "most powerful person in college sports" in 2022. He didn't deny the claim.

In truth, Sankey was the smartest guy in the Big Boys commissioner room, and he knew it. In the process he became more than willing to throw his weight around, having a major hand in shaping whatever the future of college football might look like. Sankey's involvement in major initiatives like a College Football Playoff expansion subcommittee and the NCAA transformation committee elicited skepticism about his motives, especially when it emerged he had been secretly negotiating with Texas and Oklahoma while building a twelve-team playoff model.

"The chair [of the transformation committee] being someone from the SEC—Greg Sankey, high integrity, wonderful human being—but I think there are a lot of people in the room, like, why is the SEC in charge?" said Mountain West commissioner Gloria Nevarez. "What are you trying to do? Immediately people were feeling like, 'Am I going to be voted off the island?'"

Those concerns became more real when the SEC announced a joint advisory committee with the Big Ten in February 2024. According to the conferences, the group was formed due to "recent court decisions, pending litigation, a patchwork of state laws, and complex governance proposals." The SEC and Big Ten had long been rivals, of course—Slive and Delany were constantly trying to one-up each other during their tenures—but the arrival of new Big Ten commissioner Tony Petitti and the growing gap between the Power 2 and the rest of the conferences demanded a closer working relationship. Sankey saw an equal in Petitti, a man he could work closely with in a way he never could with Warren.

"When Kevin Warren was in the room, [Greg] and Kevin hated each other," said one conference commissioner. "He didn't want to throw the SEC's weight around in a public way because he thought it would come back to bite him. He didn't have an ally at the Big Ten. As soon as Kevin's gone and Tony is in that seat, he's got an ally and now the two of them can throw their weight around."

Combined, the two power conferences could ask for everything they wanted with the threat of a breakaway hanging over any request the other conferences dared turn down. It was a multibillion-dollar game of chicken, with multiple high-ranking insiders believing deep down that Sankey was just waiting for the perfect time to leave.

"I think the SEC, if not more [conferences], are going to abandon the NCAA sooner than people think," said one influential college sports crisis communications consultant. "Start looking at Sankey's public comments and the more outspoken he's been about it. It's not just about money. It's about rules and legislative council having votes from [the University of] Akron and [the University of] Toledo on it.

"Sankey is waiting for the right spot so Sankey and the SEC aren't the villains that are blowing this up."

Sankey complained to Yahoo Sports in October 2023 that nonfootball and FCS schools had "too much influence" on important rules-making committees within the NCAA governance structure. Bowlsby, who presided over the Big 12 for a decade, sensed frustration from the SEC over how many NCAA rules seemed specifically aimed at that conference. It could range from recruiting restrictions to refusing to allow a fourth assistant coach and more scholarships in baseball, decisions that seemed to especially irk Sankey. "I, as a commissioner, can go invite Oklahoma and Texas to join," Sankey said. "I can sign media deals . . . but I can't decide who's on the women's golf team."

But with the power of major brands like Alabama, Texas, and Georgia, the SEC had the necessary ammo and motive to push for more say at the table.

The first major initiative of the two allies was the very public push in March 2024 for a substantially bigger share of the College Football Playoff revenue pie. After weeks of negotiations, the SEC and Big Ten each received a massive bump to 29 percent of the cut of the new fourteen-team, $1.3 billion ESPN deal—$21 million to $23 million each annually compared to $12 million to $14 million for ACC and Big 12 schools. The rich again got richer.

MIKE LOCKSLEY WAS MUSING ALOUD about the Cincinnati Bengals.

The Bengals, he explained, aren't in one of the biggest television markets. (Cincinnati has the sixth-smallest TV market of the thirty-two NFL franchises.) They don't have the biggest fan base or the best stadium. But because of smart evaluation in drafting and developing players like quarterback Joe Burrow and receiver Ja'Marr Chase, the Bengals emerged as one of the AFC's top teams and reached the 2022 Super Bowl. Parity was a core tenet of the NFL as it rewarded the worst teams with top draft picks and made every organization operate under the same salary cap. If college football were to survive, Locksley believed that was the direction it must head.

Locksley wanted to take a percentage of the massive television revenue coming in to create a salary cap of between $15 million and $20 million to pay football players. It would provide structure; take the onus off collectives and boosters to pay players their compensation under the guise of name, image, and likeness; and level the playing field. Just like the Bengals and New York Giants operate under the same salary cap, so, too, could Maryland and Ohio State.

"If everybody has $20 million, spend it how you want," Locksley said. "You want to spend it on a damn quarterback? That's on you. It's back on the coaches and players on managing that $20 million and developing you as a football player. Whereas now, it's whoever has the most money."

Nick Saban, Locksley's former boss at Alabama, was one of many others who saw things in the same light and believed long before the House settlement that a revenue-share model was the only way to go. It made perfect sense why coaches on the ground dealing with the chaos firsthand wanted that solution. They didn't have to worry about the legality of what a revenue-share model would look like under Title IX and the rest of the university educational enterprise, the way their bosses had to consider. Every step up the educational leadership ladder there seemed to be more people saying to pump the brakes and offer reasons why it couldn't be done.

More than anything, coaches badly wanted control, and they were forced to confront an uncontrollable market. College football looked increasingly like a professional model yet had none of the components that brought order to the NFL, like unions and collectively bargained contracts in place. Unlike the NFL, college football was nothing less than year-round free agency . . . and it was driving coaches crazy. Coaches like Locksley knew players deserved to be paid. What he and his brethren wanted were clear rules rather than ceding power and control to boosters and other third parties.

"Just call it what it is," he said. "Let's become a minor league for the NFL and make sure that these guys get degrees as much as you can. If it's going to be about the money, make it about the money. If it's going to be about degrees, how do we make that focus go back to earning degrees?"

THE COMPLEX THEORISTS OPERATING OUT of the Santa Fe Institute, the tony group of thinkers we met earlier, came up with a concept called Fitness. Not the kind of fitness one finds on a football field or your local Pilates studio, but rather the ability of a system over time to have a positive impact, like the concept of goodwill or winning.

Jim Hackett was something of a Fitness fanatic. The former Michigan athletic director who hired Jim Harbaugh had embraced the concept when trying to solve complex problems as the head of the Ford Motor Company.

"One of the first mistakes one makes is you tend to pick on the people first," said Hackett. "*Bad leader. Bad board.* [But in reality] it's the design of the system that needs to change."

Before making any decision on how a new and improved model might look, Hackett needed to decide, among all the variables, what mattered most. Given the NCAA's current state of disarray, that meant starting with the most basic question: Is there a need for a regulatory body?

"The answer was yes," Hackett said. "You can't escape that. The whole spectrum of sports requires this."

As the former AD at Michigan and CEO of Ford, Hackett sat on an advisory board along with former NFL commissioner Paul Tagliabue and ex-secretary of state Condoleezza Rice. As part of that process Hackett had been brainstorming ideas with Tagliabue and Rice about a new model. In his mind, those principles revolved around three fundamental questions: 1. Given the free agency that came with the transfer portal, how long should student-athletes be contracted to a university? 2. In the long term NIL appears unsustainable from a donor perspective, so what's the fairest way to pay players? And 3. What is the best way to resolve revenue sharing?

Under the Hackett model, when an athlete signed a grant-in-aid scholarship he would commit to remain at that school for no less than two years to better develop, personally and athletically, and allow the coach the opportunity to build a team without players heading to the portal every six months. From there, there could be an option year with incentives attached. Rather than short-term NIL, he proposed a long-term "attract and retain" idea: a 401(k)-type profit-sharing plan that college athletes couldn't access for, say, twenty years.

The third core principle, revenue sharing, was, without a doubt, the most difficult. Not the idea of sharing with the players—no right-minded person was against that—but rather how it would work for the lower-level Power 4 and Group of 5 schools in, say, the Mid-American or Sun Belt conferences, the reliable Hondas in a world of high-powered Lamborghinis.

"The 401(k) plan would replace that craziness because NIL contributions are not sustainable in my opinion," Hackett said. "It will yo-yo in and out of favor with donors, whereas television is different. You can build a system around that, not just the University of Michigan, but the Central Michigans."

With that new design in mind, Hackett was dead-set against the flavor of the early months of 2024—a premier pro-style league comprising select SEC, Big Ten, Big 12, and ACC teams with independent Notre Dame along for the ride. An association outside of the NCAA with its own budget, rules, and enforcement.

"That doesn't work in a system where you need cooperation and you're trying to be fit to compete—you can't have a superconference," Hackett said. "If you do that, you will destroy everything around it."

A YEAR AFTER LEAVING THE NCAA, former president Mark Emmert was talking about college football embracing a European soccer–style relegation system. While this wasn't quite Walter Byers admitting the term "student-athlete" was nothing but a sham, it was still striking to hear Emmert, who had frequently been criticized for an inability to articulate a clear vision for the future of college athletics, talking creatively and proactively after defending the status quo so ardently for more than a decade.

Freed from the NCAA's golden handcuffs, Emmert said aloud that he thought a football-driven breakaway was inevitable and believed the most likely outcome was a superconference of forty to sixty of the top schools. In his mind, he and his predecessors' inability to push NCAA membership into modern solutions helped pave the path for such a breakaway.

Emmert's solution? A relegation system. He envisioned a forty-team superconference broken into North, South, East, and West divisions of ten schools each. And just like the English Premier League, a specific amount of schools—he suggested five—would be relegated to the lesser conference at the end of the season with five schools moving up to a superconference. Just imagine the stakes of an Egg Bowl between Ole Miss and Mississippi State, where one was at risk of being relegated. It would supercharge already intense rivalries and give fans the ultimate bragging rights for potentially years if a school got stuck in the lower conference.

"You'd add audiences because it'd be exciting to see who's going to get to move up and who's going to get to move down," he said. "It just seems like such a media-friendly approach, and that's unfortunately all that seems to count right now. I just see that as inevitable."

The relegation model had never garnered real momentum in American sports, though the Mountain West reportedly considered it after the Pac-12 imploded and it looked for models that could include Oregon State and Washington State. Any relegation model would make it challenging to forecast year-over-year-revenue for university athletic departments, which resembled battleships in their ability and speed at changing course. Even

330 | The Price

when presented with all the reasons why it wouldn't work, Emmert stead-fastly believed TV money would find a way. "As I used to remind people in the office, these universities cracked the human genome. We can figure this out," he said. "Those are details that'll get sorted out."

In a sport ruled by self-interest, Emmert expected the heavyweight conferences like the SEC and Big Ten to continue grabbing more power and more money at the expense of the others. During his tenure at the NCAA, he witnessed what was once a Power 6 become a Power 5 as the Big East blew up. His successor, Charlie Baker, would oversee the future—a Power 5 would eventually become, as witnessed by the Pac-12 implosion, a Power 4, though it was really a Power 2.

As the SEC and Big Ten solidified their power by swiping marquee brands like Texas and USC, Emmert felt it was only a matter of time before an internal reckoning would unfold in the Big 2 just like it had within the ACC as Clemson and Florida State demanded bigger shares. Why did Van-derbilt and Rutgers deserve the same cut as Alabama and Michigan, despite delivering a sliver of the value? There would always be a desire for more, and when that didn't become readily available from television networks and streaming services, the schools would eat their own for it.

"Wouldn't it be better if we could increase the size of the pie and shrink the number of pieces?" Emmert said. "They are more than happy to raid each other's conferences, but sooner or later, they are going to have to turn on each other."

NOW NINETY-FOUR YEARS OLD, ROY Kramer's life has been shaped by college football for nearly sixty years. He won a Division II national cham-pionship as Central Michigan's head football coach in 1974 before becom-ing Vanderbilt's athletic director in 1978 and later the SEC commissioner. Among his massive contributions to the game, Kramer created the first conference championship game, added Arkansas and South Carolina to the SEC, and helped build the conference into the powerhouse it is today.

Now living in a lakefront community outside Knoxville, Kramer still loved watching college football and attended games when he could. He saw issues throughout the sport, but he also highlighted one of the great contradictions about college football. For as messy and chaotic as it had become, with coaches and administrators at their wit's end, the fall game-day experience in Ann Arbor, Tuscaloosa, Baton Rouge, and countless other locations remained unmatched.

"The game itself on Saturday afternoon is still a great, great game," Kramer said. "It still has that culture to it. It still has the impact of the game on the student-athlete, still has that competitiveness required for discipline and toughness and those things. That hasn't changed. The game today is far better. On the outside of the game, it's a whole different world.

"I think we've lost part of the heart of what was so great about college football."

Can college football survive the outside forces attacking the game that Kramer and tens of millions of others dedicated their lives to?

The ethos of big-time college football, the very soul of it all, had never felt more vulnerable to the corruption of money and self-interest. What made college football special was the pageantry, the traditions, the rivalries that dominated conversations in gas stations and diners year-round. It's Touchdown Jesus. It's a night game in Death Valley when the band plays "Neck." It's chandeliers, fine cutlery, and good bourbon in the Grove. It's Sing Second after Army-Navy. It's "Rammer Jammer" in Tuscaloosa and Rolling Toomers in Auburn. It's Dabo Swinney running full speed down a hill after touching Howard's Rock. It's Bevo, Ralphie, and Uga. It was what kept us all coming back through the ups and downs, the laughs and the tears, the love and the hate. College football was a magnificently weird yet lovable sport that succeeded despite decades of mismanagement by the people in charge.

There could always be a breaking point, and those who love college football worry that the tremendous upheaval over the last four years pushes it closer to that.

The lone certainty, it seemed, was that until something concrete happened, until a new model could be created and allowed to grow strong enough to contain the outright avarice and wanton self-interest consuming the sport, anyone and everyone who remained in or near the fallout zone of college football would continue to pay dearly for their devotion.

Acknowledgments

BOOKS OF THIS DEPTH AND scope do not come together without the guidance, input, and cooperation of a small army of professionals devoted to doing things the right way. With that in mind, we would like to thank the following folks for their help in the publication of *The Price*. We begin with HarperCollins, the iconic publishing house, and senior vice president and deputy publisher Doug Jones, a serious college football fan and the driving force behind this book; vice president and executive editor Noah Eaker, who guided and shaped our manuscript every step of the way at Harper; associate director of marketing Tom Hopke; senior director of publicity Kate D'Esmond; attorney Mike Bzozowski; and assistant Harper editor Edie Astley. We also want to send a hearty shout-out to David Vigliano, our literary agent, in helping bring this project to life; fact checker extraordinaire Kelvin C. Bias; and researcher Caroline Borge Keenan.

John would like to thank his bosses at 247Sports/CBS Sports for giving him the time and support to finish the project: Adam Stanco, Kevin Ryan, Trey Scott, Pat Tholey, Joel Cox, and Adi Joseph.

On the college football front, we'd like to recognize a long line of communications and public-relations pros who went above and beyond the call of duty to help coordinate interview requests, offer insight, and answer our follow-up and fact-checking questions. They are Meghan Durham Wright, NCAA associate director of communications; David Ablauf, associate athletic director for football communications at the University of Michigan; Jeff Bowe, associate director, communications services (football), at the University of Arizona; Craig Henderson, vice president, executive office of the president, University of Arizona; Mitch Zak, communications manager at the University of Arizona; Jason Yellin, associate athletic director and strategic communications officer at the University of Maryland; Dustin Semonavick, assistant athletic director for football communications at the University of Maryland; Mark Cohen, associate athletics director for strategic and football communications at Texas Christian University; Chuck Sullivan, assistant commissioners for communications at the American Athletic Conference; Javan Hedlund, senior associate commissioner for external communications strategy at Mountain West; Bill Hofheimer, vice president of communications for ESPN; James Riley, chief communications officer at Great Southern Wood Preserving; and Jennifer Tharpe, executive assistant to Jimmy Rane of Great Southern Wood Preserving.

Without the support of friends and colleagues, a complex and time-consuming book like this one wouldn't have been possible. We'd like to thank Lars Anderson, Jeff Benedict, Alex Scarborough, Chris Colaitis, Chuck Fleischmann, David Magee, Eric Zohn, John O'Connell, Justin Yurkanin, Katie Alexander, Kenny Voshell, Kevin Roak, Ivan Maisel, Izzy Gould, Matt Clementson, Michael Casagrande, Mike Rodak, Pavan Reddy, Peter Tartaglione, Randy and Nora Hanson, Rainer Sabin, Pam and Sonny Vaccaro, and Zack Creglow for their moral support and helpful advice to get this book over the finish line.

Finally, we thank our families, who had to bear the brunt of our obsessiveness in reporting and writing this book. They are the source of our success and the reason we wanted to tackle an ambitious project like this one.

Notes on Sources

THIS BOOK IS BASED LARGELY on firsthand observations and interviews between August 2022 and May 2024 with more than two hundred individuals at a time in which the college football landscape was changing on a near-hourly basis. The vast majority of those interviews were on the record and on tape. In dozens of cases, some individuals were interviewed multiple times. Court documents and public records were essential in support of our reporting. When necessary, we agreed to speak with certain individuals on background to protect their identity and allow them to speak freely. In addition, we traveled far and wide in an effort to bring greater authenticity and perspective to our work. The places we visited included Washington, D.C.; Ann Arbor, Michigan; Tucson, Arizona; Carlsbad and Los Angeles, California; Tuscaloosa and Abbeville, Alabama; College Park, Maryland; Nashville, Tennessee; San Antonio, Dallas, Fort Worth, and College Station, Texas; Atlanta, Georgia; Miramar Beach, Florida; Oxford, Mississippi; Phoenix and Scottsdale, Arizona; Indianapolis, Indiana; and Charlotte, North Carolina.

In addition, we'd be remiss if we didn't further acknowledge the groundwork laid by the writers and reporters who cover college football on a regular basis, often with distinction. They include Ross Dellenger, Yahoo Sports; Dan Wetzel, Yahoo Sports; Nicole Auerbach, *The Athletic*; Stewart Mandel, *The Athletic*; Bruce Feldman, *The Athletic*; Pete Thamel, ESPN; Chris Low, ESPN; Heather Dinich, ESPN; Dennis Dodd, CBS Sports; and Michael McCann, *Sportico*.

Finally, any mistakes or omissions are those of the authors and the authors alone.

PROLOGUE

This chapter is based on firsthand observations from one of the authors' attendance at the Rose Bowl in Pasadena.

CHAPTER 1: THE OLD KING I

This chapter was built around interviews with former LSU players Elice Parker, Steve Arflin, Brandon Hurley and Peter Dynakowski, former Louisiana State University and NCAA president Mark Emmert, former Cincinnati head coach Rick Minter, former LSU assistants Pete Jenkins and Rick Trickett, and former Alabama staffer Geoff Collins. All anonymous sources had direct knowledge of the situation they were quoted on. We also talked to multiple senior officials with knowledge of the lead-up and aftermath of the Saban-Fisher fight on condition of background. One of the authors attended the SEC spring meetings in Florida, and all observations are either firsthand or come from someone who witnessed them firsthand.

We'd also like to acknowledge the reporting of Mike Rodak of AL.com, Alex Scarborough of ESPN, and Bruce Feldman, Brody Miller, and Matt Fortuna of *The Athletic*.

We made multiple requests to interview Saban. According to an Alabama team spokesperson, Saban would not be "participating in any books right now" on the advice of his agent, Jimmy Sexton.

CHAPTER 2: MICHIGAN MAN

The portrayal of Jim Harbaugh and the contents of this chapter were based on an hour-long interview with Harbaugh and on other interviews, including with athletic director Warde Manuel, Tom Mars, Jim Hackett, Todd Anson, U of M regent Jordan B. Acker, and senior officials, past and present, associated with the University of Michigan and its athletic department. We would also like to cite the reporting of Dan Wetzel of Yahoo Sports, Adam Rittenberg of ESPN, Austin Meek of *The Athletic*, Pete Nakos of On3, Mark Snyder of the *Detroit Free Press*, Andrea Adelson of ESPN, Chris Balas of the *Wolverine*, Paul Myerberg of *USA Today*, Angelique S. Chengelis of *The Detroit News*, and social media posts of U of M president Santa Ono, Jim Harbaugh, Todd Anson, and John U. Bacon.

CHAPTER 3: OPPENHEIMER

This chapter was built around interviews with Sonny Vaccaro, Jon Duncan, Greg Shaheen, Mark Emmert, and Andy Schwarz. John attended the annual NCAA convention in 2023 and 2024 in San Antonio and Phoenix, respectively. The authors would also like to specifically acknowledge the 2016 book *Indentured*, a richly reported history of the NCAA by Joe Nocera and Ben Strauss, along with the work of Michael McCann of Sportico, Eric Prisbell and Pete Nakos of On3, Ross Dellenger of Yahoo Sports, Seth Emerson of *The Athletic*, and Dennis Dodd of CBS Sports. Finally, a small portion of the material in the chapter related to the Ed O'Bannon lawsuit was drawn, with permission from Sonny and Pam Vaccaro, from the pages of Vaccaro's forthcoming autobiography.

CHAPTER 4: THE PRINCE

This chapter was built around interviews with former Georgia athletic director Greg McGarity, Georgia assistant coaches Stacey Searels and Will Muschamp, former LSU assistant Leroy Ryals, Georgia players Jack Podlesny and Christopher Smith, Texas Christian head coach Sonny Dykes, and multiple former coaches who spoke to us on background.

Two books helped shape this chapter: Seth Emerson's fantastic *Attack the Day* and Kirby Smart's coauthored book with Loren Smith *How 'Bout Them Dawgs!*—an enlightening look inside Georgia's 2021 national championship. We'd also like to highlight the work of Alex Scarborough and Mark Schlabach of ESPN and Matt Zenitz of AL.com.

CHAPTER 5: CALLING COLLECTIVES

The opening scene is based on firsthand observations by one of the authors at the restaurant. The two former SEC coaches quoted in this chapter are two longtime, successful coaches who were granted anonymity to speak freely about previous tactics to get around NCAA rules. The chapter is built around interviews with multiple collective operators, among them Harry Geller, Walker Jones, Russell White, Rob Sine, and Hunter Baddour.

The on-the-record interview with Jimmy Rane was conducted by one of the authors at the corporate office of Great Southern Wood Holdings in Abbeville, Alabama, in September 2023 in the presence of James Riley, the chief communications officer of Great Southern Wood Preserving.

The Athletic's David Ubben's reporting on Spyre Sports was particularly helpful in this chapter. We'd also like to cite the reporting of Stewart Mandel of *The Athletic*, Mike Fish of ESPN, and Paul Davis of *Opelika-Auburn News*.

CHAPTER 6: RAISING ARIZONA

The story behind the rise of Arizona football was based on multiple interviews with head coach Jedd Fisch, university president Robert C. Robbins, athletic director Dave Heeke, director of player personnel Matt Doherty, Steve Voeller, vice president of government affairs, a "Next Up" YouTube interview of Fisch conducted by Adam Breneman, and Ray Wells, executive director of the Desert Takeover Football Collective. The authors would also like to acknowledge the reporting of Justin Spears and Ellie Wolfe of the *Arizona Daily Star*, Mark Snyder of *Detroit Free Press*, Carlton Thompson of the *Houston Chronicle*, and information obtained from ArizonaWildcats.com.

CHAPTER 7: THE SUMMIT

This chapter was based upon both authors' attending the University of Arizona–sponsored "Future of College Athletics Summit" in Washington, D.C., in June 2023, along with interviews with Bobby Robbins, Senators Richard Blumenthal and Tommy Tuberville, Oliver Luck, and Brent Chapman, CEO and founder of myNILpay.com. The reporting of Pete Nakos, Eric Prisbell of On3, Matt Brown of extrapointsmb.com, and Ross Dellenger of Yahoo Sports and material obtained from NCAA.org proved essential.

CHAPTER 8: MACY'S I

This chapter is based on three days spent at the University of Maryland in late September and early October 2023 for interviews with head coach Mike Locksley, offensive coordinator Josh Gattis, strength and conditioning coach Ryan Davis, associate head coach Kevin Sumlin, quarterback Taulia Tagovailoa, athletic director Damon Evans, deputy athletic director Colleen Sorem, and former basketball coach Gary Williams.

Reporting from the *Washington Post* and the *Baltimore Sun* helped with Locksley's biographical information. Galu Tagovailoa did not respond to interview requests.

CHAPTER 9: A BRAVE NEW WORLD

One of the authors attended the On3 event in Nashville, so this chapter is based largely on first-person observations, reporting, and interviews along, with a video link to the event. Individual interviews included Shannon Terry, Pete Schoenthal, and Kirk Herbstreit.

CHAPTER 10: THE QUARTERBACK

This chapter is based on in-person attendance at the Carlsbad–Castel High game in September 2023 and on multiple interviews and texts with Julian Sayin, Karen Brandenburg, Dan Sayin, Aidan Sayin, and Carlsbad head football coach Thadd MacNeal. Additional reporting was contributed by John Maffei of *The San Diego Union-Tribune* and Pablo Uggetti of ESPN.

CHAPTER 11: THE RISE AND FALL OF JIMBO FISHER

This chapter is based on interviews with former assistant coaches, personnel staffers, administrators, and others who worked directly with Jimbo Fisher, some on the record and some on background. On-record interviews were conducted with Texas Christian head coach Sonny Dykes, former Florida State University president John Thrasher, former Texas A&M University president Bowen Loftin, former personnel staffer Cody Bellaire, longtime Florida State writer Ira Schoffel, and reporter Grayson Weir.

Reporting by Tom D'Agostino of the *Palm Beach Post*, Bud Elliott of *SB Nation*, and Andrea Adelson and David Hale of ESPN proved essential.

CHAPTER 12: UNREALISTIC

The depiction of the collapse of the Pac-12 conference is based on multiple interviews both on the record and on background with several key individuals. Reporting contained in *Indentured*, particularly as related to the marriage of money and sports television, played an important role. On-the-record material included multiple interviews with Bobby Robbins and the viewing and transcription of the Robbins-Heeke Big 12 press conference. The authors would also like to acknowledge the reporting of John Canzano of JohnCanzano.com, J. Brady McCollough of the *Los Angeles Times*, Billy Witz of *The New York Times*, Dennis Dodd of CBS Sports, Ross Dellenger of Yahoo Sports, Pete Nakos and Eric Prisbell of On3, Stewart Mandell of *The Athletic*, David Gutman of the *Seattle Times*, and communications officials at the University of Arizona.

CHAPTER 13: TRYING TIMES

This chapter was based around a visit to the NCAA corporate offices in Indianapolis and interviews conducted there in December 2023. Primary interviews included Jon Duncan, Tim Buckley, and other members of the association's enforcement and administrative staff. A follow-up interview with a top investigator, in which Meghan Durham Wright, associate director of communications was present, was conducted over Microsoft Teams. Other key reporting was provided by the work of Mike McCann of Sportico, Mike Vernon of kuhearings.com, Jeremy Crabtree of On3, and *Indentured*. A small portion of the Nevin Shapiro story first appeared in *The System*. The website NCAA.org was helpful in confirming facts.

CHAPTER 14: MICHIGAN MAN II

The shaping of this chapter of Jim Harbaugh's battle with the NCAA derived from a multitude of sources. They include on-the-record interviews with Tom Mars, Warde Manuel, Jim Hackett, Todd Anson, and Jordan B. Acker. In addition, the authors would like to cite the reporting of Dan Wetzel and Ross Dellenger of Yahoo Sports, Pete Thamel and Mark Schlabach of ESPN, Michael Rosenberg and Jelani Scott of *Sports Illustrated*, Alex Kirshner of *The Ringer*, Jeff Borzello and Adam Rittenberg of ESPN, Shehan Jeyarajah and Dean Straka of CBSSports.com, Angelique S. Chengelis and Tony Paul of *The Detroit News*, Tony Garcia of the *Detroit Free Press*, Connor Earegood of the *Michigan Daily*, Dennis Dodd of CBS Sports, Ari Wasserman of *The Athletic*, and the Associated Press, along with critical texts and emails provided by various sources.

CHAPTER 15: THE POWER BROKER

Armen conducted an unrelated interview with Jimmy Sexton in November 2015 for a possible television feature, which is the basis for the quotes used here. Sexton did not respond to multiple requests for a follow-up interview for this book. We talked to multiple college administrators, on the record and on background, to put together the most comprehensive look at the mysterious Sexton. Key on-the-record interviews came from former NCAA president Mark Emmert, former Florida State University president John Thrasher, and former Utah athletic director Chris Hill. All scenes were either observed firsthand by one of the authors or described by someone who witnessed them in person.

Previous reporting on Sexton from Mark Schlabach of ESPN, Pete Thamel of *Sports Illustrated*, and Hal Habbib of *Palm Beach Post* was helpful. AL.com's Kent Faulk's reporting on the lawsuit between Sexton and Pat Dye was also utilized.

CHAPTER 16: MACY'S II

John returned to Maryland in February 2024 for interviews with head coach Mike Locksley and chief of staff Brian Griffin.

CHAPTER 17: THE AGENT

This chapter is based on multiple in-person interviews in Dallas with Jackson Zager, first in May 2023 and again for several days in December 2023. To flesh out the narrative, we also utilized the lawsuit Rusty Hardin filed on Jaden Rashada's behalf. Florida athletic director Scott Stricklin, Gator Collective founder Eddie Rojas, and Florida Victory leaders didn't respond to interview requests.

Additional reporting that was valuable in the writing of this chapter came from Stewart Mandel, Andy Staples, and G. Allen Taylor of *The Athletic*, Dennis Dodd of CBS Sports, and Chris Hummer of 247Sports.

CHAPTER 18: ONE LAST RIDE

Armen attended the Valero Alamo Bowl contest between the University of Arizona and the University of Oklahoma in San Antonio and was in the Arizona team meeting room the night before the December 2023 bowl game. Key interviews included those conducted with Jedd Fisch and Bobby Robbins. An additional interview with Fisch and attendance at a U of A football practice occurred in Tucson in September 2023. Additional reporting provided by Justin Spears and Kelly Presnell, *Arizona Daily Star* and *Tucson.com*.

CHAPTER 19: THE OLD KING II

All observations are firsthand from John, who attended Alabama games against Texas, Tennessee, Texas A&M and Georgia. On-record interviews include those with Alabama assistant coaches Holmon Wiggins and Joe Cox; Alabama players Tyler Booker, C. J. Dippre, and Jalen Milroe; and Walk of Champions chairman Elliott Maisel.

ESPN's Chris Low's extensive reporting on Saban was also cited in this chapter.

CHAPTER 20: MICHIGAN MAN III

John attended the Rose Bowl in Pasadena. Key interviews included those conducted with Warde Manuel, Tom Mars, U of M assistant football coach Rick

Minter, and Todd Anson. Reporting by Ian Rapoport of NFL Network, Kris Rhim of ESPN, and NBC Sports contributed to the storytelling. Emails and texts cited in the chapter provided by sources.

CHAPTER 21: DOMINOES

A variety of individuals and material contributed to this penultimate chapter. They include interviews with Jedd Fisch, Bobby Robbins, Dave Heeke, Todd Anson, and Karen Bradenburg, along with text exchanges with Brandenburg and Julian Sayin. The reporting and observations from Kalen DeBoer's introductory press conference were obtained firsthand by John.

Reporting by Chris Low of ESPN, Ellie Wolfe of the *Arizona Daily Star*, Caitlin Schmidt of Tucson.com, and Cameron Van Til of Associated Press proved particularly helpful, as well as staff members of the University of Arizona communications department and the office of the president.

AFTERWORD: NEW MODEL

We conducted multiple interviews with former NCAA president Mark Emmert, especially the one in person at the 2023 NCAA Convention. This chapter was also based on interviews with Sonny Vaccaro, NCAA chief of staff Tim Buckley, former Michigan AD Jim Hackett, Maryland head coach Mike Locksley, former SEC commissioner Roy Kramer, and Mountain West commissioner Gloria Nevarez. Additionally, we interviewed multiple high-level administrators and industry leaders on background.

Reporting from *Sports Illustrated*, Yahoo Sports, and ESPN was helpful in writing this chapter.

About the Authors

ARMEN KETEYIAN is widely regarded as one of the finest investigative journalists of his generation, with a twenty-six-year network television career spanning ABC News, CBS Sports, CBS News, HBO's *Real Sports with Bryant Gumbel*, *60 Minutes*, and *60 Minutes Sports*. During that time he won eleven Emmy awards.

JOHN TALTY is a national college sports reporter for 247Sports and CBS Sports. He previously worked as an SEC insider and senior sports editor for AL.com and Alabama Media Group.